HOME TERRITORIES

"This work is a tour de force, a major work of synthesis in contemporary cultural studies. In a time of rampant postmodern fragmentation, Morley evinces the generosity of spirit and expansive critical command needed to bring our scattered and disrupted notions of identity, belonging and displacement together. This book will help us make sense of the challenges and possibilities of the new century."

Ien Ang, Professor of Cultural Studies and Director, Research Centre in Intercommunal Studies, University of Western Sydney

"David Morley adroitly traces central connections between the rapidly changing notions of identity, place, and belonging, and the mediascapes within which they (and we) circulate, take root and dwell. In this subtle book Morley has given us much to think about and in the process helped to set the tone and direction for the next generation of media scholarship."

Herman Gray, University of California at Santa Cruz

"An ambitious, multi-faceted, and robust account of the politics and responsibilities of defining and locating Home. One of the most impressive features of this book is its wide-ranging engagement with issues of globalization, cosmopolitanism, migration, and the relevance of nationhood."

James Hay, Department of Speech Communication, University of Illinois

"From the TV-sitting room to the national and transnational sites we home in on, Morley makes thought-provoking interconnections and arresting, creative links across a wealth of literatures and concerns."

Gerd Baumann, Department of Cultural Anthropology, University of Amsterdam

David Morley is Professor of Media and Communications at Goldsmiths College, London. He is the author of *Television, Audiences and Cultural Studies* (Routledge 1992), co-author of *Spaces of Identity* (Routledge 1995) and co-editor of *Stuart Hall: Critical Dialogues in Cultural Studies* (Routledge 1996).

COMEDIA
Series editor: David Morley

OTHER *COMEDIA* TITLES AVAILABLE FROM ROUTLEDGE:

ADVERTISING INTERNATIONAL
The Privatisation of Public Space
Armand Mattelart translated by Michael Chanan

BLACK BRITISH CULTURE AND SOCIETY: A TEXT READER
Edited by Kwesi Owusu

THE CONSUMERIST MANIFESTO
Advertising in Postmodern Times
Martin Davidson

CULTURAL SNIPING
The Art of Transgression
Jo Spence

CULTURES OF CONSUMPTION
Masculinities and Social Space in Late Twentieth-Century Britain
Frank Mort

CUT 'N' MIX
Culture, Identity and Caribbean Music
Dick Hebdige

THE DYNASTY YEARS
Hollywood Television and Critical Media Studies
Jostein Gripsrud

FAMILY TELEVISION
Cultural Power and Domestic Leisure
David Morley

HIDING IN THE LIGHT
On Images and Things
Dick Hebdige

THE KNOWN WORLD OF BROADCAST NEWS
Stanley Baran and Roger Wallis

MIGRANCY, CULTURE, IDENTITY
Iain Chambers

THE PHOTOGRAPHIC IMAGE IN DIGITAL CULTURE
Edited by Martin Lister

THE PLACE OF MEDIA POWER
Pilgrims and Witnesses of the Media Age
Nick Couldry

SPECTACULAR BODIES
Gender, Genre and the Action Cinema
Yvonne Tasker

STUART HALL
Critical Dialogues in Cultural Studies
Edited by Kuan-Hsing Chen and David Morley

TEACHING THE MEDIA
Len Masterman

TELEVISION AND COMMON KNOWLEDGE
Edited by Jostein Gripsrud

TELEVISION, AUDIENCES AND CULTURAL STUDIES
David Morley

TELEVISION, ETHNICITY AND CULTURAL CHANGE
Marie Gillespie

TELEVISION MYTHOLOGIES
Len Masterman

TIMES OF THE TECHNOCULTURE
From the Information Society to the Virtual Life
Kevin Robins and Frank Webster

TO BE CONTINUED ...
Soap Opera Around the World
Edited by Robert C. Allen

TRANSNATIONAL CONNECTIONS
Culture, People, Places
Ulf Hannerz

VIDEO PLAYTIME
The Gendering of a Leisure Technology
Ann Gray

HOME TERRITORIES

Media, mobility and identity

David Morley

Routledge
Taylor & Francis Group

LONDON AND NEW YORK

First published 2000
by Routledge
2 Park Square, Milton Park, Abingdon, Oxon OX14 4RN

Simultaneously published in the USA and Canada
by Routledge
270 Madison Avenue, New York, NY 10016

Reprinted 2004, 2006, 2007

Routledge is an imprint of the Taylor & Francis Group, an informa business

© 2000 David Morley

Typeset in Galliard by Taylor & Francis Books Ltd
Printed and bound in Great Britain by Biddles Ltd, King's Lynn, Norfolk

British Library Cataloguing in Publication Data
A catalogue record for this book is available from the British Library

Library of Congress Cataloguing in Publication Data
Morley, David, 1949–
Home territories : media, mobility and identity / David Morley.
Includes bibliographical references and index.
1. Mass media–Social aspects. 2. Population geography.
3. Group identity. 4. Postmodernism–Social aspects.
I. Title.
HM1206 .M67 2000
306–dc 21   00-035316

ISBN 978-0-415-15764-3 (hbk)
ISBN 978-0-415-15765-0 (pbk)

To those who will also remember Slade Road,
Valentine Road, Hurst Green Road, Buckingham
Road, Dynevor Road, Brooke Road, Strathearn
Road and Alconbury Road

The question of boundaries is the first to be encountered; from it all others flow.

(Fernand Braudel)

CONTENTS

CONTENTS

CONTENTS

xiv

ILLUSTRATIONS

ACKNOWLEDGEMENTS

I would like to thank Goldsmiths College for providing me with a period of sabbatical leave in which to work on this book, and my colleagues in the Department of Media and Communications who took on extra duties to enable my absence.

A number of friends and colleagues have helped me in a variety of ways during the long period in which I have been working on this project. Some provided inspiration at key moments; some enabled providential meetings and contacts; some generously gave up their time to offer comments on the drafts of various chapters; some offered me access to their own work in draft or unpublished form; some laboured into the night when necessary to produce this manuscript in its present form (thanks, K.). Among those without whose help, support, advice and encouragement this book would have never seen the light of day I would like to thank:

Ien Ang, Gerd Baumann, Charlotte Brunsdon, Phil Cohen, James Donald, Herman Gray, Ulf Hannerz, Alec Hargreaves, Tarek Hassan, Dick Hebdige, Eric Hirsch, Krishan Kumar, Arun Kundnani, Angela McRobbie, Doreen Massey, Joshua Meyrowitz, Hamid Naficy, Kevin Robins, Viqui Rosenberg, Bill Schwarz, Kay Shoesmith, Roger Silverstone, Richard Smith, Gareth Stanton and Ken Worpole. But above all CB, for everything.

INTRODUCTION

For greater clearness, they took, as their mnemonic base their own house, where they were living, attaching to each one of its parts a distinct event – and the courtyard, the garden, the surroundings, the entire district, had no other meaning than to jog their memory.[1]

A place to start from

Shortly before completing this book I made a visit to see my mother, who still lives in the house where I grew up, and she asked me what the book was about. "Well," I began "it's about ideas of home …" I got no further in my explanation, as at that point she turned to my sister and exclaimed, in tones of what I hope were only mock outrage, "Home!! What does he know about it? He's hardly been here since he was eighteen!" Given that, as we know, all theory has its roots, in one way or another, in autobiography, and given the importance in my analysis below of questions of gender in the construction of domesticity (especially the conflation of ideas of maternity and home), I thought it well to begin with this vignette of my own experience in this respect. At a more theoretical level, ever since I first read it at some point in the early 1970s, Pierre Bourdieu's analysis of the gendering of space in the Kabyle house in North Africa has been something of a talisman to me, seeming to offer crucial insights into a variety of other domestic experiences beyond the particular one which Bourdieu himself addressed.[2] Indeed, when planning my initial audience research into the *Nationwide* programme in the mid-1970s, the questions raised by Bourdieu's analysis, and their potential applications in media research were an important dimension of my concerns. In the event, in that context it proved impossible to directly address those issues and their exploration was delayed until much later, in my work on *Family Television* and then on the *Household Uses of Information and Communication Technology*, with Roger Silverstone *et al.* at Brunel University, in the 1980s. Those concerns with the articulations of gender and domesticity have stayed with me, and the reader will find the shadow of the Kabyle house falling across the pages below at a number of points.

1

My own long interest in researching the television audience, and especially its domestic context, must in one way or another also have been derived from my childhood experience of watching television at home in my own family. If my mother was forever coming in and out of the sitting room from the kitchen, my father, who had spent the war years navigating small planes on and off aircraft carriers going back and forth across the Atlantic, seemed to me for years almost perennially fixed in place, sitting in his favourite armchair in the living room, night after night, watching the television screen. Not that my experience of home was entirely self-enclosed: there was always one particularly tantalising fragment of alterity, represented by the arrival, month by month, on subscription, of my father's copies of *Time* and *Life* magazines from America, informing my imagination with details of the texture of life in a quite different culture from the one I knew at home. Those magazine subscriptions were remnants of the fascination with the USA which my father had developed during his wartime visits there and, as I later discovered, were also the remaining fragments of his one-time desire to emigrate there after the war. The magazines represented one of the particular ways in which alterity was present within my own childhood home. As so often elsewhere, the "foreign" was thus, in an important way, represented within my domestic experience by the American – an "elsewhere" that somehow signalled other, wider horizons, beyond the net curtains of the living room in which my family sat each evening.

To return to my mother's comments with which I began, it is true that I left my childhood home at eighteen and moved to another part of the country. Of course, I have been back to visit my parental home regularly since then (though I suspect one can perhaps never visit home quite often enough for one's mother) but nonetheless, that move was decisive in my own resettled sense of home in adult life. I have now lived for more than thirty years in more or less the same part of London to which I came as an eighteen-year-old. To that extent, my own sedentarist tendencies and my investment in geographical place as form of home is evidently very strong. No doubt these predispositions must also inflect the analysis which follows. In attempting below to uncover some, at least, of the possible meanings of the idea of home, I take as another emblem Rachel Whiteread's sculptural attempt (represented on the book's cover) to reveal what is normally hidden within the four walls of the house. Rather like Bourdieu's Kabyle house (see back cover), Whiteread's *House* has a talismanic status for me and we return to that figure, too, at different points in the book. In the end, I am concerned to explicate a number of senses of what it might mean to be "at home" in a world where the sitting room is a place where, in a variety of mediated forms, the global meets the local.

Heim and Heimat

In recent years much has been made of the idea of postmodernity. Images abound of our supposedly de-territorialised culture of "homelessness": images of exile, diaspora, time–space compression, migrancy and "nomadology". The concept of home often remains as the uninterrogated anchor or alter ego of all this hyper-mobility. Certainly, traditional ideas of home, homeland and nation have been destabilised, both by new patterns of physical mobility and migration and by new communication technologies which routinely transgress the symbolic boundaries around both the private household and the nation state. The electronic landscapes in which we now dwell are haunted by all manner of cultural anxieties which arise from this destabilising flux.

If the transformations in communications and transport networks characteristic of our period, involving various forms of mediation, displacement and de-territorialisation are generally held to have transformed our sense of place, their theorisation has often proceeded at a highly abstract level, towards a generalised account of nomadology. Recent critiques of the "EurAmcentric" nature of most postmodern theory point to the dangers of such inappropriately universalised frameworks of analysis[3]. My aim here is to open up the analysis of the varieties of rootedness, exile, diaspora, displacement, connectedness and/or mobility, experienced by members of groups in a range of socio-geographical positions.

My further aim is to offer an analysis of the construction of national (or pan-national) identities (e.g. the macro-processes through which Englishness or European-ness are currently being reconstituted) which is grounded in an understanding of the (often, literally, domestic) micro-processes through which the smaller units which make up that larger community are themselves constituted. My argument is that the articulation of the domestic household into the "symbolic family" of the nation (or wider group) can best be understood by focusing on the role of media and communications technologies. These technologies must be understood as both transgressing the boundaries of the household – bringing the public world into the private – and simultaneously producing the coherence of broader social experience, through the sharing both of broadcast time and of ritual. In this I follow Foucault's strictures on the need to produce a postmodern geography which will be adequate both to the "grand strategies of geo-politics" and to the "little tactics of the habitat", in attempting to understand the articulation of "Home(mother?)land" and household in the contemporary world.[4] My concern is with making links between questions of residence, mobility, communications and cultural consumption in the construction of identities. In particular my focus is on the process through which, in different contexts, conflict is generated in the process of identity formation by the attempt to expel alterity beyond the boundaries of some ethnically, culturally or civilisationally purified homogenous enclave, at whatever level of social or geographical scale. In these processes the crucial issue in defining who (or what) "belongs" is, of course, also that of defining who (or what) is to be excluded as "matter out of place", whether that matter is represented by impure or foreign material objects, persons or cultural products.

I attempt here to bring together a set of debates concerning the concepts of home and Heimat that have, so far, largely been conducted in isolation from each other, across a range of different disciplines. My premise is that only a truly interdisciplinary (or even perhaps, at the risk of hubris, post-disciplinary) approach, which can synthesise the various potential insights generated in these conventionally separated analyses, can supply us with an effective understanding of the issues at stake in what I take to be one of the most central political questions confronting us, as we attempt to construct a viable cartography of the world in which we now live. In pursuing these questions, I am concerned to advocate what could perhaps be described as a "grounded theory" approach, which places particular emphasis on the integration of micro and macro levels of analysis. I offer an approach to the analysis of micro structures of the home, the family and the domestic realm which I hope can be effectively integrated with contemporary macro debates about the nation, community and cultural identities. My focus is thus on the mutually dependent processes of exclusion and identity construction, in relation to the domestic home, the neighbourhood and the nation as "spaces of belonging".[5]

In a sense this book can be read as an expansion of some of the issues about the articulation of the global and the local originally explored in my earlier "Notes from the sitting room".[6] The micro dimension of the analysis is rooted in my previous involvement in ethnographic studies of domestic modes of consumption of television and other information and communications technologies, through which the private world of the household or family is connected to the wider world.[7] Here the key question is one of how these various media transgress the boundaries of the "sacred space" of the home and how that transgression is regulated by various "rituals of purification". The macro dimension of the analysis derives from my previous work on the broader concept of Heimat, within the framework of debates concerning postmodern geography, identity, culture and ethnicity.[8] If, as Eric Hobsbawm has put it, "Home, in the literal sense Heim, chez moi, is essentially private ... [and] belongs to me and mine and nobody else," nonetheless, as he goes on to say, "Home in the wider sense, Heimat is essentially public ... Heimat is by definition collective. It cannot belong to us as individuals."[9] It is the articulation of these two conceptual spaces which is my principal concern.

Microwaving the macro theory

Accounts of postmodern nomadology tend to operate with one or another form of technologically determinist explanation – concerning what new technologies or modes of flexible production are somehow doing to us. Moreover, they usually fail to integrate the analysis of the macro and macro dimensions of these transformations – an integration which is, as I have indicated, to my mind crucial to the whole analytical project at stake. In his classic study of *The Sociological Imagination* C. Wright Mills presented an elegantly balanced formulation of the relation of the micro and the macro, in social theory, to the effect that "neither the life of an individual nor the history of a society can be understood without understanding both".[10] Mills' concern was with the development of a form of social theory capable of comprehending the complex interplay of biography and history, the personal and the social, the local and the global. His ambition was the development of a mode of analysis that could deal both with the intimate sphere of personal relations and with the way in which "so many of the most intimate features of the person are socially patterned". In this he argues for the need both to "grasp the interplay of (these) intimate settings with their larger structural framework" and the transformations of this framework and the consequent effects upon (particular) milieux.[11]

This approach has also been championed by Karen Knorr-Cetina and Aron Cicourel, in a collection of essays concerned with the development of modes of analysis that transcend the sterile opposition of abstracted (and empirically ungrounded) macro-social theory, which reifies social (or cultural) structures and treats the individual level as inconsequential and, conversely, the difficulties of close-grained empirical (or ethnographic) micro studies which run the risk of falling into a descriptive form of methodological individualism, which departs the proper terrain of the social, *sui generis*, in Durkheim's terms.[12] I have argued elsewhere, following Massey's work on debates in geography about "locality studies", that we should try to avoid the trap of equating the micro (or local) with the merely concrete and empirical, while equating the macro (or global) with the abstract or theoretical.[13] As Massey explains, the common conflation of these terms often follows from the confusion of the specific with the concrete and the general with the abstract: "those who conflate the local with the concrete … are confusing geographical scale with processes of abstraction in thought". Nor should the study of the local be assumed to be necessarily "only" descriptive, as opposed to "theoretical work" on the global economy, which is no less concrete a phenomenon than the locality, if more widely dispersed in geographical scale. Massey rightly warns against the conflation of "geographical scale with processes of abstraction in thought". As she notes "the local … is no less subject to nor useful for theorisation than big broad general things. The counterposition of general and local is quite distinct from the distinction between abstract and concrete."[14]

My argument here draws on insights from contemporary work in the field of cultural geography, which insists on the necessity of rethinking our sense of place in the context of the transformations and destabilisations wrought both by the forces of economic globalisation and by the global media industries. However, I am also concerned to articulate these issues of "virtual geography" to some older debates, partly within anthropology and partly within psychoanalytic theory, concerning the conceptualisation of alterity and of the foreign (the unfamiliar, or "*Fremde*", which is the negative image of "Heimat") by reference to its significance in the rituals of exclusion by means of which the home and Heimat are purified. In this connection I then address recent debates about the "territorialisation of culture", the need for "roots" and the deeply problematic re-emergence on the contemporary political scene of various regressive forms of cultural fundamentalism, xenophobia and nostalgia.[15] I offer a review of contemporary debates about cosmopolitanism, hybridity and identity and a critical perspective on some post-structuralist approaches to the "politics of difference" which seem to come close to abandoning any idea of the possibility of community – a possibility which I take to be a necessary prerequisite of any effective politics. My ultimate ambition is to offer a progressive notion of home, Heimat and community, which does not necessarily depend, for its effective functioning, on the exclusion of all forms of otherness, as inherently threatening to its own internally coherent self-identity. Clearly, in this respect, internal hybridity is the necessary correlative to a greater openness to external forms of difference, and is thus the condition of a more porous and less rigidly policed boundary around whatever is defined as the home community. Indeed, according to Renato Rosaldo, hybridity must be understood as being the inevitable condition of all human cultures "which contain no zones of purity, because they undergo continuous processes of transculturation (two-way borrowing and lending between cultures). Instead of hybridity versus purity, this view suggests that it is hybridity all the way down."[16]

Disciplinarity: multi, inter or post?

Partha Chatterjee quotes the Arab scholar Abu Bakr Muhammad Ibn Bajjah as saying that "to trouble oneself with the task of dealing with something that has been adequately dealt with before is superfluous, a result of ignorance, or a sign of evil intent".[17] While I can assure the reader that my intentions, at least, are not evil, and hope that my attempt to bring together a variety of perspectives from different disciplines is sufficiently interesting to avoid the charge of superfluity, I am well aware that specialists may feel that, in relation to their own discipline, my relative ignorance may well make it appear that I am, as we say in England (or as we used to say, before the mines closed down), doing no more than bringing coals to Newcastle. It is the articulation of a variety of disciplinary perspectives which is my objective. Thus my interest in relation to communications and urban studies, for example, is in articulating the analysis of modes of communication and of the circulation of messages with the patterns of residence and mobility of the audiences who consume them. The adequacy of my attempts to make these particular connections is, of course, for the reader to judge. However, my ambition is to go some way towards developing the mode of analysis called for by Scott Lash and Jonathan Friedman when they speak of the need to develop a perspective that can deal with the two simultaneous modes of circulation of symbolic goods – "one in which the goods, such as television broadcasts, records, videos, magazines circulate among the viewers; and the second, that of the built environment, in which the viewers circulate among the symbolic goods".[18] In the British case, this duality of mediation is perhaps best captured by reference to the phenomenon of the annual Ideal Home

Exhibition, held in London and sponsored by the *Daily Mail* newspaper. Since its inception in 1908 the exhibition has annually drawn hundreds of thousands of spectators, who come to visit it as a symbolic site of pilgrimage on which are displayed the very latest models of desirable home life – the images of which depend for much of their resonance on their own circulation in the mass media, in the form both of journalistic copy and of advertisements.[19] In effect, the exhibition has become a fixture in the national calendar of events, as an occasion when the nation celebrates the comforts and glories of the domestic home.

In what I take to be a similar spirit to my own enterprise, David Sibley offers an analysis of "how the locality and the nation invade the home … providing cues for behaviour in families as they relate to their domestic environment". As Sibley puts it, "spaces are tied together by media messages, by local rules about the appropriate uses of suburban gardens, by the state's immigration policies, and so on".[20] Similarly, in his commentary on Carol Lake's fictionalised portrait of her district of a British city in the mid-1980s, George Revill observes that, while media of various sorts transverse the urban community of which Lake writes, it is still a world of "backdoor gossip, chance encounters and casual meetings" where "national and international events are always articulated through local channels of communication, events half-heard on the radio or television". In this world, events such as the nuclear fallout at Chernobyl or riots in another British city "become local as they are mixed into conversations bound into the day-to-day problems of the community".[21] It is the attempt to interconnect, in our analyses, these different cultural processes occurring simultaneously at different scales which is my central concern.

In one sense my strategy in writing this book has been to convert Doreen Massey's substantive argument about the need to develop an "extroverted" conception of place – as a space through which a number of trajectories pass – into a methodological principle of organisation for the materials collected here.[22] I have, in effect, taken the single concept of home as my central focus and worked by attempting to identify and articulate the different discourses which pass through that conceptual space. I am, of course, well aware that my strategy brings with it many attendant dangers, not least in relation to the possible misuse of the geographical metaphors which, at various points, are central to my analysis. In their comments on the contemporary vogue for a spatialised vocabulary Michael Keith and Steven Pile argue that we see "a sense in which the geographical is being used to provide a secure grounding in the increasingly uncertain world of social and cultural theory", where this spatial vocabulary is unproblematically used in the service of "tying down elusive concepts … [and] mapping our uncertainties".[23] Drawing on the work of Kenneth Burke on the role of metaphors in "reducing the unfamiliar to the familiar" and thus redescribing the "unfamiliar event, experience or social relation as utterly known", Neil Smith and Cindi Katz note the extent to which geographical metaphors are increasingly being used as the source domain of apparently unproblematic meaning, which secures the unfathomability of meaning in other spheres.[24] As they note, it is precisely the "apparent familiarity of space, the givenness of space, its fixity and inertness that make a spatial grammar so fertile for metaphoric appropriation". As they go on to argue, it would seem that the "widespread appeal to spatial metaphors" in contemporary theoretical work results precisely from the destabilisation of all other systems of meaning in a post-structuralist, decentred theoretical universe. In this context it can come to seem that space itself has been improperly "exempted from such sceptical scrutiny, precisely so it can be held constant to provide some semblance of order for an otherwise floating world of ideas".[25] In this connection I can only hope that my own use of spatial concepts and metaphors does not fall prey to these charges. If home is not necessarily a spatial concept, it is nonetheless often lived out as if it were such.

My objective is to connect together issues and perspectives which, at least to my knowledge, have not previously been so connected. In combination with my preference for quoting authors directly (and often at length) so as to let them "speak for themselves" wherever possible, rather than paraphrasing them, this means that my project's very breadth dictates a book of considerable length, for which I can only ask the reader's forbearance. Certainly, I am aware that on a variety of occasions I have read authors somewhat against their own grain, and mobilised their arguments in quite different contexts and for different purposes than they themselves perhaps intended. In any case, where an author quoted feels that they have been dragooned into carrying an argument which is contrary to their intentions, I am sure that I can look forward to a lively exchange of views in the future. These difficulties seem to me inevitable, given my attempt to make (and perhaps on occasion force) the kind of connections I have sought, as I have attempted to synthesise my materials. Similarly the risk of, on occasion, producing a reductive analysis which blurs what are in actuality significant differences is the necessary price of my attempt to seek out parallels and analogies amidst such a disparate body of work in different disciplines. Clearly my project has a number of other inherent dangers: for instance, at many points, in my concern to concretise and exemplify the arguments made, I am reliant on journalistic sources. I am aware that I am thus involved in a precariously bifocal operation, where at some moments I am dependent on looking through the lenses of the same media which, at other points, are the object of my analysis.

At points the reader may perhaps feel the absence of a strongly stated indication of my own position on some of the issues debated here. This arises from my working method. The book's argument is embedded in the selection, editing and orchestration of my sources. Except in a small number of cases, I offer relatively little explicit critique of the work of others. My principal concern is to attempt to build on what I consider to be the best of the work available in the different fields which I survey. My hope is that the juxtapositions I offer of the different perspectives surveyed on the question of what the idea of home means will encourage readers both to make further connections of their own and to engage critically with the synthetic analysis presented here.

Where the global meets the local

The modern home can be said to be a phantasmagoric place, to the extent that electronic media of various kinds allow the radical intrusion of distant events into the space of domesticity.[26] For this reason Marshall Bermann speaks of what he calls the "internationalisation of daily life".[27] In Raymond Williams' terms the "mobile privatisation" which broadcasting offers its consumers enables them to "visit" faraway locations (via sound and image) without leaving the comfort and security of their homes. They are thus enabled to simultaneously stay home and "go places", to remain in the realm of familiar ontological security and yet to experience the vicarious thrill of exhibited difference or exotica of one sort or another.[28] In Derrida's terminology the effect of the "techno-tele-media apparatus" is to destabilise what he calls the national ontopology – that sense of the naturalness and givenness of territorialised "national belonging".[29] In this context, as Sandra Wallman observes "even homogenous populations now come up against otherness as soon as they have access to modern media of communication". Thus, she argues that, alongside increasing rates of actual physical mobility, for many people there is an increasing awareness of the *possibility* of movement as "mass media images, no doubt reflecting the mixture of people in many cities, sharpen ordinary citizens' awareness of cultural forms which are not primarily theirs".[30]

In the traditional vision of things, cultures were understood as being rooted both in time and space, embodying genealogies of "blood, property and frontiers" and thus cultures "rooted societies and their members: organisations which developed, lived and died in particular places".[31] By contrast, the contemporary world is a world of movement and that mobility (both physical and imaginative) is central to our conceptualisation of modernity and its various "posts". In the founding statement of the journal *Public Culture*, Arjun Appadurai and Carol Breckenridge declared that their starting point, in developing their mode of analysis, was the recognition that:

> The world of the late 20th century is increasingly a cosmopolitan world. More people are widely travelled, are catholic in their tastes, are more inclusive in the range of cuisines they consume, are attentive to global media-covered events and are influenced by universal trends in fashion.[32]

In a similar spirit, James Clifford writes of the "cosmopolitical contact zones" in which we live today, commonly being traversed by "new social movements and global corporations, tribal activists and cultural tourists, migrant workers' remittances and email".[33] As Bruce Robbins puts it, "We are connected to all sorts of places, causally if not always consciously, including many that we have never travelled to, that we have perhaps only seen on television – including the place where the television itself was manufactured."[34]

Drawing on the work of writers such as Chambers, Clifford, Geertz and Hart, Nigel Rapport and Andrew Dawson observe that the world "can no longer be divided up into units, territorial segments ... each of which shares a distinctive, exclusive culture" so that there are no longer such "traditionally fixed, spatially and temporally bounded cultural worlds from which to depart and return", precisely because the "migration of information, myths, languages, music, imagery, cuisine, décor, costume, furnishings, above all, persons ... brings even the most isolated areas into a cosmopolitan global framework of socio-cultural interaction".[35] This is the world of Ulf Hannerz's "global ecumene" where, rather than seeing cultures as a global mosaic of separate entities rooted in space, we see a complex system of long-distance cultural flows of images, goods and people interweaving to form a kaleidoscope of unstable identities and transpositions.[36] It is a world where, in Lyotard's well-worn formulation, the privileged metropolitan consumer can "listen to reggae, watch a western, eat McDonald's food for lunch and local cuisine for dinner, wear Paris perfume in Tokyo and 'retro' clothes in Hong Kong".[37] In this process of hybridisation and creolisation of cultures, Rapport and Dawson note that such privileged consumers "draw on a wide range of cultural resources in the securing of their own identities, continually turning the erstwhile alien into their own".[38]

As Doreen Massey puts it, the consequence is that

> few people's ... daily lives can be described as simply local. Even the most "local" ... people ... have their lives touched by wider events, are linked into a broader geographical field ... [N]obody in the First World these days lives their daily lives completely locally, entirely untouched by events elsewhere.[39]

In today's world the distribution of the "familiar" and the "strange" is a complex one, in which "difference is encountered in the adjoining neighbourhood, [and] the familiar turns up at the end of the earth".[40] Karen McCarthy Brown, an anthropologist based in New York, studied the life of a voodoo priestess based not that far from her own home, in another part of the city – in Brooklyn. As she immersed herself in the priestess's world, on her visits there, she reported that although she was "no more than a few miles from my home in lower Manhattan ... I felt as if I had taken a wrong turn, slipped through a crack between worlds, and emerged on the main street of a tropical city".[41] In the same spirit George Marcus argues that in the contemporary world, traditional anthropological notions of community or identity can no longer be mapped on to locality. As he observes, these days, the production of identity "does not depend alone, or even primarily, on the observable, concentrated activities within a particular locale or a diaspora". Rather, he argues, identity "is produced simultaneously in many different locales. One's identity where one lives ... is only one social context and perhaps not the most important one in which it is shaped."[42]

As indicated earlier, in this new context our ideas of locality have to be rethought. Above all, Arjun Appadurai asserts there is "nothing mere about the local", insofar as localities themselves are historically produced through the dynamics of the global – rather than being some pre-existing remnant (pure or contaminated) of supposedly pre-modern times.[43] Appadurai notes that the local is often held to represent "something more elementary, more contingent, and thus more real than life seen in larger scale perspective". However, he argues that we should be cautious of imagining that, in studying the local, we will finally be able to hit some "cultural bedrock, made up of a closed set of reproductive practices and untouched by rumours of the world at large" for "even the most localised of these worlds … has become inflected … by cosmopolitan scripts" derived from broader global dynamics which "forcibly enter the local imagination and become domi-nant voice-overs in the traffic of everyday life".[44] In this connection Appadurai poses the question of what locality can mean, in a world where "spatial localisation, quotidian interaction and social scale are not always isomorphic". Noting the influence of the electronic media in eroding the relationship between spatial and virtual neighbourhoods which are increasingly in disjuncture from each other, Appadurai argues that we should understand neighbourhoods as the "actually existing social forms in which locality … is realised", where this realisation may equally well take spatial or virtual form. In the logic of these arguments, a virtual neighbourhood can easily extend into and across transnational space.[45] For Appadurai, cultural spaces of connection such as this, in the form of diasporic public spheres, are increasingly part of many people's everyday lives. The engines of these diasporic public spheres are both symbolic "mediascapes" and actual patterns – or "ethnoscapes" – of geographical mobility. The combined effect of these factors, he claims is "the incapacity of states to prevent their minority popula-tions from linking themselves to wider constituencies of religious or ethnic affiliations", with the result that the era is over when "we could assume that … public spheres were typically, exclusively or necessarily national".[46]

The extent to which many locales are now awash with imports – foreign persons, goods, objects, messages and connections of one sort or another is well captured in Richard Wilk's description of contemporary Belize. As he puts it:

> the economy is open to foreign capital, the stores full of imports. Belizians themselves are transnational – their families scattered across the United States and Canada, with most of the young expecting to spend parts of their lives abroad. Those that stay at home are bombarded by foreign media … When Belizians turn off the television they can look out the window at a parade of foreign tourists, resident expatriates and students in search of authentic local experience, tradi-tional medicine, untouched rainforests and ancient ruins.[47]

Moreover, as he goes on to argue, access to these foreign goods is now much democratised, compared with earlier periods. Even the poorest and apparently isolated parts of the world often turn out, on closer inspection to be heavily connected into the global economy. Thus, in her analysis of village life in rural northern Egypt Lila Abu-Lughod observes that "while the village appears picturesque … there is not an aspect of people's everyday lives that has not been shaped by 'the modern'". This can be a matter of the state's control over local agricultural practices, schools and welfare services or of the impact of the global economy, for

> how well people eat and whether they decide to uproot cash crops to grow wheat is determined by such far away organisations as the World Bank and the IMF. Whether the men are away looking for work depends on the state of the South Arabian economy, the decisions of bourgeois investors in the Red Sea tourist developments [or] whether the *New York Times* has reported "terrorist" attacks in Cairo.[48]

The question of globalisation is, for good reason, often blurred together with the question of "Americanisation". However, in an analysis of local identities in Cairo, Farha Ghannam makes the important point that other forms of globalisation beyond that represented by Americanisation are often also present in the experience of a variety of "locals". In the case of the residents of the quarter of Cairo which Ghannam studied, besides these American influences, she argues they

> also experience the global through oil-producing countries where their children and male relatives work, as well as through the mixture of people who visit and work in Cairo from different Arab countries … Women use oil for their hair that comes from India via their sons who work in Kuwait … others visit husbands in Saudi Arabia … many have accumulated electrical appliances from Libya where their husbands and sons work.[49]

Travelling and dwelling

In the words of James Clifford, we now live amidst the possibilities of a "to-and-fro made possible by modern technologies of transport, communication and labour migration. Airplanes, telephones, tape cassettes, camcorders and mobile job markets reduce distances and facilitate two-way traffic, legal and illegal, between the world's places".[50] If the announcement of the obsolescence of the nation state is premature, nonetheless, according to Clifford, "in a world of migrations and television satellites, the policing of frontiers and collective essences can never be absolute" and "nations" require constant maintenance. Moreover, nationalisms articulate their purportedly homogenous ties and spaces selectively, in relation to new transnational flows and cultural forms.[51] However, if we take mobility to be a defining characteristic of the contemporary world, we must simultaneously pose the question of why (and with what degrees of freedom) particular people stay at home and ask how, in a world of flux, forms of collective dwelling are sustained and reinvented.[52] It would be pointless, as Clifford observes, to simply reverse the traditional anthropological figures of the sedentary native and that of the intercultural traveller, so as to turn the old margin into the conceptual pivot of a generalised nomadology which claims that "we" are all now equally travellers. Rather, he argues, we need to develop a more nuanced analysis of the specific tensions between dwelling and travelling in particular historical situations. What is required then is a "comparative cultural studies approach to specific histories, tactics and everyday practices of dwelling and travelling", and Clifford suggests that

> We need to think comparatively about the distinct routes/roots of tribes, barrios, favelas, immigrant neighbourhoods – embattled histories with crucial community "insiders" and regulated travelling "outsiders". What does it take to define and defend a homeland? What are the political stakes in claiming (or sometimes being relegated to) a "home"?[53]

While it has been claimed by Scott Lash and John Urry that the paradigmatic modern experience is that of rapid mobility over long distances,[54] John Tomlinson argues that the model of contemporary life as characterised centrally by voluntary forms of mobility is, in fact, strictly applicable only to a relatively small number of highly privileged people. Tomlinson rightly argues that it is "important not to exaggerate the way long-distance travel figures either in the lives of the majority of people in the world today or in the overall process of globalisation". Indeed, as he insists, despite the increasing ubiquity of various forms of travel, "local life ... is the vast order of human social existence ... which [still] occupies the majority of time and space", and mobility "is ultimately subordinate to – indeed derivative of – the order of location in time and space which we grasp as 'home'".[55] To this extent, the paradigm of mobile deterritorisation advanced by those such as Lash and Urry is then only applicable to the "experiences of the affluent ... information rich sectors of the most economically developed parts of the world", rather than being a truly global experience.[56] John Durham Peters also argues against the rush to declaim the "death (or transcendence) of the local", pointing out rightly that "most of the human species still lives out its days in localised spaces, dependent in various ways on people they have known for years". As he observes, distance from the local is often a luxury, and localities (whether chosen or fated) "still govern the lives of most humans, even the rapidly increasing numbers with access to global, regional, national and local media".[57] Nowadays the displaced and marginal hybrid experience of the migrant is sometimes held to be *the* central global experience. The problem is both that this abstract generalisation of the migrant experience flattens out all the specifications and differences within that category and that it ignores the experience of those vast realms of people who remain static, whether through choice or by force of circumstance.

Despite all the talk of global flows, fluidity, hybridity and mobility, it is worth observing that, in the UK at least, there is evidence that points to continued geographical sedentarism on the part of the majority of the population. Thus Peter Dickens argues that despite widespread assumptions to the contrary, geographical mobility in the UK actually declined in the 1970s and 1980s, as compared with the so-called "stable" times of the 1950s and 1960s.[58] Similarly, Diane Warburton argues that the "mobility of people in the UK has been over-played" and quotes research which suggests that "overall, there is a clear focus of attachment on the most local area"; she goes on to argue that, notwithstanding considerations of "global connexity", "most people have an environmental horizon which is very local – the end of the street or the top of the next hill".[59] While these gross statistics evidently conceal important variations (not least by class, ethnicity and gender) the evidence indicates that sedentarism is far from finished. Thus, while one recent report noted that people in the UK often now do live further away from their relatives than they did in the past, it seems that nonetheless the majority still live within one hour's journey time, and 72 per cent of grandparents still see their grandchildren at least once a week, which indicates a fairly low radius of intergenerational mobility. At its simplest, as John Gray has noted, "over half of British adults live within five miles of where they were born". It would seem that for the majority of the UK population, at least, David Sibley is still right when he observes baldly that, globalisation notwith-standing, "many people live in one place for a long time". As Ken Worpole puts it in a study of urban life in the UK: "still, for a significant proportion of any population, the town or city they are born in is the one that will shape their lives and become the stage-set of their hopes and aspirations".[60] How they make sense of their lives there, and how those lives relate both to the broader environment and to the lives of those who, through force of circumstance or choice, are more mobile, is the burden of much of the argument that follows.

However, while many people remain local and many are "kept in place" by structures of oppression of various forms, the experience which is most truly global is perhaps that of the experience of locality being undercut by the pene-tration of global forces and networks. To this extent, almost everywhere in the world, experience is increasingly "disembedded" from locality and the ties of culture to place are progressively weakened by new patterns of "connexity". It is, as Tomlinson argues, in the transformation of localities, rather than in the increase of physical mobility (significant though that may be for some groups), that the process of globalisation perhaps has its most important expression.[61] This is to suggest that though increased physical mobility is an important aspect of globalisation for some categories of people, "for most people, most of the time the impact of globalisation is felt not in travel but in staying at home". However, their experience of locality is transformed by the now banal and routinised process of "consumption of images of distant places" which, paradoxically, become familiar in their generic forms (the streets of New York, the American West, etc.) even to those who have never visited them, as they are normalised in the mediated lifeworld of the television viewer. This is to argue that the "paradigmatic experience of global modernity for most people … is that of staying in one place but experiencing the 'dis-placement' that global modernity brings to them".[62]

1

IDEAS OF HOME

Origins and belongings

It seems best to begin here with a brief survey of what the idea of home can mean. The Oxford English Dictionary defines home as "a place, region or state to which one properly belongs, on which one's affections centre, or where one finds refuge, rest or satisfaction". Angelika Bammer suggests that we might usefully think of home by analogy with Benedict Anderson's performative concept of the nation as an imagined community, as an "enacted space within which we try on roles and relationships of ... belonging and foreignness". Thus Bammer[1] argues that both nation and home are in this sense fictional constructs, "mythic narratives, stories the telling of which has the power to create the 'we' who are engaged in telling them" and to also create "the discursive right to a space (a country, a neighbourhood, a place to live) that is due us ... in the name of the 'we-ness' we have just constructed".[2] In something of the same vein, Dietmar Dath argues that "homes are 'origin stories' constructed as retrospective signposts ... they are made for coming *from*".[3] It is this which gives such poignancy to the reply given to Marina Warner by a taxi driver in San Francisco who, when she asked him where he was from, replied that he was "an illegal", as if that in itself were a well-established "place" or nationality.[4] Home is always a heavily value-laden term, and Agnes Heller perhaps inadvertently brings out some of the implicitly ethical aspects of the concept of home when she identifies place and "rootedness" with what she calls "geographical monogamy" and travel (or mobility) with "geographical promiscuity".[5]

The anthropologist Mary Douglas argues that while home is located, it is not necessarily fixed in space – rather, home starts by bringing space under control.[6] As she points out, a home is not only a space but involves regular patterns of activity and structures in time. From this point of view, home is the organisation of space over time and the "order of the day is the infrastructure of the community".[7] Douglas' argument coincides with that of Paddy Scannell on the ways in which the temporal schedules of media broadcasters function to organise and synchronise community experience. Here we also encounter the problematic relation between the home and the outside – via Scannell's arguments

16

concerning the role of broadcasting in "socialising" the domestic realm – so that we have also to consider the home as an embryonic or virtual community.[8] In his novel *Sybil* (1846), Benjamin Disraeli declares that "Home is a barbarous idea; the method of a rude age; home is isolation; therefore anti-social. What we want is community."[9] In this connection Krishan Kumar observes that the etymology of the words is instructive, in so far as

> the Latin *privatus* [carries] many of the connotations of the Greek *idiotes* "a private person" ... Private life is "idiotic" ... since it is a life spent in the privacy of one's own kind ... outside the world of the common ... A man [sic] who lives *only* a private life is not fully human.[10]

Home is not necessarily (or only) a physical place. Vincent Descombes defines a homeland as a virtual space – a rhetorical country. As he puts it, if we pose the question, "Where is (someone) at home?" the answer bears less on a geographical

> than a rhetorical territory ... The (person or) character is at home when he is at ease in the rhetoric of the people with whom he shares life. The sign of being at home is the ability to make oneself under-stood without too much difficulty, and to follow the reasoning of others, without any need for long explanations. The rhetorical country of a (person or) character ends where his interlocutors no longer understand the reasons he gives for his actions, the criticisms he makes, or the enthusiasms he displays. A disturbance of rhetorical communica-tion marks the crossing of a frontier, which should of course be envisaged as a border zone, a marchland, rather than a clearly drawn line.[11]

As Heller observes, within this "territory", "one can speak to the other without providing background information. No footnotes are needed; from few words, much can be understood."[12] However, she notes,

> to live in a home, be it one's nation ... ethnic community or family ... is ... an activity ... with formal requirements ... [in which] one partici-pates in a language game. X can say 'this is my home'; but if others (members of the family or religious community) do not co-sign the sentence, he will not be at home there. In a home, one needs to be accepted, welcomed or, at least, tolerated.[13]

Many years ago, the Italian filmmaker Federico Fellini well expressed the contingency of this sense of belonging when he remarked:

I dislike travelling and am ill at ease on journeys. In Italy, I can manage it: curiosity is aroused, I know what there is behind all those faces, voices, places. But when I'm abroad this bores me: I no longer know what anything means, I can no longer make anything out, I feel excluded.[14]

One person's exclusion is, of course, another's inclusion. Abigail Ramsey, an African-American student at Brown University in the USA, interviewed on her decision, after a year of living in a mixed-race student house, to move to the college's Harambee House, specifically set aside for African-Americans, explained her relief in her new home thus: "all of a sudden, I can talk to people going through the same things ... It feels more like home".[15] It is in this sense that Adorno argued that every language draws a circle around the people to which it belongs, a circle from which we can only escape in so far as one at the same time enters another one. It is, of course, and inevitably, also a question of power. Various contemporary forms of retrenchment and separatism may well be regrettable, but when the public world is felt to be dominated by the language and interests of some particular powerful group, others may well feel the need to put up barriers.

The domestic home: space, rules and comfort

Many approaches to the idea of home fail to pose the question of what makes possible the solidarity which is its essential foundation. While the processes that go to consolidate a country or a nation are seen to be worthy of study, the solidarity of the home is somehow often taken for granted. Against this, Douglas offers an elegant and detailed analysis of the home as a form of 'gift economy' (in Marcel Mauss' terms), an "ongoing and comprehensive system of exchanges" the daily reproduction of which is a highly complex achievement.[16] If a home is an embryonic or virtual community and not just a collection of individuals who happen to share the same household, it is above all dependent on a principle of sufficient solidarity to protect the common good. The maintenance of this principle requires highly complex forms of co-ordination and monitoring of household activities. Indeed, Douglas argues that "if we had to choose an index of solidarity from the time–space structure of our homes, the strongest indicator would not be the stoutness of the enclosing walls but the complexity of the co-ordination".[17] The burden of the home's organisation is largely carried by its adherence to conspicuous, fixed (and, indeed, often rigid) times and timetabling for the joint and separate activities of its members. Hence the emphasis on "common presence at fixed points in the day, the week ... [and] the year".[18] The requirement of common presence is often focused particularly on "family meals" and this requirement is naturally enforced all the more strongly at key moments in the national calendar. This, clearly is the basis of the importance placed in the UK on family members sharing the Christmas meal and in the USA on being home for Thanksgiving.[19] In this respect, by means of the co-ordination of domestic co-presence in space, the ordering of time, in both quotidian and calendarial terms, constitutes the infrastructure of the community.

In a fascinating analysis of the significance of the Thanksgiving meal, as a ritual through which Americans affirm their membership not only of their family but of their nation, Janet Susskind observes that "it is impossible to be an American and be unaware of Thanksgiving". It is a moment when, as if in exemplification of Benedict Anderson's phrase about the confidence that the members of a nation should have in each other's continued existence, "each household [knows] that all other households [are] celebrating in the same way at the same time". The ritual of Thanksgiving makes the "appearance of proper family relations, as demonstrated by full observance of the feast, the require-ment and proof of national identity".[20] Returning home at Thanksgiving time becomes a sentimental pilgrimage, a "ritual performance of solidarity, renewing or validating family ties". The ritual feast is a highly structured and emotionally laden celebration, not only symbolic of family and home but also of nation. Participation in this ritual "invests the value of family ties with an aura of reli-gion and patriotism" and allows its participants to connect themselves back to the cultural history of the "founding" of their nation.[21]

Homes and houses

Conventionally, in the West a home is, of course, inscribed in the particular physical structure of a house. In his investigation of these ideas, Gaston Bachelard is concerned with what he describes as the way in which inhabited space transcends geometrical space. In particular, he focuses on the ways in which the space of the house, as the first universe for the children who grow up in it, comes to shape all subsequent knowledge of the larger cosmos. For Bachelard, the house represents a metaphorical embodiment of memory and thus of identity, and is the "veritable principle of psychological integration".[22] While we might wish to resist some of the universalist and patriarchal premises of Bachelard's analysis, his insistence on the spatialisation of memory and on the potential benefits of what he calls "topo-analysis" seems nonetheless valuable as a way of understanding the inscription of affect in space, beginning at the micro level of the spatial structure of the childhood home, as the trellis on which early memory is woven.[23] Nonetheless, in Rachel Bowlby's critique, the limitation of Bachelard's analysis is that, in its romanticisation of the ideal childhood home, it finds no place for the inevitable presence within the home of the *unheimlich* or uncanny which always, for Freud, besets the tranquil vision of "homeliness". As Bowlby puts it,

> in psychoanalysis the home is no place of harmony ... [for] the house
> ... is irredeemably driven by the presence of ghosts, its comforting

appearance of womblike unity, doubled from the start by intruding forces ... untimely and dislocated hauntings of other times and places and other presences.[24]

If Bachelard is concerned with the role of the childhood home as the spatial template of memory and identity, Denis Wood and Robert Beck, in their analysis of "home rules", treat the existence of children in a domestic space as the stimulus for the enumeration of the rules which govern the inhabitation of that space.[25] Wood and Beck address the presence of alterity within the home from a different perspective. From their point of view, small children represent Outsiders or Barbarians in the home: "in so far as the child is barbarous, he is natural: in so far as he is natural he is an agent of ... dirtying", a process which disrupts the ordered system of the house.[26] Thus they argue that it is the work of their parents "to bring them in, to erase the signs of the Other, to raise them from the animal, to teach them to speak, to teach them the rules".[27] In the particular family living room which they studied over a seven-year period, Wood and Beck identified 223 separate rules governing the use of that space. Their argument is that while a room without small children (or some other category of "Barbarian") is a room whose rules are latent, their presence "excites adults to express the values manifested in the room ... in the form of prescriptive rules", thus enabling the adults to both maintain their values (in protecting the room and the objects in it from the children) and reproduce them by instilling these same values in their children. In this methodology, children play the role of a chemical agent whose presence leads to the explication of otherwise implicit domestic values, in a process which "forces the rules to disrobe".[28]

What Wood and Beck's analysis shares with Bachelard is an appreciation of the ways in which the most banal domestic objects and structures are not simply physical entities, but are also routinely laden down with values and symbolic meanings. If the childhood home gives initial shape to all later memory, this is perhaps because it is through (literally) learning to live ("behave") in the home that children learn the "habitus" of their culture. As they put it, "What is home for a child but a field of rules?"[29] A room can thus be best understood as a kind of objectified collective memory or mnemonic which "stores in the arrangement of its parts" how we behave in it. Naturally, in so far as those arrangements emerge from the pasts of the adults who furnished the room, the room is also a memory of their pasts. Their children, through learning to live in the rooms which their parents have furnished, learn the remembered values of their parents' memories – of the rooms which they grew up in. Thus is habitus transmitted through generations.

Wood and Beck offer what they call "a sort of environmental ethology" which is designed to be sensitive to the way in which a domestic space "exists not only in the material substances out of which it is composed" but is also sensitive to how "the things of the room embody the values and meanings that made, selected, arranged and preserved them". If rooms express values and also exist in the form of rules, "they form a … net of meanings and values capable of shaping the behaviour that gives rise to a room". As they note, the rules of the habitus are "a form of the room, just as the room is a form of the rules" and to know the rules of a room is to know the room itself, just as to see the room is to "see" its rules. To enter a room is to "find oneself immediately around objects whose character and arrangement admit of only certain possibilities".[30]

Just as Wood and Beck are concerned with the material embodiment of values in domestic structures at a micro level, Witold Rybczynski focuses on the parallel process on a broader scale, in relation to the architectural inscription of the idea of home.[31] He argues that "to speak of domesticity is to describe a set of felt emotions … to do with family, intimacy and devotion to the home … [and] a sense of the home as embodying … these sentiments". Rybczynski thus traces the development of the idea of this sense of domesticity, from medieval times when "houses were full of people … and privacy was unknown"[32] and where rooms did not have specialised functions, through the gradual process of the subdivision of the separate areas of the house into differentiated functions, most notably in Holland during the seventeenth century.[33] In this process, he points out that even the border between the public and private did not necessarily coincide with the outside walls of the house but sometimes with the division between downstairs and upstairs.[34] The crucial point, Rybczynski argues, is that the very idea that there should be such a clear boundary between inside and outside (wherever it might be located) was evidence of a new "desire to define the house as a separate special place".[35]

The history of home in urban space: a story of separations

Tracing a specifically European history, Kumar follows Ariès in seeing the modern idea of the family home as having emerged from the much more "promiscuous" world of the medieval household.[36] That space was less clearly bounded (more like we might nowadays think of a café or pub) and was open to the comings and goings of a multitude of diverse persons, involved in highly varied activities. As Kumar notes, it was only in the early seventeenth century that this more promiscuous world began to be ordered and tidied up, with persons and parts of the household being segregated by status and function, and boundaries much more highly drawn between work and non-work, insiders and outsiders, private and public.[37] Thus the European household gradually shrank to its nuclear "core" of the conjugal family and their dependent children.

Taking a British focus, David Chaney offers a historical analysis of changing modes of the definition and control of space in the nineteenth century, arguing that the key issue was what came to be perceived by Victorian reformers as the pre-modern city's lack of boundaries.[38] Up to that time, urban space lacked the forms of physical segregation which we now take for granted, in so far as distinct physical spaces were not necessarily reserved for particular activities – whether at the micro level, as between the different rooms in the house, or at the macro level, as between different districts of the city. For the reformers these various forms of heterogeneous mixing were seen as providing the threatening potential of pollution, destabilisation and disorder. Thus, nineteenth-century reforms were designed to more explicitly designate various forms of social and symbolic order by means of more clearly distinguishing between spaces. Prior to that time, the home had not necessarily been the exclusive terrain of a single family but often contained a mixture of biologically related persons, friends, associates and work partners. Work, recreation and the care of sick people all overlapped and co-existed within the same space. Thus reforms were designed precisely to enforce a clearer separation between the private and the public, home and work, and between feminine and masculine spheres (often designated to different parts, or rooms, of the house).

At a macro level, reforms functioned to delineate public space, by separating it off into increasingly distinct and separate specialised settings for particular types of activity (the space of the hospital or the cemetery, for example) and the city was fundamentally reorganised around "separate unities of work, residence and distraction".[39] The rise of suburbanism further fractured the urban landscape, as Chaney observes,

> through the twin strands of class segregation and domestic isolation ...
> [and] increasingly fine distinctions were made, so that each social frac-
> tion could live in a neighbourhood with a distinct and dominant
> identity ... [with] an elaborate vocabulary of physical distinctions to
> display the appropriate status of each household ... a language of class
> that has persisted as a practical mapping of urban life.[40]

In his commentary on early modern conceptions of the desirable city, based on the key principles of uniformity and regularity, Zygmunt Bauman notes that the overriding concern was how to construct clarity and order according to the requirement to "separate spatially parts of the city dedicated to different functions or differing in the quality of their inhabitants", so that "each tribe will occupy a separate district and each family a separate apartment". As he goes on to explain, from this classically modernist perspective, "logic and aesthetics alike demand functional non-ambiguity of any fragment of the city ... each function needs a place of its own, while every place should serve one and only one function".[41]

The social distribution of privacy and comfort

However, alongside the logic of the modernist rationalisation of space there remains the question of the emotional affect invested in the idea of home. The nineteenth-century Swedish painter of domestic interiors, Carl Larson, spoke of the aim of his paintings being to provide a sort of compensatory daydream, offering "that unspeakably sweet feeling of seclusion from the noise of the world".[42] However, if control over a separate and autonomous family living space, which provides some sense of that "sweet seclusion", is now something that many (apart from the homeless) in the affluent West take for granted, it is nonetheless a relatively recent historical phenomenon. In the UK, up until the nineteenth century, this kind of privatised lifestyle was open to the bourgeoisie alone, and has only become more widely available to broader sections of the population in the period of affluence after 1945. The link between domestic privacy and respectability is of key importance historically in the UK. Leonora Davidoff and Catherine Hall have traced the establishing of the privacy of the middle-class home in the nineteenth century via a whole system of room divisions, walls, gates and hedges.[43] The struggle to establish a clear division between the external world of work and community and the internal, private space of the family was crucial for nineteenth-century middle-class families in attempting to establish their respectability.[44]

In the Middle Ages, while an affluent home might have exhibited taste, or even magnificence, the modern idea of domestic comfort was totally absent.[45] Lukacs argues that the civilisation of the Middle Ages placed its primary emphasis on ceremony, in a context in which "life was a public affair", where what mattered was the external world and one's place in it. Rybczynski reminds us that the emergence of the idea of the self and the family which is taken for granted today in the West is a development specific to the last three hundred years in Europe. The evolution of domestic comfort can only be understood, Rybczynski argues, in that specific context in so far as it "begins in the appropriation of the house as a setting for an emerging interior life". In essence, Lukacs' argument is that "domesticity, privacy, comfort, the concept of the home and of the family ... are literally, principal achievements of the Bourgeois Age".[46] However, there is a further dimension to this process which, while not his principal concern, is at least noted by Rybczynski. As he observes, the classical Dutch idea of "homely domesticity" depended on the development of a "rich interior awareness", which itself was the result of a revaluation of women's role in the home. Thus, he observes, "if domesticity was ... one of the principal achievements of the Bourgeois Age, it was, above all, a Feminine achievement".[47]

As Bowlby notes in her commentary on Rybczynski's work, his "is a reassuringly evolutionary history ... of developments in bourgeois forms of living accommodation and their accompanying nations of family, intimacy and comfort", in which "the home and its pleasures were just waiting placidly to be found, at the end of the smooth historical path leading straight to the modern armchair".[48] For Rybczynski, this idea of domestic comfort is one that, if it has taken a long historical time to develop, is nonetheless one which he admonishes us to cherish and value unproblematically. The problem here, for Bowlby, lies in the price that has, historically, been paid by the housewife, in her endless labour at the altar of the ideal of domestic comfort. We shall return to this theme later (see Chapter 3), but first we must consider, in more detail, the processes through which the idea of home is materialised and symbolised.

23

The symbolism of home

Just as most forms of Western music return in conclusion to what is called their "home key", as a form of aesthetic resolution, so in her philosophical discourse on the concept of home Agnes Heller declares that

> integral to the average everyday life is awareness of a fixed point in space, a firm position from which we "proceed" ... and to which we return in due course. That firm position is what we call home ... "Going home" should mean: returning to that firm position which we know, to which we are accustomed, where we feel safe and where our emotional relationships are at the most intense.[49]

This feeling of safety and security is commonly inscribed in the physical nature of the home. Thus, in his commentary on the classic children's story *The Wind in the Willows*, Jon Bird observes that it is the space of the home which differentiates between the known and the familiar, and the loss of security and innocence.[50]

As Tim Putnam notes, research into the meaning of home "repeatedly throws up the same basic terms: privacy, security, family, intimacy, comfort and control", even if these terms are interpreted by different people, in varying circumstances, in quite different ways.[51] The home does not simply harbour or provide a background context for these sentiments – rather, it embodies them in its physical structure. In her analysis of Scandinavian household practices, Sivi Norve argues that while these days people actually build their own homes much less frequently than they did in the past, nonetheless, in the figurative sense, we still *make* our homes. As she notes, in so far as home-making us a creative practice "we still build ... we equip the home, give it colours, maintain it and arrange its patterns. We give the rooms functions and expressions." To this extent, she argues "we create something different, another ... arrangement of the material structure that has been delivered to us" – and if we fail to do this effectively, as she remarks, "the dwelling is not a proper home in the general meaning of the term".[52]

The symbolic dimensions of home and territorial belonging have always been a central preoccupation of anthropological analyses of "primitive" societies. Thus Janet Carsten and Stephen Hugh-Jones argue that the role of ritualistic property and heirlooms in sustaining the continuity of social groupings based on a particular place of residence should not be underestimated. These forms of continuity, they argue, are often assured "through holding onto fixed and movable property and through the transmission of the names, titles and prerogatives which are integral to its existence and identity".[53] However, these issues are not simply of interest in so-called primitive settings. Thus Putnam reports that in a highly mobile society such as the USA, there is evidence to suggest that "portable collections of artefacts appear to be more important in constructs of identity than attachment to house form as such, or indeed, to locality".[54] Nonetheless, and despite parallels such as this, I am conscious of the limits of the EurAmcentric history of "home" which I recount here, as it is by no means necessarily adequate to different cultural and geographical circumstances, where, for example, physical conditions may have quite different implications for home-making practices. Thus Carsten and Hugh-Jones argue that in many contexts the symbolic power of a house is also carried by the network of connections between the building and its residents, rather than simply residing in the building itself or in the objects it contains. They note, for example, that

> Malays ... do not distinguish house from home; they take it for granted that a house contains people ... Houses that are abandoned decay surprisingly rapidly and may be a source of anxiety, just as the people without houses who are a feature of present-day life in urban Britain give rise to another kind of alarm.[55]

Privatisation and domesticity

To return to the British context, since at least the 1960s, home and family centredness have been recognised as key characteristics of contemporary privatised lifestyles.[56] Thus, Ann Oakley has argued that "if society has grown more 'family-orientated', the family itself has identified more and more squarely with its physical location, the home. 'Home' and 'family' are now virtually interchangeable terms".[57] Adrian Franklin summarises the "privatisation thesis" as arguing that, in the UK at least, people have been gradually withdrawing from public life into their homes. Driven by a sense of powerlessness in the spheres of work, politics and public life, people have retreated into a "sphere of autonomy and control which would restore to them a sense of identity, attachment and belonging" – in a "place of their own", especially in the case of home owners.[58] Thus Graham Allan argues that, in the UK context, at least,

> The higher quality of housing obtainable by the majority of the population, the greater facilities and improved ambience of the home, the increasing emphasis on the ideology of conjugal marriage and "family-centredness" all foster the identification of "home" with "family" to the extent that the home then comes to be thought of as "the family's natural habitat".[59]

The increase in owner-occupation which took place in the UK in the post-war period was part of a more general trend towards a more affluent, privatised and home-centred lifestyle. Home-based consumerism and the widening ownership of consumer durables of all kinds (such as fridges and washing machines, which spread quickly in the wake of the post-World War II spread of electrification) were at the heart of this process. The "crowning object" in this process was, of course, the television, and the "television aerial above symbolised the new way of life within. Television was ... the defining symbolic object of affluence".[60]

The process of privatisation is, however, not without its own contradictions. Without falling into a technologically determinist argument, one can still note that tendencies towards home-centredness have certainly been exacerbated by technological changes in the move towards a self-service economy.[61] However, if technological pressures have worked towards a physical concentration of activity within the household, in some respects at least, they have also worked to break up the traditional family structures around which the idea of home has been based. I noted earlier the significance which Douglas rightly gives to the shared family meal as one of the key institutions through which a home is maintained. Her point is that such meals are the crucial occasion for all kinds of intercommunication. However, Kumar suggests that nowadays the microwave, as the technological embodiment of the discourse of individualism, has gone some distance (in combination with the development of freezer food) towards supplanting the practice of the shared family meal by individualised snacks often consumed at different times. Thus, he claims, "if the hearth is no longer the centre of the home, no more is the kitchen or the dining room, with the family meal symbolising togetherness".[62] To this extent, the degree of solidarity argued by Douglas to be necessary to the maintenance of the home as a "collective good" is that much more diminished, as the family fragments within the home. Clearly, in an era of multi-set television households, personal computers, personal telephones and Walkmans, home can hardly be quite what it used to be.

Homelessness in a home-centred culture

If home is an inevitably problematic space, still to be without a home in a home-centred culture is a traumatic experience. As Dick Hebdige observes,[63] full citizenship has often historically implied not just rootedness in place but property ownership, and in many places the state has long demanded a fixed address in exchange for citizenship rights. Similarly, Fontaine reminds us that a legal address is an expected attribute of a citizen.[64] Increasingly, it seems that the moral order has in effect been spatialised. Mike Davis' analysis of "Fortress LA" offers one glaring example of the contemporary bifurcation of "good citizens, off the streets, enclaved in their seemingly private consumption spheres ... [and] bad citizens, on the streets (and therefore not engaged in legitimate business) caught in the terrible Jehovan scrutiny of police helicopter surveillance".[65] As Jon Bird notes in a similar vein, in his commentary on Rachel Whiteread's *House* sculpture in the UK, within this spatialised moral order "the common experience of the homeless and the migrant is to be made to feel out of place".[66] In his analysis of the politics of representation of homelessness, Neil Smith notes that the (involuntary) presence of homeless people in the public sphere is often contested by structures of authority and "their visibility is consistently erased by institutional efforts to move them elsewhere – to shelters, out of building and parks, to poor neighbourhoods, out of the city, to other marginal spaces" in an ongoing attempt at their "erasure from the public gaze". It is against this background, he argues, that the significance of Krzystof Wodiczko's "Homeless Vehicle" project (see Figure 1.1) can be understood – in so far as it "empowers the evicted to erase their own erasure ... making home-less people visible and enhancing their identities ... dramatis[ing] the[ir] ... right ... not to be isolated and excluded".[67] Clearly, given the centrality of ideas of home as the naturalised habitat of private family life, the eruption of the crisis of homelessness in the affluent West in the Reagan/Thatcher years threw that cosy image of tranquil domesticity into sharp relief. As Marianna Torgovnick writes, it is because of our presumption that home is a natural place of shelter, where we can lock the doors against misfortune and unwanted outsiders, that

> the plight of refugees, or civilians in war, or the homeless, is so terri-
> fying. No home, no place to live, no place to shelter, no place to get
> away from it all. Home is the utopian ideal. Home is what we have to
> believe is safe, where we have to carry on as though it will be safe.[68]

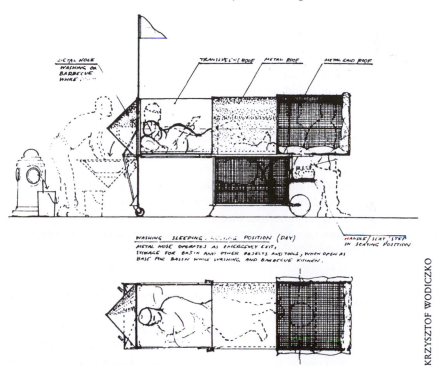

Figure 1.1 Functions of the Homeless Vehicle.

Source: Diagram by Krzysztof Wodiczko.

Homelessness, and the "sudden descent to the streets", according to Mary Ellen Hombs, precipitates not only loss of material possessions and connections but "also means a silent stripping away of rights that accompany being housed, rights that legitimate one in the eyes of society and government".[69] In a photographic essay on homelessness in the UK, Syd Jeffers noted that the problem for homeless people living in hotels or hostels paid for by Social Security was not that they were "without shelter". Their problem was that they "had little or no control over that shelter" nor over their everyday activities within it, which had to conform to a variety of imposed regulations, allowing them none of the autonomy routinely associated with being "at home". Many of them spent their time, parents and children crammed together in a small room, crowded with their possessions, trying to make what was, in effect, a waiting room (and often a room without a view, except that provided by a television) into a home.[70]

I noted earlier the way in which Rybczynski unproblematically identifies domesticity with ideas of privacy. Against this backdrop, the work of artists such as Krzystof Wodiczko and that of Martha Rosler (in her *Home Front* and *Bowery* installations, for example) dramatises the epistemological crisis in the structure of our experience caused by the way in which "homelessness brings the private into the streets".[71] In the UK context, the artist whose work has functioned most effectively to dramatise these issues has been Rachel Whiteread, with her *House* sculpture cast from the internal space of a demolished house.[72] According to Bachelard, the house is an image which bespeaks intimacy. When its walls are removed, as they were by Whiteread, then that intimacy confronts us in a wholly unfamiliar and disturbing way, as the private interior space of the house (its homely dimension) is thrust into public visibility. As Jon Bird observes in his commentary on the *House* sculpture, its particular effectivity was amplified by the public discourses in play during its period of existence, which coincided with that of the conflict in Bosnia. As Bird puts it:

> During the brief period of the existence of *House* as a media event ...
> its image appeared on television screens flowing with footage of the
> war in Bosnia. As the broadcast media emptied evidence of the world's
> broken cities into our private spaces, the fragility of homes and home-
> land was painfully evident in the images of wholly or partly destroyed
> buildings.[73]

Housing has long been central to the politics of community in London's East End, and the politics of place are equally central to the racist myth of the East End's past as a white, pure enclave ("before immigration"). Bow, where Whiteread's *House* sculpture was made, is a particularly white enclave within the East End. It was also one of the areas where a housing policy which prioritised "locals" (in effect, prioritising whites) was developed by the area's council. As Massey observes, all these factors gave the sculpture a particularly resonant symbolic charge.[74] Thus, in his analysis of local debates surrounding the *House* sculpture, Couldry notes the equivalence between the vocal, local opposition to *House* and the support for the sculpture offered by those who, so far as the locals were concerned, could be scornfully designated as "outsiders" – rich, privileged would-be gentrifiers, with no authentic claim to local legitimacy.[75] As we shall see in Chapter 9, just as, at a certain point in the race politics of the Isle of Dogs, the cockroach came to symbolise the "unwanted immigrant", Watney argues that Rachel Whiteread's sculpture *House* itself became an emblem of a similar sort and "was taken by its opponents as itself a species of unwanted, illegal immigrant", the final destruction of which symbolised the elimination of unwanted "foreign" elements from the "pure" space of community and tradition.[76] Thus is the space of home often purified.

For all but the homeless, privacy is now widely assumed to be a key feature of home life, enabling family members to live as they please without the scrutiny of others. As Allan and Crow observe, one key dimension of this is "the power to exclude others, a defensive measure to allow access to the resources of the home to a select and privileged few".[77] This access is carefully modulated – others of various types (near and distant kin, friends, representatives of state agencies) are routinely allowed varying degrees of access only to various parts of the house (some only to the hall or front parlour, some to the kitchen, a select few to the bedrooms) at different times (some on special occasions, some only in crisis, some every day). Our psychic dependence on this ability to control the physical borders of our living space is most clearly dramatised in the feelings of violation (quite apart from material loss) frequently displayed by victims of domestic burglary.[78]

For the bourgeois householder, Walter Benjamin observed that the domestic interior was the "universe for the private citizen" and its sitting room "a box in the world theatre", a sanctuary from which the world could be safely observed.[79] However, this is far from being a universal experience. The function and significance of home clearly varies with its context and, in a hostile social environment the importance of "homeplace", as bell hooks phrases it, is all the more important. She argues that for black people in America, living in a racist society, the construction of some form of autonomous domestic "homeplace" has been crucial to the development of any wider "community of resistance". To this extent, the construction of black homes, however fragile or tenuous (even in a hut or shack) has always had a political dimension, in so far as these were the places where black people could affirm and support one another, thus restoring to themselves the dignity denied them in the outside (white) world.[80] As Doreen Massey notes, the writing of bell hooks and of Toni Morrison (especially in her novel *Beloved*) "undermines ... any notion that everyone once had a place called home which they could look back on, a place not only where they belonged but which belonged to them and where they could locate their identities" as the "very meaning of the term 'home' has been very different for those who have been colonised".[81] As bell hooks herself puts it, historically for African-Americans there has long been a crucial recognition of "the subversive value of homeplace, of having access to private space where we do not directly encounter white racist aggression", so that, in this context, "domestic space has been a crucial site for organising, for forming political solidarity".[82]

Having outlined these elements of the history and politics of ideas of domesticity we now move to address the broader question of how on a broader scale, the nation comes to be figured as a place of belonging, a homeland or Heimat.

2

HEIMAT, MODERNITY
AND EXILE

At home in the Heimat

Michael Keith and Steven Pile speak of the troubling dominance, in everyday discourse of "a reactionary vocabulary of ... the identity politics of place and a spatialised politics of identity grounded in ... the rhetoric of origins, of exclusion, of boundary-making, of invasion and succession, of purity and contamination ... the glossary of ethnic cleansing".[1] As Zygmunt Bauman puts it "in an ever more insecure and uncertain world, the withdrawal into the safe haven of territoriality is an intense temptation; and so the defence of the territory – the 'safe home' becomes the pass-key to all doors which one feels must be locked".[2] In the same spirit, in her exploration of the dividing line between "home" and "hatred", Mitzi Goldman argues that there is an inextricable link between the imagining of home and the mechanisms of exclusion (and often hatred) used to define its borders, in so far as "a unified sense of self and nation depends on the exclusion or 'othering' of any foreign element that disrupts that image of unity".[3] Hatred for those who threaten its realisation is often implicit in the desire for the absolute security of home. Julia Kristeva argues that, in the regressive formulation of this desire we find

> hatred of those others who do not share my origins and who affront me personally, economically and culturally: I then move back among "my own", I stick to an archaic primitive common denominator, the one of my frailest childhood, my closest relatives, hoping they will be more trustworthy than "foreigners".[4]

It is on this basis, as Anders Johansen observes, that the nation is often experienced as a

> magnified version of the family and the circle of close friends. Its territory is our "home"; its people is marked by a common "character", much like the members of a family; its past is a "heritage" passed down from our "forefathers".[5]

31

The ascription of bodies to their proper territory does not pertain exclusively to the living. As Lisa Malkki notes, the ashes or bodies of persons who have died on foreign soil are often returned to their place of birth for burial. Conversely, there are many examples of the bodies of "foreigners" of one sort or another being exhumed and their graves despoiled as a protest against their burial in a place where they are felt by some not to "belong".[6]

Historically, the ideas of home and homeland have perhaps been most emphatically intertwined in the German concept of Heimat. Of course, as Eric Hobsbawm observes, "*Heimat* is almost always a social construction rather than a real memory ... At the limit, as when we look back across oceans or generations ... it becomes an imagined community".[7] It is nonetheless an extremely powerful signifier, notwithstanding its imagined quality. Drawing on the German tradition, Yi-Fu Tuan quotes what he calls a "superb specimen" of "Heimat sentimentality" from a South Tyrolean almanac for the year 1953:

> *Heimat* is first of all the mother earth who has given birth to our folk and race, who is the holy soil, who gulps down God's clouds, sun and storms so that together ... they give us the strength to lead a good life ... *Heimat* is ... the landscape we have experienced ... that has been fought over, menaced, filled with the history of families, towns and villages ... the *Heimat* of knights and heroes, of battles and victories, legends and fairy tales.. But more than all of this, our *Heimat* is the land which has become fruitful through the sweat of our ancestors ... for this *Heimat* our fathers have died.[8]

The German Heimat tradition takes an important part of its inspiration from Johann Gottfried Herder, who went so far as to argue that:

> prejudice is good in its proper time, because it brings happiness. It heightens the bonds of peoples grouped around their centre, it strengthens their stock, makes their nature bloom, makes them more ardent also and more blissful in their inclinations and purposes.[9]

Thus Jeffrey Peck notes that the terms Heimat and *Fremde* imply "far more than simply 'homeland' or 'a foreign place'. *Heimat* also connotes belonging and security, while *Fremde* can refer to isolation and alienation".[10] According to Celia Applegate, the Heimat of the German tradition was never "a real place, like the hometown, but an ersatz place, indeed not a place at all but a device whereby strangers could be countrymen ... a general term for the Volk in every German", and the message of the Heimat movement, Applegate claims, was "to find the village in oneself [and] make it part of one's identity".[11] Drawing on recent work on the function of metaphor in political discourse which argues that concepts of nation, home and family all operate to provide their inhabitants with different modalities of feelings of familiarity, security, unity and solidarity,

Ghassan Hage argues that national identity is "always mediated by local experience at the level of home, family, village or neighbourhood" – and even wider spaces.[12] In this process communal intimacy is reconciled with ideas of national greatness as the nation is idealised as a kind of hometown writ large, a socio-geographical environment into whose comforting security we may sink.

The idea of Heimat functions particularly to link the scattered fringes of German-speakers "to a specific past and tradition that are linked to common values, ideal, customs, and location"; thus it follows that "to be able to participate in this *Heimat* requires an identification which is at least ethnic if not racial".[13] Jeffrey Peck observes that the process of unification after 1989 moved quickly to include "all Germans", including "ethnic Germans" returning from Poland and the Soviet Union, whose "Germanness" was based on "blood links" (even when they and their families had lived elsewhere for generations and knew nothing of contemporary Germany). At the same time, the united Germany made no "room in its house for the black, brown and yellow people who live there" and a racialised definition of "who is foreign and who is German emerged again as a central issue in German life", with citizens' initiatives in various cities (especially in the former GDR) declaring their ambition to make themselves *Ausländerfrei* (free of foreigners).[14]

Rootlessness as disorder

The over-valuation of home and roots has as its necessary correlative the suspicion of mobility. As Tim Cresswell observes, the whole apparatus of state bureaucracy in most countries has long depended on the notion that people should live, work, pay taxes and vote in a fixed location, so that to be of no fixed abode is already to be a suspicious character, and mobility itself comes to be seen as a form of geographical deviance. Certainly these prejudices have long historical roots and Cresswell points both to the definition of all "vacabondes" as rogues in Elizabethan England and to the ways in which, in Nazi Germany, the persecution of the Jews and the gypsies was specifically justified by reference to their rootlessness. Clearly, as Cresswell observes, the definition of mobility as deviance derives from "the positive valuation of roots in a place-bound, property-owning society" where "mobility ... appears to be a kind of superdeviance ... [which] disturbs the whole notion that the world can be segmented into clearly defined places ... [and] becomes a basic form of disorder and chaos – constantly defined as transgression and trespass".[15]

Historically, as Peter Stallybrass and Allon White point out in their commentary on nineteenth-century discourses of social reform, Henry Mayhew's classic study of London takes as its starting point a division between two distinct "races" – the "wanderers" and the "civilised tribes", who are defined precisely by their contrast. As they note, "Mayhew's definition of the nomadic is a demonised version of what Bhaktin later defined as the grotesque", where the "nomads" confront the bourgeois spectators "as a spectacle of filth". They represent the very antithesis of bourgeois respectability, in so far as they "transgress all settled boundaries of home" and thus "simultaneously map out the area which lies beyond cleanliness" – where topography, physical appearance and morality are conflated and it becomes difficult to distinguish moral from physical filth. Indeed, it is only by means of the depiction of the unsavoury ways of the nomadic Other that Mayhew is able to negatively define what constitutes the "civilised".[16]

The production and definition of a sense of home and Heimat thus involves the designation of those – foreigners or "strangers" – against whom those within define themselves. Bauman argues that if all societies produce strangers, "each kind of society produces its own kind of strangers. In drawing its borders and charting its ... maps [any society] cannot but gestate people who conceal borderlines deemed crucial to its orderly and/or meaningful life".[17] In his analysis of Czech discourses of national identity, Ladislav Holy argues that they are characterised by a sense that the solidarity of the nation's members "springs from their all recognising the same space as their home and from all of them inhabiting that home".[18] While this much is familiar as a way of analysing such discourses, Holy then goes on to offer an extremely interesting model of the way in which foreigners or others, who do not belong to this national family, can be differentiated by reference to the modalities in which they cross the border of the Czechs' homeland. Thus Holy offers the following schema, according to which these categories can be subdivided between "guests" ("those who have been invited into the nation on a temporary basis"); "servants" ("those who do not count a specific space as their own but may live there to carry out their work"); "burglars" ("intruders who enter without invitation"); "lodgers" ("those who stay on a contractual basis in somebody else's home and enjoy, to a specified extent, the privilege of belonging") and "squatters" ("those who have entered without permission and treat it as if it were their own home").[19]

The road to the nation

Michael Billig rightly argues that a "a place – a homeland [always] has to be imagined ... beyond the directly apprehended locality ... [and] ... beyond immediate experience of place".[20] It is not only communications media which enable the construction of the imagined community of the nation, but also physical communication and transport links such as railways and motorways, which transform the functioning of what Foucault called "the three great variables – territory, communication and speed".[21] Addressing the particular historical case of the role of the construction of the autobahn system in enabling a particular form of "imagining" of the nation under the National Socialists in Germany, Edward Dimendberg writes that "the Autobahn became medium and message in one, a means to conquer spatial distance that also transformed the meaning of the territory that it traversed".[22] In the propagandistic documentaries made at the time about the building of the autobahns, emphasis was placed not only on the increased ease of travel they allowed, but also on "the gradual shrinking of distances between German cities and the advent of the *Reich* as a consolidated geographical entity". The commentary in one such documentary noted that the autobahn system would "not only contribute to the melding of the German people into a stronger political and economic unit, but will also put an end to the last remnants of particularistic thinking". The motorways were "no mere transportation system" but also a symbolic mechanism that "fostered the citizens' experience of belonging to the German nation" by making a particular aestheticised vision of the German landscape visible to the automobilised subject through his (sic) windscreen.[23] Thus the new technologies of road- and car-building were utilised in the service of a romantic pastoralism which idealised not just nature in general, but German nature and its specific landscape. As Dimendberg notes, autobahn routes were carefully inserted into this landscape and were planned so as to take in scenic views, even if that entailed otherwise unnecessary detours. Thus the autobahns facilitated an "automobilised ... gaze" directed towards an idealised natural environment, enabling "the whole German people ... to share anew together, in a national community, experience such as has for generations been lost to us", opening up for them "wide areas of their homeland of which hitherto they had known practically nothing".[24] If the German case provides an extreme example of this literal process of nation-building, it should not be seen in isolation. Thus, in his historical analysis of the construction of national feeling in America and Sweden, Orvar Lofgren stresses the role of the construction of new physical structures such as sewerage projects, road construction and the installation of electricity in linking together individual homes and previously isolated villages, building them into the fabric of the nation. As he observes, in the USA this was particularly apparent in the massive national highway construction project from the 1920s onwards, which was heralded as a patriotic project that would overcome remaining forms of regional sectionalism.[25]

The production of what Lauren Berlant calls the "National Symbolic" must be seen as an effect both of the circulation of the population around the sacred landscapes and national monuments of the community and simultaneously, of the circulation of those images, in mediated form, in the lives (and homes) of the population.[26] To illustrate this latter point I take an example from the English case, concerning the function of reproductions of one of the painter Constable's famous landscapes in the homes of many British people. In their project on the domestication of national iconography, Colin and Ann Painter investigated the various forms in which one particular visual icon of Englishness is enshrined in the homes of the nation (as reproductions, on teatrays, embroideries, pottery, etc.). The icon in question is John Constable's painting *The Cornfield*, held in the National Gallery in London – a painting which is widely understood to express a powerful symbolism of Englishness as itself enshrined in the simple pleasures of rural, bucolic life.[27] As the Painters observe, for the majority of the British population now living in urban environments, a painting such as *The Cornfield* offers them an archetypical representation of a nostalgic vision of Englishness as an idealised form of rural life. People who have one or another form of the image in their home speak of liking it "because it epitomises what I imagine country life to be like", or because it shows "a typical summer's day in peaceful rural England", or "a vision of rural England which is fast disappearing", or because "it brings back an age of innocence ... an era when things were much more green and simple". As the Painters demonstrate, this image has become "in a literal sense part of the visual furniture of thousands of people, a consistent element of their daily life, as a framed reproduction or cushion cover, as clock-face or biscuit tin". As they note, many of the people who own a reproduction of the painting

> are unconcerned with its existence as a work of art (its title, who painted it, when it was painted) and may be unaware that the original is a painting and hangs in the National Gallery. In their lives, the image and its existence as an object, has other meanings

and they relate to it and make sense of it within the fabric of their particular life.[28] In "framing" it in their world, or living with it on their cushion covers, they incorporate a crucial part of the national mythology of England as an "Old Country" directly into the symbolic structure of their own home.[29]

Perhaps even more strikingly than in the case of the sedentary, domestic English population, English landscape views of this sort have often played a particularly important nostalgic role for English exiles abroad. When Constable published a series of mezzotint plates of his rural views in 1830, his aim was to "increase the interest for, and promote the study of, the Rural Scenery of England, with all its endearing association, its amenities, and even its most simple localities, abounding as it does in grandeur and every description of Pastoral Beauty".[30] As Inderpal Grewal notes, the appeal of such peaceful "home scenery" (as Constable called it) was all the stronger in the context of emerging patterns of colonial emigration to lands far away. For the emigrants – most strikingly, perhaps, those portrayed in Richard Redgrave's famous painting *The Emigrants' Last Sight of Home* – the English landscape scenes remain as the lost secure symbol of home and peace, to treasure as a talisman while they travel.[31] According to Bill Schwarz "transporting domestic England to an alien environment – 'solemnly observing the rights of Camberley in the heart of Mudpore' – was part of the very stuff of empire" and one of the most familiar tropes of empire was "the paradox of England claiming exaggerated subjective affiliation overseas, in the white communities of distant colonies, far beyond the home shores of geographical England, where imagined England was more intensely idealised than 'at home'".[32] Focusing on the metaphor of the migrant's suitcase (to which we shall return later), Schwarz offers an illuminating commentary on a visit which the white English novelist Paul Scott made to the village of an old Indian comrade from the Second World War. During the visit, Scott suffered a combination of physical illness, discomfort and cultural dislocation to the point of nervous collapse, where a "fetishistic obsession with his suitcase" became his "only hold on his erstwhile reality", and Scott's greatest longing, as he later recounted it, was to "see another white face and to get back into my own white skin". The experience, Scott recounted, put "a severe strain on my civilised liberal instincts" and led him to better appreciate "the physical and emotional impulses that had always prompted the British in India to sequester themselves in clubs and messes and forts, to preserve some-times, to the point of absurdity, their own English middle-class way of life".[33]

Defending the national home

To move from the situation of an old country to one often designated as "new", recent Australian politics offers a number of illuminating examples of these issues.[34] Pauline Hanson, leader of the right-wing "One Nation" party, has argued that the "danger" represented by immigration in general and by the "Asianisation" of Australia in particular is such that white Australians like her "will lose our country forever and become strangers in our own land".[35] In this connection Mitzi Goldman rightly insists that it is crucial to understand the ways in which this kind of racist rhetoric appeals to downwardly mobile groups such as the struggling Anglo-Celtic smallholders, who feel most hard done by and threatened by the forces of cosmopolitan globalisation.[36] In her account of the local boom in nostalgia-driven rural tourism in Australia, Jean Duruz argues that its appeal is driven by a search for a seemingly coherent or "uncompli-cated" colonial romance of "farmhouse cooking" and peasant simplicity. Her argument is that this rural romance with the symbols of country living, where it seems that the goal is to "create the impression that one's heart is in the country", occupies a crucial place "in white Australia's dreaming". At the heart of this dream, with its "almost obsessional quest for authenticity", is a particular iconic presence – the "figure of 'grandma' – the ghostly feminine of comfort, who nourishes, cares and significantly ... always has time to listen" to the trou-bles of the escaping urban refugees, in search of respite from the Others who are now seen to colonise the cities.[37]

Similarly, in her analysis of recent debates about the meaning of home in Australia, Fiona Allon focuses on the ways in which the government of John Howard attempted to mobilise a very particular image of the traditional suburban home as the key symbol of their "mainstream" policies – "the timeless image of a white nuclear family standing in front of the white picket fence of their sprawling suburban home".[38] This imagery was clearly designed to appeal to white Australian nostalgia for the era of harmonious, middle-class suburbia, uniform in its ordinariness, quiet and safely Anglo-Saxon. According to Australian Unity Party spokesman Jason Yat-Sen Li,

It's like they're trying to romanticise an older version of this country, back to a time when you could walk down to the shops and leave your front door open. A time when there were none of these strange foreign-looking faces around. But even though that Australia doesn't exist anymore it's a period that's easy to make attractive.[39]

In this politics of (white) memory, the symbolic picket fence is firmly placed round a very narrow, conservative and socially exclusionary vision of the supposed quintessence of the Australian family and its home. As Allon argues, much of this debate was conducted in a displaced form, through a discourse ostensibly concerned with the preservation of architectural heritage, by reference to the nature and design of the materials out of which the family home should be constructed.[40] The visible signs of cultural disorder were the replacement in immigrants' homes of leadlight windows by aluminium frames, the rendering over of the houses' traditional brick structure with whitewashed cement in the Mediterranean style, and the tiling over of what had been the lawn areas. These represent the preferred architectural styles of the various immigrant groups who have now come to inhabit the Earlwood suburb of Sydney, where Howard grew up, and who are responsible for the "Mediterranianisation" of the area, which has now become "a space that contains the traces of perhaps a hundred homes and homelands and histories, imaginary and imagined places and traditions, each laying claim to the meaning of place". This restless geography is now inhabited by other nostalgias than those of white Australia – in particular, by what is now officially designated as "Post-War Immigrant Nostalgia Style".[41] As Allon observes, the lexicon of conservation and heritage which describes the transformations made by immigrant groups as "inappropriate" or "unsympathetic" is a powerful weapon. Given the central symbolic position in Australian culture of the traditional brick home as "the cornerstone of society, a buttress against social, moral and national collapse", Howard and his allies have been able to present these physical transformations as a grievous form of disfigurement of the symbolic home of white Australia's suburban childhood and as a brutalising infringement of the proper character of the period housing in Earlwood, and thus, at one remove, of Australia's national heritage.[42] This is a rhetoric of community, memory and "quality of life" designed to appeal to the country's "forgotten (white) people", and represents what one might call the revenge of the mainstream. In Howard's selective vision of the national past (and of Earlwood's, and thus Australia's possible future) his "conflation of home with stability, tradition and continuity ... excludes all those perceived not to 'belong' ... the cosmopolitan impurities of multiculturalism, cultural difference, change and translation".[43]

At the level of emotional affect, the sense of national belonging is often inscribed in the taken-for-granted practices of everyday life – how you buy stamps in France, as opposed to in Poland; how you order a burger in Amsterdam, as opposed to in New York, or, as Lofgren puts it "the many tiny details which make a Swedish supermarket or post office different from a Norwegian one".[44] In this analysis, national culture is understood to be both firmly rooted in what appears trivial and to be continually reproduced through the cultural practice of everyday life. In a similar vein, Anders Linde-Laursen explores the way in which small differences in home design (and in the conduct of purification rituals – such as washing-up) function as identity makers establishing the distinction between Swedes and Danes. Linde-Laursen (a Dane) thus reports one of his hosts reprimanding him, on a visit he made to Sweden, about his own washing-up practices: "You're not washing-up properly – you're doing it the Danish way."[45]

Sedentarism, mobility and the hearth

To the very extent that the nation has been made to seem more "homely" to its inhabitants in the recent historical period, those such as refugees who are nationless are made to seem all the more homeless. The pervasive assumption of a natural – or originary – world in which people are (or in happier days, were) rooted in their own proper soils or territories is described by Lisa Malkki as the "metaphysics of sedentarism" – through which a culture is equated with a people and that people with a particular geographical place or territory. Clearly the assumptions of homogeneity and purity built into this model are at odds with the actual state of flux of peoples and cultures in many parts of the contemporary world. However, this racialised and territorised model of culture continues to have enormous influence in popular consciousness. From this metaphysics then flows a further set of binary oppositions – between "us and them", "here and there" and "our own and other" cultures or societies. According to Malkki this sedentarist perspective "actively territorialises our identities, whether cultural or national ... [and] directly enables a vision of territorial displacement as pathological".[46] Against the "metaphysical sedentarism" that seeks to keep people(s) in their "proper" place, Malkki observes that we must pay urgent attention to the

> global social fact that, now perhaps more than ever before, [many] people are chronically mobile and routinely displaced, and invent homes and homelands in the absence of territorial, national bases – not "in-situ", but through memories of, and claims on, places that they will never corporeally inhabit.[47]

However, refugees are not always inert in the process of their signification. To take one example, Malkki observes that, for some Hutu refugees in exile from Burundi, in so far as the true nation was imagined as the moral community formed centrally by those in exile, their very displacement became a form of categorical purity to which they clung.[48] In a similar vein, in his study of Palestinian refugee camps George Bisharat reports that for many in that situation their refugee status became a badge of entitlement and a moral claim which meant that their reluctance to leave the refugee camps for better temporary accommodation elsewhere was "a deliberate, conscious statement of their determination not to be assimilated ... [in their place of exile] but to return to their ancestral villages" and their refugee ID cards were felt to be the "promissory note" on their right to return to their lands.[49]

If the traditional home was the axial point securing the unity of the spiritual and the domestic, it also served to connect the individual horizontally in space to contiguous resident kin and vertically, in time, to their ancestors. As Yi-Fu Tuan observes, in classical times the idea of home stood at the centre of an astronomically determined spatial system, the vertical axis of which, linking heaven to the underworld, passed through the family hearth as the focal point of this cosmic structure. The altar or family hearth often held the sacred fire which represented the ancestors to whom offerings had to be made: "the altar ... symbolised sedentary life ... Duty and religion required that the family remain grouped around its altar; the family was ... thus ... as much fixed to the soil as the altar itself." In such a world view, place has a supreme value as the home not only of a people, but of their gods and guardian spirits, and the ruin of a settlement implied the ruin of the corresponding cosmos.[50]

However mobile people become, some sense of home often remains as the "sacred" or central location, from which they still map and measure their advances and travels.[51] Nonetheless, for those who are mobile, this sense of home cannot easily be fixed in geographical place. Thus, in his analysis of the increasingly cosmopolitan nature of contemporary Belize, Richard Wilk notes that the economy itself is open to foreign capital, the stores full of imported goods, the airwaves full of satellite media and the island itself replete with foreign tourists and resident expatriates. Moreover, Wilk notes, Belizians themselves are increasingly transnational – "their families scattered across the USA and the Caribbean, with most of the young expecting to spend parts of their lives abroad".[52] As Daniel Miller observes in this connection, in many parts of the Caribbean, "families even at the nuclear level often unite various countries ... [and] to consider oneself only in relation to one's home state would itself be an artificial parochialism". Miller goes on to point to the particularly striking demographics of the island of Nevis, studied by Karen Fog-Olwig, which has reached the point where perhaps "the majority of people who would associate their origins with Nevis live abroad" and the island's cultural activities have "thereby become largely directed towards the concerns of 'authentication' for the visiting émigrés who want a taste of home". In this respect, Miller notes, Fog-Olwig is right to note that "Home is where you leave it".[53] However, it should not be assumed that feelings of national loyalty or of assumed emotions such as patriotism are necessarily confined to sedentary persons. A television documentary on the Tuareg nomads in North Africa included one such tribesman's fervent avowal that "your own country is always better than any other. A country which is not your own is worthless."[54] We shall return to these issues concerning the relation of migration, exile and home at the end of the chapter.

Geographical monogamy and promiscuity

The very vocabulary in which we discuss questions of mobility is, as we have seen, inevitably value-laden. Heller attempts to reconfigure the conventional contrast between traditional, place-based notions of home or identity and the contemporary experience of globalisation in such a way that we might see this not as a contrast between the presence and absence of an experience of homeliness but rather as two different modalities of this experience.[55] She contrasts two different personal encounters which throw light on these issues. In the first, she met the owner of a trattoria in Rome's Campo dei Fiori, who was unfortunately unable to advise her when she asked how she might best find the shortest way to another district of Rome, because, as he explained, he had never in his life left his own district of the city. In the second case, she fell into conversation with a fellow-passenger on an aeroplane, who was employed by an international firm. This woman spoke five languages and owned apartments in three different places, and, on being asked where she felt at home, was quite taken aback and could only reply that her home was where her cat lived at a given moment.

Heller argues that the resident of Campo dei Fiori experienced a form of "geographic monogamy that wedded him to his tradition" and to his geographical place and that this, no doubt, included a strong sense of "familiarity" embedded in his "language, the mother tongue, the local lingo … the commonplaces, the gestures, the signs, the facial expressions [and] the minute customs" of his locality. However, she argues that it is not the case that the second, international businesswoman's "geographical promiscuity" simply entailed a sense of pathos in respect of her "de-territorialisation". Heller argues that this woman participates not so much in the culture of a place but of a time:

> what she carried on her back was not a particular culture of a particular place … but a particular time shared by all the places … [she visited] She remained herself in so far as she moved together with all the present times common to all the places she ever visited.[56]

Thus, Heller argues

> on her constant trips … she stays in the same Hilton hotel, eats the same tuna sandwich … eats Chinese food in Paris and French food in Hong Kong … uses the same type of fax, telephones and computer, watches the same films and discusses the same kind of problems with the same kind of people.[57]

Heller's point is that this woman also has a "home experience", if of a different kind to that of the Italian restaurant owner. She knows where the electric switch is likely to be in any hotel bedroom and is familiar with how the room's electric door-lock will probably work; she knows what kinds of choices will be likely to confront her on the restaurant menu wherever she goes. In her world of international business travel she too can "read the gestures and allusions" of the people she meets and, on the whole, can understand these others "without further explanation", in so far as she participates in the culture of an internationalised "universal contemporaneity" in which her sense of familiarity is inscribed in the very "cosmopolitanism of the things we use (cars, televisions, kitchen utensils, magazines)".[58]

At home in modernity

According to Nikos Papastergiadis, we are perhaps bedevilled by too stark a contrast between the realm of the traditional and that of the modern, which are often understood as being opposed to each other as stasis is to mobility. In this stereotyped image the traditional home is a space of integration and conformity, "locked into the frozen time of the past: bound to unchangeable customs; restricted to pure members; ruled by strict authoritarian father figures; stifled by religious beliefs".[59] This is the realm of closed tradition, and to stay there is to atrophy. The space of the past is thus envisaged as embedded within a closed territory – inhabited by a settled and unitary community. By contrast, modernity is usually defined by reference to its potential to sweep away tradition, prioritising mobility over stasis, openness of perspective and enquiry over fixed traditions, and reason over prejudice. The problem, as Papastergiadis notes, is that modernity is haunted by the image of its lost home and by the stress of living in a permanent state of homelessness. One solution might perhaps be to pose matters in less starkly oppositional terms.

In the first place, Nestor Garcia Canclini argues that many theorists have over-emphasised the extent to which tradition was, in earlier times, "fixed to a specific place, mired in atavistic rituals and enclosed within specific kinship networks".[60] Moreover, the idea that tradition simply represents a "source of mystification, an enemy to reason and an obstacle against progress" is a vast over-simplification, in so far as tradition itself is often a flexible form, a way of dealing with change and disruption and making sense of it. Traditions themselves have to engage in a continuous process of modification and adaptation to new circumstances – if they ossify, they then become irrelevant and may die out. This is to suggest that we should think of tradition itself as a complex mix of continuities and breaks, of similarities and differences – what Paul Gilroy calls "the living memory of the 'changing same' ".[61] In exactly this spirit of innovative traditionalism, a Saami reindeer farmer poses the rhetorical question, "What can you call 'traditional'?" and answers it by saying that "Young people who have grown up with the snowmobile will say that it is part of their tradition".[62]

If we see tradition not so much as the enemy of all reason and progress but in this new light, we can also afford a somewhat less briskly dismissive attitude to the fear of homelessness generated by the hustle and bustle of modernity. Just as nostalgia need not be seen as an entirely regressive and negative phenomenon, we can also regard the search for some sense of home more positively as a "future-oriented project of constructing a sense of belonging in a context of change and displacement".[63] In his analysis of notions of habitation and belonging in the shifting geography of postmodernity, Roger Rouse argues that the ways in which we now define our identities can no longer be articulated through the traditional terminology of place-based belonging.[64] However, this is not to suggest we have simply all become nomads in some kind of post-modern hyperspace. Thus Rouse suggests that we can find the "raw materials for a new cartography ... in the details of people's daily lives" in which the idea of home is remapped by migrants, so that it no longer represents simply one particular place (of origin or destination), but rather a dispersed set of linkages across the different places through which they move, "a single community spread across a variety of sites".[65] He argues that through their constant back and forth migration and their use of telephones and other long-distance communications media, the residents of the Aguilillan community he studied are able to reproduce their links with people who "are 2000 miles away as actively as they maintain their relations with their immediate neighbours ... through the continuous circulation of people, money, commodities and information ... [so that] the diverse settlements ... are probably better understood as forming ... one community dispersed in a variety of places".[66]

These migrants' lives routinely straddle national borders, and they exist in a multi-local social setting, juggling a variety of forms of cultural understandings, economic, political and legal pressures. Rouse's concern is with "the widespread tendency to assume that identity and identity formation are universal aspects of human experience" and with the dangers of ethnocentrically projecting "onto the lives of people who may think and act quite differently" what are, in fact, quite culturally specific conceptions of personhood developed in the affluent West in the recent period.[67] The experience of the migrants Rouse studied was not so much one in which people possessing one culturally formed identity had to deal with the pressures to take on or accommodate another identity, different in content. Rather, he argues, more fundamentally they moved "from a world in which [personal] identity was not a central concern to one in which they were pressed with increasing force to adopt" a particular concept of personhood (as bearers of individual identities) and of identity as a member of a collective or "community" (rather than as a family) which was quite at odds with their own understandings of their situation and their needs. For these migrants, the taxonomic pressures of various state authorities to enumerate and certify their individual identities was often something to be avoided or neutralised wherever possible, in order to maximise their own flexibility of manoeuvre and action. When they needed to join with others in action, and mobilise for some particular goal, their preference was to do so through a highly personalised (and often extensive) hybrid network of contacts of various kinds, rather than necessarily with others of the same (ascribed) ethnic, racial or cultural identity.

Many contemporary commentators have followed Heidegger's famous dictum that "Homelessness is coming to be the destiny of the world", without stopping to pose the question that Orvar Lofgren raises, concerning, as he puts it, "how short the history of homesickness is".[68] His point is that it may well be that we tend to back-project our own anxieties about homelessness on to a historical past in which, in actuality, many people had a far less sentimental and more pragmatic attitude to the place where they lived, in so far as the home "had not yet been transformed into a space of longing, for dreams, ambitions and a project of self realisation". Lofgren's argument is that, in earlier times, people were often less home-centred than we are now, and could feel sufficiently at home on a more pragmatic basis, as they passed through a variety of spaces, as "life flowed through the house ... [which] was not yet the special place of beginning and endings that we imagine it to be".[69] Contemporaneously the question of who can (literally) afford what degree of sentimentalisation of their idea of home may vary with social cultural and economic circumstances: as a Turkish migrant worker interviewed in Germany put it, "Home is wherever you have a job."[70]

The migrant's suitcase

Sometimes a particular symbolic object – such as the key to the house from which the refugee has been expelled – is taken on the exile's journey and comes to function as a synecdoche for the unreachable lost home, and to act as a focus for memories of the exile's past life.[71] According to George Bisharat, many Palestinian refugee families "retained the keys to their [original] homes, prominently displaying them in their camp shelters as symbols of their determination to return".[72] On some occasions, for the migrant home may perhaps come to be symbolised not by a key but by the suitcase containing their most talismanic possessions, as we saw earlier in the case of Paul Scott. Thus, in his analysis of the conditions of life of migrant workers in Europe in the 1970s, John Berger reported that when, in some places, the *Gastarbeiter* were forbidden to keep their suitcases in their dormitories (because these things made their rooms untidy) they went on strike precisely because:

> in these suitcases, they keep their personal possessions, not the clothes they put in the wardrobes, not the photographs they pin to the wall, but articles which, for one reason or another, are their talismans. Each suitcase, locked or tied round with card, is like a man's memory. They defend the right to keep their suitcases.[73]

Hannah Arendt, having escaped from the Nazis to arrive in New York, is said to have stayed for the rest of her life without unpacking her suitcases.[74] Perhaps the most poignant form of the symbolism of the migrant's suitcase appears in Charlotte Salomon's autobiographical paintings of her life as a Jewish refugee, hiding from the Germans in Vichy France. In one of the paintings, her fictional alter ego "Lotte" is shown sitting dejectedly on the edge of her bed preparing for exile, staring at the debris of her previously cultured life, which she is forlornly failing to pack into the suitcase she will take with her on her flight. As Irit Rogoff has remarked, luggage always functions "as a sign imbued with an indisputable frisson of unease, displacement and dislocation", a double inscription of both "concrete material belongings and of travel and movement away from the materialised anchorings of those belongings".[75] In a recent interview, Edward Said expressed exactly this anxiety when he said that "like all Palestinians" he has a tendency to overpack for any journey, because he is always plagued by a "panic about not coming back".[76]

Even when the migrant arrives at their destination, the suitcase often remains a potent symbol both of the journey they have made, and of the unstable potential for further movement. In her autobiographical novel, describing growing up in the UK of Indian parents, Meera Syal gives a compelling account of the symbolic significance of the large suitcases which had sat on the top of her mother's bedroom wardrobe for as long as she could remember. She explains that as a child she had

> always assumed this was some kind of ancient Punjabi custom, this need to display several dusty, bulging cases, overflowing with old Indian suits, photographs and yellowing official papers, as all my Uncles' and Aunties' wardrobes were similarly crowned with this impressive array of luggage.[77]

Her mother tried to brush off her questions about the significance of the suitcases with the practical observation that they were just a good place to keep "all the things that do not fit into these small English wardrobes". However, her daughter was not convinced that matters were so simple, as she had

> already noticed that everything in those cases had something to do with India – the clothes, the albums, the letters from various cousins – and wondered why they were kept apart from the rest of the household jumble, allotted their own place and prominence, the nearest thing in our house that we had to a shrine.[78]

Nor is this simply an account of how life used to be among Indian immigrants living in the UK in the 1960s. In a recent edition of the BBC2 television comedy show *Goodness Gracious Me* (also scripted by Syal), one of the most effective gags was that in which an Indian estate agent offered to his Indian clients houses with "built-in" suitcases on top of the wardrobes, as a way of signifying to his would-be customers that he was familiar with their most private domestic habits.

It is not only the suitcase he carries with him that performs this talismanic function for the migrant. If the suitcase is usually full of things brought from home, for many migrants there is often also another crucial physical container, standing empty in their homeland. Thus Lofgren notes that these days, all around the world one can find hundreds and thousands of empty houses, paid for or built by migrants,

> investing a lot of their dreams, ambitions and resources in building and furnishing houses "back home" [which] may be briefly visited now and then, but really stand as a materialised utopia of returning home ... [which] in all their emptiness ... are full of longing, nostalgia and dreams.[79]

In a similar vein, Russell King observes that in many places, migrants have transformed their districts of origin by the building of houses in the style of the countries to which they emigrated. As he observes,

> in Southern Italy, in the early twentieth century many towns and villages had whole streets of "American houses" – new houses built by the *americani*, the local emigrants who went to America; in Hong Kong houses built with money earnt in England are called "sterling houses"; in the Punjab ... *pukka* houses stand out above the local dwellings as testimony to a certain level of success abroad on the part of their owners.[80]

Similarly, there is a strong tendency for Turkish migrants to Germany to buy apartments in middle-class areas, furnish them and spend their annual holidays there, and to endlessly prepare them for an eventual return which is, in fact, unlikely to ever occur.[81] Beyond the suitcase and the house, there is also a third "container": the coffin. Writing in the context of France in the 1980s, Azouz Begag writes that when they die, the bodies of the North African immigrants often make a "journey home to be buried in their native soil".[82] Similarly, Alec Hargreaves notes that for many immigrants in France the receding horizon of their much-anticipated return home is often pushed to its ultimate point: "only after death, with a burial place in the land of their birth, will many immigrants finally accomplish the return journey of which they have dreamed since their initial departure".[83]

Home is not always symbolised by any physical container – whether suitcase, building or coffin. At times language and culture themselves provide the migrant with the ultimate mobile home. According to John Berger, in our contemporary mobile world, we need a much more plurilocal concept of home which, for many of the world's mobile population, may be inscribed not in a building or a territory but in "words, jokes, opinions, gestures, actions, even the way one wears a hat", in routinised practices and habitual interactions, in styles of dress and narrative forms.[84] Thus home may not be so much a singular physical entity fixed in a particular place, but rather a mobile, symbolic habitat, a performative way of life and of doing things in which one makes one's home while in movement.[85]

In his account of Adorno's difficulties during his years of exile in the USA, Jamie Daniel emphasises that, in the end, it was principally Adorno's determined continuation of the use of the German language that provided him with some sense of home. Unlike other exiles, such as Paul Lazarsfeld, who went out of their way to hide the cultural and linguistic signs of their otherness and to assimilate as best they could into North American culture, Adorno always resisted such pressures. He said that he experienced his decade in the USA "as an active impingement on his European selfhood".[86] His refusal to behave like an American, or to attempt to assimilate into the melting pot of the (American) "family of man" was unequivocal, and Daniel reports that he refers to his attitude, in this respect, as the "lifeboat that kept his identity from going under".[87] Adorno felt his psychological and intellectual integrity threatened with obliteration by pressures to assimilate, and felt that to do things "the American way" would be to relinquish what made him German. As Daniel notes, drawing on the work of Ruth Mandel, an interesting parallel might be drawn between Adorno's intransigence in refusing to give up the cultural signs of his "Germanness" as the price of acceptance in America, and contemporary debates in Germany and in France as to whether Muslim girls should be compelled to abandon their headscarves as the price of acceptance in the secularised schools of Western Europe.[88]

During his years of exile in the USA, Adorno felt strongly that he was living in an environment which, however flawless his knowledge of the local laws and customs might become, would always remain fundamentally incomprehensible to him. As Daniel notes, Adorno came to feel that "the only site left for retaining ... and actively practising his identity was in the language of his home, childhood, friendships and thought – in German itself".[89] In this respect his sense of his predicament is paralleled by Jimmy Durham's story of the man who, when in a foreign land, always carried a book in his own language, which functioned, he said, as a mirror so that "I can see myself by reading a book of my own language, my own people".[90]

Language, recognition and silence

It can be argued that the journeys of modernity (and postmodernity) are necessarily underwritten by the "maternal" reassurance of the possibility of return and stability, so that, as Papastergiadis puts it, "despite the geographical migrations, social upheavals, personal crises and cultural differences there is one privileged place where origin and destiny intersect ... where security and integrity are not compromised".[91] This space is, of course, that where, in the words of the North American sit-com *Cheers* theme song, "everybody knows your name". Here we return to the point made earlier by Descombes that a person is "at home" in the rhetoric of those with whom they share a mutual understanding of life, such that interaction is not dependent on long explanations but can proceed on the taken-for-granted premises of a set of shared assumptions.[92] Home is where you can be recognised (as the particular person you are and as one of the category of normal persons) by others.

In this context Azouz Begag recounts the story of a Tunisian friend who, on returning from France to live in Tunis, said that the main difference he experienced was the way he felt walking down the street, in relation to how people looked at him. The fundamental point, as Begag observes, is that as soon as one leaves home one must submit to the gaze of others and negotiate with their "look". Begag's friend, back in Tunis,

> felt safe, free from the gaze of ... people unlike himself, Westerners. He could walk freely in the streets with a feeling both of anonymity and presence. He could be himself, among people like himself without getting strange looks from anyone.[93]

The question of who has to submit to the problematic gaze of which others is also, of course, a heavily gendered one. The extent of the space in which a person may feel "at home" can vary – from the space of a house to that of a street, a neighbourhood or a whole country. This depends on extent of their confidence and the geographical area in which they feel that their public presence will be confirmed ("normalised") as welcome in the looks of others, rather than their presence inviting looks of either hostility or curiosity.

One of the most deeply wearing effects of exile is the undermining of a person's dignity and self-confidence as a result of the predominant lack of such recognition. Correspondingly, in his account of the plight of migrants, John Berger notes that it is only when the migrant returns home that he can "choose to be silent".[94] Indeed, Papastergiadis claims that the status of silence can be used as a key marker in distinguishing, in his terms, between the home and the "anti-home", observing that in the home "silence signifies tranquillity ... whereas in the anti-home silence is filled with a deafening anguish". As Heller confirms, "where silence is not threatening we are certainly at home".[95] To be a foreigner is, Kristeva argues,

> to be of no account to others. No one listens to you, you never have the floor, or else, when you have the courage to seize it, your speech is quickly erased by the more garrulous and fully relaxed talk of the community ... You do not have enough status to make your speech useful ... Your speech, fascinating as it might be on account of its very strangeness, will be of no consequence, will have no effect.[96]

Exile: living in the past

If the past, as the saying has it, is a foreign country, it is both a time and a place for which many exiles continue to yearn. John Durham Peters quotes Lord Acton's maxim that "exile is the mother of nationality" as signifying the fecundity of exile in producing compensatory fantasies of and longings for the "sweet place" of the lost homeland.[97] Likewise Ganguly, writing of members of the Indian diaspora in the USA, argues that the past becomes increasingly important for people whose perspective on the present is destabilised as a result of enforced displacement, and argues that the stories people tell about their pasts "have more to do with the continuing sharing up of self-understanding than with historical 'truths' ".[98] Similarly, Kristeva writes of

> the foreigner who survives with a tearful face turned toward the lost homeland. Melancholy lover of a vanished space, he cannot ... get over his having abandoned a period of time. The lost paradise is a mirage of the past that he will never be able to recover.[99]

In her study of one group of Italian migrants in Australia, Loretta Baldassar reports that even "after a century of emigration, San Fior [the migrants' home town] still plays a very big part in the lives of the emigrants" and they and their descendants remain oriented by a continued sense of loyalty to their place of origin. Many of the migrants, she reports, would simply say, "*E sempre il mio paese* (it is and always will be my town)."[100]

Exile is often a form of temporal as well as geographical dislocation, in which, in the course of their physical mobility, cultural forms get artificially frozen. Ashis Nandy makes the point that exiles often develop a fixed and backward-looking image of their homeland. Thus, he argues that, in the Indian case, diasporic Hinduism is often more exclusive and homogenic than that in India. Similarly, he notes, "in matters of culture the diaspora tends to emphasise only the classical components and expects the nation state that represents their mother country to act as a repository of this high culture".[101] Nandy's argument is that in an understandable, but regrettable, response to the racism of which they are the object in their host country, migrants commonly look to an idealised and fossilised image of their mother country to redeem their own self-respect, and are enraged when their home country falls short of their expectation. He argues that these expectations often constitute the most chauvinistic and homogenising pressure groups in their effects on politics in their home country, so that, for example, some of the most traditionalist, nationalist South Asians are those who themselves are geographically located in the West.

In a related vein, Hamid Naficy offers an account of the significance of the particularly intense fetishisation of the images of their lost homeland produced by Iranian exile television stations in Los Angeles. As Naficy puts it:

> exile television clings to a fetishised televisual construct of homeland
> ... that fails to take into account the realities of changes taking place in
> Iran. As present-day Iran is found wanting ... this myth of a secular
> pre-Islamic Iran continues to act, through ... [exile television] like a
> series of Lacanian mirrors, within which exile members ... [can] find
> themselves.[102]

In Naficy's analysis, the continued production and circulation of fetishised
images of that lost homeland dramatises and memorialises the exiles' sense of
loss in a tragic and masochistic mode, but can never assuage it. The glorious
past is endlessly celebrated and commemorated, in a process in which "in exile,
'home' colonises the mind".[103] The fundamental changes going on in the
present-day Islamic Republic of Iran are ignored, and the exiles focus on an
idealised, static and dehistoricised image of the "authentic" Iran which they feel
themselves to have lost. These exiles thus construct for themselves a heavily
ritualised lifestyle, dominated by the consumption of Iranian exile media, in
which news about their lost homeland dominates and "the newscasts ... [efface]
the fact of exile and [give] the impression of living and watching news in Iran",
news of a "dreamland in the far, far away".[104]

In her analysis of life in Southall in West London, an area populated by many
families of South Asian origin, Marie Gillespie identifies another aspect of this
dislocation of time frames, as between the place of exile and the place of home.
In this case, Gillespie argues that Southall itself has, at least in the eyes of many
of its younger generation, been transformed by their parents into a rather backward, tradition-bound community which is in fact much less cosmopolitan than
the actual Indian cities from which their parents emigrated – which are seen as
being much more open to change. In the words of one of Gillespie's interviewees, a sixteen-year-old "Punjabi Londoner" (as he describes himself):

> Now Delhi is much more Westernised than Southall ... They've got
> more variety there – more ... shops with brilliant and very modern
> styles. Lots of people in Southall are living in the "India" they left
> behind and they don't realise how ... things have changed.[105]

The plight of the Yugo-zombies

Many writers have addressed the plight of migrants and the difficulty (or impossibility) of their eventual homecoming. However, Stef Jansen's analysis of the
plight of the "Yugo-zombies" – intellectuals with a continuing commitment to
the multicultural Yugoslavia in which they grew up, but which no longer exists
– addresses the question of what happens when someone's past is destroyed, so
that it is now only available, if at all, in a nationalist and exclusionist form which
they cannot recognise as home. As Jansen argues, even when people stay at
home they can find themselves displaced, for many borders are travelling as well

and the "history of the Balkans is the history of migrations, not just of people but of lands".[106] The recent years of Balkan conflict can thus be understood as a series of conflicts about the nature of the idea of home – over whose story as to who "belonged" where was to prevail – "a conflict about the right to a home in the name of different 'we's' " – as a result of which the meaning of home was drastically transformed for all the inhabitants of the various republics of the former Yugoslavia.[107]

For these Yugo-zombies, would-be citizens of a multicultural state that no longer exists, homecoming would involve not a spatial but a temporal journey, back to a now non-existent era. Moreover, their very attachment to a cosmopolitanism in which "you lived in different cultures and you experienced them as part of yourself" is unacceptable to the new states which now define their erstwhile homes in exclusionist, nationalist terms.[108] Thus a number of Croatia's leading women writers who espoused this form of cosmopolitanism, such as Slavenka Drakulic and Dubravka Ugresic, were subsequently denounced in their own country as "witches" for their refusal to espouse Croatian nation-alist ideology and for their continuing commitment to a multicultural vision of the Yugoslavian "home" in which they had grown up. The many members of "mixed families" (such as Drakulic herself, whose husband was a Serb) consti-tute a profound and problematic practical anomaly for the new nationalist governments of the territories in which they live, just as, in intellectual terms, the commitment of these "witches" to multiculturalism was seen to pose a threat to the new nationalist ideology of the Croatian state. Against the post-structuralist tendency to romanticise all forms of mobility, flux and destabilisation as *ipso facto* liberatory, in the light of her experiences, Ugresic resorts to a bleak vision of her future home as being perhaps in the transit area of an airport, "in a place that belongs to nobody", and she declares that she will "live in the artificial light of the airport, as an example of the post-modern societies, in a transit phase, in an ideal shelter, in purgatory, in an emotionally sterile room".[109]

Migrants' homes and alien environments

For the migrant in an alien environment the space of the domestic home carries a particularly strong affective change. Thus in her study of the home-making strategies of Vietnamese immigrant families in their new country in Australia, Mandy Thomas explores the ways in which, for these migrants, their house often serves both as the focus of their emotional anxieties about the loss of their original homeland and as the idiom through which they try to articulate this sense of belonging to their new and old homes.[110] As she notes, "for those dislocated from a homeland, the house is often the concrete manifestation of the more abstract notion of home". Given their geographical displacement, the house comes to function particularly strongly as a sanctuary and nucleus of identity. The difficulty is that their home has to articulate the conflicts between

51

traditional Vietnamese conceptions of how household spaces should be organised, how many people and/or animals of what sorts should live there and how household life should be conducted, as against Australian regulations governing household density, overcrowding and family life. These regulations express quite different cultural values which are literally embedded in the physical design of Australian houses and are quite antithetical to Vietnamese ideas of what a home should be like.[111]

While attempting to negotiate these difficulties and contradictions between the values and cultural norms of the two worlds which their home now straddles, the vital function of the house for many Vietnamese migrants is to provide a haven in what is otherwise perceived as a hostile environment. As one Vietnamese woman migrant puts it, "we set up everything to look like back home". Relationships with the past are represented by photos. Vietnamese flowers and herbs may be grown in the garden, so as to create familiar sights and smells, along with all the "little things that make us remember everything back home" which allow the migrants to re-experience the sensual world of their past. To this extent, these migrants' homes create a private climate of comfort to facilitate the expression of their cultural differences without "bothering" anybody else, and, hopefully, without being subject to their scrutiny or judgement.[112] Thus, as Thomas puts it, despite the constraints imposed by state authorities, for these migrants the "home remains the key site for the expression of a Vietnamese cultural aesthetic. It is also seen as the only space in which one's actions are not entirely regulated by others", and is the key site in which these displaced people deal with the sense of loss that has accompanied leaving their original homeland and extended families behind.[113] The symbolic burden the home must carry in this situation is all the heavier for the lack of external confirmatory cultural supports, and it must often function as the sole bulwark against what is felt as the intrusion and undermining influences of the new host culture in which they must make their lives. In this same spirit, Gary Younge reports that, growing up as the child of an immigrant family in the UK in the 1960s,

> for as long as I remember, there was a tiny adhesive flag stuck to our front door ... It was the Barbadian flag and the rule was that whenever we entered the house we were not English – we were in Barbados and we would behave accordingly ... "You can do what you want out there but step into this house and you're in Barbados," Mum used to say.[114]

Transnational migration: Australian Italians

However, if the house is a crucial symbolic environment for the migrant it is by no means necessarily the case that it contains the whole family: transnational migration necessarily implies transnational patterns of kinship. Geographically based identities can extend over great distances and may be better understood as articulated through ideas of place, rather than being necessarily rooted in particular territories. Ulf Hannerz makes the point that, as collective systems of meaning, cultures belong primarily to networks of social relationships and "only indirectly and without logical necessity, do they belong to places". As he points out, the less people are sedentary and the less exclusively dependent they are on face-to-face modes of communication, so the link between culture and territory becomes the more attenuated.[115] To that extent, as we saw in the Aguilillan case reported by Rouse, originally place-based identities can be transplanted across space.

In her study, referred to earlier, of the patterns of transnational migration through which Italian emigrants to Australia and their descendants articulate, sustain and develop their identities, Loretta Baldassar examines the fluidity and flexibility of their spatially defined identities in a way that closely parallels Gerd Baumann's observations concerning the shifting nature of community boundaries among immigrant communities in the UK.[116] Baldassar argues that for the Italian migrants she studies, notwithstanding the length of time they had been away from their home town (in the Veneto region of Italy), they still thought of it as home. In their sense of belonging, the central concept is that of *campanilismo*, which literally translates as an attachment to the territory within earshot of the town tower's bells.[117] The concept connotes a strong sense of parochialism and refers to "the identity shared by people who live in the same place, who share the same town time and who respond to the same death knells".[118] Underlying the identification with space is an idea of consocialisation – of a shared temporality which may transcend spatial distance. Thus Baldassar reports that in one of the towns she studied, it was the migrant families in distant Argentina rather than the inhabitants themselves who principally funded the restoration of the bell tower when it was needed. However, Baldassar's central point is that the boundaries of these migrants' spatial identities "can expand or contract along provincial, regional or national lines, depending on the context", so that, if at times their *campanilismo* is signified by their home town in Italy, at others it is signified by the Australian city in which they live or, more specifically, by the community of Italian fellow migrants in that city. Thus, she argues, the symbolic nature of *campanilismo* is best understood as a fluid boundary-forming and maintaining device whose form can persist while its content varies contextually.[119]

As against the traditional conception of societies or communities each occupying separate discontinuous spaces, these transnational migrants sustain multi-stranded networks of social relations which link together their old and new homelands, as part of the same social and communicative field. As migrants they understand themselves to be morally obliged to make regular return visits, as they negotiate the respective claims of their "home and away" identities, and continually refashion their identities as they travel through time and space. Alongside the regular return visit, with all its attendant difficulties in reconciling geographically fractured family histories, ties with the extended family at home are maintained through a continual flow of letters, photos and gifts.[120]

While it would be possible, using a model of virtual pilgrimage, to understand the migrants' return visits home as no more than visits to a shrine, the situation is more complex than that. Baldassar argues that, among other things, the returning immigrants wanted to demonstrate, by virtue of their having retained their Italian identity, that they were still *paesani* (townspeople). If their home town is the centre of gravity at the core of *campanilismo*, visiting migrants not only strive to retain a profile in the town but also to "extend the boundary of *campanilismo* to include their community abroad".[121] In this context they understand themselves to have also attempted to maintain their *campanilismo* by re-creating, in the form of cluster migration and the construction of exclusive social clubs in their place of settlement in Australia, a kind of "home away from home" where they can still preserve their Italian identity in exile.

Home is where you leave it

It is not only that those who have left a place often go to great lengths to retain some emotional claim on the home they left behind. Sometimes absence itself functions as a badge or emblem of a fundamental sense of belonging which transcends mere physical presence. Just as reported by Fog-Olwig in Nevis and by Baldassar in Italy, a recent study of local identities in Cairo found a similar tendency for people to continue to identify with places of origin which they may have left many years ago. Farha Ghannam notes that "relocated people still refer to themselves as 'people of Bulaq', despite the fact that they have been living in al-Zawiya for 15 years. Many also still identify with their old villages and towns they left more than 50 years ago".[122] Similarly, Bisharat reports that, even after fifty years of exile, many Palestinian refugees still refer to themselves as "coming from" their original home villages.[123] Moreover, it seems that there are also occasions in which, in order to truly "belong" to a community, it may well be stipulatory to leave it, at least for a time. Thus, in his analysis of a dispute over relative degrees of authenticity or "belongingness" in a pit village in the north-east of England, Andrew Dawson articulates a revealing dynamic between fixity and mobility. In the course of this dispute, the middle-class group who claimed authenticity by virtue of their unbroken long-term residence in the village were effectively trumped by the representatives of the working-class group who argued that their very itinerary of mobility, in so far as it had been forced on them by the need to find mining work elsewhere when their local pit closed down, made them the more authentic part of the pit village tradition. They thus effectively insisted that labour migrancy is, at key moments, an essential part of the mining life, and the mobility entailed should be recoded as a necessary part (a rite of passage) of true membership of the mining community, where "community identity is effectively dislocated from the objective referent of place" and "community is represented as beyond the place one calls home".[124] To this extent, as Karen Fog-Olwig puts it in her commentary on Dawson's analysis, "attachment to a mining industry that …

involved intermittent labour migration" to destinations elsewhere was, in this case, held to be a stronger index of community belonging than "unbroken residence [in one place] through time".[125]

In her own analysis of understandings of community and culture in St Kitts–Nevis, Fog-Olwig argues that the Nevisian community is similarly deterritorialised in many ways, including family and household relations. While the island is heavily dependent on money sent home by the large population of the island's people who work abroad, these migrants are still, in a crucial sense, part of the community, in their own view and that of their significant others. Historically, such migrants

> did not leave the island with a view to discontinuing all relations with Nevis, but regarded their migration as a temporary move and expected to return, once they had improved their condition. If at all possible they sent economic support to their relatives on Nevis who then, in turn, maintained the family home in a state which made it possible for them to return at any time.

Fog-Olwig reports that the transnational orientation of Nevisian culture is reflected in everyday experience at the level of the household: in her survey of Nevisian schoolchildren, she found that a third of them had at least one parent outside the island, and virtually all had relatives absent working abroad, whose remittances were vital to the survival of their households. She notes that "in the eyes of the children [these] relatives remained central members of the households, despite their physical absence, and many of the children listed absent relatives when asked ... who lived in their household". Here, she argues, we see a thoroughly deterritorialised, transnational form of kinship. Her argument is that it is the very closeness of these ties, embodying as they do feelings of affection and networks of rights and obligations, which "make it possible to extend them to distant migration destinations abroad and yet sustain them for years".[126] If, as Trinh T. Minh-ha has put it, "our present age is one of exile", nonetheless we must avoid essentialising movement itself and recognise that movement and mobility are polythetic categories, containing within them a variety of types of experience.[127] Thus Arjun Appadurai distinguishes between "diasporas of hope, diasporas of terror and diasporas of despair", and Hamid Naficy observes that "all displaced people do not experience exile equally or uniformly. Exile discourse thrives on detail, specificity and locality. There is a there *there* in exile".[128]

Having now introduced a range of micro and macro considerations in relation to ideas of sedentarism, exile, mobility, home and Heimat, we turn to examine the domestic home in more detail and in particular the question of its gendering. I begin with the deconstruction of conventional ideas of domesticity.

3

THE GENDER OF HOME

Deconstructing domesticity: family propaganda

The idealised image of domesticity and familial life remains an enormously powerful discourse. Outside the realms of feminist theory, the dominant imagery of the home is still almost invariably set in benign terms. According to Lee Rainwater there is

> a long history ... of the house as a place of safety ... the place of maximum exercise of individual autonomy ... The house acquires a sacred character from its complex intertwining with the self and from the symbolic character it has as a representation of the family.[1]

Thus in his critical commentary on Bachelard's "happy phenomenology of the home" David Sibley notes that there is little recognition, within prevalent discourses of domesticity, of the conflictual aspects of domestic life.[2] In pointing to this crucial silence Sibley follows a long line of feminist work on this topic, from landmark works such as Ann Oakley's *Housewife*, through to the works of Lynn Segal and Elizabeth Wilson, addressing the questions of oppression, exploitation and violence within the hallowed realms of the family home.[3] The home as a locus of power relations has often been almost entirely neglected. As Sibley argues, the problem is that "What is missing from the 'house as haven' thesis is a recognition of the ... tensions surrounding the use of domestic space, tensions which become a part of the problem of domination within families".[4] It is in this spirit that Nancy Fraser refers to families as "sites of egocentric, strategic and instrumental calculation as well as sites of usually exploitative exchange of services, labour, cash and sex, not to mention, frequently, sites of coercion and violence".[5] In her analysis of current discourses of disease, Sara Maitland argues that the repeating media panics about the various strange and frightening diseases which are nowadays seen to threaten us often serve to displace our attention from the fact that statistically, the main risks to our health and happiness do not in fact derive from the outside world, but lurk within the home. As she notes, it is "in the home, the normal social milieu of our daily lives … where our physical and mental health are really at risk".[6]

If some family homes are benign environments, the celebratory idea of home is evidently far too simple. As Karen Fog-Olwig observes, we must recognise that often home is "a contested domain: an arena where differing interests struggle to define their own spaces within which to localise and cultivate their identity", whether this takes the form of conflict between different sub-units of a household, a community, a region or a nation.[7] Fog-Olwig argues that homes may perhaps be better thought of as places where certain kinds of trouble and conflict have to be fought out and resolved – whether in the process of children struggling with their parents in the process of coming to maturation or that of different parts of a divided community struggling with each other over the meanings of the space which they must share with others. In this connection it is interesting to note that Liz Greenhalgh and Ken Worpole's *Park Life* study discovered that many people valued their local park as a public place where, paradoxically they could often enjoy more effective privacy than they experienced at home. The home is for many people not only a physically contested site which has to be shared with others with whom one is often in conflict, but is now so heavily "connected" to elsewhere via the technologies (phone, fax, e-mail, television, etc.) installed in it, as to no longer function for them as a haven of peace and tranquillity. Thus Worpole reports that:

> many people, particularly young people, went to the park to escape from the overly *public* nature of domestic life … to seek an element of personal privacy on a park bench … as a space that was seen as more respectful and trustworthy than domestic space.[8]

In her analysis of the images of home held by a sample of German women, Nora Rathzel notes that for the women in her study who held particularly cosy images of home (as always a place of warmth, acceptance and belonging) the price of this image of "harmonious Heimat" was a series of necessary deletions/repressions. In these women's images of home, "rooms and houses are free of people who want to see a different television programme [who] are disturbed by music one wants to hear, or are … themselves listening to music that ruins one's nerves".[9] However, it is not simply the existence of humdrum domestic tensions that gets written out of the idealised image of the home. There is no place in that imagery for the recognition of the fact that the family home is also a place whose inhabitants sometimes abuse each other and their children, and where dysfunctional family communications systems have to be recognised as the source of various forms of individual "madnesses" and disorders.[10]

Commenting on the ideological remobilisation of the virtues of the "traditional family" in the UK during the 1990s, Suzanne Moore notes that it "has become part of the heritage industry, a kind of emotional theme park, which we visit from time to time to remind ourselves how things used to be". As she observes, while that might be nice for a nostalgic day out, "would you really want to live in one?" in the light of all that we know about the hidden pathologies of that supposedly ideal form of household.[11] Given the ideological framework within which our ideas and images of family life are constructed, it follows, as Andrew Palmer observed in his review of Val Williams' "Who's looking at the family?" exhibition, that "by definition, photographed families are happy families". It rarely occurs to us to photograph family rows or moments of domestic distress. To this extent, "each family album is, in its own way, an exercise in conformity" as we strive to represent our own family lives in the terms of our idealised imagery of how it should be.[12] Family photography has thus long tended to present "family life as it might be, or as what we would wish it to be" and to act not so much as a record of activity but as a "talisman against the real".[13] As Moore has also observed, when we pose for family photographs and holiday snapshots we tend to impersonate the idealised version of family life which we carry round in our heads – perhaps subconsciously derived, as she suggests, from the imagery on the back of cereal packets, routinely placed in front of us on the altarplace of the domestic kitchen table.[14]

As Williams observes, for at least a generation of post-war British children the stereotyped representations of family life in the *Ladybird* book series seemed somehow to represent the very quintessence of normality. However, it was, of course, a quite idealised vision of what normality *should* be like – not at all "how it was" for a child growing up in any actual family. Seen this way, family photography then becomes "part of a universalised fiction and national narrative".[15] Larry Sutton records how when revisiting his elderly parents, one night they all sat down to watch a collection of the family's old home movies. As he remembers:

> sitting in the living room, we watched thirty years of folktales – epic celebrations of the family. They were remarkable, more like a record of hopes and fantasies than of actual events. It was as if my parents had projected their dreams onto film emulsion.[16]

The potential for buried trauma in this terrain is nowhere better expressed than in Alexandra Artley's study of the photographs of smiling children in seemingly idyllic domestic and holiday scenes, taken from the family album of a father whose two daughters subsequently murdered him to halt his sexual abuse of them. Artley, twisting Shakespeare, observes simply that "these conventional family photographs confirm that one may smile and smile and be a victim".[17] The father's snapshots (see Figure 3.1) of his smiling daughters "acted as propaganda, both within and outside the family, and positioned him as a seemingly loving storyteller who dealt persuasively in idylls".[18] Here we begin to see the shadow of the *unheimlich* falling across the bright doorstep of the home – an issue to which we will return later in the chapter.

58

Figure 3.1   June and Hilda Thomson with Beauty, photographed by their father, July 1958.

Masculine premises, gendered anxieties

Space is a gendered on a variety of scales. As Akhil Gupta and James Ferguson put it, the opposition in which the local is understood to be that which is natural, authentic and original, while the global is seen as the realm of the external, artificially imposed or inauthentic, is often a gendered one. The local is often associated with femininity and seen as the natural basis of home and community, into which an implicitly masculine global realm intrudes.[19]

According to Rybczynski, "the feminisation of the home in seventeenth century Holland was one of the most important events in the evolution of the domestic interior".[20] The domestic remains a site of specifically gendered anxieties: however much the masculine-coded perspective of modernism attempts to present itself as universal, it can never quite banish its own shadows, especially in this domestic realm. As Doreen Massey well argues, the essential point is that in a taken-for-granted way "the Universal, the theoretical, the conceptual are, in current Western ways of thinking, coded masculine. They are the terms of a disembodied, free-flowing, generalising science" while, conversely, the feminine is often equated with the (merely?) local.[21] In a similar vein Sharon Haar and Christopher Reed argue that the Heideggerian tradition of phenomenological discourse on home, exemplified in the work of Gaston Bachelard and Emmanuel Levinas, is nonetheless ultimately vitiated by its unreflexively masculine premises. These authors' perspective on the relations of domesticity, dwelling, childhood and memory is "the prerogative of men, positioned as the beneficiaries of domestic nurturance", Haar and Reed argue – an induction which is "confirmed by Bachelard's casual linkage of domestic love with motherlove in the bosom of the house" and by Levinas' assertion that "the

woman is the condition for recollection, the interiority of the Home and inhabitation".[22]

At a philosophical level, Alison Ainley glosses Luce Irigaray's critique of this
Heideggerian tradition to the effect that "Heidegger builds his philosophical
'house' at the expense of the feminine" and argues that this "debt he owes to
the feminine" is one that Heidegger never acknowledges.[23] Irigaray's argument is that while the feminine provides a "dwelling" for men, the woman
herself is, in effect, left homeless, in the process – or else she is imprisoned.[24]
Thus "in exchange for what the philosopher has 'borrowed' from the feminine, in order to construct his spatiality ... he buys her a house, even shuts her
up in it ... either way, the result is a denial by immobilisation or exclusion".[25]
An interestingly concretised example of this psychoanalytic perspective on the
gendering of home is offered by Roger Bromley in his reading of Wim
Wenders' film *Paris, Texas*.[26] In the film, when we first meet the hero Travis,
he is himself abject in his lostness and in his homelessness – which he experiences as a form of exile from "the maternal body, conventionally the
em-bodi-ment of home and family".[27] In his search to reconstitute his family,
Travis strives to return to that place (the original, maternal Home) "where
distance did not yet count".[28] The problem is, that in an almost literal enact-
ment of Irigaray's analysis, Travis has earlier attempted to transcend the
symbolic distance between himself and his wife Jane by "giving up work so he
could be close to [her] ... confusing love with possession ... yet also alienating
her, attaching a cowbell to her and tying her up to a stove" until "in an
attempt to achieve some space and power, Jane burns down [their] trailer and
escapes with the child".[29] Set within these initial terms, Travis' subsequent
quest, if at points heroic, is bound to end, as it does, in failure, at least in
terms of its literal objective. Clearly, we must avoid any romanticised image of
the domestic which fails to recognise its darker sides, which are normally
screened out in the conventional idea of home. In this respect Haar and Reed
note the importance of the work of artists such as Eric Fischl, depicting
"domestic corruption" among "unhappy suburban families". As they note, for
Fischl, privacy (one of the cardinal components of the ideal of domesticity) is
no simple good but also includes "whatever you're not supposed to be doing
... stealing ... having sex with your neighbour ..."[30]

Domesticity, modernity and modernism

In its combination of the features of separation of living space from that of
work, and its valuation of privacy, comfort and family-centredness, domesticity
is a "specifically modern phenomenon, a product of the influence of capitalist
economics, breakthroughs in technology and enlightenment notions of individuality".[31] However, the twentieth-century avant-garde of modernist art and
architecture has continually defined itself in opposition to the values associated
with domesticity. Thus domesticity itself has come to be positioned as the

antithesis of High Art. Reed traces the modernist avant-garde's disavowal of domesticity to Baudelaire's analysis in "The Painter of Modern Life", in which the artist is represented as a flâneur, the "man of the world", who resents time sacrificed to domestic existence when he could be out and about recording the life of the city.[32] In this connection Penny Sparke's historical account of what she calls the "sexual politics of taste" offers an exemplary analysis of the ways in which masculinist forms of modernism have repeatedly equated the feminine with despised forms of mass culture and (at best) middlebrow taste – to the point where woman and mass consumer can seem to be "indistinguishable from each other". As Sparke argues, modernism was defined at key moments by virtue of its high-minded contrast to the comforts of the Domestic Ideal, most significantly perhaps in the wake of the Vietnamese architect Adolf Loos' clarion call for the "separation of the functional from the ornamental" in his celebrated essay of 1908, "Ornament and crime".[33] Reed's further concern is to trace the roots of the specific antipathy to domesticity which has influenced modernist architecture throughout the twentieth century. As he observes, the "anti-domestic tenor of avant-garde architectural theory" not only famously equated ornament with crime but despised the "absurd bric-a-brac" of domestic décor produced, according to Le Corbusier, by the "sentimental hysteria surrounding the cult of the home", which distracted architects from the proper business of producing machines for living in for "healthy and virile, active and useful" people.[34] This modernist aesthetic is quite antagonistic to the idea of the home as a "refuge of privacy and an assertion of individual – or family – identity" expressed in "the knick knacks on the shelves, the antimacassars on the armchairs, the filmy curtains at the windows, the screen before the fireplace".[35] On this terrain a symbolic battle emerges between the figures of the housewife and the modernist architect.

In the UK, in the post-war period, it was only at the point of being rehoused from working-class areas of the inner city into the suburban "New Towns" of the 1950s that many working-class families were able to secure a house of their own (even if still one provided by the local housing authority). In her account of how the residents of one such "New Town" (Harlow, in Essex) set about transforming it into a "place of their own", Judy Attfield traces the way in which these housewives came into conflict with the modernist aesthetics of their homes' architects and designers through their household decoration practices, in which they attempted to impose their own particular lived sense of place on the architecture they came to inhabit. One particular site of such conflict was located at a key boundary of the household privacy: the window. As Attfield records,

> windows designed by architects to let in light were veiled behind
> Venetian blinds and layers of curtains, topped with double pelmets and
> an array of ornaments. Through the appropriation of privacy by the
> concealment of the interior from the unlimited gaze, people took

control of their own interior space and at the same time made a public declaration of their variance from the architects' design.[36]

In their struggle to turn the houses into which they had been placed by the public authority into homes of their own, these housewives subverted the architects' and town planners' modernist aesthetic with the "cosy clutter" of their curtains and heavy drapes.

If from the modernist point of view "excessive" decoration is to be avoided as improperly sentimental, then the post-war American modernists went a step further by staking their claim to the mantle of the contemporary avant-garde on the Abstract Expressionists' denunciation of the whole tradition of European easel painting – as itself overly domesticated in its production of "pictures for the home ... for over the mantel".[37] If domestication was the enemy, then so was its close associate, decoration, which Clement Greenberg described as the "spectre that haunts modernist painting". Indeed, for Greenberg, domesticity and decoration were the antithesis of art (hence his well-known critique of the decorative aspects of Matisse's work) and he famously defined avant-garde art by means of its opposition to "Kitsch". For Julius Meier-Graefe, if art becomes decorative it is then in danger of functioning like a "gentle little housewife", surrounding its domestic consumers with "tender attentions" designed to merely "distract tired people after a day's work" rather than inspire them to critical thought, as true art should.[38] As Reed observes, in formulating this opposition between art and domesticity so aggressively, and in struggling so hard to free art of any taint of unseeming (unmanly?) decorativeness, the modernist critics replicate the classical trope of the Odyssean adventure, in which the masculine hero is forced to leave the domestic hearth in order to undertake his quest and has "no time to spare for the mundane details of home life and housekeeping". However, as Reed also argues, behind these compulsive and vehement denunciations of all merely domestic arts still, if it is "perpetually invoked in order to be denied", the domestic "remains throughout the course of modernism, a crucial site of anxiety and subversion".[39]

In her analysis of Australian discourses of gender, domesticity and modernity in the post-World War II period, Lesley Johnson argues that the very idea of the modern subject who transcends the nostalgic desire for the secure world of traditional ways to become an autonomous and self-defining being, at ease in the maelstrom of modernity, is implicitly gendered.[40] Johnson is concerned to demonstrate that this particular conception of modern subjectivity is itself defined in terms of a specifically masculine set of values (separation, autonomy, adventure) of which we should be wary, and that other conceptions of that subjectivity are conceivable, such as the idea of "a self that is not closed off, separated from the social relations that shape it ... [that] does not have to imagine itself 'leaving home' to become a self" which might be of rather more relevance to women.[41] In the same vein, Doreen Massey argues that the very "need for the security of boundaries, the requirement for such a defensive and counterpositional definition of identity", rather than being some universal truth, is rather, in fact, a specific and " 'culturally masculine' tendency".[42] According to Johnson, in the Australian post-war case, for many women home was "not a place separate from the contingencies of the modern world to withdraw into ... a bounded space where ... processes of modernisation could be excluded ... but a place to be created".[43] Rather, she argues, these women were involved in what de Certeau calls "an active practising of place", and home, for them was not a retreat but rather "the site of their agency".[44] As Johnson puts it:

> The modern, for them, did not mean undertaking heroic voyages or making great scientific discoveries in a world from which the traveller could then return to existing security, to home as tradition. No such place existed for them. Home was not a bounded space, a fortress into which the individual could withdraw and from which all others could be excluded. Their modernity was about actually creating a place called home.[45]

The housewife, the home and the Heimat: woman as home

According to Gillian Rose, place is "always associated with the timeless, infinite vanishing point of the maternal".[46] Certainly, there is a long and well-established tradition of writing on the mutual identification of the woman, the mother and the home. In his portrait of working-class family life in the north of Britain in the 1950s, Richard Hoggart claimed that at the core of working-class culture was a "sense of the personal, the concrete, the local ... .embodied in the idea of ... .family ... and neighbourhood". At the epicentre of this terrain we find the figure of the mother, "Ma", who, in Hoggart's words is "the pivot of the home, as it is practically the whole of her world" – a world which "she, more than the father, holds ... together".[47] In this powerful imagery the mother both represents and literally (daily) constitutes the home. While many things have changed since the date of Hoggart's analysis, it is still undoubtedly true that at a simple, material level, most women (and certainly married women) in the UK at least, notwithstanding their far greater presence in the workforce outside the home, are still much more subsumed in the home than are men.

To return to the level of the symbolic structuring of gender addressed earlier, Doreen Massey writes that from a masculine perspective, woman still "often stands as a symbol both for Nature and for all that has been lost or left behind", so "that place called home is frequently personified by and partakes of the same characteristics as those assigned to Woman/Mother".[48] From this point of view, as Genevieve Lloyd puts it,

> Woman's task is to preserve the sphere of intermingling of mind and body, to which the Man of Reason will repair for solace, warmth and

relaxation. If he is to exercise the most exhalted form of Reason, he must leave soft emotions and sensuousness behind; woman will keep them intact for him.[49]

As Massey also observes, the identities of the woman and of the home-place are frequently blurred: "home is where the heart is (if you happen to have the spatial mobility to have left) and where the woman (mother, lover-to-whom-you-will-one-day-return) is also". Thus she notes, the idealisations of home in the British literature and films produced by the working-class "Angry Young Men", who left the North for London in the 1950s, not only "looked back north with an unforgivable romanticism" but also constructed their view of home around the image of "Mum": "not as herself a living person ... engaged in her own ... history but [as] a stable symbolic centre – functioning as an anchor for others" as "a mother, assigned the role of personifying a place which did not change".[50]

Gender, mobility and visibility

As Kevin Robins and I have argued elsewhere, the very concept of Heimat is predicated on a particular concept of gender.[51] The term Heimat, as Stephen Keane observes, conflates "the motherly and the homely, Heimat also means 'birthplace', 'settled', 'identity', 'a sense of belonging'".[52] One of the crucial dimensions along which Heimat is defined is by contrast to all that is foreign or distant. The characteristics of the traditional Heimat film genre involve a conflict between the stable word of the Heimat and the threatening assault of the *Fremde* (foreign) so that America, in particular, becomes the very antithesis of Heimat. Edgar Reitz's film *Heimat* (1984) follows exactly this pattern, in so far as it is structured around a central contrast between those (principally women) who stay in the village (*die Dableiber*) and those (men) who represent a culture of immigrants, who left home (*die Weggegangenen*). The moral universe of the film is structured around a set of contrasts: tradition/rootless-ness; village/city; local/foreign; natural/modern; eternal/changing; feminine/masculine. Of these contrasts, the final pair is perhaps the most significant. At the centre of Reitz's film is Maria Wiegard, who as daughter, wife, then mother, never leaves the Heimat. She is always at home (*daheim*). Indeed, as Anton Kaes has suggested, "Maria embodies security, safety and permanence. The film's secret message is: Wherever she is, there is *Heimat*."[53] In German litera-ture in the Heimat genre, Celia Applegate observes "the identification of *Heimat* with femaleness ... takes a number of forms: women preserve the folk ways, weave the folk clothes, sing the folk songs, prepare the folk foods". In this literature

women exist ... according to their roles in the family. There are no superfluous women, no excess of widows and unmarried women, no women at work outside the farm, no women with short hair ... no modern or new women at all.[54]

In our analysis of the way in which popular current affairs magazine programmes in the UK construct the domestic spectator's perspective on events in the wider world, Charlotte Brunsdon and I pointed to the way in which the home is usually presented as the unchanging backcloth to the world of "real" historical activity in the outside world.[55] Moreover, within this perspective, there is a collapsing of the image of the wife/mother into the image of the home itself. The woman in the family is not only the "still point" in a changing world, the protector of the "true community", the place to which the (male) labourer/traveller returns. The woman and the home seem to become each other's attributes, just as James Joyce used to refer to his wife Nora as his "portable Ireland".[56]

In a similar vein, Marina Warner claims that "at the heart of romantic nationalism lies the interdependency of home, identity, heritage and women", a veritable "mythology of the hearth" in which to "go home" is to manage the blissful return to "a golden afternoon in the past". As Warner notes,

> this romantic figment of the "folk hearth" returns us once more to "Mum", she who embodies birthplace ... and by extension nation ... But she can only fulfil this role at the price of shedding personal history, of claiming timelessness and unchangingness.

In this mythology, home symbolises "an end to questing, to wandering, to trouble – home is closure; the arrival [there] brings the story to an end ... return signals ... escape from misadventure ... [to the safety of] the domestic hearth, coded female".[57] This is, of course, a return to the safety of the private, familial realm, in which the door can be shut on the outside world.

Home, tradition and gender

It is not simply the home itself which is coded as feminine. It is also the very realm of tradition – the cultural equivalent of the process of biological reproduction – which is also often understood as "women's business". Drawing on the work of Nira Yuval-Davis, Phil Cohen argues that women as mothers are frequently positioned discursively as responsible for the transmission of the cultural patrimony to the next generation. As he notes, "oral traditions conveyed through the 'mother tongue' are thus naturalised by association with mother's milk, and the maternal lap becomes the privileged place where the national heritage itself is institutionalised".[58] This is particularly so among migrant or displaced groups, where cultural continuity is often felt to be under threat, and thus particular efforts are felt to be needed to preserve it. Celeste Olalquiaga notes that in the west ... home came to mean intimacy and protection, the site of individuality. In the East, home was the last bastion of millenary traditions, a refuge from the incessant attack of modernisation. For both, home was the last territory to be penetrated [sic], a feminised domestic space where women and children – the guarantors of tomorrow – were to be kept from the outside world.[59]

The home, the harem and the veil are here closely connected. In her introduction to Malek Alloula's study of French colonial representations of Algerian women, Barbara Harlow argues that "more than analogy links the imperialist project of colonising other lands and peoples with the phantasy of appropriation of the veiled exotic female".[60] For the colonialist, whether in Algeria or in India, the seclusion of indigenous women behind the veil or within the harem was deeply problematic. As Inderpal Grewal notes in her study of the British in India, the veil and the harem symbolised the opacity of the indigenous culture which the colonisers were determined to render transparent, so as to better include the private (feminine) sphere of the native home within their surveillance. As Grewal observes, "the move to 'civilise' eastern women functioned to make them less opaque, to strip them of their veils and to remove them from the harem" where they might otherwise live hidden from the colonisers' scrutiny.[61] It was in response to similar forms of colonial surveillance that, during the nationalist struggle in Algeria, the veil was at some points taken up specifically as a symbolic protest against the French attempts to impose their authority. Similarly, in India, as Grewal reports, the feminine space of the home or harem came to be seen as the crucial repository of nationalist culture, and specifically "Indian women's location in the women's part of the house [became] the symbol of what is sacred and private for Indian nationalist culture".[62]

In this spirit, Trinh T. Minh-ha writes of "the naturalised image of women as guardians of tradition, keepers of home and bearers of language".[63] In the contemporary context, Gillespie notes the way that, among the "Punjabi Londoners" she studied who are constantly attempting to balance the contradictory demands of tradition and progress, this contradiction itself is also articulated through gender divisions.[64] Many of the adult women in this community speak little or no English, living almost entirely in their domestic/local world, with little interaction with the broader society, relying on their husbands, sons and daughters to deal with this outside world on their behalf. Their daughters are much more strictly controlled than their sons. As Gillespie notes, the girls "are usually socialised to remain within the domestic realm and often participate in strong and supportive female cultures in the home, where the viewing of (traditional) Indian films on video plays an important part".[65] To that extent it is on their (gendered) shoulders that the traditions of the community are seen to be secured. As Gillespie reports, many of my informants reported that they viewed their mothers, grandmothers and aunts as the prime carriers of culture and tradition within the family, as it was to them that the responsibility for the maintenance of religious traditions and moral values was assigned.[66]

For many of the girls in this community, their confinement to a domestic environment dominated by such traditional values (and forms of in-house entertainment) is such that "they might as well be in India", in the words of one of Gillespie's interviewees.[67] These matters are by no means only of consequence to migrant or displaced groups, even if they sometimes achieve a particularly dramatic quality in those circumstances. This idealised image of the "realm of the pure" (the chastity of the culture?), in which community, tradition, and home are conflated, is also powerfully resonant within the mainstream of British contemporary culture, as evidenced, for example in Suzanne Moore's comments, quoted earlier, on the mobilisation of an image of the "traditional family" as a key resource in our national heritage, an image which has in recent years been reheated in various ways in the media.[68]

The gender of the modern public

If the idea of home can only be understood as one part of binary relation, in which the private is defined by distinction from the public, the further point is that this distinction is itself gendered. Thus Janet Wolf argues that, in so far as the theoretical literature on modernity focuses so strongly on the public sphere – the life of the streets, where the (male) *flâneur* wanders – it effectively equates the modern with the public and simply fails to describe women's experience. Her point is that "the literature of modernity describes the experience of men" – focusing on the "public world of work, politics and city life … from which women were excluded, or in which they were practically invisible". As she goes on to argue,

> the public sphere … despite the presence of some women, in certain concentrated areas of it, was a masculine domain, and in so far as the experience of 'the modern' occurred mainly in the public sphere, it was primarily men's experience.

To this extent it follows that "The heroes of modernity [the *flâneur*, the stranger with the freedom to wander] … share the possibility of lone travel, of voluntary uprooting, of anonymous arrival at a new place. They are, of course, all men."[69]

In her later analysis of metaphors of travel, Wolf argues that the

> problem with terms like "nomad" and "travel" is that they are not usually "located" … they suggest ungrounded and unbounded movement –

since the whole point is to resist fixed selves/viewers/subjects, but the consequent suggestion of free and equal mobility is itself a deception, since we don't all have the same access to the road.[70]

Such discourses have functioned historically to limit the access that women have generally had to mobility, in so far as the traveller has, in effect, almost always been constituted as "he". Women who have travelled, such as the great nineteenth-century "lady explorers", often had to do so as men, or under the aegis of men, so that travel has both been gendered and itself functioned as a technology of gender.[71]

To be confined to the realm of home is to be precluded from the advantages that are offered by mobility in its various forms. Thus Enloe argues that historically

in many societies being feminine has been defined as sticking close to home – masculinity, by contrast, has been the passport for travel ... A principal difference between women and men in countless societies has been the license to travel away from a place thought of as "home".[72]

In a similar vein, Meaghan Morris has observed that:

There is a very powerful cultural link ... dear to a masculinist tradition inscribing "home" as the site both of frustrating containment (home as dull) and of truth to be rediscovered (home as real). The stifling home is the place from which the voyage begins and to which, in the end, it returns ... The tourist leaving and returning to the blank space of the *domus* is, and will remain, a sexually in-different "him".[73]

At this symbolic level, Mary Gordon writes of a "habit of association that connects females with stasis and death: males with movement and life" in a symbolic system in which the woman functions as "the centripetal force pulling [the masculine hero] not only from natural happiness but from heroism as well", so that men's journeys are often represented as (necessary) flights from constraining women.[74]

Drawing on Wolf's work on the "invisible *flâneuse*", Doreen Massey argues that the social spaces of modernity and of its symbolic site, the modern city, were always uninhabitable for women except as objects for male consumption (visually and sexually). At its simplest, as Massey puts it, "the public city which is celebrated in the enthusiastic descriptions of the dawn of modernism was a city for men ... the *flâneur*, the stroller in the crowd, observing but not observed ... is irretrievably male ... [and] the *flâneuse* was an impossibility".[75] Thus Trinh Minh-ha writes of women's "lack of mobility in a male economy of movement", and Ashraf Ghani notes that, for many women, historically "the distinction between the private space of the house and the public space of work

... [resulted in] a pronounced gendering of space ... [and] the monopoly of spaces of power by men".[76] Similarly, Gillian Rose suggests that still today in advanced Western societies, only white heterosexual men can fully enjoy an unproblematic sense of spatial freedom and that "women know that spaces are not necessarily without constraint; sexual attacks warn them that their bodies are not meant to be in public spaces" just as "racist and homophobic violence delimits the space of black and lesbian and gay communities".[77] Elizabeth Wilson argues that, historically,

> women have fared especially badly in western visions of the metropolis because they have seemed to represent disorder. There is fear of the city as a realm of uncontrolled and chaotic sexual license, and the rigid control of women in cities has been felt necessary to avert this danger.[78]

Access out of the home is often as carefully controlled as access into it. Neil Smith notes that

> as a means to control access to women's bodies ... the scope especially of young women's mobility can be severely restricted to the environs of the home, whether formally, in many Islamic cultures with the tradition of purdah, or less formally, as in many inner cities in the USA.[79]

In the UK Worpole reports that, based on his empirical evidence, space is often timetabled by gender: thus, for example,

> in many ways women are the majority users of town centres for shopping, voluntary activities and social meetings – but only in the daytime. At night the pubs open and the town centre once again becomes predominantly the domain of men.[80]

If it is problematic for a woman to be mobile, we must also recognise that the concept of home is so much a gendered one that, as Lesley Harman notes in her study of homeless women in Toronto, "the very notion of homelessness among women cannot be invoked without noting the ideological climate in which this condition is framed as problematic, in which the deviant categories of 'homeless women' and 'bag lady' are culturally produced".[81] It is by the same token that agoraphobia – the fear of going out and making oneself visible in the public realm – has always been gendered as a feminine disease.[82] The continuing strength of these presumptions about the proper place for a woman is also strikingly revealed in Tim Cresswell's analysis of media coverage of the Women's Peace Camp at Greenham Common in the UK in the 1980s. As he observes, the women were seen as out of place – and thus not "proper women" – by virtue of their abandonment (seen as neglect or even betrayal) of their homes. They were also seen as doubly out of place by virtue of their presence in a particularly unfeminine space – on the perimeter of a military base.[83] The extent of the women's transgression of the gendered rules of place and role can perhaps be judged precisely from the hysterical and grotesque responses which their actions produced both from media commentators (Auberon Waugh describing them as "smelling of fish paste and bad oysters"), local youth (who smeared their camp with excrement and pig's blood) and soldiers (who on one occasion ritually bared their buttocks to the women as they were driven past the women's camp in a coach).[84]

The women were condemned either way: if they had left their children at home, this was a reprehensible abandonment; if they had them with them at the camp it was irresponsible, as the camp was seen as no place for children. As Cresswell points out, the key signifiers of the discourse through which the Greenham women were represented were all domestic: they were designated abnormal by virtue of their mistreated/neglected children; and by their black-ened teapots, cooking pots and kettles and their unfeminine standards of dress. Cresswell also notes the frequency of the words "rancid" and "burnt" to describe their food. These allegations of dirtiness take on specific significance in relation to women, given their particular and contradictory association both with dirt itself (moral, sexual and material) and with its removal. As the house-wives of the world, women are expected to be the epitome of cleanliness themselves. The images of dirt at the women's peace camp index a double transgression, in so far as the women were condemned for failing in their femi-nine duty to keep both themselves and their environment clean. In the face of this media/public fascination with their supposed odour and dirtiness, the women then most dramatically scandalised their opponents at the point when they used signifiers of their own menstruation – supposedly the most private and hidden of all taboo phenomena – in their "decoration" of the airfield's perimeter fence, thus bringing the private/feminine into the realm of the masculine/public in the most transgressive way possible.

The place of the housewife

The place of the housewife is, of course, principally to make a home for her family. In her analysis of late nineteenth-century aesthetics, Joyce Robinson observes that implicit in the discourses of housewifely care, in popular literature and handbooks of the time designed to aid the housewife "in her creation of a quiet and restful enclave within the urban jungle", was the belief that "the decoration of the home fell within the purview of the wifely activities" and the related assumption that "such domestic activity was undertaken primarily for the benefit of the male occupant of the home".[85] Addressing the issue of the role of the housewife in home decoration in *fin-de-siècle* France, Lisa Tierstein writes that the bourgeois housewife's role was explicitly compared to that of the artist, to the extent that she was portrayed as "modern artist of the domestic interior" who "with the taste with which she is gifted" is able to orchestrate the disparate contents of her domestic interior. Tierstein further notes that the identification of the housewife with the physical structure of her family's home itself was "so great that the bourgeois woman herself became a part of the décor" and bourgeois wives were admonished to "use your rugs and curtains to dress yourself" by selecting domestic furnishings which blended with their own particular hair colour and skin tones.[86]

However, these are by no means issues of only historical concern. As Allan and Crow note, still today the "ideology which requires of home life the presence of a wife (and ideally, mother) remains powerful", given the extent to which home as a set of relationships is still built around the roles of wife and mother.[87] If historically "the home was ... the bastion of family life, the kitchen its command centre and the woman its sergeant", still, as argued earlier, changes in women's participation in the workplace have not abolished the "radical split between the lives of women as the centre (pivot) of home life and as the periphery (margin) of social (outside) life".[88] I make this argument in Chapter 4, in relation to the continuing effectivity of gender as a determinant of domestic viewing practices, but those evidently represent only one tip of the iceberg of domestic gender relations. Principal among the internal pivots of home life is, of course, the question of cooking. Notwithstanding the empirical tendencies noted earlier for the family meal to be replaced by separate microwaved snacks in many households, it retains a central symbolic significance in the culture of domesticity. The significance of "proper meals" and their centrality to the structuration of the household is rightly stressed by Stevi Jackson and Shaun Moores.[89] As they point out, whether at a quotidian level, when a meal is cooked to be ready for a husband's return from work in the evening, thus symbolising his reinclusion in the family group, or in the elaborated form of Sunday (or Christmas, or in the USA Thanksgiving) dinner, when meals may celebrate the "homecoming" of kin from beyond the immediate household group, "such occasions have a high symbolic value, representing home comforts and family unity" and are designed to symbolise these values by being "eaten with all co-resident household members present at the table".[90] In her analysis of traditional domestic practices in Wales, Ann Murcott argues that the symbolism of the "proper meal" cooked by a wife for her husband was very precise:

> its composition and prescribed cooking technologies involve prolonged work and attention; its timing, for homecoming, prescribes when that work will be done. To do so demands that the cook be working at it, doing wifely work, in time that corresponds to that spent by her husband earning for the family ... [just as] a car worker's lunch, prepared by his wife the evening before, is symbolic of the domestic relationship which constitutes the rationale for his presence in the workplace.[91]

The housewife often spends her time negotiating her way round the contradiction between public norms of her job, which would demand that she keep her home clean and orderly, and the private norms, which demand that her family experience their home as a place with a free and easy, comfortable atmosphere.[92] As a result, she often spends her time allowing the creation of various forms of disorder which she tidies up later. Her skills are, as Pauline Hunt observes, largely directed towards meeting the needs of others. Just for herself she is unlikely to keep the house warm throughout or cook a "proper meal" – these are things she does to make the home welcoming for when the family comes home, and much of this labour will be invisible to all but her. She rarely has disposal over her own time. As Hunt puts it, "the hallmark of a houseworker's relationship to her husband and children is her availability. She puts herself at their disposal. Her time is tailored to their needs." She literally waits on others, and "all this waiting expresses subordination, for it is those with power who command the time of others".[93]

Changes in gender ideologies notwithstanding, it does still seem that women maintain primary responsibility for the smooth running of the home and for the reproduction of domestic order and comfort. This means, among other things, that domestic leisure remains heavily gendered. In so far as the home remains women's workplace, "the continued presence of household duties and obligations means that it is difficult for women to set aside time for leisure".[94] The same applies to space as to time. Just as few housewives have time of their own, it is extremely rare for a housewife to have a room of her own other than the kitchen, the heart of the process of domestic labour (although her children, and often her husband will have a room or demarcated space – a "den" of some sort of their own).[95] Hunt reports her women interviewees as being baffled by her questions about the desirability of a room of their own, interpreting such questions as being about what they might do when they felt depressed (take a long bath, have a good cry) and as irrelevant because, as one of them puts it, "I'm on my own a lot here in the daytime," or in another's words, "This is my room, the house ..."[96] However, when the house is empty, although she notionally has access to the whole of it as a potential leisure space, in practice not only is the housewife highly unlikely to keep the whole space heated in winter, but undone domestic chores often make it impossible for her to treat the house as a space of potential leisure at all, rather than a site of continuous housework.

The process of identification of the mother/housewife with "her" house is not simply an internalised psychic process on the part of the woman concerned. As Hunt reports, "the strong identification between the houseworker as a person and her home is reflected in the type of gifts she receives ... household items are frequently seen as appropriate gifts for the housewife".[97] So much is the housewife perceived by others as inseparable from her house that a gift for the house can be represented as a gift for her. The physical character of the home necessarily carries a strong charge of affect, and a well-decorated home is usually seen as a symbol of united family.[98] As Mikhali Csikszentmihalyi and

Eugene Rochberg-Halton observe, decorative objects are signs of the ties that bind the family together, and it is such objects that are often particularly cherished by housewives.[99] Thus, one of Pauline Hunt's interviewees says that she particularly treasures her china cabinet because it contains gifts "from everyone in the family, plus friends and relations".[100] It is in this context that we can perhaps usefully return to the "scandal" of Rachel Whiteread's *House* sculpture referred to earlier. In his commentary on the debates surrounding this sculpture, Nick Couldry observes that

> as a public monument under a woman's direction, *House* ran counter
> to important stereotypes: the gendering of the public/private distinc-
> tion; the historical exclusion of women from monumental and their
> confinement to domestic art; and the regulation of women's circula-
> tion in public space.

Not only did it also negate the traditional stereotype of woman as defender of the home (in so far as Whiteread was (wrongly) seen as responsible for this home's destruction as a living space) but "*House* (a home filled in to become unliveable) negated Ruskin's classic image of home as a place of Peace".[101] Perhaps part of what made Whiteread's sculpture scandalous was the fact that, as a woman artist, her work represented a highly visible and enormously contentious antithesis to the traditional concept of feminine responsibility for housewifely care of the privacy of the home.

The gendering of global space

While I wish to argue for the continuing importance of gendered divisions in the domestic life of the affluent West, some caution is necessary here. I have argued earlier for the continuing usefulness (allowing for contextual variations) of Bourdieu's classical analysis of the gendering of space. Certainly, one can find resonances with the patterns Bourdieu identifies in some parts of the UK even today, in these matters. To take an obvious case from a contemporary rural context, in her study of the organisation of domestic space in farmhouses in the English countryside, Mary Bouquet reports a particularly strongly demarcated boundary between the farm and the house which is itself principally organised along gender lines.[102] The farm is the men's concern: for them the house is where they come inside to wash, rest, eat and sleep before returning to their proper place (exactly in Bourdieu's sense) in the world of outdoor work. The house is the area of women's business – and, again, in parallel with Bourdieu's analysis, there are specific areas within it (in this case the whole of the upstairs, access to which is demarcated by particular rituals of washing, taking off outside clothes, etc.) which are particularly reserved for family privacy and most closely associated with feminine control.

However, the gender-coding of space and domesticity is by no means a phenomenon particular either to so-called primitive societies or to rural areas. There is plenty of evidence of a strong thread of continuity in this respect in the history of the organisation of domestic space in the industrialised urban West. Thus Ruth Madigan and Moira Munro offer historical evidence of the extent to which, in the UK, the design of the Victorian town house "reflected the internal hierarchy of the bourgeois family with the public 'masculine' domain at the front of the house and the private 'feminine' domain confined to the rear".[103] Indeed, they argue that, among all classes, the same ideal was aspired to and that "the more respectable and status conscious a household, the greater the differentiation between front and back, the public [masculine] sphere of the street and parlour and the private [feminine] sphere of the kitchen, the yard, and the backlane". This gendered division of space also informed the whole later development of suburbia, which allowed an even greater separation of home and work and thus provided for the creation of a "protected, semi-rural environment for wives and children" within the enclosure of the suburban "private household behind the formality of the public façade" where the private, feminine realm could be all the more clearly protected from the travails of the public world.[104]

None of this need blind us to the dangers of an incautious application of Bourdieu's analytic structure. Thus, in the introduction to their cross-cultural comparative study of the symbolic function of the house in South-East Asia and South America, Janet Carsten and Stephen Hugh-Jones warn against the dangers of universalising Bourdieu's model.[105] As they note, in Bourdieu's analysis the "outside" world is associated with men and the "inside" world with women in a hierarchical relation so that "the house is defined ... from the outside by men; women, on the inside, are subordinate to them. Movement inwards is intrinsically female movement; movement outwards, intrinsically male." However, as they note, this ordering simply does not apply universally and "in different contexts, the Malay, Tukanoan or Velabit house can be associated with women, with women and men, or with men". Given that in different cultural contexts "houses can be simultaneously 'private' and 'public', associated with women or with men or both ... we should ... be wary about describing the house as a structure of unchanging gendered oppositions". Indeed, they argue, in some cases,

> the opposition between outside and inside may not be perceived in gendered terms at all. It may be linked to oppositions based on other kinds of perceived social differences ... [and] inside or outside may be linked with siblingship or marriage, with descent or affirmity, with unity or difference ... or with high rank or low

rather than always being primarily linked to the gender differences between men and women.[106] Certainly this is a caveat that must be borne in mind in considering the culturally bounded limitations to the application of Bourdieu's model.

Nonetheless, if we turn our attention to the question of current debates about globalisation, it must also be noted that much of the writing about global space has been conducted without paying any attention to the question of its gendering. In an important corrective to this blind spot in the literature, Petra Weyland[107] offers an analysis of the Istanbul-based lives of the wives of a set of international businessmen and of their female domestic maidservants, many of whom are also migrants (often illegal ones from the Philippines). As she notes, while the businessmen's accompanying wives and their female maidservants are very differently placed with respect to wealth and status, spatially their lives are both largely circumscribed by the domestic space of the house or apartment provided to the businessman by his company. Much in the manner of the traditional harem, this enclosed, protected, luxurious and secret female space is "often well-hidden in a dead-end street on a hill overlooking the Bosphorus ... surrounded by high walls, situated in a park-like landscape ... protected by guards ... not accessible from, nor even seen by the outside world". For the accompanying wives, their sequestration in this protected space is a matter of social isolation. Unlike their husbands, they have no ready-made structure of activity through which to engage with the particular city they find themselves posted to, and for them their homes are often the "only stable, known and controlled places in a periodically changing and each time alien setting". For their Filipina maidservants, the city represents an alien cosmos – incomprehensible, potentially threatening – which they are reluctant or unable to enter or get to know. For them it is above all a space of male domination – "an alien and potentially hostile male territory"[108] – through which they attempt to manoeuvre unobtrusively (especially those who fear the attentions of the police in relation to their immigration status). The maids thus exist in an informal feminised network, made up of islands of domestic space hidden from the public life of the city – their own rooms or those of their friends, in their employers' houses: from which fastnesses they send home the money which supports their own faraway families in the Philippines.[109] In this example we see the regeneration of the most traditional patterns of the gendering of space, in the context of the contemporary organisation of some of the most advanced forms of transnational capital.

Gender essentialism?

One of the dangers here is, of course, the risk of falling into a backward-looking form of gender essentialism, which ascribes too deterministic an effect to structures of gender and fails to recognise the extent to which gender is a performative category and the corresponding extent to which people are not always and inevitably "prisoners of gender".[110] Thus, in relation to the question of patterns of media usage which I discuss in detail in the next chapter, David

Gauntlett and Annette Hill criticise both my own earlier work and that of a number of feminist scholars for taking too deterministic a view of the influence of gender roles and subjectivities.[111] Critiques such as that of Gauntlett and Hill also call attention to changes in patterns of employment for women and changes in household structures, which are also held to make the impact of traditional gender roles less relevant to contemporary life in the advanced industrial societies of the West, at least. These two issues – the one epistemological, concerning the nature of generalisations about gender (or by implication, about any other social category), the other based rather on substantively different generalisations about contemporary structures of gender, must be dealt with separately.

In the first case, in relation to the viability of generalisations about gender, as a matter of principle, Susan Bordo observes that

> gender never exhibits itself in pure form but in the context of lives that are shaped by a multiplicity of influences which cannot be neatly sorted out. This doesn't mean, however … that abstractions or generalisations about gender are methodologically illicit or perniciously homogenising of difference.[112]

In a parallel argument, Bruce Robbins critiques Chandra Mohanty's objection to what she describes as the improperly universalising tendencies of "easy generalisation[s]" about "women in the Third World", by remarking that the problem here is that Mohanty's comments tend to encourage a politically and intellectually disabling presumption that generalisation *per se* is undesirable. In that case we are left ultimately with a methodologically individualist position, from which all we can say is that everything is unique. Against this disastrous conclusion, Robbins urges that "if we agree that there is no 'easy generalisation', don't we want to retain the right to difficult generalisations?"[113] I have elsewhere argued a similar case that the post-structuralist critique of essentialism in the invocation of gender or any other social category always runs the risk of falling back into a form of methodological individualism which leaves one, ultimately, only able to tell particularised stories of (logically) infinite difference.[114]

In relation to the second question, my own reading of the available evidence indicates that traditional patterns of gender relations are surprisingly resilient, and as we have seen, often reassert themselves in new forms, and in changed circumstances. Thus, in her analysis of contemporary family lifestyles, Fiona Devine argues that even if more women go out to work in the UK compared with earlier times, nonetheless, at crucial stages for those who have children, their lives remain thoroughly home-centred.[115] To take another example, in her study of a group of male Cambridge scientists, Doreen Massey observes that when they say that they feel that the boundary between work and play has disappeared from their lives (so that they do not mind working very long hours) this does raise a problem about their home lives. As she puts it, those long hours and the flexibility of their organisation is someone else's constraint. Who goes to the launderette? Who picks up the children from school? ... [T]he whole design of those jobs requires that these employees do not do the work of reproduction and of caring for other people; indeed, it implies that ... they have someone to look after them.[116]

As Massey notes, the unspoken premise of these men's flexible labour is a very constrained role for the women who care for them and their children. She elsewhere observes that when these men talk about the boundary between home and work breaking down, what they fail to take into account is that it tends only to break down in one direction: while work increasingly enters the domestic sphere, it is very rare for domestic concerns to find comparable ease of access into the sphere of work.

In relation to the breakdown of the traditional idea of the home and of gender relations within it, Donna Haraway has notably argued that, in the cybernetic era home has to be redefined to take into account all the following developments:

Home: Women-headed households, serial monogamy, flight of men, old women alone, technology of domestic work, paid homework, re-emergence of home sweat shops, home-based businesses and telecommuting, electronic cottage, urban homelessness, migration, module architecture, reinforced (simulated) nuclear family, intense domestic violence.[117]

She is, of course, entirely right to insist on the significance of all these trans-formations. They do not, however, mean that we can dispense with generalisations about gender, nor that the content of previous generalisations is now entirely irrelevant. The task is surely to produce better, more adequate generalisations which more effectively address our contemporary situation.

It is now well attested that statistically, the conventional nuclear family, consisting of married parents and their dependent children, accounts for a steadily declining population of households throughout the countries of the industrial West. Nonetheless, as Cynthia Carter puts it, the "politics of normalcy still operate so as to privilege the image of the traditional nuclear family as the hegemonic and (naturally?) preferable form of familial configuration".[118] As Jackie Stacey observes, fewer and fewer people in the West choose to themselves live in households of this type, being involved instead in "a multiplicity of family and household arrangements, which [they] inhabit uneasily and reconstitute frequently in response to changing personal and occupational circum-stances".[119] However, there remains a strong sense of nostalgia for this form of familial configuration, given the poverty of the available vocabularies for the description (and evaluation) of non-family forms of relationships and households.

As Jeffrey Weeks puts it, despite all we know of the actual shortcomings and limitations of life within the traditional nuclear family, we fall back, in the absence of an alternative discourse, on "the security of what we know, or believe, to be secure and stable, a haven ... where those who feel besieged may find protection".[120] The question is, what price must be paid for this "protection" behind the walls of the purified space of domesticity, and who does the paying?

Heimat's darker shadows: domesticity, dirt and femininity

Just as Mary Douglas argues that if we can abstract pathogenicity and hygiene from our notion of it, dirt consists in no particular essence but only in matter out of place within the terms of some particular cultural system, so Phyllis Palmer argues that "dirt is not a scientific fact but a principal means to arrange cultures".[121] Most particularly, in Palmer's view, dirt is crucial to the organisation of gender relations, in so far as femininity has long been defined by its relation to that category. If, as Frazer Ward argues, it is "in the nature of dirt to be cleared up", the image of the middle-class housewife, the historically dominant model of femininity in the USA, "has long been constructed around domestic cleanliness".[122] As Palmer argues, the concept of dirt is inextricably linked to the organisation of sexuality, the family and domesticity, and "sex, dirt, housework and badness in women are linked in Western unconsciousness". Conversely, as she notes,

> the home has been reified as the setting for good women, virtuous wives and mothers. Its work has been haloed with maternal imagery. Yet the work carried on in the house is unconsciously identified with dirt and decay, which threaten to taint the character of the woman who does it.[123]

To this extent, then, femininity has been, at least in part, defined by how women manage dirt. The solution for the middle-class housewife, at an earlier stage, was to hire servants to do this work for her, and thus "dirty" themselves rather than her (these servants being replaced, in the post-World War II period, by mechanical appliances) so that she was symbolically removed from contact with dirt and thus clean for her husband.[124] A woman who had servants to deal with dirt was perceived as "more feminine, more ladylike" while the "negative, unfeminine connotations of dirt had to be absorbed by the body of the servant" and "the 'good' woman could be responsible for the disappearance of dirt in the home, but never have to touch it herself".[125]

Historically, marital success or failure was in general terms judged by the wife's moral standing, as evidenced by her ability to properly keep house. As Cara Mertes observes, more specifically, "the middle class housewife was expected to maintain a good reputation, provide a proper education for the children and be socially presentable". It was her duty to keep the home clean, not only physically but also morally and it was equally important that no stain appear on either her household or her own reputation – as the condition of both functioned as "a marker of social significance that reflected on the male head of household".[126] In contemporary culture Sibley observes that, in the imagery of advertising, the children in various detergent adverts are depicted as wild barbarians, with a tendency to become dirty as they play. In this latter context, the family home is the setting for the struggle against their natural wildness and dirtiness, as they are "purified by the civilising influences of mother, home and detergent".[127]

If femininity represents the troublesome realm of the emotions, of sexuality and the body, the irruption of any of these elements within the confines of the ordered bourgeois household clearly represents matter out of place. This is the realm of the abject (often identified with the feminine) in Kristeva's terms – the "improper and unclean 'refuse' thrown away in the proper and clean family home".[128] However, if it is femininity which is most associated with the origin of these troublesome, irrational elements, it is also the housewife's job to control and manage them, just as she keeps at bay all the other forms of dirt that would otherwise threaten the integrity and security of the household.

In his analysis of the developments of concerns with hygiene from the end of the nineteenth century, Anders Linde-Laursen notes that the general principle applied "to prevent ... foreign bodies from spreading and causing disease" was the attempt to organise the physical environment so that "there was no improper mixing of substances". To this end, the "disorder of contamination" was to be avoided by a "general struggle for purity, which transforms sterility into both an aesthetic and a moral category". However, if this educational project was to be successful, there had to be someone delegated to be respon-sible for its execution at a local level. This someone, as he observes, was the housewife, who thus took up the struggle against symbolic impurity as the "little chemist" who maintained hygiene, and thus moral order, in the home: "since she is concerned with clean and unclean, order and disorder, the house-wife's work to achieve cleanliness at the same time concerns identity; she becomes the person who draws the boundaries that are the basis for iden-tity".[129]

The *heimlich*, the *heimisch* and the *unheimlich*

Ideologies of domestic bliss notwithstanding, Angelika Bammer insists that "home, in a sense, has always been *unheimlich*: not just the utopian place of safety and shelter for which we supposedly yearn, but also the place of dark secrets, of fear and danger, that we can only inhabit furtively".[130] Jon Bird spec-ulates that Freud's analysis of the uncanny is concerned with the process through which the familiar transposes itself into its opposite. Thus, while the meaning of *heimlich* begins with "belonging to the house", or "familiar" or "friendly", as it is elaborated it turns into something concealed or kept from sight, "finally becoming the negative compound *unheimlich*: 'gruesome fear ... ghostly ... a haunted house ...' thus *heimlich* is a word the meaning of which develops in the direction of ambivalence, until it finally coincides with its opposite, *unheimlich*".[131]

While the *heimlich* can be seen as the realm of the tame, of intimacy, friendliness and comfort (as in the realm of the *heimisch* – the known and familiar world) nonetheless, as Stephen Keane observes, the second meaning of *heimlich* is that of concealment, so that "*heimlich* contains *unheimlich*, because to conceal is the exact opposite of making familiar ... thus *unheimlich* is the hidden core of *heimlich*".[132] Similarly, as Anthony Vidler notes, for Freud

> the apparently warm and all-enclosing interiors of intrauterine existence were ... at the same time, the very centres of the uncanny. At once the refuge of inevitably unfulfilled desire and the potential crypt of living burial, the womb-house offered little solace to daily life.[133]

In her commentary on questions of belonging and dislocation, Jenny Bourne-Taylor observes that, in Freud's analysis, *unheimlich* does not simply mean the opposite of that which is homely. Rather, she argues that the notions of *heimlich* and *unheimlich* are better seen as inverted replications, rather than opposites of each other. *Heimlich* itself, she notes, means both cosy and also hidden or secret. As Freud himself puts it: "the uncanny is that class of the frightening which leads back to what is known of old and long familiar".[134] Thus, "the strangeness is not without but within, there is no home per se that is a safe place from the strangers, since home is the site of the uncanny, the double. ... sleep, madness, dreams, beasts, sex".[135]

The uncanny art object

These issues have also been a topic of some concern in recent art historical writing. In her analysis of Robert Rauschenberg's use of domestic fabrics in his collage work of the 1950s and 1960s, Lisa Wainwright argues that its significance lies in its contrast to the high modernist ideals of the Abstract Expressionist school, which was then dominant in the USA, whose heroic masculinist limits Rauschenberg wished to escape.[136] As Wainwright observes, "against the heavy weight of high culture, high modernism and its attendant high masculinity ... Rauschenberg posed an alternative aesthetic which some commentators have read as proto-feminist, others as gay". In choosing to feature domestic fabrics in his work, Rauschenberg was making a fundamentally symbolic choice, in so far as fabrics were understood as a feminine medium: "fabrics related to the home: to curtains, clothing and bedspreads and so cloth evokes the gender-assigned characteristics of domesticity and comfort". If, as Wainwright notes, "in fabrics, Rauschenberg found a readymade sign for the familiar or *heimlich*", in collaging his "found" objects from the everyday world into an artistic frame he "rendered his found objects uncanny" and they became both familiar (as recognisable objects) and unfamiliar (as inscribed with new meanings in different contexts) – perhaps most notably in his celebrated paint-splattered sleeping bag *Bed* of 1955 (see Figure 3.2). As she argues, Rauschenberg's attempt to "wed his gayness to concepts of domesticity only furthered the *unheimlich* effect of his work". To this extent, Rauschenberg's aesthetic strategy, using "paisley fabric backgrounds [to] conjure up old-fash-ioned sitting rooms where things are dark and worn but somehow also familiar and reassuring" can almost be seen as a textbook explication of Freud's theory of the essential ambiguity of the terms *heimlich/unheimlich*.[137]

Figure 3.2　Robert Rauschenberg, *Bed*, 1955. The Museum of Modern Art, New York. Gift of Leo Castelli in honour of Alfred Barr Jr, 1989.
Source:　Photo © The Museum of Modern Art.

A number of other contemporary artists besides Rauschenberg (especially in the USA and including, notably, Ed Keinholz) have also addressed the question of the uncanny in their representations of domesticity. For example, Elizabeth Diller and Ricardo Scofidio's work (see Figure 3.3) also involves the transformation of domestic spaces and furnishings into pathological combinations, in which familiar objects are displaced from their proper domains and functions (chairs suspended in the air or attached to tables by locks; beds split in two). Commenting on their work, Anthony Vidler argues that this aesthetic strategy again exploits the ambivalence of the uncanny dimensions of domesticity.[138] As Vidler notes, the use in the work of well-known, everyday objects such as old chairs and televisions lulls us into a false sense of security, based on their banal familiarity. However, as they are recontextualised in problematic contexts they

> take on more sinister overtures. Returned from their proper burial, discovered in the wrong place, invested with an uncanny life of their own, they break the long process of deterioration ... that leads from the familiar, the ordinary, to the banal, returning once more to the status of the unhomely.[139]

Figure 3.3 Elizabeth Diller and Ricardo Scofidio, installation view from *the withDrawing Room*, 1987. The Capp Street Project, San Francisco.

Source: Photo: Ben Blackwell. Courtesy of the artists.

From another perspective, in her commentary on the work of Vito Acconci (see Figures 3.4 and 3.5), Christine Poggi traces the ambivalence of masculine perspectives on domesticity, even within the discourses of postmodernity.[140] On the one hand Acconci's ambition is to deconstruct and destabilise any harmonious image of domesticity, declaring that one of his installations should be "the kind of home that makes you a stranger inside it" which "makes you itch … [and] do a double-take", rather than enabling you to "snuggle" into any nostalgic imagery of reassuring stability.[141] Acconci uses deliberately shocking tactics to achieve this effect: *Bad Dream House* plainly fails to offer its inhabitants either privacy or shelter; other pieces dramatise the display of privacy in public space; *High Rise* specifically satirises the American (frontier?) mythology of man-as-Housebuilder. Nonetheless, Acconci himself claims to have "a great fear of the notion of home and family", and his work can be seen as still linked to "the modernist ethos of the singular, heroic, transgressive male, whose independence drives him from home". [142] The work is still, if paradoxically, imbued with modernism's masculinist sense of domesticity as a "bad dream" and of the man who stays in the house as a "sissy stay-at-home".[143]

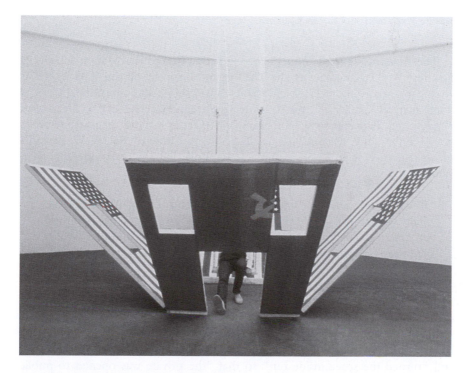

Figure 3.4 Vito Acconci, *Instant House*, 1980.

Source: Photo courtesy of Barbara Gladstone.

Figure 3.5 Vito Acconci, *Bad Dream House*, 1984.
Source: Photo courtesy of Barbara Gladstone.

The *Womanhouse* installation created in Judy Chicago and Miriam Schapiro's Feminist Art Programme at the Californian Institute of the Arts in 1972 attempted, according to Haar and Reed, to destabilise all conventional ideas of domesticity as familiar and banal, by using surreal imagery – of the *Nurturant Kitchen* and *Fear Bathroom*, for example.[144] From a more explicitly feminist point of view, the *Womanhouse* installation foreshadowed Rachel Whiteread's *House* sculpture, in so far as, in this case symbolically rather than literally (as in Whiteread's case),

> *Womanhouse* turned the house inside out. The isolation and anger that many women felt in the single-nuclear-family dwelling in every suburb of America was flung out at the public … exposing a sadness which had been covered by the roofs of many in their own private homes.[145]

In the case of Whiteread's *House* sculpture, its impact was due, according to Massey, to the way in which it disrupted conventions of both space and time. As she notes, it set "a familiar past in the space-time of today; it made present something which was absent; it was the space of a house no longer there". More immediately shockingly perhaps, it exposed the intimacies of the inside and "turned the space inside out" so that "the private was opened to public view". In this, the sculpture "exposes the private sphere to public view and thus to questioning … it defamiliarises house and home … [and] exposes the normal, comfortable mythologising of 'home' ... the things which should be hidden are ... exposed".[146] To this extent, as Simon Watney argues, *House* was seen as threatening, or even obscure, precisely because "it exposes an interior ... shows us something we are not supposed to see", something which is perhaps particularly troubling to English notions of domestic respectability and their rigid divisions of gender and sexuality, public and private moralities.[147]

These are some of the contradictions and difficulties embedded in the concept of home. Having established a working perspective on its gendering, we now turn to the question of its function as a site of mediated consumption.

4

AT HOME WITH THE MEDIA

Domestic media/mediated domesticity

In the research into the Household Uses of Information and Communication Technologies which Roger Silverstone, Eric Hirsch and I conducted, our central interest lay in trying to formulate an analytical framework for the understanding of the role of various communications media in the articulation of the private and public spheres.[1] The key issues arising from the HICT project which I wish to explore here concern the role of these technologies in disrupting boundaries of various sorts (at both the domestic and national levels) and in rearticulating the private and public spheres in new ways. Our interest was in understanding how different families mobilised the various technologies with which they lived, and in countering any techno-determinist model, in which new technologies were simply assumed to be (in some straightforward casual process) necessarily transforming the home or the family.[2] Despite its theoretical sophistication in other respects, a great deal of postmodern theory does seem to be underpinned by exactly that kind of hypodermic "effects" model, which presumes the unilateral power of macro–technological forces to simply effect the realm of the micro–domestic. In that research, our concern was to pose household cultures (and their material constraints and settings) as independent variables, which could then more helpfully explain, not only (in a negative sense) the differential impact of particular technologies on different households, but also (in a more active sense) how and why particular members of particular households perceived (and therefore adopted or rejected) particular technologies as (ir)relevant and/or (in)appropriate to them.

Having rejected hypodermic theories of technological power, it is also then necessary to acknowledge the "double life" of various technologies which allows them to be mobilised in different ways in different contexts, sometimes for other purposes than those foreseen by their designers.[3] Within the terms of this contradictory dynamic, if these technologies themselves do not simply have effects on the home, but have rather to be analysed in terms of how they come to be embedded within pre-existing domestic routines, they are, simultaneously, technologies which also have a disembedding effect – in so far as they potentially function to connect individuals within the home to others, geographically elsewhere.[4] This is to speak of communications technologies as having the simultaneous capacity to articulate together that which is separate (to bring the outside world into the home, via television, or to connect family members, via the phone, to friends or relatives elsewhere) but, by the same token, to transgress the (always, of course, potentially sacred) boundary which protects the privacy and solidarity of the home from the flux and threat of the outside world. In this connection, Margaret Morse captures something of the liminal place occupied by the television set, at the junction of the inside and the outside, the channel through which the news of the public world enters the domestic realm. She suggests that it is as if "inside the hollow television, the ultimate box, is a personal reliquary for fetish objects, or sacra, at the cross-roads of everyday life, the commodity world and our common culture".[5] If it is now a commonplace to note that television has replaced the hearth as the totemic centrepiece of the family's main living space, we should note that this replacement occurs literally at the centre of the symbolic space of the family home: a sacred space, by any definition, within our culture. Morse goes on to note that television is "premised upon private reception in an environment isolated from events 'out there', which determine the conditions of life outside the home". The question is one of how the media connect the place of "our idyll, our self-sufficient and bounded place ... the space in front of the television set" to other, geographically distant but communicationally present places.[6]

The central point for my present purposes concerns the fact that media industries are implicated in these social–spatial processes in significant and distinctive ways. Thus, as Kevin Robins argues, "issues around the politics of communication converge with the politics of space. Questions of communication are also about the nature and scope of community."[7] Such theoretical work as has begun to take on board these questions has largely done so at a very abstract level. As indicated earlier, if one of the central functions of communications systems is to articulate different spaces (the public and the private, the national and the international) and, necessarily, in doing so, to transgress boundaries (whether the boundary around the domestic household, or that around the nation) then our analytical framework must be capable of being applied at both the micro and the macro level.

TV in the modern home

It was during the period 1880–1940 that the cultural ideal of domesticity, which had emerged long before for the bourgeoisie "was codified in the spaces of suburbia and became a reality for the majority of the population in Britain and in the USA". As Eric Hirsch argues, this process entered its golden age during the period from the 1940s to the 1970s when "processes of technological miniaturisation and the rapid expansion of consumer electronics further enhanced the domestic ideal".[8] Hirsch's point is that forms of domesticity have not developed solely through some internal dynamic but always in relation to the broader societal development of technologies on which these forms of life themselves depend for their viability. In a striking application of a parallel perspective, in his analysis of the cultural politics and symbolic significance of the process of "home electrification" in post-war Japan, Shunya Yoshimi traces the ways in which the processes of modernisation of the home and the nation were intertwined there.[9] In the early part of the twentieth century, the *Seikatu Kaizen* ("better standard of living") movement stressed the importance of using modern electrical appliances. Subsequently, Yoshimi notes, the Life Improvement Union stressed the importance of "removing all waste from the home, taking away all ornaments [and] introducing more rationalisation" as a way of promoting "efficiency in the activity of the nation" and constituting to "the growth of national fortune". Throughout this period, the modern home was characterised by its possession of the "three sacred things", in the form of consumer appliances. In the 1950s these were the washing machine, the refrigerator and the black-and-white television; in the 1960s they were the car, the air conditioner and the colour television. However, notwithstanding the shifting referents of the phrase, its significance, Yoshimi argues, lies in the way in which it so closely echoes the traditional formula referring to the "three sacred treasures" (sword, jewels and mirror) which "are national symbols for authenticating the position of the emperor as the ruler of the Japanese archipelago". The point, Yoshimi claims, is that, in a parallel sense, the possession of the three sacred consumer appliances (whichever particular ones might be specified at a given time) functioned "as a symbol for authenticating the identity of the individual household as being a 'modern family' ".[10]

In the context of the post-World War II America, television was famously described as "the shining centre of the home" by NBC network head Pat Weaver in 1954.[11] This phenomenon is now rather more widespread. In his research on the impact of new media in Iban society in Malaysian Borneo, John Postill reports that the television now usually takes pride of place there among a family's possessions. Moreover, he notes, it has also penetrated Iban religious practices to the extent that, at one funeral he witnessed, the dead person's television set was placed at the foot of his grave and its screen smashed (in the back-to-front Iban afterworld, television can only be watched on a broken set) as were the rest of the grave goods that would accompany their dead owner into the afterworld.[12] In an analogy with Ondina Leal's findings from her work in Brazil, Postill also argues that in Iban society family albums and photos placed in symbolic settings (such as on top of the television set) serve to transcend the time–space gulfs between present and absent family members, whether those who are absent are so by virtue of migration (temporary absence in space) or of death (permanent absence in time).[13] In either case, the presence of their image keeps alive their memory or spirit, at the site of the family's sacred (electrical) hearth (see Figure 4.1).

Figure 4.1 Television with family photos in Chinese home.
Source: Photo: James Lull.

I have argued elsewhere for the importance of analysing what we might call the "physics" of television as a material and symbolic object in the home.[14] Having recognised the symbolic centrality of the television set as a sacred physical object in many homes, it is perhaps also worth noting one particularly interesting case, reported by Sean Moores in his study of satellite television, where it is the shared possession (in this case rented, rather than owned) of the television which seems, in effect, to constitute the very definition of the household. For the purposes of official surveys in the UK, a household is often defined as those who eat together. It seems, however, that in some cases a household may perhaps be better defined as those who view together. In the case that Moores reports, a group of university students, only some of whom actually lived on the premises where the set was housed, clubbed together to rent satellite television. Their agreement was that even those who did not live in the household "could be round to watch Sky television at any time of the day or night that we wanted – [on] an open door policy". To this extent their joint subscription to Sky television meant that "for the routine purposes of everyday life ... they ... [were] effectively members of the same domestic group".[15]

The media and the construction of domestic routine

The study of the media's articulation with patterns of everyday life has become more widely recognised as an important area of research in recent years. In their study of television viewing habits in the UK, David Gauntlet and Annette Hill argue that it would seem that "television is, at the very least a catalyst for forms of organisation of time and space – or, to be more emphatic, often a primary determining factor in how households organise their internal geography and everyday timetables".[16] Many of their respondents record that they normally eat their evening meal while watching a particular television programme. The meal is deliberately planned to coincide with a regular feature of the television schedule, and thus the meal and the programme function together as an integral element in the scheduling of household time. For the unemployed, retired or elderly, who lack external structure in their lives, the broadcast schedule itself often provides a desperately needed way of regulating what would otherwise be depressingly unstructured acres of time. Just as, on a quotidian level, being allowed to stay up to watch particular types of programming is characteristically associated with the passage from childhood to adult status, and the adoption of particular viewing choices (especially news and current affairs) is associated with maturation, so for the unemployed, conversely, their dependence on television can be experienced as a guilty return to childish ways. Thus Gauntlett and Hill report one 30-year-old unemployed man who is ashamed of "some of the childish programmes" he watches which, in his own eyes, "don't fit in with [the proper activities of] a 30-year-old man. So when I admit I watch them, I expect others to laugh me down for still watching them at my age."[17]

The integration of television viewing into the spatial geography of the home constitutes a core part of how household life is organised. Thus when one of Gauntlett and Hill's respondents reports that, in their household "each family member watches TV in a different place. Mum and Dad in the living room, my sister in the bedroom and I usually watch TV in the kitchen", the authors note that one or another such form of routinised dispersion of viewing is common to 80 per cent of the households in their study.[18] Here we see one aspect of the much-heralded move to the fragmentation of domestic viewing. In line with his earlier argument about the relationship between the development of particular forms of domestic life and broader socio-technological changes, Hirsch observes that in the recent period, in the UK, "new configurations of television (less centred on the broadcast form) in the shape of cable, satellite [and] video ... and the new technology of personal computers ... position themselves in a politico-moral environment of 'choice'" which is based on the desires of the private individual, rather than the household as a unit.[19] Picking up the theme of fragmentation within the home referred to earlier, Silverstone has noted the extent to which the future of the family itself has been widely perceived to be threatened by the arrival of "portable, individual ... privatising technologies" which function as "isolating and fragmenting machines". In this dystopic vision Silverstone observes, beyond the issue of withdrawal from the public sphere into the home, nowadays, inside the home itself, we face a situation where "parents and children could be seen to occupy separate domestic times and spaces, isolated by personalised stereo systems ... passing each other like ships in the night in a jamming fog of electronic communication and information over-load".[20] From this perspective the personalisation of technologies (the Walkman, the Gameboy, Playstation, the multiple television sets in many homes) makes for the fragmentation of the family or household – an effect which as Silverstone notes, echoing Kumar's comments quoted earlier, "is further enhanced by the 'time-shift' capabilities of both the VCR and the microwave". [21]

Negotiating difference in the family

In many cases the fragmentation of domestic viewing may function to avoid, if not resolve, what would otherwise be conflicts over viewing choices. Certainly conflicts and disagreements about television and other media are often a site of family and household tensions. In some cases it seems that it is hard for people to tolerate the idea of differences of opinion and judgement as between different members of the family. Thus, when one of the respondents in Lelia Green's study of television viewing in the Australian outback states rather defen-sively, "we are a close family. Generally we all like the same shows", we perhaps glimpse the tip of an iceberg of anxiety about the toleration, organisation and management of difference (and thus potential conflict) within the home.[22]

These matters are commonly dealt with, or at least demarcated by, systems of differentiation by which household members negotiate the occupation of separate (and often complementary) physical and/or symbolic spaces. Thus, Graham Murdock and his colleagues argue that children in their study used their time on their computer "to win space and privacy within the household and assert their separation and independence from their parents".[23] In a more developed case, an adult young man living at home with his parents is reported by Moores as inhab-iting a "masculine world of gadgets, fast cars and sci-fi fantasies" in which he assembles a collection of electrical goods as "signs of a struggle to fashion some limited degree of autonomy in the face of parental authority". For him, as for one of the young men in the HICT study, whose family customarily referred to his room (full of similar gadgets) as his "Womb", this young man's special area of expertise is inscribed in (and demarcates) his particular symbolic and geographical territory within the house. He puts it this way:

> I'm the only one who knows how to use my electrical equipment. Nobody else comes in my room – I think of it as my space ... Up here I can watch anything I want ... As soon as I go into my room, it's like I'm on another planet.[24]

The son in this family is heavily identified with satellite viewing and dismisses established terrestrial television as traditional, boring and old-fashioned. In a sideways move which produces a differentiated and thus complementary position for himself in the household, in response to the son's increasing interest and involvement in new technologies his father has become increasingly absorbed in restoring antique furniture. Similarly, in another of the families on which Moores reports in the same study, the wife invests her energies and interests in antiques exactly to the (growing) extent to which her husband has become obsessed, as she perceives it, with modern, electronic gadgetry.[25]

In the context of the HICT study, Eric Hirsch further reports the tensions in one household arising from the placing of the husband's computer equipment in their lounge, in so far as it impinges on their joint living space.[26] At the point of upgrading the relevant computer equipment, Hirsch reports that each member of the family perceived the new equipment as offering different (and partly contradictory) possibilities. The same piece of technology (a new computer modem) was variously envisaged by the husband of the family as "a tremendous potential"; by his wife as a threat to her use of the telephone line; by the son as an exciting potential for the use of email, and by the daughter as of only "marginal interest in comparison with television". As Hirsch observes, the family faced a very difficult situation, where their variously conflicting interests would need to be reconciled in dealing with the arrival of this new piece of technology and the multiple connections which it potentially offered with the outside world – in a situation where any one of these connections potentially vitiated others. Clearly, the advent of multiple phone lines in many houses, since the time of the HICT study, has gone some way to alleviating some of these contradictions, but the essential point remains, so long as the various members of a household still have competing and contradictory priorities for the use of essentially scarce resources such as money, time and space.

As indicated earlier, the HICT study attempted to utilise an anthropological approach, which focused on the symbolic and ritual significance of domestic objects. Thus in another paper arising from that project, Hirsch draws an analogy between Western and so-called primitive societies, arguing that "we are not really so different from Melanesians in the way we sustain relationships through material forms".[27] In a particularly graphic example of the symbolism of how communication technologies are domesticated, he reports how one family concealed all their technologies so far as possible, at the wife's insistence, within reproduction antique cabinets. This seemingly innocent aesthetic choice makes better sense when we realise that family life in this particular household is continually disrupted by the calls and interruptions caused by the husband's work as a policeman, much to his wife's distress. In this context his wife's attempt to hide "any sign of an intrusive technology that might indicate a relationship with the outside world" becomes perfectly understandable as part of her struggle to erase the "signs of connections with the outside world that might interfere with their home life".[28]

The gendered forms of media consumption

In this section I shall return to some of the questions about the gendering of domestic life developed in Chapter 3 and address the question of gendered differences in patterns of media usage and the forms of domestic conflict to which they sometimes give rise. In this context Hirsch reports a struggle (see above) between a woman and her husband who kept his portable computer in the living room, so that he could work on it in the evenings. His wife wanted the computer taken back to his place of work, where in her view it properly belonged, because it took up too much space, claiming that "he has it everywhere where it shouldn't be".[29] From the anthropological perspective noted above, this woman's comments take exactly the form specified by Mary Douglas' classic definition of dirt (see below, Chapter 6, on this). In this case her husband's work is every bit as much "matter out of place" in the sitting room as mud would be, so far as she is concerned. In her commentary on Hirsch's analysis in this study, Karen Fog-Olwig rightly observes that the key dynamic was that in which these new technologies created a new space within the home which was in effect colonised by the men (and boys) of the house. The consequent conflicts in these households over the appropriate use of these technologies must then be understood, she argues, as being the result of the technology-driven "intrusion of male domains … [and] spheres of activity that had traditionally taken place outside … into a home traditionally defined by female home-makers, whether as mothers, wives or educators".[30]

In a further striking example of the gendering of (and differentiation of) attitudes to and uses of technology, Moores reports the complementary cases of a woman and a man in his study who both work at home, but take completely opposed attitudes to the difficulties posed for them, as homeworkers, by the telephone. Thus, in one case the wife in the family is so concerned to maintain some boundary round her private space that not only does she use the answering machine to screen calls, but in the evenings and weekends she unplugs both the phone and the answering machine so as to avoid being disturbed. Conversely, the male homeworker has such a "phobia about … people not being able to speak to me" that he makes himself available by phone "seven days a week, 24 hours a day", using telecommunications, as Moores observes, "to create a constantly permeable external boundary to the home" as he is so anxious not to lose potential custom.[31]

There is now considerable evidence to support the idea that masculine and feminine modalities of telephone usage exhibit clear differences. Thus in her study of the gendering of telephone usage in Australia, Ann Moyal reports that she discovered "a pervasive, deeply rooted … feminine culture of the telephone in which 'kinkeeping', caring, mutual support, friendship … and community activity play a central part … which … contributes substantially to women's sense of autonomy, security, participation and well being".[32] As Linda Rakow reported from her American study of the same phenomenon, "telephoning is a form of care-giving ... gendered work ... that women do to hold together the fabric of the community, build and maintain relationships".[33] By nature of this telephone involvement, which links together women in different domestic households, a mediated "psychological neighbourhood" is created and sustained. Moyal's study reveals the existence of a "marginalised but vibrant culture of the telephone – a network of callers which constitutes an 'electronic community' of friendships, mutual support and kinkeeping" as the technology "provides access to a 'neighbourhood' structured across space and time".[34] This kind of "kinkeeping" use of the phone is very rarely found among men and then only when men are playing what is, in effect, a feminine role.[35]

In one of the families in Moores' study, the wife keeps in touch with her relatives in Malta and Australia by phone. When he enquired about the expense of this practice, she defensively replied that her relations usually rang her, rather than vice versa: a response that became clearer when her husband interjected that if he had his way he would "get rid of the phone" because of the expense of these kinkeeping calls.[36] However, just as the HICT study revealed tensions around the use of the telephone, which on closer examination turned out to be not so much to do with cost as to do with the phone's effects in "de-linking" teenage children from the family group and plugging them more firmly into their peer group, so Moyal discovered similar tensions between the husbands and wives in her study concerning the women's use of the telephone.[37] While the financial cost of heavy telephone use was at times the issue, more often it seemed that the husbands in her study were simply jealous of telephonic others' claims on their wives' attention.

Perhaps not surprisingly, given the tenacity of gender roles, new technologies such as the mobile phone also tend to be incorporated into existing patterns of gender differentiation. Rakow and Navarro's research on the gendered uses of cellular telephones demonstrates that while the men in their sample tended to use their phone during their leisure time as a way to better connect to their place of work, by contrast the women they studied tended to use it during work time, as a way of accomplishing their domestic tasks and obligations by remote control.[38] In a context where many employees (and especially successful middle-class ones) work long hours and often have to travel away from home on business, the phone becomes an essential tool for the maintenance of familial relationships between husband and wife, and between parent and child. In the most common case, where it is the man who is absent from home most of the time, it seems that he will often disengage from all use of the phone while he is at home so as to protect the little "family time" that he experiences, and he will be likely to disapprove of (and often attempt to discourage) his wife and children's use of the phone to contact others (and thus to separate themselves from the family) during the brief period of his presence in the home.

The one case where the phone seemed regularly to be used by men in what would conventionally be understood as a feminine manner is that noted by Christine Castelaine-Meunier in her study of the use of the phone by divorced and separated fathers to maintain contact with their young children, living with their mothers. She notes that, in this context, the telephone is often used in a heavily ritualised manner with father and child telephoning each other at prescribed times on particular days of the week. In this situation, she argues, the telephone functions as a kind of umbilical cord, linking the separated father and child in a form of virtual parenting.[39] This is, however, a very clear exception to the dominant pattern of masculine telephone usage.

The end of gender?

In their study of patterns of television viewing among the UK audience quoted earlier, Gauntlett and Hill are very critical of what they call the "polarised distinctions between men's and women's tastes and uses of media which some previous studies had emphasised".[40] As the studies they have in mind include my own, along with work by Ann Gray, Christine Geraghty and Charlotte Brunsdon, this is a point of some interest to me.[41] At one level, Gauntlett and Hill's argument is a simple historical one, in so far as they claim that things have changed substantially, in matters of gender, since the time of mine and Gray's studies in the mid-1980s. Indeed, they go so far as to say that "in our experience, students in the 1990s reject these gender-divided approaches completely, finding them bewildering and laughable", even if these ideas might "have made some sense 20 years ago". They argue that, from their more recent work, there is little evidence either of differential gender competences in the operation of the relevant technologies (as opposed, for example, to the strongly gendered appropriation of video technology revealed in my own and Gray's work) and little evidence of "there being distinct women's and men's tastes and interests" of the type that Brunsdon, Geraghty, Gray and I all discuss.[42]

In the first place, I would most certainly accept that in the UK, many things have changed in recent years. Certainly, when Gray and I were studying the gendered appropriation of video technologies as "toys for the boys", we were doing so in the very early period of that new technology's distribution. At that time, as a new technology barely out of its hobbyist phase, it was only to be expected that it would principally be appropriated, in the first instance, by technically minded young men, just as radio was before it and as computers were later. Equally, the whole point about the domestication of such a technology is that in this process of "democratisation" (beyond the hands of the technical specialist) it becomes effectively "feminised" as it is made more consumer friendly.[43] To this extent it would be just as surprising if an established consumer technology such as video were to still now be highly gendered as it would be were the next new leisure technology not to pass through a similar, initially gendered, trajectory. However, I am less convinced by the argument that the very idea of gendered differences in programme tastes is now outdated. Naturally, it is important to note the extent to which, for example, in the UK the genre of soap opera has in recent years been transformed so as to more effectively also address masculine viewers. That a relatively minor shift of this kind should lead us to abandon the basic idea of gendered competences, subjectivities and taste patterns seems less clear to me.[44]

Continuing divisions of gender

Evidently, questions of gender division depend, among other things, on geographical and cultural context. In her study of viewing patterns in rural Western Australia referred to earlier, Lelia Green supplies evidence that supports the hypothesis that still, in that particular context, "gender is often a determinant of what is viewed, and of the ways in which programming is viewed". She reports almost hysterical responses from men, the urgency of whose need to disidentify with "soppy" programming such as soap opera is a clear index of their continuing investment in a very unreconstructed form of masculinity. Most graphically, one respondent explains, "I go out of my way to totally avoid [soap operas] ... I think they're sickening ... they drive me crazy. I can't stand them", and another opines that "they're bullshit – I'm a definite non-soapy fan".[45] The strength of these men's expressed disidentification with the idea of such "soapy" programming (whatever their actual viewing practices) gives some indication of just how difficult it can be for people to abandon (at least, publicly) their ascribed gender identities. Within the specific cultural context of Green's research, for a man to explicitly identify with television material of this type is clearly very difficult, even if in other contexts viewing patterns may well not be gendered in the same way – all of which plainly indicates the need for caution in our generalisations on these matters.

Drawing on Judith Butler's view of gender as a "stylised repetition of acts", Green argues that one of the ways in which gender is actually constructed is through differentiated television viewing patterns, so that "one of the ways in which men perform 'male' and women perform 'female' is through their consumption of genre programmes".[46] This process is particularly visible at puberty, as the child negotiates the transition from absorbed dependence within the family to independence as a gendered adult. One of the fora in which this occurs is through viewing practices, as the child's relatively ungendered viewing is abandoned and adult, gendered viewing identities are adopted. Indeed, Green argues that in her sample there was clear evidence of mothers recruiting girls to soap opera viewing at this stage and fathers recruiting sons to the sports audience, to the extent that "young women who watch sports with their fathers and young men who watch soap opera with their mothers gradually find their viewing behaviour at odds with others in their age groups, and eventually reject the familial pattern" in favour of their peer group's norms of viewing.[47] Thus the disciplinary effect of peer pressure, especially at puberty, continues to tie individuals strongly to their ascribed gender identities. Just as women's viewing of soap opera has been argued to constitute the basis for a feminine culture of workplace gossip based on this common viewing pattern,[48] in a parallel fashion in other situations one can find an equivalent masculine office peer group culture, based on the exchange of information about both the hardware and software of satellite television (focused on sports shows and action movies) and involving the exchange of taped materials. As Moores notes, the desire to achieve membership of this type of subculture can also constitute a strong motivation for the acquisition of satellite television in the first place – and in his study it was almost exclusively men, in the families in his sample, who initiated the acquisition of satellite television [49]

To return to the questions of the gendering of domestic labour discussed in Chapter 3, there are clear parallels between work on the gendering of domestic viewing and the findings of the work of Nikkie Charles and Marion Kerr on gender, domesticity and eating patterns.[50] The pattern of masculine dominance reported in a number of studies of domestic viewing patterns is paralleled by Charles and Kerr's findings of the dominance of husbands' tastes in family food provision. Many of the women studied by Charles and Kerr "expressed a desire to be more creative and adventurous in their cooking – to experiment with alternative or exotic dishes – yet found themselves constrained by [their] husbands' demands for so-called 'proper meals' consisting of meat and two veg".[51] Again, in a parallel to findings of the tendency for housewives to occasionally indulge in the "guilty pleasures" of solo viewing of their favourite soap opera when they were alone in the house, Charles and Kerr report similar instances of women, frustrated by their husbands' reluctance to try more adventurous dishes, who would cook such things ("solo servings" perhaps) for themselves, when they were alone. As one of these women put it, "I have a curious notion of what's a treat. For me a treat ... it's anything that I like and nobody else in the family likes."[52]

Boundaries and technologies: communities on the phone wires

The delineation of gender identities is, of course, but one of the many processes of boundary drawing in which households are involved. Nowadays, in the affluent West, as we have seen, a whole range of technological innovations have made the boundaries between the household and the outside world far more porous in both directions.[53] The capacity of technologies to transform the boundary between the private and the public is perhaps most dramatically illustrated by the mobile phone. The user of a mobile phone in a public space is "no longer walking in the street, wandering in the park, or driving along the road in the way that others are. The speaker is not with us, nor we with them." Indeed, J.G. Ballard goes so far as to suggest that the real function of the mobile phone

> is to separate its users from the surrounding world and isolate them within the protective cocoon of an intimate electronic space. At the same time, phone users can discretely theatricalise themselves, using a

body language that is an anthology of presentation techniques and offers to others a tantalising glimpse of their private and intimate lives.[54]

For the user, the mobile phone offers a powerful form of security and solace. Michael Bywater, speculating on the nature of his own desire for the latest designer mobile phone, realises that what he actually wants (which is momentarily symbolised for him by a new Nokia mobile) is, he as puts it, "The Ultimately Desirable Object" which will simply have the capacity to "Make Everything Alright": the object "the size of a cigarette case, made of platinum ... [which will] slip into my breast pocket and never leave me. With it by my side, I will be at home anywhere on the planet."[55]

As argued earlier, technologies often display multivalency, any particular technology being capable of being deployed for various purposes, depending on the social context. In a study of the functions and uses of the telephone answering machine in France, Patrice Flichy points out that "The answering machine affords a whole range of possibilities between instantaneous and permanent communication, and total disconnection".[56] Present day mores (especially in the business arena) in the West increasingly stress the necessity of being available to others for communicative purposes. Thus, as Pierre Alain Mercier puts it, "disappearing, even for a short time, is no longer acceptable" as absence is seen as anti-social.[57] In this context, he notes, the primary purpose of the answering machine is to avoid gaps in the flow of information, to be always reachable. However, for a growing number of users the supposed primary function of the answering machine, as a way of simulating presence or of making up for absence, is declining. That primary function is being supplanted by the machine's supposedly secondary function – of enabling the receiver to screen or filter incoming calls before deciding whether or not to answer them. In this case, the answering machine thus simulates absence and frees the receiver from the tyranny of the demand for perpetual communicative availability.

The telephone itself, as well as the answering machine, does not always serve to perform the purpose for which it was originally designed. Rather than being a device for maintaining contact between those who are geographically distant, there is also considerable evidence that the telephone is often used to make contact between those already living in close geographical proximity.[58] Claisse and Rowe note that two-thirds of the telephone calls in their study "are closely related to [their subjects'] daily mobility and that they replace, lead to or organise their movements", so that the phone consolidates communication "between close relations in all the emotional, metric, sociological, demographic and economic senses of the term".[59] One very clear example of this kind of use of the phone is provided by Vanessa Manceron's study of the telephone use among a group of young Parisians. Among this group, Manceron argues, the phone does not simply enable communication between group members, in a functional sense, but is also a key component of the group's identity, symbolising their connectedness. Members use each other's phones when visiting as common property, both making and receiving calls on them as a matter of course.[60] Some members regularly call their own answering machines at home while they are out, to check if there are messages from other group members. The aim of their phone calls is principally to keep in touch with others' plans as they develop through the day, and thus to confirm their availability to take part in the group's activities. In this case, the phone is "a tool for constructing an intensive communal lifestyle", allowing the group's schedule of activities to be constantly renegotiated. Manceron describes this group's almost constant use of the phone as bulimic. The calls are frequent and of a very short duration and often consist of little more than information on where someone is now and where they will be later, principally serving a "phatic" function of confirming their ongoing membership of the group's network.[61] If, as Raymond Williams observed, community is necessarily constructed through patterns of communications, we have here a very graphic example of the role of these technologies in the construction of this particular subcultural group.

Television in the Outback

If the specifications of its urban Parisian context are crucial to understanding the significance of Manceron's study of phone usage, by striking contrast Green's study of the consumption of television in remote areas of Western Australia allows the problems of time–space compression to be considered in the context of a strikingly contrasting situation, where matters of physical distance retain a clear and obvious pertinence.[62] The geographical isolation of communities in the Outback has long been a important issue in Australian culture and politics. As one of Green's respondents, living in one such community, puts it, "as it is now, the rest of Australia could disappear and we'd be the last to know. The lack of outside communication in the town is very frustrating and tends to make the town insular and self-centred." As another says, after the introduction of satellite, people in remote communities "became more aware of the rest of Australia ... Before there were just words, then they saw that there actually were other places in the world".[63] However, the introduction of satellite television in these areas did not simply "dispel the mental and geographical distance separating urban and regional dwellers" but also often provided "more material through which that distance can be articulated and negotiated".[64] Rather than simply lessening the experience of the remoteness of Outback life, it "became the trigger for a redefinition of what it is to be remote or regional" so that, in many instances, "the introduction of ... television heightened that sense of difference". The availability of commercial television advertising was sometimes perceived by people in such remote communities as "a statement of inclusion; of finally having made it as attractive and desirable consumers, economically worth advertising to".[65] However, commercial advertising also had the effect of aggravating their sense of exclusion, in so far as the goods shown were simply not available in the places where they lived: as one respondent put it "nearly everything [on the advertisements] we can't get up here. We say – Come off it, you're wasting our time!" To this extent, television advertising can also communicate to the periphery its very distance from the core centres of production and consumption.[66]

Television news coverage of events in remote communities is appreciated by their residents in so far as "it's nice to see local things on television … it just shows that we do exist. And things actually happen here."[67] However, the content of most of the news shown on television, as one respondent says, "is just so unrelated to our everyday problems and our everyday happenings that I don't take much notice of it"; another perceives television news as "not really much my business" but something "like a busybody talking on television".[68] The question of distance is, of course, no simple geographical matter, but also a matter of social and cultural definition. In this connection we now turn to the articulation of forms of virtual and actual travel.

Virtual and actual travel

Here I want to try to make a case for the necessity of understanding various forms of media choices, for example the choice to subscribe to satellite or cable television, in the broader context of people's overall attitudes to and valuation of opportunities for travel and mobility. One of the respondents in Moore's study of satellite television reports that: "when I'm watching Sky – because it's from a European satellite … I very much get the sense of being a European". For this man, "it's quite something when you can sit in your front room and watch what's on in another country". It may be no more than a form of armchair tourism, but satellite television nonetheless enables him to reimagine the boundaries of his own community and identity. For him, Sky television offers "the feeling of not being restricted in the Good Old British Way".[69] Similarly, the young merchant sailor in the study referred to earlier, who lives (when he is not at sea) in an upstairs flat in his parental home, with a collection of sophisticated electronic gadgetry in his bedroom, reports feeling himself limited by terrestrial broadcasting services. Again, ideas of travel and mobility, both actual and imaginary, are important to him in constructing his choices. His work as a sailor has taken him to the USA, where his experience of multi-channel cable enthused him to subscribe to satellite when back in the UK, in order to try to recreate that experience. In his case it is America rather than Europe which symbolises the desire for escape from the limits of Britishness – but the desire for that sense of escape is constant in both cases. In another example, a married couple point to the role of their interest in actual travel to foreign places in motivating them to get satellite television. For them, it was not a question of substituting virtual for actual travel, but rather of supporting their interests in "going somewhere" with the virtual sense of "transatlantic reach" supplied by satellite television. Again, in this case, it is America which is the symbol of desirable alterity. The couple describe themselves as "Americo-philes" for whom "watching things on CNN and ABC keeps us in touch" and enables them to escape the quotidian constraints of their provincial existence.[70] In the case of the student household referred to earlier, satellite television was again very positively associated with the idea of escaping from the limitations of the narrowly British perspective of terrestrial television. As this group put it, "when you're plugged into satellite, you're plugged into a European nation, where Britain doesn't take centre-stage ... I mean the MTV weather is European weather ... it gives you a wider view of what's going on".[71]

Conversely, the positive valuation of the space of home can have equally important effects on media choices. Thus, in one British Asian family in Moores' study, the father had explicitly agreed to install satellite television as a bribe to keep his young sons indoors within the safe boundaries of the home and family unit.[72] In the wake of the continuing moral panic in the UK about the danger posed to young children by strangers of one sort or another, parental concern about their children's safety in public places has contributed massively to their willingness to provide them with media-rich environments in their bedrooms where they can play safely, rather than allow them outside in the public world.[73] It is to the relation of the outside and the inside – and the boundary between them – that we must now turn more directly.

Bounded realms: household and nation

As noted earlier, communications technologies inevitably transgress the boundaries of the household, and in the HICT project, our interest was in the variety of ways in which households of different types regulated this transgression. Elsewhere, I have offered a detailed account of these modalities of regulation – most notably, in relation to parental concerns about protecting "family time" from the intrusions of others, and about the prospect of deregulated satellite television broadcasting bringing pornographic or violent programming within their children's grasp.[74] Deregulation is not only a concern for the state, at the level of the disruption of national boundaries by transnational broadcasters: it is also a question of fear of the family's boundaries being transgressed directly by unwanted "foreign" elements. Thus, in their analysis of responses to the Minitel system in France, Josiane Jouet and Yves Toussaint reported anxieties of a very similar kind among families who perceived this technology as a threat to the intimacy and safety of their households, in so far as it enabled a myriad of social problems to penetrate the home. In earlier times, it had seemed easier to keep such problems at bay, by virtue of their confinement to particular geographical locations outside the household. A number of parents among those surveyed by Jouet and Toussaint forbade their children to use the Minitel system precisely because they feared its capacity to bring them into contact with prostitution, drugs or other modern-day evils.[75]

Such anxieties about the ways in which communications media transgress (and thus potentially destabilise) the boundaries of the household can readily be seen to have parallels at other levels of social scale. Thus Diane Zimmerman Umble offers an illuminating account of a situation in which a whole community came to feel its boundaries (and potentially its coherence and solidarity) threatened by such technologies.[76] The Amish community in Pennsylvania has formalised a clear set of rules to control the impact of the telephone on their community (outgoing calls only, except in emergency; community phones, carefully managed by church leaders, physically located outside the home, etc.). The objective of the rules is to allow the Amish such access to communication facilities as are necessary for their survival, without allowing the intrusion of that wider world into the sacred space of the Amish home. The Amish perceived the telephone as a cultural threat, first, because it encouraged the use of English rather than German, and second, because it decontextualised personal communication from community control and created access to outside information that was not filtered through the boundary-maintaining rituals of the community. The crucial issue was to defend the sacred space of the home from the impurities of the outside world and the Amish's control strategy addressed this central issue directly – "rules about the telephone marked the edges of appropriate association – who could be connected to whom, in what context and under what circumstances".[77]

Virtual borders, virtual homes

It is a short step from the analysis of strategies for the maintenance of household and community boundaries to the analysis of the strategies for the maintenance of its boundaries mobilised by the nation-state. This is especially so in an era of satellite broadcasting, when governments increasingly find their populations consuming, via satellite, material generated outside their national boundaries. Maria Bakardjieva's survey of Bulgarians' motives for adopting home satellite television concludes that these motives ranged from getting an understanding "of the Truth", to learning about "the aesthetics of a world radically different from the Bulgarian reality", one viewer claiming that satellite television "makes me feel … integrated into the world". For these Bulgarian viewers, satellite technology generated a "tension zone" between the local, daily environment and the satellite screen reality, which is the product of a foreign culture, technology and experience. From a governmental point of view the difficulty is that, as Bakardjieva concludes, "even when a society does not want … the media information age to come in through the door, the latter slips through the roof, or in this case through the balcony".[78]

In recent years, governments in many countries have attempted to ban or at least control the consumption of foreign media material via satellite by outlawing the possession (or by requiring the licensing) of satellite dishes, thus spawning, among other things, a whole industry in the manufacture of disguised, camouflaged and miniaturised dishes. At one point the Iranian government banned the possession of such dishes on the grounds that foreign programmes were part of a Western "cultural offensive".[79] Conversely, it was reported that, in France, the mayor of Courcouronnes, a poor area of (mainly tower block) council housing south of Paris with a large population of North African immigrants, had banned satellite dishes from its tower blocks. The ban was ostensibly initiated on grounds of public safety – because of the supposed danger of a dish being blown off by the wind and falling on someone below. However, the ban was widely interpreted as a concession to the demands of the French National Front, in whose eyes the dishes represented a symbol of cultural treason by means of which the migrant families were able to inhabit a space of virtual Islam, while living physically on the geographical territory of France.[80] We shall return to a more detailed consideration of this case in Chapter 7.

Just as many governments have attempted to control the impact of foreign cultures transmitted into their territories via satellite television, so the growth of the Internet has also been a source of great concern to governments every-where, anxious to control their informational borders. In the West, much of the panic has revolved around the perceived threat of unregulated access to pornog-raphy on the Net. The governments of the Association of South East Asian Nations (ASEAN) have attempted to set up a regulatory body to control what they see as the potentially destabilising effects of their populations' ability to evade state censorship of information via these new technologies, by setting up what the opposition Vietnam Freedom Party refers to as a "bamboo curtain", screening their populations from the influence of unwanted foreign materials.[81] The control of virtual "invaders" is now a key dimension of international poli-tics. In an era of electronic communications, conflict is conducted by the invasion not only of geographical but also of virtual territory. Thus the Serbian ethnic cleansing of Kosovo in the spring of 1999 was foreshadowed in the autumn of the previous year by a cyberwar between Serbian and Kosovan computer hackers invading, infiltrating, rewriting and in some cases attempting to "cleanse" or close down each other's web sites.[82]

Equally, in the world of those exiled from their geographical territories, a virtual home can come to have enormous importance. The exiled Greek Cypriot community of the town of Morphou, now taken into Turkish control and renamed as Güzelyurt, a number of whom ended up living in Barnet in the UK, have created a town of virtual-Morphou, still elect a mayor-in-exile and have now organised a formal "town-twinning" arrangement between virtual-Morphou and the actual town of Barnet. On a larger scale, for the Kurdish exile population scattered across Europe, their satellite television station MED-TV functions daily to recreate the culture of officially non-existent Kurdistan in the virtual form of what they call their electronic "little nation", which, as a volun-teer worker in MED-TV's Brussels studio put it, is "for us … like a family".[83] MED-TV functions as a cultural and informational lifeline for this, the world's largest stateless nation, and is for them the object of passionate attachment.

A visitor to the Kurdish area of eastern Turkey reports that, although it is illegal, huge numbers of Kurds crowd into friends' homes to watch MED-TV, and that sometimes the only electricity in the village will be reserved for the MED-TV supply. Against this loyalty, as Nick Ryan reports, the Turkish government continually attempts to police this informational border by the crudest physical means: "viewers have been beaten and jailed; satellite dishes have been banned or smashed by the army; satellite vendors are targeted and electricity is often cut off in villages to stop the peasants watching".[84] Thus are virtual and physical "border controls" entwined.

Having identified some of the dynamics through which communities and their boundaries are mediated at different geographical scales, in both quotidian and dramatic ways, we now turn to consider the dynamics of the construction of the nation and the National Family as a symbolic home. As we shall see in our analysis of the dynamics of the public sphere, ultimately its homeliness is premised on a significant series of exclusions, and the shadows thrown by structures of gender, "race" and class are visible in its construction.

5

BROADCASTING AND THE CONSTRUCTION OF THE NATIONAL FAMILY

The mediated nation as symbolic home

In raising questions about how the mediated public sphere constructed by the institutions of national broadcasting functions as a symbolic home for the nation's members, I shall attempt to move beyond the narrowly rationalist modality in which discussions of the public sphere have predominantly been cast. My focus will be on the question of who feels included in or excluded from symbolic membership of the nation, and how they participate in the idea of the nation as represented in its mediated culture. The original public service model of broadcasting was figured as one in which "all the citizens of a nation can talk to each other like a family sitting and chatting around the domestic hearth".[1] Ominously, from the point of view of the inclusiveness or otherwise of that model family in the UK, the daughter of the BBC's first Director General, Lord Reith, reported in her biographical memoir of her father that "he just could not accept the otherness of members of his family". As we shall see later, Lord Reith's domestic problems in this respect have uneasy echoes at the macro level of the national audience.[2] In this respect, heritage, as Mike Phillips observes, "is a fence which marks out the boundaries of exclusion".[3] The principal form of symbolic articulation, in this respect, concerns the relation of the family home to the image of the National Family. It was King George V who declared that "The foundations of the national glory are set in the homes of the people", but it was the mass newspaper, the *Daily Mail*, which subsequently adapted this statement as the credo of that central Institution of British Life, the Ideal Home Exhibition.[4]

The role of the media in articulating the dispersed members of the nation to the centres of symbolic power is crucial here. The question is through what kinds of mechanisms this effect is achieved. In this connection Daniel Dayan and Elihu Katz make the analogy between religious processions, in which the image of a saint is paraded through a physical neighbourhood, and media events in which the same "sacred" image is transmitted simultaneously into households throughout the land. In both cases public values "penetrate the private world of the residence, with the world of the house being integrated into the metaphor of public life".[5] This sense of interpenetration of the sacred into the realm of the household is perhaps nowhere given clearer expression than in the example of the royal Christmas broadcast in the UK. Thus, when Lord Reith finally persuaded King George V to "make a national moral impression" by addressing the media and Empire in a Christmas message in 1932, the King's words were "I speak now from my home and my heart to all of you. To men and women so cut off by snows, the desert or the sea that only voices out of the air can reach. To all, to each, I wish a Happy Christmas. God bless you!"[6] Here we see one aspect of the crucial role of broadcasting in forging a link between the dispersed and disparate listeners and the symbolic heartland of national life, and of its role in promoting a sense of communal identity within its audience, at both regional and national levels.

In parallel with Paddy Scannell's analysis of the role of the BBC in the construction of a sense of national unity in the UK, Lofgren offers a convincing account of the role of broadcasting in the construction of a sense of national identity in other European countries in the twentieth century.[7] Lofgren's central concern is with the question of how people have come to feel at home in the nation and with the educative role of broadcast media in the everyday process of what he calls the "cultural thickening" of the nation state. Lofgren calls this the "micro-physics of learning to belong to the nation-as-home, through which the nation-state makes itself visible and tangible … in the lives of its citizens".[8] In this analysis these media are seen to supply "the fragments of cultural memory" that compose "the invisible information structure" which constitutes a person's sense of their homeland as a virtual community.[9] In Sweden, Lofgren observes that by the 1930s, national radio had constructed a new *Gemeinschaft* of listeners tied together by the contents and myths of national radio broadcasting. This synchronised experience of radio came to provide a stable national frame of understanding for local events and topics, in an educative process which turned the nation into something resembling a vast schoolroom. This broadcast national rhetoric took many forms – not least ritual ones, such as familiarising people with the national anthem and inscribing it at key moments in their own domestic practices. Even the weather was nationalised and its national limits clearly demarcated, so that "in the daily shipping forecast, the names of the coastal observation posts of Sweden were read like a magic chant, as outposts encircling the nation".[10]

In a similar vein, in his introduction to the catalogue of Mark Power's photographic project on *The Shipping Forecast* in the UK, David Chandler notes that while the information on weather conditions at sea around the UK is plainly of practical use only to seafarers, the size of the listenership of BBC radio's shipping forecast (broadcast four times a day since 1926) and the affection in which the broadcast is held by many who never go to sea, indicates that "its mesmeric voice and timeless rhythms are buried deep in the public consciousness … For those of us safely ashore, its messages from 'out there' [and] its warnings from a dangerous peripheral world of extremes and uncertainty are reassuring".[11] Nikos Papastergiadis has argued that "the symbols and narratives of the nation can only resonate if they are admitted to the chamber of the home".[12] Radio often achieves, as Chandler notes, exactly this kind of intimacy. His argument is that if the shipping forecast enhances our sense of comfort in being safe at home, this is also a matter of national belonging in the profoundest sense:

> The shipping forecast is both national narrative and symbol; for seventy years it has given reports on an unstable, volatile "exterior" against which the ideas of "home" and "nation" as places of safety, order and even divine protection are reinforced. In those brief moments, when its alien language of the sea interrupts the day, the forecast offers to complete the enveloping circle and rekindle a picture of Britain glowing with a sense of wholeness and unity.[13]

National broadcasting can thus create a sense of unity – and of corresponding boundaries around the nation; it can link the peripheral to the centre; turn previously exclusive social events into mass experiences; and, above all, it penetrates the domestic sphere, linking the national public into the private lives of its citizens, through the creation of both sacred and quotidian moments of national communion. Not that this process is always smooth and without tension or resistance. Lofgren notes that, historically, what was at stake here was both the nationalisation of the domestic and the domestication of the national, so that "the radio turned the sitting room into a public room, the voices from the ether spoke from the capital and united us with our rulers, but also with all other radio listeners around the country".[14] Nonetheless, this socialisation of the private sphere, in the service of the "civilisation of the peripheries" of the nation, could also give rise to resentment. As one Swedish listener recalls, "when the radio was on, the room wasn't really ours, the sonorous voices with their Stockholm [accents] ... pushed our own thick [regional] voices into a corner where we commented in whispers on the cocksure statements from the radio".[15]

In her analysis of national fantasy and the construction of the landscape of national iconography, Lauren Berlant traces the processes through which a common national character is produced. As she puts it, through the accident of birth within a particular set of geographical and political boundaries, the individual is transformed into the subject of a collectively held history and learns to value a particular set of symbols as intrinsic to the nation and its terrain. In this process, the nation's "traditional icons, its metaphors, its heroes, its rituals and narratives provide an alphabet for collective consciousness or national subjectivity; through the National Symbolic the historical nation aspires to achieve the inevitability of the status of national law, a birthright".[16] Berlant's central point, for our purposes, concerns the ways in which desire and affect are harnessed to political life in the cultural forms of the National Symbolic. For her, it is both through the mediated circulation of images and narratives and through geographical perambulation to symbolic monuments and sites that national culture becomes local and rooted in the public forms of everyday life. In line with Martin-Barbero's analysis of the role of cultural institutions in converting the (potentially distant) realm of the national into the quotidian, Eley and Suny remark that "we are 'national' when we vote, watch the six o'clock news, follow the national sport, and observe (while barely noticing) the repeated iconographies of landscape, history and citation in the movies".[17] Moreover, in the construction of this national symbolism, the national is often figured in the powerful imagery of the familial. Thus, in her analysis of the figuring of national space through familial and domestic imagery, Anne McLintock notes that:

> The term nation derives from natio: to be born – we speak of nations as "motherlands" and "fatherlands". Foreigners "adopt" countries that are not their native homes and are nationalised in the "national family". We talk of the "family of nations" of "homelands" and "native" lands. In Britain, immigration matters are dealt with at the Home Office; in the United States the president and his wife are called the First family.[18]

Participatory models of the media: from ideology to sociability

In his analysis of the socialising function of broadcasting, Scannell argues that radio and television "brought into being a culture in common to whole populations and a shared life of a quite new kind".[19] In an extension of this argument Stuart Hall argues that the BBC did not in any way simply reflect the make-up of a pre-existing nation, but rather was "an instrument, an apparatus, a 'machine' through which the nation was constituted. It produced the nation which it addressed: it constituted its audience by the ways in which it represented them."[20] In his recent work, Scannell has done much to extend and further develop his earlier influential analysis of the role of broadcast scheduling in the temporal structuring of public experience.[21] Ultimately, he links this structuring to Braudel's concept of the *longue durée* of historical time, as opposed to the *histoire événementielle* of the everyday world of events – in relation to which, as Braudel puts it, the "newspaper offers us all the mediocre accidents of everyday life".[22] For Scannell, the important contrast is between the flux of the ever-changing contents of the media (and of that daily life itself, on which the media report) and the relatively unchanging nature of the stable structures which contain and frame these events. The issue is then how these basic structures themselves are continually reproduced over time.

One of broadcasting's principal achievements lies in the way it links the "biography" of an occasion or event with the "geography of situation" of its audiences.[23] The broadcast schedules become so much a part of the audience's everyday domestic routines that change to them can be the occasion of some personal distress for audience members – as witnessed by the comments earlier on the importance of the shipping forecast for many UK radio listeners, and by the outcry of protest that has attended recent changes to the long-established schedules of BBC Radio 4. In order to achieve this degree of intimacy with their audiences, Scannell argues, broadcasters have had to take responsibility for understanding the nature of their audience's domestic circumstances and have had to learn to produce their materials in forms fitted to the circumstances of their audiences' lives and concerns. If the development of broadcasting had involved the "socialisation of the private sphere" it has, correspondingly, also involved what David Cardiff had described as the "domestication of public utterance".[24]

For Scannell, broadcasting is not simply involved in ordinary life but (at least in part) constitutive of it. He follows Harvey Sacks' argument that being an "ordinary person" involves, among other things, a certain amount of daily television viewing, which is performed, at least in part, so as to be "among those who have seen" in Claus Dieter Rath's terms.[25] To this extent, anyone who is unable (e.g. some categories of prisoners who have been deprived of the privilege of television viewing as punishment for some misdemeanour) or unwilling (some eccentrics) to do this may well be deemed not to attain full membership of the culture. Cultural citizenship, it transpires, entails responsibilities (to have seen crucial television broadcasts) as well as entitlements. Rather than conceiving of cultural citizenship as a simple binary in/out mechanism, we might do better to think of it as a graduated incline, in which fuller membership depends, among other things, on particular types and amounts of media consumption. However, for Scannell, it is, above all, the temporality of broadcasting which is the key to its understanding. On the one hand, this is the production for the audience community of a patterned temporal regularity at a calendical level, as broadcasting marks (and helps construct) the annual regular festivals and occasions of the culture's yearly, seasonal and weekly cycles. On the other hand, it also involves the continual reproduction of the temporal structure of everyday life at a quotidian level, or as Scannell puts it, the production of a sense of "dailiness" which "retemporises time", in "an endless … narrative of days and their dailiness … attending to the present moment and producing it as the moment it is … 'time to get up' … or whatever … orienting … [the audience] to the day today".[26]

James Carey observes that Benedict Anderson's analysis was decisive in offering us a model of the nation as a sociological organism that moves calendically through a homogeneous time – which is not simply historical time, but media time.[27] This social community is effectively united by the production of a shared sense of reality, which is materially inscribed in the dailiness of the newspaper or media broadcast. In a similar vein Rath argues that the broadcasting of a live media event:

guarantees our being in time, or being up to date ... live television thereby functions as an apparatus of synchronisation ... from the angle of the viewer, the apparently empty time of his or her everyday life is transformed into "full" time – time filled by public or publicised ... "significant" events ... the viewer becomes part of the social fabric ... The viewer's life becomes a story ... [and] the individual ... appears as part of a symbolic structure.[28]

In all this, the news of the public world of the centres of economic power and political control is woven into the fabric of our ordinary days, as broadcasting articulates the spheres of private and public life for its audiences.

In relation to these issues I am very much in sympathy with much of Scannell's approach. I have argued elsewhere for the need to complement the analysis of the vertical dimension of media power with a corresponding analysis of the horizontal dimension of the media's ritual functions, in organising its audience's participation in various forms of collective life.[29] The difficulty is that, for Scannell, it seems that it is not so much a question of developing any such complementary, or multi-dimensional model of analysis but, rather more simply (especially in his "Public service broadcasting and modern life") of entirely replacing the vertical dimension of analysis with the horizontal and of "correcting" cultural studies' (apparent) errors, in focusing, so much as it has done, on the media's ideological role and on the politics of representation. That is, for Scannell, an approach which "systematically misunderstands and misrecognises its object", and he argues that broadcasting is not to be understood as any

> form of social control ... cultural standardisation or ideological misrepresentation ... [but] as a public good that has unobtrusively contributed to the democratisation of everyday life most notably through its promotion of a "communicative ethos" of more inclusive and extensive forms of sociability among its audiences.[30]

While the rather shrill tone of denunciation employed in this attack on cultural studies is somewhat muted in Scannell's later work, the realm of power and politics is still simply set aside there, in favour of a phenomenological analysis of the media's contribution to the production of "ordinary *unpolitical* daily life".[31] Thus, Scannell explains that the starting point and clear focus for his approach is what he calls "the sociable dimension of radio and television broadcasting as its basic communicative ethos".[32] If this was all there was to it, while I might personally feel unable to share Scannell's desire to simply set aside the vocabulary of power and politics, I could nonetheless applaud the elegance of many of his analyses of the dynamics of the programme forms and genres he studies. However, even on his own terms, and focusing exclusively on the question of broadcasting's role in the inculcation of sociability, there is a major difficulty with Scannell's Panglossian approach. Sociability is simply not the indivisible Good which Scannell assumes it to be. By the very way (and to the very extent that) a programme signals to members of some groups that it is designed for them and functions as an effective invitation to their participation in social life, it will necessarily signal to members of other groups that it is not for them and, indeed, that they are not among the invitees to its particular forum of sociability. Only a programme constructed within the terms of some form of cultural Esperanto could hope to appeal equally to all, without favour or division. Sociability, by definition, can only ever be produced in some particular cultural (and linguistic) form – and only those with access to the relevant forms of cultural capital will feel interpellated by and at home within the particular form of sociability offered by a given programme.

On some occasions this might be a matter of gender or of generation, on others a matter of class. Thus, Suzanne Moore reports the views of Anthony Smith, an influential figure in the world of British broadcasting, who confessed himself unable to watch daytime television talk shows, featuring ordinary people such as those hosted by Oprah, Jerry Springer or, in the UK, Vanessa Feltz. The ostensible reason for Smith's unease, it seemed, was his (somewhat patrician) concern that the people on these shows were being exploited, notwithstanding their own willingness (and indeed, enthusiasm) to appear on the shows (presumably from Smith's point of view, they were suffering from some form of false consciousness, in this respect). However, one could take the view that the problem was rather that the form of sociability offered by these shows just failed to fit with the cultural predilections of someone of Smith's background. To him, the shows' invitation to this particular form of sociability clearly seems either grotesque or offensive.

Moore concludes ironically that perhaps from the point of view of those such as Anthony Smith, it "would be better if ordinary people were banned from our screens altogether and then we could just convince ourselves that the world really is (exclusively) populated by articulate, rational, middle class types". As for the question of why people volunteer to appear on these shows, Moore points to the simple but powerful capacity of the media to offer these participants some form of recognition, however perverse, of their existence. As she notes,

> ordinary people enjoy appearing on television enormously, even if they come across as mad, bad or sad. They video themselves with pride. Why? Because somehow appearing on television feels more real to them than their real lives. Rightly or wrongly, it is a vindication, a validation that they are somebody.[33]

As an answer to the potentially puzzling question as to why people are often eager to appear on talk shows, given how humiliating the situations on such shows can be, Margaret Morse similarly offers an explanation in terms of television's ability to confer confirmation on whoever appears on its screen. As she puts it,

> perhaps even a minor role of being bad on television is good, a kind of confirmation that, yes, one has lived or even mattered in the social drama; the largely thwarted desire to speak and to be recognised and to know and be known is such a powerful motivating force in ordinary social life that any context serves better than oblivion.[34]

However, Moore's point goes further. If Smith is offended by (and/or feels excluded from) this kind of representation of working-class life and culture, there are others who are correspondingly offended by or excluded from the forms of sociability offered by the kinds of programming which someone like Smith probably regards as "normal" and with which he feels more "at home". Thus Moore herself notes that she has never been able to listen, without unease, to Radio 4, as the "relentless middlebrowness" of its population, she says, "makes me want to join Class War".[35] The question is always which forms of sociability feel foreign to whom. Any one form of sociability must have its constitutive outside, some necessary field of exclusions by which the collective identity of those whom it interpellates successfully is defined.

The question of the necessarily limits of sociability can also sometimes take a starker form, in relation to the politics of representation of which Scannell is so dismissive. Thus, in his analysis of what he describes as broadcasting's role in the production of "the merely sociable", he argues that "public displays of sociability on radio and television ... provide models of appropriate behaviour ... [and] affirm that interaction with and between strangers can be not merely non-threatening but positively enjoyable and relaxing".[36] The difficulty here is perhaps best captured to referring to Alec Hargreaves' work on the representation of immigrants on French television.[37] The whole force of Hargreaves' analysis is that, on the whole, immigrants only get to appear on French television in genres associated with problems and conflict, such as news and current affairs. Correspondingly, they are largely excluded from what Hargreaves calls the spaces or genres of conviviality, such as game shows, quiz shows and the like.[38] By the same token, of course, those who do not see themselves represented in such shows can hardly be expected to be effectively interpellated by them or to feel much of an identification with the culture that they represent. In France, at least, it seems, there are limits to how strange a stranger can be, if broadcasting is still to offer the kind of positive model of interaction which Scannell unproblematically assumes it to do for all, as a matter of course. But broadcasting only does that within the limits of normality – and it is precisely the question of how those limits are reproduced, reconstructed (or transformed) over time that is precluded by Scannell's dismissal of politics.

Beyond the singular public sphere?

My discussion of the work of Scannell, and the joint work of Dayan and Katz has thus far not questioned one of the major premises on which much of their work is based – that there indeed is a public sphere, in the singular, and that it is a Good Thing. As indicated above, I have high regard for some aspects of the contributions made by these scholars to our understanding of how mediated public spheres work, especially in relation to their role in the articulation and synchronisation of the public and the private. However, underlying all this work are certain premises derived from the authors' appropriation of a Habermasian model of the public which do stand in need of interrogation. Thus, for example, I would argue that, despite Scannell's attempts to distance himself from Habermas, his own model of the role of broadcasting in the construction of an undifferentiated sense of sociability replicates, if in a different form, one of the most problematic features of Habermas' model. [39]

The basic narrative of Habermas' work on the public sphere can be argued to represent a "tragic rise and fall myth" in which that sphere is seen to have arisen in reaction to the limits of an old aristocratic culture but then to have been corrupted by the artificialities of our contemporary mediatised world. In this model the contemporary media function as a corrupting influence on the supposedly "pristine state of rational openness in which citizens once communicated transparently".[40] To this extent Habermas' work has been recruited into a kind of conventional wisdom, as Paolo Carpignano *et al.* describe it, in which public life is seen as having been corrupted by a process of commodification, resulting in a "form of communication increasingly based on emotionally charged images rather than on rational discourse, such that political discourse has been degraded to the level of entertainment and cultural consumerism has been substituted for democratic participation".[41] In this narrative, as Bruce Robbins notes, the media are held to have corrupted the habits of self-reliant critical thought, which are taken to be the foundation of democracy. However, there is a substantial problem with the nostalgic model of the Good Old Days of nineteenth-century liberalism, from which the "Fall of Public Man" (in Richard Sennett's phrase) is calibrated. There may be good reasons to suggest that the "mythic town square in the sky" in which the sovereign and omnicompetent citizens of liberal democracy were imagined to have conducted their business was, in reality, a "phantasmagoria: an agora (public forum, assembly) that is only a phantasm".[42] Similarly, Jacques Derrida argues that public opinion, while being constantly cited or ventriloquised by politicians, pollsters and others, is in effect a spectre which is never actually present in any particular place and is best understood perhaps as "the silhouette of a phantom".[43]

The central problem with this phantasmagoria, Robbins argues, is best revealed by posing the simple question of for whom the public sphere is supposed to have previously operated more democratically than it does now. As he puts it,

Was it ever open to the scrutiny and participation, let alone under the control, of the majority? Was there ever a time when intellectuals were really authorised to speak to the people as a whole about the(ir) interests … If so, where were the workers, the women, the lesbians, the gay men, the African-Americans?[44]

The appropriate response, according to Robbins, is to try to get away from the unhappy lament for some lone, lost, idealised single public and to accept that "no sites are inherently or eternally public". Instead, we must pay attention to "the actual multiplicity of distinct and overlapping public discourses [and] public spheres that already exist … in diverse forms … [as] a multitudinous presence among the conditions of postmodern life", but which are actually screened from view by the idealisation of the single public sphere of the Habermasian tradition.[45] We must recognise the constitutive exclusions on which the definition of the classical public sphere was based – not least those which, as Rosalyn Deutsche among others has argued, in effect defined it as a masculine gendered sphere.[46] We need to pay attention to the role of a variety of alternative public spheres and counterpublics based on divisions of ethnicity, "race", generation, region, religion or class. [47] As we shall see later, we shall also need to abandon the Habermasian assumption that the public sphere is necessarily (or intrinsically) national in scope and address the issues raised by the existence of cross-cutting transnational and diasporic public spheres. In the end the issue is also one of creating public spheres which are open to the expression of agonistic difference as the core of the democratic process.[48]

The masculine public

Nancy Fraser rightly argues that not only does Habermas' account idealise the liberal public sphere, but that it is because he fails to examine other non-liberal, non-bourgeois, competing public spheres – what she calls subaltern counterpublics – that he ends up idealising the uninterrogated class- and gender-based assumptions of the claim that the bourgeois public ever fully represented the public in the singular. In the first place, Fraser argues, the bourgeois republican public sphere rested on and was constituted by a set of masculinist assumption in its very definition of the topics and modes of rational debate appropriate to that sphere, despite its rhetoric of accessibility and openness. As she observes, the network of philanthropic, civic and professional clubs and associations that constituted the basis of the liberal public sphere in Europe was far from accessible to everyone by virtue of these exclusions and was, in effect, "the arena, the training ground and eventually the power base of a stratum of bourgeois men".[49] Conversely, in her analysis of contemporary cultural politics in Egypt, Lila Abu-Lughod argues that television has had a profoundly democratising effect in so far as it gives access to "stories of other worlds" to women, the young and the rural illiterates as well as to urban men. Echoing Meyrowitz,

Abu-Lughod argues that television's central importance is that it "brings a variety of vivid experiences of the non-local into the most local of situations, the home". Thus, she notes, when someone like the Nobel prize-winning author Naguib Mahfouz laments the decline of the traditional public sphere, in the form of the Cairo coffee house, where people would go to listen to storytellers, he "forgets that this older form of entertainment, with the imaginary non-local worlds it conjured up, was only available to men".[50]

Fraser argues that Habermas and his followers ignore not only the existence of competing and alternative public spheres but also the evidence that relations between them and the bourgeois public were relations of power and conflict, in which the representatives of the bourgeois sphere combated the critiques of its exclusionary nature and blocked demands for wider social participation, as much as they combated absolutism and traditional authority. From Fraser's point of view, these exclusions were always constitutive of the bourgeois conception of the public sphere, so that we need to see it not so much as a utopian ideal which happens not yet to have achieved its full realisation, but as "a masculinist ideological notion that functioned to legitimate an emergent form of class rule".[51] For Iris Marion Young, the effective exclusion of women from the universalist model of the public sphere, far from being accidental, follows directly from the equation of masculinity with the (unmarked, invisible) category of the normal (or the rational) and of women, by contrast with the particular, the self-interested or the merely private. The civic public is identified with the general interest or the impartial viewpoint of Reason, as expressed, equally ideally, by a self which has "no particular history, is a member of no communities ... [and] has no body".[52] This means that, given the equation of the realm of femininity with the spheres of desire, affectivity and the body (by opposition to which Reason is constituted) this civic public is a masculine one by definition, from which femininity is excluded as a matter of principle. As Michael Warner notes in his commentary on Pier Paolo Pasolini's observation (made shortly before his murder) that "tolerance is always and purely nominal", the bourgeois public sphere has, from the outset, always been structured by a logic of abstraction which systematically privileges the normalised (unmarked or disincorporated) male white middle-class heterosexual body.[53] At the same time, this discourse exercises a minoritising logic of domination, in which to be particular (and thus visible) is always to be something less than fully public, whether the particular minority concerned is tolerated or condemned.

In her critique of Habermas' public sphere theory, Joke Hermes also points to the gender-blindness of the dominant models, which unproblematically equate citizenship with masculinity as the unmarked norm, against which femininity is defined by its defects. To this extent, Hermes argues, what has been called the "Public Knowledge" project in media studies is badly compromised by its masculinist premises – which can be traced back to its equation of femininity with the negative characteristics of "passivity, emotionalism, irrationality, gullibility, consumerism ... all those things ... that ... clash with honest politics and upright citizenship and ... can be characterised as deviations from the male norm".[54] At a more concrete level, Fraser observes that the rhetoric of the public sphere has traditionally functioned to exclude issues of concern to many women from public debate by casting them as personal matters, beyond the realm of public, political debate. As she notes, a viable conception of the public sphere would necessitate the inclusion of all the issues and interests such as these which are labelled private and treated as ipso facto inadmissible by bourgeois masculinist ideology. In this connection we might usefully return to consider the role of the television talk show as a particular form of public sphere.

Drawing on Masciorotte's work on *The Oprah Winfrey Show*, Hermes argues that such shows represent the embodiment of a distinctively feminine perspective in popular discourse which is disruptive of conventional standards of rational discussion in the public sphere. Hermes thus argues that such shows, with their "participatory chaos and spectacular emotionalism ... multiple points of view, rather than arguments pro or contra, deferring solutions or closure", represent a significant feminisation of the previously unrecognised masculinism of the culture of citizenship.[55] Certainly, Oprah Winfrey herself has been quoted as claiming that "we do programme these shows to empower women", and Masciorotte claims that "talk shows afford women the political gesture of overcoming their alienation through talking about their particular experience as women in society".[56] In relation to their formal characteristics, Livingstone reports that women viewers among their audiences are less likely than men to find such talk shows problematically chaotic in their presentation, and also less likely than male viewers to side with the experts, against the perspective of the ordinary people on the shows.[57] As we have seen earlier, these shows tend to be perceived by many commentators as representing a regrettable bowdlerisation of properly informed public debate. However, historically, these shows were also the arena in which many social problems, which had been traditionally designated as merely "women's issues" (such as domestic violence and eating disorders, for example), were first given public voice. To this extent, such shows can be seen to have performed a valuable function as a feminised counterpublic. This is not to suggest that "subaltern counterpublics are always necessarily virtuous". As Fraser observes, some are explicitly anti-democratic and anti-egalitarian, and it is easy to think of examples of talk shows that mobilise explicitly reactionary forms of public opinion. Nonetheless, whatever liberals may think of the views expressed on such shows, they are, Fraser argues, properly part of our public life – "parallel discursive arenas, where members of subordinated social groups invent and circulate counter-discourses, so as to formulate oppositional interpretations of their identities, interests and needs".[58]

Against the criticisms made by many liberal commentators of the television talk show's supposedly exploitative nature and its reduction of rational discussion to the mere spectacle of dramatic conflict, Carpignano *et al.* argue that the talk show represents an important structural transformation of the conventional divisions between the producers and consumers of culture, and between the expert, or professional authority, and the lay audience. To this extent, they claim, these shows represent a "contested space in which new discursive practices are developed in contrast to the traditional modes of political and ideological representation".[59] In so far as these shows provide "a forum for the disenfranchised ... who are not represented in the current knowledge-based community culture", they function as empowering contexts for minority and marginalised discourses. The central thrust of their argument is that in previous eras and in other genres, the public has only tended to appear on television anonymously – as the audible public of a sit-com soundtrack; as the visible but inarticulate and de-individualised public of televised sports events; as "real people" in unusual (and normally humorous) situations, on shows such as *Candid Camera*; or as ventriloquised vox pop representations of public opinion in news and documentary programming. Only in the talk show does "the public gain full recognition ... in ... the role of protagonist", where the show is not simply put on for the public, but is "constructed around the audience ... [with] the camera ... as the instrument of the viewers' presence ... and the public ... literally centre-stage".[60] This is a quite new form of mediated public sphere which, if fractious and sensationalist, nonetheless allows previously disenfranchised sections of the population to be the public stars of their own show.

By contrast to the enthusiasm of Carpignano *et al.*, Sonia Livingstone and Peter Lunt, on the basis of their empirical investigation of participants in and viewers of UK television talk shows, seem ultimately to be equivocal about their role. While they recognise that such shows give voice to ordinary people, they point out that this is not necessarily to be equated with giving them power over "real decision-making and power relations" and may, indeed (to return to the terms of Habermas' original critique) perhaps amount to no more than "the illusion of participation" in public affairs. After all, they observe, their participation only occurs in a heavily managed forum in what, in the end, remains "a bounded region of access ... in a particular region of television", which is, they argue, ultimately "a backwater, a trivial and unimportant realm".[61] However, despite such scepticism, one can argue that the rise of the talk show, with its carnivalesque and dialogic qualities, in which a wide range of voices clamours for expression (based on the authority of their own lived experience, challenging the monophonic authority of the experts who would claim to speak in their names), has rather to be seen as part of the long-term process in which the voices of those who were historically drowned out by the patriarchal and imperialist metanarratives of modernism are finally allowed to speak in public.[62] Of course, beyond this there remains the further question of the relations of power which set the terms within which these voices are represented, or allowed to represent themselves.

The need for a variety of counterpublics is premised on the recognition that public spheres themselves are not spaces of zero-degree culture, equally hospitable to any form of cultural expression. To return to my earlier critique of

Scannell's over-simplistic model of the media, as producing some indivisible form of sociability, equally inviting and accessible to all, we have to recognise that public media necessarily function as "culturally specific rhetorical lenses that filter and alter the utterances they frame; they can accommodate some expressive models and not others".[63] To this extent, an egalitarian multicultural society depends on the creation and maintenance of a plurality of public arenas in which a wide range of groups, with a diverse range of values and rhetorics, can effectively participate.

The whiteness of the public sphere[64]

If the national media constitute the public sphere which is most central in the mediation of the nation-state to the general public, then whatever is excluded from those media is in effect excluded from the symbolic culture of the nation. When the culture of that public sphere (and thus of the nation) is in effect "racialised" by the naturalisation of one (largely unmarked and undeclared) form of ethnicity, then only some citizens of the nation find it a homely and welcoming place. The imagined community is, in fact, usually constructed in the language of some particular ethnos, membership of which then effectively becomes a prerequisite for the enjoyment of a political citizenship within the nation-state. On this argument, the Englishness of the public sphere in the UK is its most crucial characteristic. For George Orwell, the English are most quintessentially so in the diversity of their everyday leisure activities at home:

> We are a nation of flower-lovers, but also a nation of stamp-collectors, pigeon fanciers, amateur carpenters, coupon snippers, darts-players, crossword-puzzle fans. All the culture that is most truly native centres round things which even when they are communal are not official – the pub, the football match, the back garden, the fireside and the "nice cup of tea". The liberty of the individual is still believed in, almost as in the nineteenth century, but this has nothing to do with economic liberty, the right to exploit others for profit. It is the liberty to have a home of your own, to do what you like in your spare time, to choose your own amusements instead of having them chosen for you from above.[65]

But this is not a merely domestic issue. The public sphere of national broadcast culture is the place where Englishness is then articulated and reflected back to the domestic audience in its own leisure time. Much of popular television is given over precisely to reflecting back to the audience an image of the nation as comprised of a vast range of individualities, eccentrics, hobbies, local and regional traditions – out of whose very differences the unity of the nation is secured symbolically. As Brunsdon and I have argued in our retrospective comments on our earlier analysis of the television magazine *Nationwide*'s presentation of ordinary life, what that programme can actually be seen to have been primarily engaged in was "the construction of a particular type of white lower middle class national (ethnic) identity as Englishness".[66] As we have seen, in Scannell's argument, the broadcast schedule is assumed to construct a domesticated public life in common for the whole population, allowing them to then feel at home in this mediated public sphere. In his insightful analysis of the transcript of the *Harry Hopeful* radio show in Britain in the mid-1930s, Scannell observes that in the voice of an elderly member of the public who appears on the programme, "Miss Lomas", what he hears above all is an expression of "a rootedness in time and place, a secure achieved identity". However, one could suggest that what Scannell actually hears (although he fails to register it) is precisely an expression of a secure ethnic identity, which he shares with the speaker and which is so taken-for-granted as to be invisible. However, its invisibility (or – better, in the context – inaudibility) should not be mistaken for its absence.[67] Once we recognise Englishness itself as an ethnicity, we see that not everyone can feel at home in the public sphere, in an easy, naturalised way, as opposed to feeling particularised and, at best, tolerated (as others) within it. Indeed, one could argue that it is precisely through the orchestration of the vernacular forms of English ethnicity that broadcasting has embedded itself in the ordinary lives of the population and thus domesticated a particular ethnic version of the nation.[68]

Conventionally, only minorities have been understood to possess or inhabit ethnicities (which can be tolerated so long as they are confined to the private sphere of family and community) whereas the dominant/majority culture is presented as if it were universal (or modern, by contrast to the "traditional" ways of ethnic peoples). Once ethnicity has thus been confined to the private sphere, which is where it is seen to be reproduced, the political realm can then be presented as if it were not simply white, but colourless, or ethnically neutral.[69] As Catherine Hall has argued, "the recognition that Englishness is an ethnicity, just like any other, demands a decentring of the English imagination. For ethnicities have been constructed as belonging to 'others', not to the norm, which is English."[70] The difficulty in this matter is exactly the same as that involved in recognising "whiteness" as a particular (rather than the absence of) colour. As Richard Dyer argues, whiteness when universalised disappears:

> in the realm of categories, black is always marked as a colour ... and is always particularising; whereas white is not anything really, not an identity, not a particularising quality because it is everything – white is no colour because it is all colours. This property of whiteness, to be everything and nothing, is the source of its representational power.[71]

Scannell's celebration of broadcasting as a public good, "a culture in common to whole populations"[72] which needs to be defended against the fragmenting forces of deregulation, simply fails to recognise that this public culture itself is already an ethnic culture and has a colour which is only common to some of the citizens of the nation which it supposedly reflects, and which it attempts to address. As Yasmin Alibhai-Brown has remarked, the most influential programmes on British television and radio still remain predominantly white.[73]

White broadcasting in the UK

"If you flick through the national channels for ten minutes, everything is White, White, White". [74]

In his research on the development of debates about "race" and ethnicity in British broadcasting, Arun Kundnani has traced the ways in which, from the Annan Committee's deliberations in 1977 on the need for broadcasting to better reflect the pluralism of British culture, so as to serve minority groups' "special needs" (including those of ethnic minorities), through to the enshrinement of multiculturalism within the brief of Channel Four, when it was established in the early 1980s, the media have been seen by black critics as orchestrating a largely white perspective which is out of step with the UK's development as a multicultural society.[75] By the time that Channel Four was launched, in the wake of the riots in black areas of many British cities in 1981, the connection between debates about the racialisation of geographical space and the racialisation of the airwaves had become much more apparent. As Kundnani observes, if we understand the media as layers of public space that extend and connect with geographical space, then the demands for better, fuller and more varied representation of black and Asian peoples on and in the British media have to be seen as continuous with the parallel demands for less discriminatory policing of public and private space.[76] Kundnani argues that what we need, in this respect, is a "history of broadcasting that parallels the history of space, understood in terms of movement … ghettoisation, policing of boundaries, mobility out of boundaries and consolidation within them".[77]

Certainly the Home Secretary at the time of the riots in the UK in 1981, William Whitelaw, understood the connection between real and symbolic geographies only too well. If the price of keeping black people off the streets of Brixton and Toxteth after the 1981 riots was their greater visibility on the screens of the nation (or at least, on some of those screens, at marginal times, on Channel Four) this was evidently a price he was happy to pay.[78] Thus Angela Barry notes that if the images of the black teenage rioter "slotted easily into the spaces formerly occupied by the mugger and the … immigrant", their appearance on British television screens in the early 1980s nonetheless ran in parallel with a sudden increase in the number of black faces making more respectable television appearances. As she puts it, in that same year, in those same organisations, a curious thing happened – Moira Stewart began to read prime time news; *Nationwide* seized upon a black female presenter, Maggie Nelson; on ITV, Trevor McDonald became more visible. The BBC introduced *Ebony*, a programme for Afro-Caribbean viewers.[79]

As Paul Gilroy noted at the time, "the storm which swept through Britain's inner cities in July 1981" was also "the wind which blew black television onto our screens".[80]

The question then also arises as to whether a greater presence of minorities (of all types) in the (singular) public sphere is a sufficient remedy to our existing difficulties, or whether we might be better advised to consider the various ways in which (and the sites on which) a variety of alternative, independent or oppositional public spheres might be created in a genuinely multicultural society.[81] For some people Channel Four in the UK was seen, at its inception, as the potential institutional site of such an alternative public sphere, though many have had their hopes disappointed by the channel's subsequent performance overall, notwithstanding its occasional brave forays into difficult territory.[82] In 1999 the channel's Chief Executive, Michael Jackson, declared that the channel no longer wished to be seen as "a minority channel for minority audiences", as he felt that British culture had now "moved on", to the point where concerns of ethnically (or sexually) defined minorities were now so much more a part of mainstream culture that a strategy of ghetto broadcasting was anachronistic. The difficulty, from the point of view of Jackson's critics such as Clive Jones, Chief Executive of Carlton Communication, is that, in the end, honourable exceptions notwithstanding, "television is still White Anglo-Saxon, Britain is not".[83]

In this connection the recent report on ethnic minority views of British television by Annabelle Sreberny concluded that television is still lagging behind current social developments by failing to reflect the multicultural nature of the country.[84] One substantial criticism that emerges in that report is that still today, on the whole, British television fiction offers only a limited and stereotyped representation of characters from ethnic minorities, so that they still carry the "burden of representation" of portraying social problems, rather than being presented as rounded persons, as white actors more commonly are. In their earlier report on black minority viewers' responses to British television, Sreberny and her colleague Karen Ross similarly reported that a significant number of African-Caribbeans preferred imported American programming to British, because "American programmes more routinely use the principle of integrated casting, so characters are not always acting their skin".[85] Similarly, the migrant Asian community which Gillespie studied in the mid-1980s felt ill-served by the broadcasting media, and for that reason had a particular interest in video, cable and satellite media.[86] In the same vein, the father in one middle-class British Asian family in Moores' study in the early 1990s much prefers Sky television news to that of the BBC – precisely because of the non-Britishness of the newsreaders' mode of address on Sky. As he puts it,

> with the BBC, you always feel as though the structure of society is there – the authority. Their newsreaders speak just like schoolmasters ... "telling" the kids. I think Sky News has more of a North American approach. It's more relaxed. They treat you like equals and don't take the audience for a bunch of small kids.[87]

In this case, his preference for Sky is produced by his dis-identification with the BBC, precisely in so far as he sees the latter as the embodiment of the white British Establishment and its values.[88]

Despite the recent mainstream success of the *Goodness Gracious Me* series on BBC 2, featuring a British Asian cast, the majority of the UK's Asian population still feels largely excluded from British television. In this context it is perhaps not surprising that, according to a survey of British viewers conducted by the Independent Television Commission in 1994, both Asian and Afro-Caribbean households were more likely than British viewers in general to subscribe to satellite or cable television stations.[89] That report concluded that members of ethnic minorities were considerably less satisfied than the general population with the programme services provided on terrestrial television. They were much more likely to regard those channels as biased against their interests and to regard cable and satellite programming as preferable, overall, to that on terrestrial channels (specifically among Asian households, targeted channels such as Zee TV, Asianet and now B4U – Bollywood For You; and among African-Caribbean households, channels such as BET International).

The study of ethnic minority views of British broadcasting conducted by James Halloran *et al.* in 1995 also reported considerable dissatisfaction. One respondent felt that "Television is not doing well for us [Gujeratis] – not enough programmes for the Asian community"; another said that "the Asian community is not getting value for money from any channel"; another that "there is not much for ethnic minorities in television", that "there is nothing – they only know about Diwali, and that only on the news for a few minutes"; yet another that "TV doesn't really portray us" (Bengali-speakers).[90] These findings were confirmed by Sreberny and Ross' study in the same year, where one of their respondents said, "as it is today the BBC are not providing anything for us, so why pay [the licence fee]? If I could opt out I'd do it today."[91] As another respondent put it, "I feel cheated. They're asking for £90 a year and you just watch 'mainstream' [white] stuff all the time – or you pay more to get cable and see the American stuff – it's much better for ethnic minorities." The key issue was that respondents felt that "American cable has channels dedicated to black programmes. You can see the difference in quality, with situations that black people can relate to."[92] At its simplest, from this point of view, as an

Asian viewer put it in Sreberny's later study, "on Asianet, on cable, they have more realistic images".[93]

A Bangladeshi group in Burnley interviewed by Sreberny and Ross similarly expressed strong preference for cable and satellite services. In their view, as "these new cable companies have got Asian programmes, the BBC will have to catch up ... Compared with cable the BBC is forty years behind". As one of them puts it, "I've got to spend £15 a month to see my favourite programmes because the BBC aren't up to it". Another explains that "since it's been installed, everybody is subscribing to cable and that's ... £15 or £30 a month" but, as he said, "that's for thirty channels to choose from, including Asianet".[94] In the light of these comments Sreberny and Ross concluded that

> instead of complaining, or simply switching off, many black minority viewers are registering their protest silently by subscribing to new cable and satellite services ... The success of these alternative media bears eloquent testimony to the consummate dissatisfaction that many black minorities feel with terrestrial television.[95]

Four years later, at the time of Sreberny's repeat study, 36 per cent of the ethnic minority viewers in her sample had subscribed to either cable or satellite services – certainly a higher figure than for the UK population overall.[96] In that 1999 study, Sreberny quotes the same refrain of complaint heard over the years: "We pay for Zee TV and cable TV because we want more of our programmes – for the money ... they [the BBC] aren't giving us enough." To this extent many ethnic minority groups clearly continue to feel that they need satellite and cable services because they are ill-serviced by terrestrial television – a situation, as we shall see later, with ready parallels in other countries.[97]

New public spheres also arise and are sustained in different ways, in particular local circumstances, and often involve a recombination of the physical and virtual geographies of community. Black and Asian pirate radio stations in London are frequently structured around the active participation of listening groups, via phoned-in dedications, and "shout-outs" to their local "crews" and "massives". These practices are perhaps best understood as a ritualistic process of continuous re-confirmation of a virtual community of listeners, through the recitation of their names and of their familiar local landmarks and symbols. Through this process, the listeners are granted (and grant each other) recognition as members of this virtual community, which is overlaid on the geographical space of their lives. As one listener to a London pirate radio station put it,

> It's so down to earth. You hear people that sound like you on the radio, which is unbelievable and [you can] relate to that. [You] know the DJs aren't changing their voice to sound more "street". If you

know a station's coming out of your area, you feel close to it and want to support it.[98]

In a similar spirit, in relation to these questions of recognition, Trevor Phillips explains that, as the producer of the television show *Black on Black*, his decision to use a visible studio audience was informed by the simple but striking fact that he had

> never seen a television programme in this country which brought together a lot of black people in the studio … People in this country are afraid of seeing a lot of black people together. They think we're going to riot, or eat somebody, or something.

As he explains, his purpose in opting for the "actual visual representation of our community" was to "give the viewer a sense of solidarity with a community".[99]

Towards a multi-ethnic public sphere?

As Negt and Kluge remark in their criticisms of the class structure of the public sphere, the claim that it represents the totality of society as an equal, if not homogenous, community cannot be sustained precisely because of its own mechanisms of exclusion. One can not simply bracket status differentials based on ethnicity, class or gender and proceed as if they did not exist. These factors naturally continue to have very real effects – which are all the harder to deal with if their status is not recognised. The problem with attempting to integrate a multi-ethnic society through a single public sphere is that the "idea of the public as universal and the concomitant identification of particularity with privacy makes homogeneity a requirement of public participation".[100] To this extent, the dominant group is enabled to monopolise the public sphere in the name of seemingly universal values. The idea that citizens must somehow transcend their particularities in order to participate in the public sphere is, Charles Husband argues, a myth: "the public sphere that seeks to articulate the public opinion of such a citizenry is already partial and inadequate". His conclusion is that we must rather "theorise and realise a politics of citizenship which recognises and empowers difference" – through a variety of particular and differentiated public spheres in the plural.[101]

The difficulty with the conventional view of citizenship is that the idea of the "same for all" is often translated, in practice, into the requirement that all citizens be should be the same. As Young puts it, "we must develop participatory democratic theory not on the assumption of an undifferentiated humanity, but rather on the assumption that there are group differences and that some groups are actually or potentially oppressed or disadvantaged".[102] Her argument is that there is a democratic virtue in explicitly recognising difference within a universal formal citizenship. Thus, in his extension of Young's argument towards the specific case of multicultural citizenship, Steven Castles argues for the "rejection of the conception of all citizens as equal individuals and its replacement by a recognition of all citizens as having equal rights as individuals and different needs and wants as members of groups with specific characteristics and social situations".[103] It is through a perspective based on premises such as those that we shall perhaps also be best able to arrive at an adequate analysis of the public sphere and of the media's role in it.

Transnational and diasporic public spheres

Thus far, we have considered the limitations of conventional accounts of the public sphere as the national symbolic home from the point of view of those groups whose concerns are not effectively addressed and who do not feel at home within it. However, we must now turn to the question of the extent to which, given the undermining of the nation state by the processes of globalisation, we must also consider the extent to which public spheres are themselves, for many people, transnational in form, as contemporary media enable migrants to sustain up-to-the-minute links with events in their homelands.[104] To attend to the divisions and complexities within the public sphere of any one (imagined) national community is nowadays in itself quite insufficient. Societies all over the world increasingly tend to include a variety of migrant and mobile populations, for whom the public spheres of the host nation in which they geographically reside are far from being the only source of interpellations and identifications. As Dayan puts it, in many places the local has itself become cosmopolitan and "the masses are no longer confined to the local. They are themselves in motion: they are made of tourists, of television watchers, of *Gastarbeiter*."[105]

To make these points is not necessarily to fall into some historically naive or uncritical vision in which mediated processes of globalisation are assumed to have entirely swept away national cultures. In this respect, James Curran makes cogent criticisms of the presumption that global television is undermining national cohesion and political participation in some unstoppable process. In broad historical terms, as he observes, television's post-war defeat of cinema (and thus of Hollywood, which had come to dominate world cinema) in terms of overall popularity "represented a dramatic shift towards the restabilisation of *national* media systems".[106] Indeed, television, radio and the press are, in most places, still (and despite globalising tendencies) in many respects national media, based on nationally generated content and, where such material is available, majority audiences often prefer it to imported products. However, the difficulty, as we have seen, is that alongside the majority community in many nations, there exist a variety of minorities who often do not feel themselves to be effectively addressed by the discourses of the national media. The members of these diasporic communities are often spread over the geographical territories of various different nation-states, and are typically exposed to a wide range of potential discourses of identity – between which they must choose – or alternate, in different circumstances and on different occasions. As Khaching Tölölyan puts it:

> Diasporas have played a major role on both sides of the prolonged struggles between Israelis and Palestinians, as well as in supporting Armenians, Croatians and Chechens in their conflicts. Through television, faxes and electronic mail, the commitments of diasporas are reinvigorated and sometimes polarised by constant contact with their former homes; "former" no longer means what it did.[107]

Minority and immigrant groups cannot be satisfactorily treated as marginal exceptions to a simple norm of sedentarism. These "travelling cultures", disassociated from direct territorial inscription, require new models and methods of analysis which focus on the communication networks that sustain them.[108] These networks, which link personal, individual choices to grander, diasporic narratives of identity, are often sustained through a complex mixture of physical mobility (pilgrimages, back and forth travelling, family visits) and symbolic communications through a variety of "small media" such as exchanges of letters, phone-calls, photographs, and videos.[109] One index of this is the way in which districts of cities with substantial immigrant populations in the UK now tend to feature a plethora of high-street call-centres, offering discount rates for phone calls to the many places that count as home for their residents. Similarly, in Margolis' study of migrants living in "little Brazil" in New York, it is reported that

> 95 per cent of the immigrants in [the] sample call Brazil on a regular basis … they spend sizeable sums on long distance calls; most spend between $85 to $150 a month, while quite a few (sheepishly) admit their bills regularly come to $200 a month or more.[110]

As Roger Rouse observes in his study of Mexican migration patterns referred to earlier,

> Today, Aguilillans find that their most important kin and friends are as likely to be living hundreds or thousands of miles away as immediately around them. More significantly, growing access to the telephone has been particularly significant, allowing people not just to keep in touch periodically, but to contribute to decision-making and participate in familial events from considerable distance.

As Clifford notes in his commentary on Rouse's work, immigrants such as these often establish transregional identities "maintained through travel and telephone circuits that do not stake everything on an increasingly risky future in a single nation".[111] Such immigrants often improvise what Aihwa Ong has called forms of flexible citizenship, deterritorialised in relation to any one particular country but highly localised in relation to the places (often in different countries) where the members of their family network live.[112]

In our analysis of all this we must certainly attempt to avoid falling into any kind of romanticisation of mobility *per se*. Nor indeed, in the words of Pheng Cheah's critique of Clifford and Bhabha, should we "endow cosmopolitan mobility with a normative dimension" which uncritically valorises the often painful nature of diasporic existence, as if it were some kind of state of cultural grace.[113] However, and despite these cautions, it is also true that any analysis of the role of the media in the construction of contemporary cultural identities which assumes the existence of a unified and sedentary population occupying a unitary public sphere, within the secure boundaries of a given geographical territory, is unlikely to be adequate in understanding significant aspects of our contemporary situation.

We shall return to these issues in the following chapters. We now move to address a variety of practices of inclusion and exclusion which constitute communities of different sorts, in both their physical and virtual modalities. In addressing these questions I attempt to develop a perspective which integrates the conventional concerns of media and communications studies with perspectives from urban studies concerning patterns of residence and physical mobility. My premise in doing so is that there are strong parallels between the questions addressed in this chapter as to who feels at home in the public sphere of national broadcasting and the question of who feels at home in which forms of material public space. [114] My concern here is with the articulations of forms of media consumption and the geography of how these media consumers' lives are organised. We shall begin with the exploration of the relationship between television as a medium and suburbanism as a way of life.

6

THE MEDIA, THE CITY AND THE SUBURBS
Urban and virtual geographies of exclusion

Television as a suburban medium

If television occasionally presents us with problematic and potentially disturbing events, nonetheless, by virtue of its modalities and its structure (and by means of the predictability and reliability of its scheduling), it also performs a reassuring function. The epitome of this is the 24-hour television news channel, which is reassuring by its very persistence – thus contributing, in Silverstone's terms, to our sense of ontological security, sustained through the presence of the familiar and the predictable.[1] In a similar vein, in the context of a discussion with Doreen Massey on the relationship between space and the media, Karen Lury observes that "through its manipulation of space and time – in its linearity, repetition, circularity and implementation of a largely spurious authority – television often closes down or fixes social relationships".[2] In his analysis of television and everyday life, Silverstone argues that there is an elective affinity between television and the suburb. He argues that television is not simply the result of the suburbanisation of the world, but is itself responsible for the "suburbanisation of the public sphere".[3] It is characterised for him by what he calls the suburban genres, par excellence, of soap opera and situation comedy, largely devoted to the representation and working through of the problems of domestic life. As Andy Medhurst argues, the secure rhythms of suburban life are textually mirrored in the safely predictable narratives of sitcom, and the very "newslessness of suburbia is a cornerstone of the vision of tranquillity that ... [sells] the suburban dream".[4] In this scenario, it is not just news *per se* which is troubling – in the fictional genres which Medhurst discusses, he notes that any element coming from outside the community (letters, phone calls, faxes) is liable to function in the narrative as the occasion of potential trouble.

For Silverstone it is precisely the combination of broadcasting schedules and the practical routines of domestic life which create the framework within which the ontological security of our normalities can be sustained. The particular form of everyday life that has characteristically developed in the suburbs is the result, according to him, of a concatenation of developments, such as road building, the private car and improved transport links, which have allowed the dispersal of

128

the population from the city. However, the present consolidation of this form of life, he argues, "can be ascribed to the electronic communication technologies: the telephone, the radio and the television, that followed".[5] The suburb is then best seen as the embodiment of what Raymond Williams called "mobile privatisation", a form of living at once self-sufficient and home/family-centred, yet always potentially mobile, rather than entirely fixed or sedentary.[6] Because of the inscription of various electronic media in the constitution of the suburban home, the "horizons of reach" of its citizens are complex and contradictory.[7] We live in homes in which television and other media bring hostile and threatening images and messages from the outside world into the private world of the household. At the same time, they give us access to the wider world of shared or imagined communities through which we construct our feelings of security. It is a situation, in Meyrowitz's words, where "television escorts children across the globe even before they have permission to cross the street".[8]

The suburbs: home for whom?

If, as Silverstone argues, suburbs have become models of homeliness for our time, the key questions are: what kind of homeliness, and for whom? As he notes, central to suburbanism is the impulse towards conflict-avoidance, which gives rise to "an anti-politics of withdrawal from the public sphere ... of conformity, self-interest and exclusion".[9] It is a defensive, possessive, anxiety-driven politics, based on a normalised homogeneity of experience, and on a relative absence of "strangers" which is the result of the general exclusion from suburban life of all those forms of otherness associated with city life (the poor, ethnic minorities) who might tarnish the suburban ideal. This is characteristically, the racist, sexist, homophobic and segregationist ideology of the narratives of suburbia's indigenous genre, the sitcom. Medhurst offers an excellent example of this in his comments on the narrative structuring of the 1980s British sitcom *Ever Decreasing Circles*, in which, as he puts it, the suburbs are presented as the site of "petty, status-seeking, unimaginative repetitions and a ferocious hostility to difference".[10] The process of exclusion is, of course, rarely made explicit in quite these terms: in suburbia

> the exclusionary laws are not completely explicit: there are no zoning maps divided into racially or economically restricted areas, so labelled. But there are thousands of zoning maps which say, in effect, "Upper-Income Here"; "Middle to Upper Income Here"; "No Lower Income permitted except as Household Employees".[11]

Often these anxieties are only visible in displaced form. Thus, in her analysis of the metaphors of alterity occurring in American television's science-fiction programming in the 1950s and 1960s, Lynn Spigel points to the way in which the paranoid fear of difference in suburbia (and especially the fear of racial and ethnic difference) was characteristically articulated through representations of aliens, monsters and extraterrestrials. This is no merely historical point – a recent report on current American network plans for autumn 1999 notes wryly that "there will be more aliens and intergalactic psychopaths on TV this season than there will be minorities".[12] As Spigel notes, American television's "liberal cautionary tales about interplanetary race relations" often included didactic elements designed to encourage their audience to question their own regressive attitudes to racial difference. Nonetheless "white flight", from the city to the suburbs, has continued unabated in the USA – as Spigel notes "in 1993, 86 per cent of suburban whites still lived in areas with a black population below 1 per cent".[13] If, as Homi Bhabha observes in his comments on the suburbs of Chicago, "the conservative suburban attitude is founded on fear of difference ... and a narrow-minded appeal to cultural homogeneity", this is by no means a specifically North American phenomenon.[14] As Simon Frith notes, in the UK on the whole, "suburban culture is white culture, white English culture, white south-eastern English culture".[15]

Speaking up for the (gendered) suburbs

Against their conventionally negative image, in his spirited defence of suburbia John Hartley observes that one of its key problems has always been its association with the petit-bourgeoisie, "the social class with the lowest reputation in the entire history of class theory", and that, partly as a result of this, "in the semiosphere, the suburbs generally occupy the position of the Ugly Sister ... a rhetorical foil for whichever desirable *urbs* they *sub*-tend".[16] Thus, suburbia is often held to symbolise the lamentable decline of the body politic, as part of the process in which the urban, informed, rational public sphere proper is undermined and corrupted by the rise of suburban, commercial, commodity culture. Against this conventional pessimism, Hartley argues that "contemporary suburbia is the physical location of a newly privatised, feminised, suburban, consumerised public sphere" which, if its virtues are not easily recognisable from a Habermasian standpoint, are nonetheless real for all that.[17]

Certainly, as Medhurst observes, the conventionally negative image of the suburb (in Dennis Potter's *Pennies From Heaven*, for example) as "a trap, offering nothing but drab conformation and frigid respectability" relies on an uninterrogated conceptualisation of gender. As argued earlier in relation to the gendering of mobility, in this schema it is only men who dream of adventure and/or escaping from routine drudgery, while suburban conformity is almost always feminised – and it is women who "embody the shackles of suburban constraints". What we have here, of course (especially in genres such as the "kitchen sink"/social realist tradition of British cinema such as *Saturday Night and Sunday Morning*), is, as Medhurst shows, a deeply problematic and juvenile opposition between "working class patriarchal mastery" and the "soft, suburbanising dangers" of femininity. In this narrative, the suburb functions as an emasculating device, and while men are presented as needing to "resist the closing, feminising jaws of domestic containment", that is nonetheless their symbolic destination – "where the aggressively masculine protagonists are liable to end up, once their proletarian defiance has been tamed through marriage".[18]

However, if the conventional critique of suburbia is problematically gendered, that is not to say that suburban family life is without its difficulties. In this connection, in her commentary on Young and Wilmott's early study of British families who had moved from a working-class urban area to an outlying suburb, Vicky LeBeau offers a disturbing picture of what she characterises as the autistic nature of family life in the suburb. This life, she says, is largely characterised by "a withdrawal back into the protective shell of the nuclear family, a refusal to engage with the world 'outside these four walls' ", and this retreat is often reinforced by the way these families use television to forge a rather oppressive sense of family cohesion.[19] One of Young and Wilmott's respondents put it this way: "I'm only interested in my little family. My wife and my two children – they're the people I care about. My life down here is my home."[20] Forty years later, the credo of Silvio Berlusconi's "alternative city" *Milano 3*, "a town conceived for children" (sic), is "the family is the domestic church".[21]

Other suburbs

The dominant Western model of suburban life has certainly been widely exported internationally. In their commentary on middle-class lifestyles in the new suburbs of Istanbul, Ayse Öncü and Petra Weyland suggest that these people have adopted an internationalised image of their ideal home derived from Western media. They have thus been willing to invest heavily in moving to high-rise housing developments on the periphery of the city so as to distance themselves, symbolically and spatially, from what they have come to perceive as the urban chaos and social pollution of metropolitan Istanbul. As they observe, it is the homogeneity and uniformity of these new antiseptic housing developments which are now seen as the symbolic markers distinguishing a middle lifestyle in contemporary Istanbul.[22]

Öncü quotes from an estate agent's advertising brochure which claims that these new housing developments offer "clean, happy, peaceful settings" for life, for those who wish to escape the pollution which contaminates "not only the air, water and soil of the city, but its people, its traffic, its culture".[23] From the point of view of the aspiring middle classes, Öncü explains, the city has become "dirty-fied" by the emergence of the hybrid and mixed forms of culture which have arisen in the "informal" neighbourhoods and squatter camps which have invaded the city.[24] As Öncü observes, for the middle classes this emergent culture "with its mixed forms of music, grammar and dress, represents a half-breed world of pseudo-urbanism … which contradicts and pollutes the cherished purity of their own 'westernised' way of life".[25] It is in embracing the image of the ideal home represented by the new suburban housing developments that they distinguish themselves from these forms of urban cultural pollution. What is appealing about these new forms of "site" housing is that they are clean (the phrase most often used to describe them) not only physically but socially and culturally. Thus "site residence means a homogenous, safe, orderly environment, distant both spatially and socially from the heterogeneous populations of Istanbul". They are places "cleansed of the urban clutter, of poverty, of immigrants, of elbowing crowds, dirt and traffic" and they represent a dreamland world of safe and antiseptic social spaces.[26]

Clearly, the origins of the particular image of the ideal home which the middle classes of Istanbul are buying into lie principally in its representations in television, film and commercial advertising. Öncü argues that in the post-war era, "cultural spaces emblematic of the middle class ... were translated into the physical space of the mass-produced suburbs and transposed onto television". The point, however, is that this global myth, although deriving historically from particular national and class specific situations, has now travelled, via the international media, across national boundaries and has acquired the "moral superiority and legitimacy of a timeless and placeless truth" to which aspirant citizens everywhere pay obeisance.[27]

However we must be cautious in our generalisations about suburbia. In a commentary on Silverstone's model of suburbia, based on his own ethnographic work in Latin America, Thomas Tufte cautions that models of domesticity and suburbia based on the experiences of affluent West European (or North American) societies do not always travel well.[28] Tufte rightly observes that both my own and Silverstone's description of television watching as a somewhat mysterious process taking place "behind the closed front doors" of the home hardly applied in the area of Paraguay he studied.[29] There, most television viewing took place outside "the front door and not behind it". In a situation where life is largely lived outdoors, the boundary between private and public is rather blurred, and domesticity clearly signifies something quite different in the "semi-public everyday life of a Paraguayan family".[30] His central point is that it is, of course, quite inappropriate to generalise about the nature of domesticity without recognising that "home as a construct varies from a middle class white North European [context] ... To [that of] a low income mestizo urban dweller in a Latin America metropolis, [to that of] peasants in different regions of the world".[31]

Moreover, one should be wary of over-generalising, as Tufte believes Silverstone does, about the suburbanisation of the world, as if that were a uniform socio-cultural and political-economic process. As he points out, the suburbs of which Silverstone mainly speaks can hardly be compared with huge low-income urban *periferias* of the larger cities and towns of Latin America.[32] This is a quite different form of modernity, where things work in other ways than in the suburbs of Europe, for contrary to Silverstone's ideas of suburban way of life … the people living here are not middle-class, they do not live in an ideal place (far from it), they have not moved there by their own free will, but are often forced to migrate looking for jobs/income … Finding a place to stay in the huge *periferias* becomes a survival strategy. Given that many of these areas started as squatter camps with self-built houses, most of them are far from standardised.[33]

Clearly, *periferias* are quite unlike EurAmerican suburbs and the doors there may well be open rather than closed, contrary to both my own and Silverstone's Eurocentric presumptions. If, for Silverstone, the suburb is characteristically lacking in any sense of community, for Jesus Martin-Barbero the neighbourhoods of the *periferias* "provide the individual with basic references for the construction of an 'us' … Belonging to a neighbourhood means, for the popular classes, to have a recognised identity."[34] Equally, in these quite different circumstances, the telenovela may well play a quite other role than that played by its notional equivalent, the soap opera, in an English suburb.

The ecology of fear: white flight

Within the urban ecology of the affluent West, the drift towards suburbanisation has been one of the key trends of recent years. Paul Barker argues that the new form of suburbanism identified by Joel Garreau as the "Edge City" is "created by the car, the computer and the fax machine as surely as New York or Liverpool were created by ocean-going ships and Chicago or Manchester by the railway".[35] Without falling into a technologically determinist mode of explanation, one can recognise that new transport and communication technologies enable new scales of the organisation of living. Thus, to take a UK example, Barker argues that "Oxford … has become a exurb of London. Structurally, Oxford is to late twentieth century London what Hampstead was to mid century London."[36] As John Lichfield puts it, "Edge cities are a symptom of the 1980s information revolution. They exist, in part, because of the demand for lots of cheap, bright, quality office space in buildings wired for computer terminals." As he goes on to point out, although Edge Cities are not, in themselves, necessarily racist places (not least in so far as, in their American version, they may contain members of the black middle classes) they are certainly "cities without an underclass", and the

> basic Edge City impulse – to abandon wholesale the cities from which they've sprung – is racially motivated. The more the white middle class removed their homes, the more inner cities became dominated by blacks – and the more the white suburbanites [then] wanted to take their jobs and shops with them.[37]

As Deyan Sudjic puts it, summarising the comparable processes in the UK: "the home migrated first, then the jobs and now the shops, the cinemas and the sports centres".[38]

In so far as these new suburban Edge Cities have anything resembling a centre, it is, of course, the shopping mall. In his attempt to defend the virtues of the malls against their critics, Barker argues that they replicate, for a new age, the sense of "safety among strangers" within a walled space that Jane Jacobs defined as the bedrock attribute of a successful city.[39] The problem, evidently, is that the price of the feeling of safety enjoyed by the mall's consumers is only bought at the price of the exclusion of those who do not fit the protocols of the mall's owners. Barker speaks warmly of shoppers "walk[ing] down the arcades of Lakeside or Metro centre with happy smiles on their faces". Unfortunately, it transpires that the premise of this happiness is the exclusion of the misery of others – because, as Barker puts it, in these malls "there are no panhandlers, no alkies, no sad folk peeing in the street".[40]

In his analysis of Los Angeles in the wake of the 1992 riots, Mike Davis offers a gloomy perspective on the further development of what he calls the "carceral city", as a series of separated communities or enclaves obsessed with purity, order and social exclusion.[41] In this scenario, the city is increasingly divided between the physically gated, electronically surveyed and heavily policed districts of the affluent and the lawless barrios and slums of the poor. In this situation, members of each group are increasingly confined to their own area or locality, and being geographically out of place comes to be criminalised as an inherently suspicious form of behaviour (a form of status crime). Hamid Naficy reports that, in the USA, the fear-driven trend towards the balkanisation of public space has gone so far that one third of new housing developments built in Southern California in the years between 1990 and 1995 were gated communities. However, as he observes, the phenomenon is by no means any longer confined to rich areas, and many of the houses of the poor in American cities (and increasingly in poor urban areas in the UK) are now defended by bars and iron grilles designed to keep out robbers and attackers in an atmosphere of ambient fear.[42] Similarly, Davis observes that in Los Angeles in the mid-1980s, "gated communities" were largely confined to very wealthy neighbourhoods, but that since the riots of spring 1992 an increasing number of ordinary residential neighbourhoods have demanded the right to gate themselves off. As he notes, while fear of crime and concern with safety are the primary motivations for these moves towards urban fortification, gatedness also has the further effect of increasing property values. Thus, as communities (including some black middle-class areas) hurry to reap this equity windfall, the security differential between the inner city and the suburbs widens – and along with it, the class divisions based on the consequent property price differences.[43] For the affluent, as Davis puts it, physical gatedness is matched by an increasingly comprehensive system of electronic surveillance which constitutes a virtual scanscape – a space of protective visibility that increasingly defines where white-collar office workers and middle class tourists feel safe Downtown ... [as] the workplace or shopping mall video camera ... [becomes] linked with home security systems ... in a seamless continuity of surveillance over daily routine.[44]

In this context CCTV surveillance becomes a way of singling out those who do not belong in a particular environment and taking pre-emptive action to exclude them. These exclusions are also embedded in the architecture. Worpole and Greenhalgh report that in the city centre of Houston in the USA there are now in effect two separate public spheres – one for the "legitimate" population of (largely white) office workers and one for the (largely black) poor inner-city residents. A new (and in effect privatised) tunnel system

connects all the main office buildings ... and is sealed off from the street. It is only possible to enter the system from within one of the office blocks, ensuring that there exists a separate public realm where white Americans can now walk safely through the area without fear of crime or of rubbing shoulders with those they perceive to be the criminal classes.[45]

Conversely, the areas of the poor come to fall off the new electronic map, except for such surveillance mechanisms as are deemed necessary for policing purposes (e.g. satellite monitoring of electronically tagged suspects, to ensure that they do not leave their designated territories). Thus Davis argues that urban cyberspace may come to be even more segmented than the traditional built city. Certainly, he observes,

South-Central LA ... is a data and media black hole, without local cable programming or links to major data systems. Just as it became a housing/jobs ghetto in the early twentieth century industrial city, it is now evolving into an electronic ghetto within the emerging information city.[46]

Davis notes that, throughout the poorer areas of the city, the police exercise increasing control over freedom of movement, containing problematic population elements such as the homeless and other pariah groups within confined areas and excluding them from public spaces such as parks and shopping malls. This is a process which amounts effectively, to a form of status criminalisation of these "dangerous classes". The official slogan of LA's *Neighbourhood Watch* programme is "Be on the look out for strangers" – as concise a summary of social attitudes in this respect as one could find. From such a perspective, to be a stranger in a given area is to come under suspicion by nature of being out of place. Here we might, of course, usefully recall Foucault's observation that

135

"discipline proceeds from the distribution of individuals in space".[47] This is by no means simply an American phenomenon, but is a tendency which is increasingly replicated in many British cities. Reporting on Comedia's Out of Hours study of urban space, Worpole notes that black or Asian people living in the towns included in that study said that they quickly learned where they could and could not go safely in the towns in which they settled. As Worpole observes, "a young black person getting off at the 'wrong' bus stop, and finding themselves in the 'wrong' neighbourhood in many British city suburbs becomes almost immediately an object of police suspicion".[48]

To return to the American case, the end result of this process of geographical separation by racial or ethnic category was captured dramatically in a *Time* report of the aftermath of the Los Angeles riots in the spring of 1992, when a group of black people from South Central Los Angeles drove to the courthouse in the white suburb of Simi Valley where the policemen charged with assault on Rodney King were to be arraigned, to be met by the hurt and puzzled cry from one of Simi's white residents, "Why do you bother us? ... Let us get on with our lives, like you are."[49] The last thing those engaged in white flight want is the reappearance, in their secluded spaces, of the problems which they left the city to escape. That they cannot escape the representation of these problems on television seems perhaps galling enough to them – to be also physically reminded of that which they have succeeded in excluding geographically from their lives can clearly feel just too much to bear. We shall return later in this chapter to the question of the ways in which mediated forms of what we might call virtual alterity can create difficulty.

There is some evidence that, in America, these questions of residential segregation by race are further reinforced by segregated patterns of television viewing. Although there is some "crossover" viewing of black programming by some young middle-class white viewers, on the whole, and with the singular exception of *The Cosby Show* (1984–92), there has never been a television show in the USA watched in equal numbers by whites and blacks.[50] Melinda Whittstock reports 1998 figures demonstrating that not a single television show was in the Top 10 for both blacks and whites. As she notes, what we see here is little less than a form of televisionally mediated apartheid, in which the virtual public sphere in the USA is thoroughly segregated by race. As she puts it:

> white Americans over the age of 21 just don't watch black American shows. And the converse is also true. Fourteen of the twenty most popular shows among African American viewers don't even rank among the Top 100 shows white people watch ... Few whites have even heard of ... the number-one rated series among blacks ... *Between Brothers* ... Conversely, the biggest hits among whites ... are anything but [that] for blacks ... *Friends* ... the fourth most popular show among whites ... ranks one hundred and eighteenth with blacks.[51]

Indeed, it has been argued that in the USA it is "increasingly hard to distinguish segmentation of the audience from segregation of the audience".[52] Social and ethnic balkanisation, combined with the proliferation of narrowcast media outlets and the virtual whitewash of network programming, with fewer and fewer black and minority characters on prime time network television, have produced a situation where, in their search for the white high-school audience wanted by advertisers, "the networks seem to have become de facto white, middle-class channels, catering to some kind of imaginary suburban American whose racial composition is about as multi-ethnic as the cast of *Friends*". In this situation, Patterson notes, now that minority viewers have access to niche cable channels such as BET, WB and UPN, they correspondingly are deserting the major networks, in a clear parallel with the process we saw earlier in relation to British ethnic minority viewers' preferences for imported, cable and satellite programming.[53]

The tendency for patterns of physically entrenched withdrawal and social separation to be replicated in the realm of virtual media spaces is also apparent in some cases at the national level. Thus, in August 1996, during the war in Bosnia, the London *Evening Standard*'s reporter Lanette Ziener visited Peoria, the traditional symbol of Middle America, and reported meetings with interviewees who, on the whole, had never set foot outside the Midwest ("Why would I want to do that?" asked one). It seemed that though they might watch the television news and read the *Peoria Journal Star*, they largely ignored their minimal international coverage ("Those things don't matter to me"). Kindergarten teacher Shirley Wade, interviewed by Ziener, explained why, in her view, most people in Peoria are uninterested in current affairs outside the USA:

> We're the type of people who want a peaceful life … I've never been overseas. I've never even been to New York or Los Angeles – they're full of peculiar folk. I choose to live my life here and want to know what's going on here … I feel safe in Peoria. Even the Oklahoma City bomb didn't frighten me. It wasn't here.[54]

The process of social withdrawal takes place at different geographical scales and in both actual and virtual forms, affecting both patterns of residence and patterns of media consumption. Thus John Tomlinson notes that, throughout the affluent West, "news coverage of foreign events on television seems to be shrinking", quoting a fall of two-thirds in North American network news coverage of foreign affairs over a twenty-year period according to one analysis, and an even more dramatic fall of 42 per cent between 1988 and 1996 according to another. According to Ryzard Kapuscinski, only 5 per cent of American network news output is now devoted to other countries, while 72 per cent of material is local in character.[55] Tomlinson notes that this trend is visible throughout much of the developed world, quoting the then Chief Executive of BBC News Tony Hall's comments that "most news organisations are spending less on foreign news" and that, ironically, "at a time when most of our futures are decided globally, the audience of our broadcast programmes appears to be less interested in the world".[56] According to Cleasby,

> the trend towards insularity ... stems ... from a broad assumption that programmes on international affairs are inevitably unpopular with the British audience ... Viewers want to see more programmes of relevance to their own lives and experiences and this is interpreted as meaning more programmes about Britain.[57]

Suburbanism – the politics of withdrawal

If the discourse of multiculturalism does describe inner-city street life by day (and sometimes club life by night) in some parts of Britain's cities, still, according to Michael Ignatieff,

> most of us continue to live separate lives. Notwithstanding the rise in inter-marriages, most of us continue to live apart. In reality, like continues to live with like, and the practice of tolerance looks much more like polite – or not so polite – avoidance.[58]

Certainly, compared with the USA, ethnic residential patterns in the UK are more mixed. Raj Patel suggests that on a 'segregation index' (whereby 0 per cent signifies that an ethnic minority is evenly spread across a whole city and 100 per cent means they entirely live in ghettos) "American blacks are typically 80 per cent segregated; for their British counterparts this figure is about 40 per cent". Clearly, even this is a high level of segregation.[59]

In his definition of the positive attributes of city life, Lewis Mumford argued that "in its various and many-sided life, in its very opportunities for social disharmony and conflict the city creates drama, the suburb lacks it".[60] This is a utopian concept of the city as a theatre of social drama where, through their common inhabitation of space and common use of facilities, people of different sorts come to experience and deal with many forms of alterity. The alternative is the organisation of social and geographical space as a co-existing series of inward-looking monocultures devoid of social diversity, in practice, as Patel notes, as a result of the fear-driven process which leads social groups to flee from each other into homogenous social enclaves.[61]

The tendency of the new professional and managerial elites in the USA to physically separate themselves off from the society in which they live by moving into gated communities has been well analysed by Christopher Lasch.[62] However, this tendency is no longer confined to the Americas. A parallel development has recently been reported among Russia's new elite, who are increasingly building heavily fortified estates for themselves to keep out the poor who surround them.[63] Similarly, the emergence of "a new housing apartheid" in the UK has been "creating a social laager for the new superclass who are migrating from the rest of the country to live in the streets and districts where they know they can find others as rich as themselves".[64] Jonathan Glancey notes that they offer "security and seclusion … and peace of mind" to their rich inhabitants and that while the names ("Virginia Water") and architectural styles "are designed to connote English traditions these … houses could hardly be less English … What we have here, in salubrious Surrey, is an unexpected slice of Florida, New Jersey, Cape Town or Guangzhou." As Richard Thorney observes, the motto of the new secluded rich (like that of Tom Wolfe's "masters of the universe" in his *Bonfire of the Vanities*) is "Insulate! Insulate!" and he observes of the particular gated community in Buckinghamshire on which he reports that "the whole point about the place is that no one knows where it is, that people can't find it" (the residents are strongly resistant to any sign-posting which would assist "outsiders" to find their location). As he puts it,

> People can only come and go at your command … strangers don't clutter your pavement. Salesmen, Jehovah's Witnesses, Gypsies … can't knock on the door … Whatever happens inside the insulated island is planned. The wealth of the inhabitants has bought them a new product: predictability.[65]

What these gated communities sell is clearly similar to the attractions of the Disney-built community in Celebration, Florida. Mary Dejevsky observes that what the town offers is

> a traditional sort of safety you can rely on … the small town of imagined childhood memory; a town with a centre, with walkable streets and houses that look as houses ought to look; a town where you feel safe enough to leave your door unlocked, to let your children walk to school and lend your neighbour a cup of tea.[66]

This is the same vision of an almost existential condition of tranquillity and security that inspired Silvio Berlusconi's "alternative city", *Milano 3* in northern Italy, referred to earlier, which was described by one of its residents as having "everything that Milan lacks: clean air, ordered silence, efficiency" – and, of course, no poor people.[67] The question, in such a place, is who can afford to be your neighbour? And the answer is – only people as rich (and usually white) as you are. As Dejevsky notes, the appeal of a community such as Celebration is "identical to that of [any] upmarket white suburb … Its residents select themselves by income and aspiration."[68]

Geodemographics: "Where you live is who you are"

The process of self-selection which leads to the increasing internal homogenisation of residential areas has been the basis of one of the commercial success stories of consumer market research over the last thirty years: the development of geodemographic analyses of consumer types by residential area. These systems work extremely well in enabling marketers to identify and predict the predominant forms of consumer behaviour in any given residential area. The basis of their success is the inbuilt tendency of the price mechanism in the housing market to work towards the homogenisation of any one area and its segregation from others.[69]

Perhaps the best known system of geodemographic segmentation in the UK is CACI's "ACORN" ("A Classification of Residential Neighbourhoods") which works by classifying people according to the type of area in which they live. The system is based on the division of the UK population into 150,000 enumeration districts for census purposes (extremely small geographical areas which will thus tend to have a relatively high degree of internal homogeneity), all of which are readily converted into one or another of the UK's 1.3 million postcodes for marketing purposes. The ACORN system then divides the whole of the UK into fifty-four types of neighbourhood (ranging from "wealthy suburbs, detached houses" to "partially gentrified, multi-ethnic area" to "council flats, greatest hardship, many lone parents") identified with particular postcodes in different geographical areas. Clearly, within any one area there will always be a small residue of untypical residents but, given the pressures of the housing market referred to above, the clear majority of those in any one area of ACORN's fifty-four neighbourhood types will tend to have similar demographic and social characteristics and share similar lifestyle and consumption patterns. In the USA there is a similar geodemographic segmentation system known as PRIZM ("Potential Rating Index by Zip Market"). The "zip" number is the five-digit American postal code, and PRIZM divides these 35,000 zip codes into forty market clusters, identifying types of relatively distinct population segments and their geographic locations (ranging from "blue blood estates", through "sun belt singles" to "blue collar Catholics" and "back country folks"). The clusters are again constructed from a combination of demographic and social variables including housing stock, education, ethnicity and urban/rural division, so as to identify each of them with a particular dominant lifestyle identifiable in the geographical areas with the relevant zipcodes. At its simplest, all these systems are based on the premise that place of residence is the single best predictor (or from another point of view, index) of lifestyle and consumption patterns, and their commercial success goes some way to proving the soundness of this premise. As Decca Aitkenhead has noted more particularly, in relation to the recent boom in the UK property market, the effect of the market mechanism is increasingly that "mixed neighbourhoods are being reorganised into homogenous zones" as different types of people are "all relocated to the appropriate parts of town where only people like them can afford to live".[70]

Having now established some of the dynamics of the key processes of exclusion and withdrawal in both urban and virtual space, let us turn to consider these geographies of exclusion from a more theoretical viewpoint.

The purification of space

There is a long history, from the Greeks and the Romans onwards, of imaginary geographies, in which the members of a society locate themselves at the centre of the universe, at the spatial periphery of which they picture a world of threatening monsters and grotesques.[71] In this logic, the further out from the centre one goes, the stranger the creatures one encounters. In these matters the question of boundary maintenance is crucial. Here "the determination of a border between the inside and the outside [proceeds] according to the simple logic of excluding filth" or the "imperative of distancing from disgust".[72] This is a process which operates both on a societal level and at the level of everyday, familial experience through various forms of limitation and closure which function to provide ontological stability. The family may, of course, be mobile as it moves through this threatening, external world, but its boundaries must remain secure. Thus, as Sibley notes in his analysis of the Volkswagen advert from the early 1990s showing a small girl being driven in a Volkswagen through the threatening streets of New York City, the car here symbolises a pure/safe space (a mobile home) in a defiled environment: "the commercial implies that the car will transport [the child] safely through the city, where street people – homeless, mentally ill, drug addicts – are represented as remote, but threatening, part of another world, viewed from the safety of the Volkswagen".[73]

Drawing on Foucault's comments on the "hidden presence of the sacred" in the "oppositions that we regard as simple givens ... between private space and public space, between family space and social space", where he notes acerbically that "we may not yet have reached the point of a practical desanctification of space", Sibley argues that "in order to understand the problem of exclusion in modern society, we need ... an 'anthropology of space' which emphasises the rituals of spatial organisation".[74] In relation to questions of residential segregation, the shaping of social space organised around ideas of who is (or is not) felt to belong there – and the corresponding resistance to a different sort of person moving into a neighbourhood – can be traced back to questions of anxiety and fear in relation to various forms of alterity, even if their primary expression is articulated as a concern about property values.

In his path-breaking study of the "uses of disorder", Richard Sennett outlined the positive benefits which accrued to the inhabitants of North American cities in earlier times, who had a greater variety of contact points with others different from themselves, as they went about their daily lives. As Sennett notes, in those days not only was residential life more mixed up with commercial and industrial activity, but the old neighbourhoods themselves were also more complex and cosmopolitan – simply because no one group had the economic resources to indulge whatever desire they may have had to shield themselves from others. In this respect, Sennett points to what he sees as the highly negative role which affluence has had in enabling people to form homogenous "communities of self-conscious solidarity".[75] Thus, he argues, nowadays, with the advent of greater affluence for many, these "desires for coherence, for structured exclusion and internal sameness" (where the "image of community is purified of all that might convey a feeling of difference, let alone conflict, in who 'we' are") can be more fully played out. The result, he argues is the "simplification of the social environment in the suburbs" where "physical space becomes rigidly divided into functional areas". By this means, people are enabled to "live with people like themselves" in a "functionally separated, internally homogenous environment" and "potentially diversifying experiences can be shut out with the feeling of performing a moral act".[76] The price, evidently, is the reinforcement of the most regressive desires for the elimination of any potentially enriching experience of alterity.

Matter out of place

In his analysis of the dynamics of what he calls the "purification of space" Sibley draws on the work of Mary Douglas and that of Basil Bernstein to offer a number of insights into the significance of processes of boundary maintenance.[77] He is concerned with the "problem of boundary erection ... in the shaping of social relations and the creation of social space", and argues that the dynamics of this process are motivated by the socially produced "distaste for or hostility toward the mixing of unlike categories".[78] Douglas' work, which originated in the analysis of the role of abjection and exclusion in the social structuring of small-scale, traditional societies, is, in fact, of wider application, and has much to offer the analysis of contemporary cultural dynamics. The essentials of Douglas' thesis are that

> (1) there is a need to classify (people, behaviour, objects) in order to make sense of the world; (2) that which fails to fit a classification is viewed adversely and (3) purification rules are developed in order to exclude that which is unclassified. The unclassified residual category is dirt, pollution, a threat to the integrity of the collectivity.[79]

Wherever there is dirt there is a system, in so far as "dirt is the by-product of a systematic ordering and classification of matter ... as ordering involves rejecting inappropriate elements." [80] For Douglas, "dirt is that which must not be included if a pattern is to be maintained". As she puts it,

> shoes are not dirty in themselves, but it is dirty to place them on the

dining table; food is not dirty in itself, but it is dirty to leave cooking utensils in the bedroom, or food bespattered on clothing; similarly ... outdoor things indoors; upstairs things downstairs; underclothing appearing where over-clothing should be, and so on.[81]

This applies at both micro and macro levels: just as the home may be profaned by the presence of dust or mud (or a particular space within it profaned by the presence of an object properly belonging to another space), similarly the homeland may be profaned by the presence of strangers, or the national culture profaned by imported, foreign films.

In her commentary on the categorisation of dirt, Douglas observes that hybrids (such as fish that crawl, for example) are always deemed particularly offensive, in so far as they intermingle and confuse elements and characteristics which, in a properly ordered universe, should be kept separate. These things are deemed problematic in so far as they are "imperfect members of their class" or because their class itself "confounds the general scheme of the world".[82] Hybrids thus unsettle fixed schema based on clear and separate categories – their ambiguity and ambivalence creates a crisis of "decidability". Thus, as Frazer Ward argues, following Kristeva, "hybrids, as embodiments of ambiguity, threaten identity itself".[83] According to the terms of Douglas' analysis, the key problems always pertain to elements, objects or persons which lack the virtue of clarity of belonging. From this same perspective, Madan Sarup argued that "strangers are, in principle ... unclassifiable. A stranger is someone who refuses to remain confined to the 'far away' land or go away from our own. S/he is physically close while remaining culturally remote." Thus, in much contemporary political discourse, "the deviant has been replaced by the immigrant. In traditional folklore, there were demons, witches, devils. Now we have visible deviants, foreigners."[84] Because group membership is usually the main definer of individual rights, it is often felt to be essential to maintain the boundary separating members from strangers by expelling polluting individuals or symbolic objects (whether they be witches, members of other ethnic groups, AIDS victims or foreign television programmes). Far from being particular to so-called primitive societies, purification rituals are a pervasive feature of contemporary cultural life. [85]

The spatial separations of contemporary urban societies symbolise a moral order every bit as much as they do in tribal societies. In this connection, Martin Walker notes the spread of the private swimming pool club in the USA as a further element in "the discreet and self-deceiving way of modern American apartheid. It is now justified as a way to avoid the crowds, crime and drugs of the municipal pool, these being code words which are used to signify black people."[86] Boundaries are inscribed both in social institutions and in material structures. Thus Steven Flusty addresses the architectural practices that have been developed to protect the physical security and isolation of elite groups' areas from penetration by the less privileged. Flusty's concern is with the design of what he calls interdictory spaces, which are designed to intercept, repel or filter undesirables. Zygmunt Bauman argues that what we see here is a "contemporary equivalent of the early-modern enclosures" of yesterday's commons, as public spaces are gradually replaced by "privately produced ... owned and administered spaces ... [where] access is predicated upon ability to pay ... [and] exclusivity rules".[87]

In attempting to understand the dynamics of the process of boundary-construction described here, one question is how and why people come to value homogeneity (and to abhor difference) in the ways that they do. According to Sibley, it is in some part due to consumer advertising, which encourages "the creation of private worlds which are ... well-ordered, pristine, and pure". Such model domestic environments may "reinforce personality characteristics which are associated with a low tolerance for disorder or ambiguity". However, this does not simply apply to the level of the micro-domestic environment. Rather, we may expect an "endless relation of reciprocal conditioning between global and micro contexts" where we can see played out, at all levels, the consequences of an inculcated abhorrence of "mixed categories or blurred identities ... experienced as a pollution, endangering the sacred".[88] If the individual, the home, the locality and the community are interlinked elements in the process of social structuration, we should "expect the inability to tolerate disorder or impurity to be reinforced if the well-ordered home is located in a well-ordered suburb".

In so far as social divisions are inscribed in patterns of residence, the mere presence of difference can then be seen as implicitly threatening. While the creation of residential submarkets minimises the likelihood of encountering difference and otherness, by the same token "when such encounters do occur, the greater the likelihood that a moral panic will ensue".[89] Zygmunt Bauman similarly observes that "intolerance of difference, resentment of strangers and ... demands to ... banish them ... tend to climb to their highest pitch in the most uniform ... racially, ethnically and class-wise segregated, homogenous local communities".[90] As he points out, this is a vicious circle because, in such an area, people have little opportunity to develop the necessary skills to deal creatively with such encounters, and when they occur they are therefore all the more likely to breed reactions of panic. At a political level, various forms of zero-tolerance policing policies (such as those developed by Mayor Giuliani in New York and now advocated by the New Labour government in the UK) have been designed in recent years to banish undesirables such as the homeless, beggars or car windscreen washers from the streets. According to Bauman, what such vagabonds represent to the respectable citizens of our "risk society" is a worrying vision of what they might themselves become, given a sufficient run of bad luck. In "sweeping the vagabond under the carpet – banning the beggar and the homeless from the street, confining him to a far-away 'no-go' ghetto, demanding his exile or incarceration", what the respectable citizen desperately (if vainly) seeks is in fact "the deportation of his own fears" – the very converse of Kristeva's admonishment that we should rather learn to recognise and accept the "stranger" in ourselves.[91]

Problematic smells and signs

If we step back and take a historical perspective on these issues of spatial purification, we see that in the growth of the cities of the West, it was the "unclean poor" from whom the middle and upper classes wished to segregate themselves. Thus, Alain Corbin notes that Baron Hausmann's plans for Paris in the nineteenth century were designed to eliminate "the darkness at the centre of the city", which symbolised not only the foul-smelling environment of the poor but also the poor themselves. As he points out, the nineteenth century's sanitation schemes, designed to improve living conditions in poor areas, led to a symbolic association of the poor with their own excrement, and he suggests that "the bourgeois self separated itself from the working class Other through ... fear of smell".[92] Similarly, the nineteenth-century English urban reformers such as Chadwick, Booth and Mayhew all equated the moral status of the poor with the physical dirt of the conditions in which they lived, so that the poor themselves became a form of dirt, and the separations which the middle classes were able to achieve in their suburbs had their meaning by virtue of the contrast with the improper mixings of persons and polluting matters in the slums.[93]

The slum was metonymically linked to filth, filth to disease and disease to moral degradation. Ultimately, the poor themselves came to be seen as a source of physical or moral contagion (cholera or gambling) to be avoided: denizens of a dark, public realm of disease and dangers from which the civilised realm of respectable domesticity must be protected. The problem was that "even as the separation of the suburb from the slum enabled a certain class difference, the development of the city simultaneously threatened the clarity of that segregation", for the public places, thoroughfares and means of transport remained shockingly promiscuous – and the "fear of that promiscuity was encoded above all in terms of the fear of being touched".[94] Such fears are clearly still with us. In 1995, Steven Norris, then the Minister for Transport in the Conservative government in the UK, explained that he always preferred to travel by car rather than by public transport because that way "You have your own company, your own temperature control, your own music. And you don't have to put up with the dreadful human beings sitting alongside you."[95]

However, as can perhaps be evidenced by any number of scandals involving Establishment figures, this desire to protect the civilised self from the lower orders is not without its ambivalences. As Stallybrass and White argue, the secular magic which governs these laws of exclusion is often accompanied by a simultaneous fascination "with the criminal of the night, a landscape of darkness, drunkenness, noise and obscenity". The problem is that while the bourgeois subject continuously redefined itself through the exclusion of the dirty and the contaminating, "that very act of exclusion was constitutive of its identity". The objects of disgust often also bear the ambivalent imprint of desire and "these low domains, apparently expelled as Other, return as the object of nostalgia, longing and fascination". Ultimately the "imperative to eliminate the debasing 'low' conflicts powerfully and unpredictably with a desire for this Other" – which can, in fact, never be excluded without returning in the form of neurotic symptoms and desires which threaten to undermine the fragile domain of civilisation.[96]

Nowadays, concern with pollution has largely changed its focus towards racial or non-conforming minorities, rather than reflecting bourgeois anxieties about the unwashed masses. Sibley argues that it is possible to identify in popular discourse "a number of building blocks or key sites of nationalistic sentiment, including the family, the suburb and the countryside, all of which exclude black people, gays, gypsies, etc. from the nation" – i.e. those who are defined as different by virtue of "race" or sexuality or lifestyle.[97] The work of the black photographer Ingrid Pollard dramatises the ways in which the countryside in particular is still largely represented as the essence of white Englishness – as a stable, culturally homogeneous, historically unchanging territory in which racial difference can only be seen as an uncomfortable and destabilising presence (see Figure 6.1).[98] It is, of course, not only racial others from whom sacred spaces must be defended. Recent legislation in the UK has also been designed to clamp down on the incursions of deviant youth cultures into the countryside and to protect the lifestyles and pastimes of the (white) "country people". The latter are seen to embody the quintessential national virtues which express the homogeneity and harmony of rural England. Here again, the city – as a cosmopolitan space and the home of deviant sub-cultures – provides the source of unwanted invasions of English rurality.[99]

The writing on the wall

Just as Douglas defines dirt in relative terms, so Julia Kristeva argues that the power of pollution is "proportional to the potency of the prohibition that founds it".[100] In his analysis of the panic in New York over the appearance of graffiti in the city during the 1970s and 1980s, Tim Cresswell observes that its appearance was reported in the media as an epidemic or a plague or a cancer – a symptom of illness appearing on the body of the city. Graffiti was thus articulated to other forms of urban disorder – garbage, noise, broken-down buildings – indexing the breakdown of good order and the eruption of "the dirty, animalistic, uncivilised and profane" on the streets of the city.[101] As Cresswell observes, in de Certeau's terms, graffiti can be understood as a tactical art of the dispossessed and marginal groups, asserting their fleeting triumph over the legitimate authorities' control over urban space by means of the assertion of private meanings in public space, and by their refusal to respect the laws of place. Just as the poor came to be equated with their smell in the nineteenth-century city, here there is a collapse between the perceived foreignness of

... its as if the Black experience is only lived within an urban environment. I thought I liked the Lake District; where I wandered lonely as a black face in a sea of white. A visit to the countryside is always accompanied by a feeling of unease, dread ...

Figure 6.1   Ingrid Pollard, *Pastoral Interlude.*
Source: Courtesy of Ingrid Pollard.

graffiti and its presumed sources among the youth of immigrant ethnic minorities. As Cresswell puts it,

> the description of graffiti as a plague ... implies foreign origin ... [and] the metaphorical inscription of graffiti as dirt and disease is combined with a notion that graffiti comes from and belongs in the metaphorical "jungle" of the third world ... [and] that graffiti writers are probably from some distant place (some other context, where graffiti is more appropriate).[102]

In a similar vein Kristin Koptivich observes that in many American cities, graffiti can often be read as "cultural inscriptions of resistance etched in the 'war zone' along a new frontier where ghetto meets gentrification", where the graffiti "answers back with its ephemeral but insistent repetitions of the signature tags of those most cut off" from the rewards of the affluent society which surrounds them.[103]

To this extent these signs of foreignness are often interpreted by the majority population as sacrilegious defacements of their city, announcing its estrangement

147

from them. Thus the anti-hero of Juan Goytisolo's novel *Landscapes after the Battle* is greatly troubled by the graffiti which he perceives as a sign of the gradual de-Europeanisation of the French city in which he lives. What he finds unsettling is the "gradual penetration of the disastrous, disintegrating action of mostly foreign elements" which make him feel less and less at home in his own city. This transformation is partly physical: "the appearance of Oriental souks and hammams, peddlers of African totems and necklaces", the "emergence in the perfectly ordered Cartesian perspectives of Baron Haussman of bits and pieces of Tlemcen and Dakar, Cairo and Karachi, Bamako and Calcutta". He senses that his city is being colonised by the barbarians, and that he and his fellow "aborigines" are more and more out of place each day, as the city goes over to "Byzantium time". This is partly a result of the creeping presence of "incomprehensible graffiti on the walls", which began as a "few inscriptions in chalk ... written in a strange alphabet" but which have gradually come to seem to him more like "an accumulation of signs ... in a secret language", threatening that "they're out to get us". The problem for Goytisolo's hero is that these threatening "veritable algebraic equations reproduced ... with obsessive regularity" are written in words in "their" alphabet which "the good Lord himself couldn't read ... written all backward the way they are". The crucial issue though, is where these signs now appear – and he nostalgically recalls that "there was a time when they wrote them only in their own country, but now they're coming nosing about up here, daubing and dirtying up our walls as though they owned the city".[104] Similarly, in the context of his commentary on the reactions of the local population to the building of a mosque in my own area of north-east London, Gilsenan poses the question of:

> the effect that outside forces, over a relatively short period of time, can have on the transformation of the whole of the relations that make up urban space, including its sacred geography. Imagine, not only one building being constructed on an alien model, but an entire system of urban life ... [and] its symbolic cultural forms being imposed upon already existing towns and cities that have been organised on quite different bases.[105]

As we have seen, in the contemporary world the migration of messages, objects, persons and cultures from their perceived places of origin serves to continuously destabilise existing borders and boundaries and it is to the confluence of media, mobility and migrancy that we now turn.

7

MEDIA, MOBILITY AND MIGRANCY

Exclusion, withdrawal and mobile privatisation

We can usefully explore the relationship between patterns of media consumption and patterns of residence by reference to what Raymond Williams called "mobile privatisation". Williams understood this as a form of activity centred on the home (and to that extent involving a withdrawal into domestic space). However, he stressed that this is not simply a "retreating privatisation ... because what it especially confers is an unexampled mobility ... It is not living in a cut-off way". If it does involve living in some kind of shell, "it is a shell which you can take with you, which you can fly with, to places that previous generations could never imagine visiting".[1] Thus, like Arnheim, Williams saw the television set as part of the same set of technologies as the motor car – as Moores puts it, technologies "designed to transport the individual or small family group to destinations [physical, symbolic or imaginary] well beyond the confines of home or neighbourhood, combining privacy with mobility". The experience of domestic television consumption is then one of "simultaneously staying home and imaginatively, at least, going places". If broadcasting is able to "transport" viewers and listeners to previously distant or unknown sites, mediating between private and public domains, then, as Moores notes, "we need to specify the kind of 'journeys' that are made. Who chooses to go where, with whom and why?",[2] asking "to what new destinations is it promising transport".[3] Without wanting to overstate the contrast between modern and pre-modern periods, it is still possible to accept James Carey's argument that modern technologies, from the telegraph to satellite television, give rise to "communities ... not in place, but in space, mobile, connected across vast distances by appropriate symbols, forms and interests".[4] It is in this context that Anthony Giddens argues that while in pre-modern societies space and place largely coincide, by contrast "the advent of modernity increasingly tears space away from place, by fostering relations between 'absent' others, locationally distant from any given situation of face-to-face interaction".[5]

Communications technologies can function as disembedding mechanisms, powerfully enabling individuals (and sometimes whole families or communities) to escape, at least imaginatively, from their geographical locations. When people's situation is particularly constrained, such escape becomes all the more important, as is demonstrated by the importance given by many prisoners to the privilege of access to television, to take one stark example. To take another, Andrea Ashworth has written of growing up as an abused child in a family in Manchester in the 1970s in a situation where the media (and particularly, in her case, the radio she listened to alone at night) provided a crucial psychological escape route from her oppressive family life and enabled her to make some sense of it. As she puts it, for her, tuning into the BBC World Service on the radio "was like tuning into the future, learning the language they spoke there".[6] As Edward Relph has it,

> the places to which we are most committed may be the very centres of our lives, but they may also be oppressive and imprisoning. There is a sheer drudgery of place, a sense of being tied inexorably to *this* place, of being bound by the established scenes and symbols and routines.[7]

In relation to the oppressiveness of being trapped in "locality" in a poor Third World country, the hero of Romesh Guneseka's novel bemoans the fact that

> in those days we had no television ... Only the newspapers gave some inkling [of elsewhere], but not enough to give shape or sense to the place ... I could not visualise the lie of the land, the real geography of the city, or the sea between countries; only walls everywhere ... I was trapped inside what I could see, what I could hear, what I could walk to.[8]

In this respect Hamid Naficy has argued that, alongside the dynamics of nostalgia for the lost homeland, we must also pay attention to the correlative dynamics of wanderlust or "what in German is called *Fernweh* which means ... a desire to escape from one's own homeland". Naficy argues that for those in their homeland, "this wanderlust for other places can be just as insatiable and unrealisable as is the desire for return to the homeland for those who are in exile".[9] Thus, as noted earlier, for particular types of people within the UK, satellite television has come to symbolise and represent just such a form of desirable freedom of viewing, by contradistinction to the constraints of the old national broadcasting institutions such as the BBC.[10] However, if imaginative forms of mobility are, for some people a positive response to their disidentification with their place of residence, still, as we have seen in the last chapter, the more basic tendency is that which works towards the exclusion of alterity from the sacred space of the familiar.

Virtual and physical alterity

Threatening encounters with those defined as alien – those held responsible for various forms of cultural miscegenation – can take place not only in physical but also in virtual, or symbolic, space. In so far as the television set is placed within the symbolic centre of the home, it can serve to disturb viewers' symbolic sense of community by bringing unwanted strangers into their homes. In her study of viewers' letters written to the producers of the black sitcom *Julia*, made by NBC in America in the late 1960s, Aniko Bodroghkozy discovered a particularly striking one from a white viewer, pleased with his continuing success in keeping black people out of the physical neighbourhood in which he lived, who was outraged at their invasion of his territory via television. This viewer declared that "I believe I can speak for millions of real Americans ... I am tired of niggers in my living room".[11]

As Bodroghkozy notes, in 1968, when this viewer's letter was written, the American networks in the wake of that year's black inner-city riots had broadcast an unprecedented number of television documentaries on "Black America" and its problems. Viewers seemed to make little distinction between these documentary programmes on civil strife and civil rights and the fictional world of *Julia*, and for some white viewers it all just clearly amounted to too much visibility for blacks. She quotes one who says, "we have had so much color shoved down our throats on special programmes this summer, it's enough to make a person sick" and another who comments that "after the riots and the network-filled 'Black American' shows all summer, white people aren't feeling too kindly towards colored people shows". Or, as yet another correspondent dramatically puts it, in the words from which Bodroghkozy's article takes its title, "Is this what you mean by color TV? Ugh! Click!"[12] It is, however, worth noting that this is not necessarily a one-way street. Although the racialised power relations in this case are evidently quite different from those in the context which Bodroghkozy investigated, in his study of satellite television in Australia Philip Batty notes that many of the Aboriginal people in the area he studied also thought of the images that satellite television would bring into their homes as precisely analogous to an unwelcome physical encroachment of others on their space. As one member of the Ernabella Aboriginal community put it, "unimpeded satellite transmission in our communities will be like having hundreds of whitefellas visit without permits, every day".[13] Unfortunately these issues also continue to have a clear pertinence in contemporary Britain. An African-Caribbean woman in Sreberny and Ross' study of black minority viewers reported that she had a friend whose father would still not watch any news programme fronted by a black presenter. As she continued, in a disturbing echo of Bodroghkozy's comments on 1960s America,

> there are white people who switch the television off if a black person or programme comes on. It's their last bit of power. They know we can

move around and live where we want, but they're stuck and they want to keep their traditional things.[14]

In a world where many people live in multi-ethnic cities, for some viewers, unhappy with this hybridity and with what Kobena Mercer has called the sheer difficulty of living with difference, the television set can also sometimes offer majority viewers the solace of symbolic immersion in a lost world of settled homogeneity. Thus Bruce Gyngell, the former head of TV-AM in Britain and now returned to work in television in his native Australia, has claimed that Australian soap operas such as *Neighbours* and *Home and Away*, which receive far higher ratings when they are shown in Britain than they do in Australia, appeal to many within the British audience precisely because they are, in effect "racial programmes", depicting an all-white society for which some Britons still pine. Gyngell trenchantly claims that: "*Neighbours* and *Home and Away* represent a society which existed in Britain ... before people began arriving from the Caribbean and Africa. The Poms delve into it to get their quiet little racism fix."[15] The exclusion of ethnic minorities from these programmes is conversely a matter of resentment among black and Asian viewers. As one of them notes, "things like *Neighbours* and *Home and Away* they just show absolutely no ethnic minorities in the cast at all".[16] Conversely, it has also been argued that the particular popularity of the British soap opera *Coronation Street* among British expatriates in Australasia and elsewhere is evidence of their nostalgia for the (white) "past they have lost". Indeed, although other British soap operas, such as the BBC's *EastEnders*, have at times featured Asian and Afro-Caribbean characters, it was only in 1998, thirty-eight years into its run, that *Coronation Street* got its first Asian family, when the Desais took over the Street's corner shop.[17] Even now, on the whole, as Sallie Westwood and John Williams argue, the UK's television soap operas "are suffused with notions of Englishness and belonging which exclude ... the Other British – the myriad and diverse peoples who are part of the nation".[18]

Clearly, this is to raise complex issues concerning the question of nostalgia for a lost (if mythical) world of secure and settled identities. A Cambodian woman refugee in Paris puts it simply: "we are a disturbance. That's the word. Because we show you in a terrible way how fragile the world we live in is ... You don't know this in your skin, in every second of your life."[19] In his work on the impact of immigration in contemporary Swedish culture, Gunnar Alsmark details the myriad ways in which the mere physical co-presence of alterity in the same space can create difficulties. Whether it is the differential use of a particular space (whether stairways are understood as spaces to move through rapidly or places for a chat) or of a technology (which clothes can be washed with which others in a Laundromat), the mere presence of cultural differences in everyday life has a relativising effect. As Alsmark says, in this situation "the power of tradition ... loses ... its self-evident nature. It is constantly questioned instead of being taken for granted. The simple things we once did without

152

thinking must now be adjusted, changed or abandoned."[20] Similarly Baldassar, in her study of Italian migrants' return visits to their home town, referred to earlier reports that their visits have a troubling impact on the locals, who experience a sense of dislocation rather like that of the migrants themselves, in so far as the migrants' very arrivals and departures "call into question the existence of a quintessential 'San Fiorese' identity based on unbroken connection to place".[21] In general terms, as Phil Cohen argues, "if immigrants put down roots, if ethnic minorities make a home from home, then they are perceived to threaten the privileged link between habit and habitat upon which the myth of indigenous origins rests".[22]

In the context of these regressive desires for certainty and closure, it is worth noting that recent research in the UK found that three-quarters of potential house-buyers in the UK would prefer, if possible, to live in a leafy, village-style cul-de-sac, secluded from all traffic and passing strangers. As Worpole notes in his commentary on these findings, it seems that "the urge to leave Albert Square or Coronation St to live in Ambridge still remains a pervasive ingredient of the English dream".[23] These regressive desires are not specifically English. In a recent discussion of the popularity of reinvented forms of "new urbanist", traditional architecture in the USA, Susan Marling observed that

> it seems that the desire of the common man [sic] is very clear. He wants to live in the neighbourly world of the soap opera *Peyton Place*, to return to Fifties America, when houses had porches and picket fences and all the folk were cheery.

And, perhaps one feels tempted to add, in so far as once again the traditional form of the architecture seems to symbolise a racialised form of memory, where all the folk were white.[24] In this respect, it would seem that the media both supply needs unmet in the reality of people's experience of the contemporary city and also give shape to their dreams of how they would ideally prefer to live. We shall return to these questions in later chapters. For the moment, though, we must turn to the broader context of the cultural politics of migrancy and mobility.

Worlds in motion: moving images and deterritorialised viewers

In the discussion of transnational and diasporic public spheres at the end of Chapter 5, I argued that given the extent of mobility of both populations and media flows across national boundaries in the contemporary world, any model of culture and communications that operates solely within the assumptions of a national framework is inadequate. In his analysis of contemporary cultural flows, Arjun Appadurai addresses the conjunction of electronic mediation and mass migration where, in many cases, both audiences and messages are often in simultaneous circulation. He insists that we attend to the "mutual contextual-ising of motion and mediation" as we live in a world where "moving images meet deterritorialised viewers". As he notes, while many people are not migrants (cf. the UK evidence cited earlier), and some media remain local in scope, it is also true that even local media carry messages and influences from far afield and many "local people" have either relatives, acquaintances or colleagues who are "on the road to somewhere else, or already coming back home, bearing stories and possibilities".[25] Because of this unstable conjunction between mass-mediated events and migrating audiences, Appadurai notes,

> persons and images often meet unpredictably, outside the certainties of home and the cordon sanitaire of local and national media ... [in] a space of contestation in which individuals and groups seek to annex the global into their own practices of the modern.[26]

While Appadurai fully accepts that mass migration itself is no recent develop-ment, he nonetheless argues that its juxtaposition with contemporary global flows of mass-mediated imagery and discourses produces a "new order of insta-bility in the production of modern subjectivities". As he notes, "as Turkish guest workers in Germany watch Turkish films in their German flats, as Koreans in Philadelphia watch the ... Olympics in Seoul through satellite ... and as Pakistani cabdrivers in Chicago listen to cassettes of sermons recorded in Mosques in ... Iran", important new diasporic public spheres are created and sustained that quite transcend the orbit of the nation-state.[27] Thus, Appadurai insists that we must attend to the role of the media in the construction of what he calls "migratory scripts". As he puts it:

> More people than ever before seem to imagine routinely the possibility that they or their children will live and work in places other then where they were born ... those who wish to move, those who have moved, those who wish to return and those who choose to stay rarely formu-late their plans outside the sphere of radio and television, cassette and videos, newsprint and telephone ... and are deeply affected by a mass-mediated imaginary that frequently transcends national space.[28]

In his discussion of the role of television in the Albanian migration process, Nicola Mai explores this issue in the context of recent large-scale flows of illegal immigration by young Albanians into southern Italy, which they see as the "gateway to Europe".[29] This physical immigration has to be seen as an exten-sion of the long previous immersion of young Albanians in watching Italian television in Albania, while dreaming of escape. Although, under the Hoxha regime, it was illegal to watch foreign television (with a seven-year jail sentence, if caught doing so), as Mai notes, via their televisions a virtual Italy was in people's homes for six or seven hours every night. Mai rightly points to the parallel symbolism, in Albania, of the hundreds of thousands of convex concrete bunkers installed by Hoxha around the country, designed to defend the country against invasion by its foreign enemies, and the concave satellite dishes through which foreign culture invaded Albanian airwaves. Of course, to speak of "invasion" here may be misleading – for many Albanians, oppressed by the Hoxha regime, consuming Italian television (with its "landscapes of colour and beauty", by contrast to the drabness of life in Albania) was an act of symbolic resistance in which people developed their dreams of freedom.[30] For Albanian youth, having learnt Italian, watched Italian television, taken part in the overthrow of the Hoxha regime and then experienced the traumas of post-Communist Albanian life, physical migration to Italy was but the logical extension of their long-term disavowal of Albanian culture and their emotional investment in "Italianness" (as the locally available version of the West), an attempt to finally reach, physically, the promised land of their televisual dreams.

Migration and representation – symbols of impurity, rituals of purification

If the West commonly represents the land of the migrant's dreams, for the West itself the migrant is often still figured as the scapegoat. Giovanna Campani argues that in the Italian media, African immigrant women are often presented as prostitutes, despite the fact that, in actuality, a far higher proportion of them work as domestic cleaners – an ironical transformation of their actual "purifying" role into a symbolically "contaminating" one.[31] Similarly, Bruno Riccio argues that the Italian media predominantly represent immigrant Senegalese men as associated with "illegal trade".[32] However, in his analysis of Senegalese migratory paths and their media representations, Riccio also offers some striking examples of how European cultures appear from the point of view of the migrant. By contrast to the conventional fears of host communities of being polluted by incoming foreigners, a number of Riccio's Senegalese respondents are very concerned not to be themselves polluted by the corrupt environment of the country to which they have migrated. As one of them puts it:

> this society [Italy] has lost a lot of values ... Italians do not give importance to their parents ... Children ... forget their responsibility, putting them in an old persons' home. This is the worst thing that can happen to a family. In Senegal it would never happen. Here the children have lost their sense of family too ... [because they] spend their time in the kindergarten ... Here there is less faith ... people are too materialistic. We need to recognise that the life and the wealth are inside. We need to be clean inside.[33]

These Senegalese migrants are very aware of the dangers of the temptations provided by the Italian environment in which they move. One of them says explicitly, "what I am afraid of is to be captured by the material"; another explains that, because of the temptations, "it is difficult to be a good Muslim in Italy".[34] In response to these dangers, the immigrants devise a repertoire of strategies designed to maintain their own cultural identity and moral dignity. These include keeping themselves mainly separate from Italians, staying in close touch with their families back in Senegal, revisiting home whenever possible and supporting the visits of their religious leader (the Marabout) when he comes to Italy to give them his blessing.[35]

Moreover, as Riccio argues, a number of these migrants provide a striking reversal of the conventional discourse which portrays migrants as primitives in a more developed country – by portraying themselves as more knowledgeable and more worldly than the Italians among whom they live. In a parallel to the cultural distinction which Ulf Hannerz reports among Nigerians between the naive "Bush" (as in "never left the bush") and the sophisticated "Beento" (i.e. those who have "been to" London, Paris or New York), these Senegalese migrants explain the Italians' racism as a regrettable consequence of their ethnocentrism and ignorance.[36] Thus, the migrants construct for themselves a superior, cosmopolitan position – as one of them points out:

> The person who has been abroad will always be better than the one who stays at home all the time … The Italian is not informed, he does not travel, and television gives bad information about Africa, always with bad images. When they show bad things, they always show Africa. Italians think that being black, I am a wild person who lives with animals … And then you discover that you have experienced much more than them, and travelled more than them.[37]

Having established, in general terms, the significance of the question of migrancy in contemporary culture, I now want to focus, by way of illustration, on the situation of two particular categories of migrants in different parts of Europe – Arabs in France and Turks in Germany.

Spaces of difference: migrants, residential space and media representations in France

My concern here is with the interface between physical and symbolic forms of cultural division as registered in residential patterns, in media representations and in patterns of cultural consumption, as between migrant and host populations in France.[38] Questions of representation, of cultural and of spatial division are closely articulated with each other. As noted in Chapter 4, the question of the need to control the flow of television images coming into the homes of immigrant families from Islamic countries via satellite television has been debated in France in close parallel with the issue of immigration itself. If in the UK the appearance of a satellite dish on the walls of a house was often taken to

signify its inhabitants' abandonment of the space of national public broadcasting and citizenship in favour of the pleasures of international consumerism,
in France, as we have seen, these dishes have "become the symbol of ... immigrants as an alien cultural presence, threatening the integrity of French national
identity".[39] In a pun on the normal term for a satellite dish (*antenne
parabolique*) these dishes are now often referred to as *antennes paradiabolique* –
signifiers of trouble, if not evil.[40] In the words of a French Ministry of Social
Affairs report:

> There are risks of the people concerned [i.e. those with satellite
> receivers] being manipulated by foreign powers, all the more so in
> that the number of DBS dishes is constantly growing, particularly in
> the *banlieues* ... In addition, the various channels broadcast in Arabic,
> which could undermine years of literacy classes and other efforts at
> Gallicising these people. Moreover, the religious content of certain
> programmes will probably increase the Islamisation of the *banlieues.*[41]

Increasingly it seems that the people of the banlieues are considered by
mainstream French society as a threat, in so far as they are seen as living in
"their own Muslim world ... courtesy of local mosques and satellite television
beamed in from North Africa and Saudi Arabia".[42] The issue for the French
National Front is ostensibly to what extent these transborder communication
patterns prevent migrant families from becoming fully assimilated into French
culture – or rather, allow them to maintain a separate and independent cultural
identity. Certainly, there is a marked difference in the extent of take-up of
satellite television between migrant households and the general population in
France. A 1995 Eutelsat survey indicated that while only 4 per cent of the
general population of France subscribed to satellite television, 21 per cent of
Arabic-speaking households had subscribed to these channels.[43] More recent
figures indicate that while the general level of satellite penetration in France
has increased to 20 per cent of households, the figure for Arabic-speaking
households has now increased to almost 50 per cent, a striking difference
which clearly represents a burgeoning form of cultural division within
France.[44]

The Arab-speaking migrant population of France is heavily concentrated in
the outlying, poor suburbs (banlieues) situated on the edges of the larger
French cities. As is well attested, rates of unemployment (especially among
young people), poverty and other indicators of social exclusion are extremely
high in these areas.[45] The impoverished quality of life in these banlieues has
been given strong fictional expression in the *beur* literature, such as Mehdi
Charef's novel *Tea in the Harem,*[46] and in film, by Mathieu Kassovitz's *La
Haine* (1995) which offers a graphic representation of the impoverished lives
of young, second-generation Arab-speaking migrants living in the run-down
banlieues outside Paris.[47]

Whereas in most of Britain (though not in Scotland and the North) and the USA, the poor districts in which migrant families live are often situated in the inner city, in France the social isolation of these poor districts and their separation from the host community which surrounds them is further intensified by their being placed in geographically peripheral areas. These outlying districts characteristically have very poor transport connections. In this context, these physical transport links to the city, besides their practical function, also take on an important symbolic dimension. Thus, when North African young people in the banlieues outside Lille (living in the *quartiers difficiles* – the sink suburbs) rioted in the autumn of 1997, the *Independent*'s reporter John Lichfield reported that they chose the buses which linked their suburbs to the city centre as the particular symbolic target of their rage. One of the neighbourhood commentators interviewed by Lichfield suggested that "what you have [here] with the younger kids is a collapse of all sense of citizenship. They live from day to day, to survive. They're attacking buses because there's nothing much else left." Another interviewee suggested that one might say that, in fact, these young people were quite rational in attacking the only means of transport that might take them to the city because, after all, there is little point in them going into town – "they know that, even if they could afford to go to a nightclub in town, they wouldn't be allowed in". However Rabah Aliout, a French–Algerian social worker interviewed by Lichfield, perhaps grasps the symbolic significance of the attacks on the buses most accurately. As he put it:

> If you live at the end of the bus route, the bus becomes a symbol of the life, and wealth of the city which you can't afford to enjoy. Even if you have the fare ... you have no money to do the things, or buy the things the city offers ... Attacking buses becomes the symbol of the rage of the kids in the *banlieues*.[48]

In a similar way, in the autumn of 1995 in Strasbourg local unemployed youth from the city's outlying banlieues firebombed one of the new trams which the city's socialist local authority had just installed in order to provide a lifeline which would reduce both the practical and symbolic distance between the deprived estates and the city. At a time and in a region where the National Front was very strong – and the city's attempt to tackle the problem of racism thus all the more notable – the attack on the trams clearly signalled the depth of the despair of those whom they had been designed to serve.[49] A clear echo of this phenomenon can be found in the events in Bolton, in the UK, in December 1996, when thirty-seven buses were destroyed, in the words of the Chairman of the local Bus Users' Society, "by the calculated, if perverse action of people incensed at being robbed of their mobility by the withdrawal of all bus services over the Christmas holidays", in what he described as "a cry of protest from those who see their enforced immobility as yet another symptom of society's accelerating bias against the poor".[50]

The fundamental economic processes which drive the poor away from areas of affluence are put simply by Worpole in his comments on the parallels with changing patterns in the retail trade: "only high-turnover retailers can afford to be in the town centre and other services and facilities have been forced to the perimeter, where rents and land are cheaper. These forces combine to deter the 'low-value' user from the town centre".[51] However, it is not simply a question of poverty. Although that is part of the issue, there is also a sense of psychic isolation that often pertains to the experience of peripheral or suburban life – especially for the young. As the British rock musician Brett Anderson recounted of his own teenage years: "being born on the outskirts of London, being able to peer in but not quite see what's going on, is a really tantalising experience".[52]

Incarceration in the banlieues

As a result of their physical separation, Mary Dejevsky notes

> in big French cities such as Paris and Lyon, it is possible for the city-dwellers never to have anything to do with the *banlieues*, or those who live in them, and vice versa. There is a "comfortable France" and an "uncomfortable France" and the paths of the two need never cross.[53]

Kristin Ross argues that the building of the Péripherique motorway around the outskirts of the city of Paris between 1956 and 1972, as a key part of the city's adaptation to the coming of the automobile, was central to the process through which the isolation of the banlieues was constructed. As she puts it, the Péripherique:

> replaced the old fortifications with a kind of permeable wall of traffic that, for the Parisian inhabiting and working within the charmed inner circle, made the ... *banlieues* seem some formless magma, a desert of 10 million inhabitants and grey, undifferentiated constructions, a circular Purgatory cordoned off, with Paris – Paradise – in the middle. From the perspective within ... the suburbs were, and remain, that vague terrain "out there" ... a purely provisional space of transient populations, a makeshift world.[54]

Historically, the area to the north of Paris where the now most run-down banlieues exist was "where they buried the rubbish and dead horses from Paris".[55] At a later stage it was the site of the "dirty industries" considered undesirable inside the walls of Paris and of the homes of those who worked in them. Nowadays, with the collapse of those rustbelt industries, it is simply the zone of the unemployed and excluded, stranded without work, prospects or transport in the Great Beyond outside the city. At each historical stage, the difference between those within and without the city limits has been clearly marked and "living on different sides of the constraining line, the Parisians and the others had reason to feel different from each other". Francois Maspero notes ironically that the logical consequence of the fact that the banlieu estates were built on the cheapest land is that "only two things [are] missing ... work nearby and public transport".[56] Nowadays, an area like this is "no longer a town, even a very poor one but a simple storage zone" for surplus labour – a place, in Bauman's terms, of incarceration for the unwanted poor.[57] These are "pieces of badly stuck together space", places made only for travelling through (preferably by car) where nobody stops who doesn't have to. The prison-like, static world of the estates is literally bordered by the parallel world of perpetual motion of the motorways. As Maspero writes of one such estate: "The *3,000* [estate] was out of the way, with no train or metro. Far from ... everything else. The motorway cut it off like a ditch from nearby neighbourhoods, from nearby estates, from the rest of the world".[58] The overall result is

> an urban planning policy which has shut up the most destitute people far from town centres, though all the while subjecting them to the torment of Tantalus thanks to the RER [the rapid transport train from the suburbs to central Paris] which leaves them twenty minutes away from the attractions of consumer society like Les Halles.[59]

Just as it is difficult to get from Dakar to Cairo without travelling via Paris, so Maspero and his photographer companion Anaik Frantz discovered on their research tour that things really get tough when you try to travel between outlying areas. The hardest journey to make is to get laterally from one part of the banlieues to another without going into central Paris, changing trains and coming back out. Moreover, if you are without a car (as, of course, are many of the banlieues' poor inhabitants) life is very constrained. What would have once been long but viable journeys on foot (in the absence of other modes of transport) are literally made impassable, as Maspero and Frantz discovered on their sojourn, as old footpaths are now blocked off by motorways and fences.

If the estates are an area of effective incarceration for those who live there, this is not only a matter of physical but also of symbolic and emotional forms of containment. The problem with the estates, according to Akim, one of the young people of the *beur* generation who Maspero interviews, is that

> they don't let go of you easily: they're shut in on themselves, they offer a territory, a form of security. There are kids growing up on the Auber estate who have never really searched for other horizons. Even Paris exists only for the odd excursion.

Moreover, as he says, it's hard to "try going out of the estate when its reputation sticks to you". Even for Akim, whose perspective is quite worldly by comparison to the lives of the younger kids of whom he speaks, the estates slightly to the north of his own are "Zulu country", and when he is working in a nearby area he still likes to go back to his own estate for lunch, saying, "as soon as I see the sign for Aubervilliers I feel better – I'm home".[60] The world of the estates is a heavily localised world – and directions are hard to come by for strangers. Many people seem to only know the name of their own tower block, or only know their own route from the house to the station, supermarket or school, without knowing the way to anywhere else. From here, the metropolitan city seems very far away.

In Britain, the nearest equivalent to the French banlieues and their problems are the poor estates on the edges of some northern cities, of which Beatrix Campbell has written in her study of what she calls "Britain's dangerous places".[61] Like their French counterparts, these estates are effectively cut off from the centre of the cities on whose edge they perch. Inadequate transport, prohibitive bus fares and high local unemployment mean that their inhabitants are in effect quarantined in a miasma of economic and cultural deprivation and high criminality. As she observes, in the early 1990s the symbolic location of criminality and of problems of social order was seen to shift from the "frisson of chaos and cosmopolitanism in the inner city ... to the edge of the city, archipelago, out there, anywhere" – to estates such as Meadowell on Tyneside, in the impoverished North East – now envisaged as "a thrown away place, imagined as akin to Botany Bay, a place to which folks had been transported".[62] When these impoverished estates, riven with unemployment, crime, drugs and dereliction erupted in riots in 1991,

> the stars of the riots were boys, lads who rarely travelled more than a mile or so from home ... hopeless terrestrials, who didn't talk much ... [who] were suddenly globalised [and] became international icons, seen on television screens from Toulouse to Tokyo. They achieved not just Andy Warhol's fifteen minutes of fame, but a fortnight of it.

Their briefly mediated global fame could, of course, be re-wound for further local display – for they "preserved their activities on home-made videos of stolen cars doing pirouettes around suburban streets".[63] If they themselves remained locked out, on the outskirts of the city, nonetheless they perhaps felt at least their own images had now travelled, if briefly, from the poor estates to which they remained confined.

Territorial symbols

Kevin Robins and I have commented elsewhere on the symbolic significance of the decision taken by Mme Edith Cresson, when Trade Minister in the early 1990s, that all Japanese electrical goods imported into France were to be required to pass through the inland customs port at Poitiers, as a protectionist device to slow down the import of foreign goods into France. The hidden point is that Poitiers was the site in 732 of the battle at which the French king, Charles Martel, defeated the invading Arab armies marching up from Spain, and saved France from Arab domination.[64] These national symbols are remarkably hardwearing over time, as Joanna Helcké reports in her study of French viewers' interpretations of a fictional television series featuring a number of Arab immigrants, *La Composition Française*. In one scene in the programme, a little Arab boy asks his uncle the name of the famous French leader who defeated the Arabs at Poitiers. His uncle says that he does not know the answer, as when he arrived in France he didn't come through Poitiers.[65] The respondents in the study considered this to be an ignorant answer, attributable to either the uncle's lack of (French) schooling or to his "cultural difference". To not know the dominant symbolic meanings of the nation's geographical places and spaces is, it seems, to fail to achieve full cultural citizenship.

In this respect, as Hargreaves observes in his study of French media, "during the 1990s a new social space has been delineated in France: that of the *banlieues*. A term that once served simply to denote peripheral parts of the urban areas has become a synonym of alterity, deviance and disadvantage", so that the word "banlieue" signifies "first and foremost, a concentration of urban problems rather than (simply) a peripherally located place" – a space of "criminality" and "foreignness". By virtue of the French media's exaggerated and stereotyped reporting of events in these areas, their actual difference from the natural, mythical space of France proper[66] is even further exaggerated. Thus, as Hargreaves puts it, "a newspaper reader taking the 'banlieues' tag at face value might well conclude that poor, criminally inclined people of immigrant origin are threatening to take over the whole of the country's major cities".[67] The parallel with Hall *et al.*'s analysis in *Policing the Crisis* of the British media's role in the consumption of "race" as central to the problem of social and cultural "disorder" in the UK is clear:

> In lieu of explanation and analysis, the media offer "descriptive" conglomerates in which, through repetition and contiguity, each component comes to signify the others, in an endlessly circular process. Thus, people of immigrant origin live in run-down, dangerous areas because they are poor; because they are poor, they commit crimes; because people of immigrant origin commit crimes, normal law-abiding citizens do not want to live near them; because of this, the *banlieues* are ethically alien places which are fundamentally threatening to the social order.[68]

Just as Mayhew and other social reformers investigated the poor East End of nineteenth-century London as if it were an outpost of the Empire, from this "space of difference" the French media then report the exotic news brought back by their intrepid explorer/reporters from their "*Voyage(s) dans les cités barbares*" as if they were bringing back news from another planet.[69]

162

Geographies and genres of representation

As I have indicated, my principal interest is in the articulation of these physical and cultural divisions with their mediation in electronic form. In their work on various forms of participation in and exclusion from public space in contemporary Britain, Greenhalgh and Worpole make a good case for the need to connect up the debates about the media as a public sphere (discussed earlier in Chapter 5), with discussions in urban studies.[70] At different points, physical and virtual public spheres can function, in effect, either as complements or as substitutes for each other. In the example which Worpole gives from Liverpool, he notes that naive dreams of multicultural urban spaces aside, in fact,

> It is still the case that few young black people come into Liverpool city centre as a rule; their most important form of public space and time is Toxteth Community Radio ... which gives them freedom of the airwaves to play the music they like, discuss the issues of importance to their community and directly address their peers.[71]

However, for Greenhalgh and Worpole, the question of who is visible in and who is absent from which places is not only a matter of spatial divisions but also of time, and they argue that we have to attend to the question of how public space itself is timetabled. To take the crudest example, if for much of the day some areas of the professional districts of big cities are mainly populated by highly paid white men, at other times these same spaces are populated by armies of lowly paid women cleaners, many from ethnic minorities. As Saskia Sassen puts it, "the fact that at night a whole other, mostly immigrant workforce installs itself in these spaces ... and inscribes the space with a different culture (manual labour, often music, lunch breaks at midnight) is an invisible event".[72] In many places the people on the streets on their way to work at 5.30 a.m. are a very different group again from those whose travel to work at 8 a.m.; and a very different group from those (children, women, the old, the unemployed) who mainly populate those same streets during the day.[73] In her discussion of Marguerite Duras' film *Les Mains Négatives*, featuring black street sweepers in modern-day Paris, Christine Holmland reports Duras' own account of how she came to make this film about who is visible, when, in which parts of the city:

> I suddenly found myself at 7 a.m. in a colonial mass of humanity. There was an enormous number of blacks who were cleaning the sidewalks, the streets, the gutters. There were Portuguese cleaning women ... who came out of banks, cafes, and all these people, one knew, would disappear in the coming hour, to make way for us. This film is dedicated to that humanity which peoples the great cities of the occident in the morning.[74]

In a similar vein, in his novel *Moses Ascending*, the Caribbean writer Sam Selvon comments ironically on the time-schedule of the black Londoner's life:

> The alarms of all the black people in Britain are timed to ring before the rest of the population. It is their destiny to be up and about at the crack of dawn. In these days of pollution ... he is very lucky, for he can breathe the freshest air of the new day before anybody else ... He does not know how privileged he is to be in charge of the streets whilst the rest of Britain is still abed.[75]

It is perhaps useful, in this connection, to make an analogy between the geographical question of which social groups inhabit which physical spaces and the representational question of which groups inhabit which genres – or "virtual spaces" of representation in the media. In this respect, the timetable of visibility of different social groups in the city is analogous to the broadcast schedule. There are prime and marginal times and spaces in both contexts, and the question of which groups have access to and are represented within (or excluded from) them is a crucial one. Here we can profitably return to Hargreaves' work on migrant communities in France. In his analysis of the representation of immigrants on French television, Hargreaves observes that just as, physically, immigrants tend to be confined to locations such as the poor, outlying banlieues, so they are on the whole only visible within particular media genres. His analysis demonstrates that, on French television, members of ethnic minority groups are principally represented as "problems" of one sort or another – in news or current affairs – and even in those genres, of course,

> they occupy a very disadvantaged position in the hierarchy of media power structures ... Even when they appear on screen, they do so largely in silent and often marginal roles ... [and are rarely] given the opportunity of giving their own point of view in their own words.

Moreover, by contrast, they feature in "none of the intimate relationships seen in French-made programmes of 'ordinary life' (soaps, sitcoms. etc.) and ... are largely excluded from areas of inter-personal conviviality, such as game shows and drama programmes of a non-transgressive nature". Centrally, Hargreaves' point is that, because of their confinement to "problem" genres and their exclusion from light entertainment (and, on the whole, from television advertising), ethnic minority and immigrant groups "are simply not represented as part of everyday life". To this extent, Hargreaves claims, "French broadcasters reinforce popular perceptions whereby these groups are seen as fundamentally alien, rather than as ordinary people".[76]

To this extent it seems that French broadcasting still replicates the pattern of racist representation identified by Husband in the UK in the 1970s, whereby non-whites rarely appeared in the media except as negative stereotypes, and rarely appeared as ordinary members of the public, either in interviews, news stories or fictional dramas.[77] If the situation in the UK has improved to some extent since then, especially since the launch of Channel Four, it clearly remains an issue of concern, as the critical comments by ethnic minority viewers quoted earlier indicate.[78] As noted in that discussion, Trevor Phillips' insistence on showing a black studio audience on screen in the *Black on Black* programme was an important move in the (literal) politics of racial representation in Britain. To take another example, the crucial importance of these simple forms of inclusion, representation and visibility for ethnic minority families is graphically portrayed in the scene in Meera Syal's autobiographical novel *Anita and Me* where she recounts that, as a child of Indian parents growing up in the UK in the 1960s, her impression was that:

> According to the newspapers and television we simply did not exist. If a brown or black face ever did appear on television, it stopped us all in our tracks "Daljit! Quick!" Papa would call, and we would all crowd round and coo over the walk-on in some detective series, some long-suffering actor in a gaudy costume with a "goodness-gracious-me" accent ... and welcome them into our home like a long-lost relative.[79]

This is no mere matter of historical record. In her 1999 report on this issue, Sreberny reports, as we have seen, that her ethnic minority respondents still feel that when they are represented on screen it is even now all too often only as part of a "social problem".[80]

Beyond the Orientalist image

It is useful to set the findings of Hargreaves' study of actual satellite viewing patterns among ethnic communities in France in the general context of Appadurai's concept of ethnoscapes – diasporic identities "spread over vast and irregular spaces, as groups move, yet stay linked to one another through sophisticated media capabilities".[81] Hargreaves' empirical investigations reveal a far more complex picture than one in which these migrant families simply bind themselves into a common cultural space, centred on their "home" country, and remove themselves entirely from Gallic culture. Here again we see the importance of integrating macro and micro perspective on these issues, as advocated in Chapter 1, so that generalisations about (in this case) migrants' usage of the media can be grounded in an understanding of their domestic consumption practices. Hargreaves' study shows that these immigrant families' viewing habits are, in fact, less dominated than might be imagined by programmes from Islamic countries. There are significant differences between first-generation migrant families and their offspring, with only the former being much interested in religious programming on these satellite channels. There are also significant gender divisions in these families – some first-generation immigrant women with a poor command of French being particularly keen on having Arabic channels available.[82] These patterns are also replicated to some extent among ethnic minorities in the UK, as demonstrated by Sreberny's study. She also reports that older and female viewers may prefer satellite channels for linguistic reasons. As one of her interviewees puts it, "my aunt doesn't know English and she just watches Zee TV all the time". That study also reports a tendency by the older generation of Asian viewers to maintain their links to what they still think of as their home country, and thus their cultural identity, through their use of satellite. As one young respondent explains, "our parents like [Zee TV] because it's the closest thing they've got ... it's cultural contact with India, keeping that cultural thing".[83]

The main motivation for first-generation migrants, in Hargreaves' study, in getting satellite channels was often the simple one of wanting to "see more of what was going on in their home country".[84] However, in generational terms, it seemed that viewing patterns were often heavily divided within any given migrant family. Hargreaves found a very common pattern in which, while the main television set, in the living room with a satellite feed, would be dominated by the adults (and especially the man of the house), the children would frequently report a preference for watching French television channels on the sets in their bedrooms. Even more strikingly, when the children did get access to the set with a satellite feed, it seemed that their viewing preferences were for MTV, TNT and CNN rather than Arabic channels. As Hargreaves concludes:

> When second generation minority ethnic viewers tune into French stations, they participate in popular forms of entertainment and information that increasingly transcend the narrow boundaries of France. To the extent that this represents a challenge to conservative conceptions of French national identity, it points in a very different direction from the nostalgic longing of their parents for images of their country of origin. Instead, young minority ethnic viewers join, to a very large extent, those of majority ethnic origin in embracing popular cultural forms which are at root more American with a French accent than Maghrebi or Turkish.[85]

The situation in France at the time of Hargreaves' study showed some contrast with the situation in the UK given fictional portrayal by Hanif Kureishi in his story "My son the fanatic", where a group of British Asian teenagers are portrayed as reaffirming a radical Islamic identity which they see their parents' generation having lost.[86] By contrast, the predominant pattern among Hargreaves' respondents was one in which there seemed to be a steady intergenerational erosion of Islamic beliefs and practices, with the younger generations expressing little interest, for example, in religious programming made available by satellite, as compared to their parents. However, in the absence of recognition by French culture, in more recent years some at least of these young people have increasingly felt forced back on an Islamic identity, for lack of any other cultural alternative.[87]

Hargreaves makes plain that many children of Maghrebi immigrants, just as much as those of French descent, have "assimilated elements of both black Atlantic and white American culture through the US-dominated mass media ... [which] are now *de facto* parts of the culture of France". Indeed, he makes plain that, for many members of the gang cultures in the banlieues, "while physically confined to small localities within particular banlieues, in their signifying practices they are part of a global post-colonial culture ... situated somewhere between Manhattan, Dakar and Saint Denis". As he observes, members of these groups construct new forms of ethnicity based on shared linguistic and cultural codes and identifications with both geographical and symbolic territories. These are by no means simply a straightforward continuation of their parents' ethnic traditions, as they "owe far more to the youth cultures of France and the Black Atlantic, with which they interface through the mass media".[88]

German Turks? *Ausländer* and others

Just as in France, in Germany too there has been considerable anxiety in recent years about the perceived "cultural withdrawal" of immigrant populations into satellite television – in this case into the separate audio-visual space now offered by Turkish-language satellite television stations. This withdrawal has, in some cases, been taken to constitute an index of the essential "foreignness" of these immigrants and to constitute evidence of a culpable lack of willingness, on their part, to integrate into German culture and society.[89] However, based on his research on the media and cultural practices of the Turkish diaspora population in Europe, Kevin Robins argues that the question is not an "either/or" of whether immigrants have withdrawn into their own cultural space or are assimilated into the host culture.[90] Rather, he argues, the question is one of how these migrants are not so much caught between two worlds as engaged in constructing various forms of hybrid identities which enable them to participate simultaneously in both. From this perspective, the question is how, for different members of different parts of these migrant communities, it is possible for them to engage in a new kind of "commuting migration" (between German and Turkish virtual and geographical spaces) which allows them to be both assimilated *and* withdrawn at different times, in relation to different topics and issues.[91]

According to Ayse Caglar,

> the persistent presence of Turkey in migrants' lives in Germany has to do more with their quest for social mobility than their 'traditionalism', the immobility of their "belonging" to Turkey, or the question of whether they will in reality return to Turkey.[92]

Drawing on Bourdieu's analysis of "rates of exchange" between different forms of capital (social, cultural and economic) in different spheres, Caglar argues that the crucial issue is that, however much economic capital Turks may gain in Germany, it is almost impossible for them to convert it into social or cultural capital there. Given the greater ease of converting their monetary wealth into social status in Turkey, it follows that Turkey – as a symbolic space of display of their achievements – remains crucial in these migrants' lives, even if they physically visit the country only for a few weeks a year, and even if their much-planned return there is often endlessly delayed. Given the resistance of German society to recognising them in the terms they would wish, it is in Turkey that they must seek such recognition, even if as nouveau-riche *Almançis* they also encounter substantial social resentment on their visits "back home".

The availability of satellite television has the fundamental effect of synchronising cultural experiences across large distances.[93] In the case under discussion here, it is undoubtedly true that the availability of satellite stations allows migrant populations a crucial sense of synchronisation, from day to day, with events in Turkey itself and throughout their diaspora (as indicated earlier by my comments on the role of MED-TV for the Kurdish diaspora). However, new technologies such as satellite not only disrupt national boundaries as containers of cultural experience. They also help to constitute new, transnational spaces of experience – in this case, the transnational space of a Turkish diaspora which stretches beyond Germany, right across Europe. New technologies such as the Internet are also often recruited to consolidate the institutional foundations of this diasporic culture. Thus there is now an increasingly important Muslim marriage agency operating by website and email right across Europe. As we have seen, if sometimes these new technologies are disruptive of tradition, they are also often simultaneously colonised by their users to consolidate and reinforce traditional patterns (in this case, that of arranged marriage) in new forms.[94]

Differences of gender and generation are always crucial here. As noted earlier, in relation to the discussion of immigrant communities in the UK and in France, the greater tendency for first-generation immigrant women to be confined to the house, and their consequently less developed skills in the language of their host culture, often leads to them being particularly attracted to satellite broadcasting in their language of cultural origin. Moreover, there are significant differences by generation among the immigrant communities in Germany, and there is some evidence of younger second- and third-generation Turks taking, in response to the hostility which they perceive as surrounding them, if anything an increasingly militant Turkish-nationalist stance in their self-identification.[95] Beyond questions of gender and generation, there are, of course, further very substantial differences within the population of Turkish origin in Germany – not least between Sunni and other Muslims; between Turks and Kurds; and between Turkish families established in Germany since the 1960s and recently arrived rural Turks from Anatolia – all of which must be taken into account, rather than subsuming all these different sub-groups into some Orientalised group: "the Turks".[96] As Ruth Mandel puts it:

urban Turks from Western Turkey often feel little if any kinship with their poorer rural compatriots. Worse yet, from the perspective of some, are the Kurds from Eastern Anatolia, who they regard as little better than primitive. The self-designated "westernised" urban Turks often feel shame and resentment towards their "backwards" compatriots, who, they say, give all Turks "even well-integrated, modern ones" a bad name.[97]

At one time, the predominant term in use to denote Germany's "foreigner problem" was that of *Gastarbeiter*. Over time, that term largely disappeared from both official and popular discourse and the key formulation became the opposition between Germans and *Ausländer* – with the latter largely functioning as a synonym for Turkish. In more recent times, the further distinction has increasingly been made between the *Ausländer* and the *Asylanter* (asylum seekers) with the latter group often most vilified (and not infrequently, physically attacked). As Mandel notes, it has become increasingly apparent that now, in the discourse of foreignness in Germany, there are several different classes of outsiders – especially after the problems of German reunification:

> On the one hand, the Turks are more "foreign" than the Germans of the eastern "new states", yet in many cases the Turks are much better integrated into the (West) German social and economic structures. Consequently, they have become victimised, as they serve as targets for the anger, frustration and violence of some desperate (East) Germans ... The Turks in Berlin have a saying ... "When the Wall came down, it fell on us".[98]

According to Mandel, many members of different immigrant groups reproduce the Germans' own hierarchically ordered scheme of degrees of "foreignness", in which Christian European *Gastarbeiter* are at the top and those drawn from nationalities held to be at the furthest cultural distance from Germany (such as the Turks) are at the bottom. The most ironic situation, it would seem, is reserved for Greek immigrants. Mandel notes that "in Greece the most salient Other has nearly always been the Turk, to the extent that Greekness is often conceived of in direct opposition to imagined and feared Turkishness". However, in Germany the "labels, treatment and concept of *Ausländer* and 'Turk' are frequently used synonymously and interchangeably" – so that, to their dismay, Greeks are often mistaken for and called "Turks".[99] The irony here concerns the extent to which, historically, the Germans' own construction of their racial purity as Aryans was founded on a very particular reading of Greek history and of their own supposedly privileged relation to the traditions of classical Greece – as the guarantee of Germany's claim to represent the true inheritance of European culture. That the actual citizens of Greece should nonetheless be indistinguishable from the lowly Turks in the eyes of the

German population only goes to show both the extent of the possible disjuncture between patterns of migration and structures of cultural representation, and the extent of the cultural burdens and fears which are often projected on to the figure of the migrant.[100]

We shall return to these questions of who does and does not belong in Europe in Chapter 11. However, having now considered sedentarist, urban and suburban patterns of life, alongside questions of mobility and migrancy and in relation to modes of media representation and consumption, it is time to address the question of postmodern geography in more general terms.

8

POSTMODERN, VIRTUAL AND CYBERNETIC GEOGRAPHIES

Virtual geographies

As long ago as 1913 we find Marinetti observing that

> An ordinary man can in a day's time travel by train from a little dead town of empty squares, where the sun, the dust and the wind amuse themselves in silence, to a capital city bristling with lights, gestures and street cries. By reading a newspaper the inhabitant of a mountain village can tremble each day with anxiety, following insurrection in China [and] the heroic dog-sleds of the polar explorers. The timid, sedentary inhabitant of any provincial town can indulge in the intoxi-cation of danger by going to the cinema and watching a great hunt in the Congo ... Then back in his bourgeois bed he can enjoy the distant expressive voice of a Caruso or Burzio.[1]

Rolf Arnheim argued in 1933 that "television turns out to be related to the motor car and to the aeroplane – as a means of transport for the mind".[2] Earlier discussions of what television would mean, in the British trade press, had explored many of the same arguments. Thus, one commentator, Shaw Desmond, writing in the trade journal *Television* in September 1929 on "How television will kill time", put it like this:

> what the motor car was to the horse, and the aeroplane to the motor car, the "televison" will be to the aeroplane ... and to the world ... For it is television that is going to wipe out space and above all, time. In the world of the future, time as such will have no existence. We will no longer reckon our little lives by watches and clocks, but by events.[3]

By 1944 J.B. Priestley was optimistically arguing that the new forms of travel and communication which had emerged in the twentieth century would trans-form national identifications and forms of government.[4]

Nowadays images abound of our new disembedded status, within the virtual geography of postmodernity: from Marshall McLuhan and Quentin Fiore's declaration that time has ceased and space has vanished, in the global village, to Giddens' assertion that "time–space convergence has brought individuals and families into the presence of places that were previously unknown".[5] Paul Virilio asserts, perhaps somewhat overdramatically, that "with the interfacing of computer terminals and video monitors, distinctions of here and there no longer mean anything", and he heralds the advent of a final generation of "vehicles" that have "nothing in common with those associated with the revolution of transport". He argues that if the late nineteenth century and early twentieth century experienced the dynamic vehicles of the railroad, the street and then the air, then the end of this century seems to herald "the next vehicle, substitute for the change of physical location, and extension of domestic inertia". These vehicles, he argues, are "less a vector of change in physical location" than they are a

> means of representation, the channel for an increasingly rapid optical effect of the surrounding space. The more or less distant vision of our travels thereby gradually recedes behind the arrival at the destination, a general arrival of images, of information that henceforth stands for our constant change of location.[6]

It was Marx who first spoke of the role of communications technologies (in both their physical and symbolic senses) in effecting what he called the "annihilation of space by time".[7] Precisely to the extent that capitalism "by its very nature, drives beyond every spatial barrier", it comes to depend increasingly on the exchange of goods over longer and longer distances compared with earlier economic systems, where much trade was local. To that very same extent, the communications system, which was but a peripheral phenomenon within feudal society, comes to have a central place within the development of capitalism. As Yves de la Haye notes, these communicative links "create the basis for the dissolution of the narrow limits of the local community".[8]

Nowadays it is not just the limits of the local community which are undermined by communications technologies, but also those of the home – which is now a nodal point in a complex flow of people, goods and messages. In this context, Margaret Morse speaks of the freeway, the mall and the television as "non-spaces of privatised mobility" which constitute a continuous elsewhere of "experience and representation ... which inhabits the everyday". Following Williams, Morse explores the paradox of mass culture and social isolation – the "increasing functional isolation and spatial segmentation of individuals and families into private worlds which are then mediated into larger and larger entities by new forms of communication". Her argument is that not only have "mass circulation media constituted the nation as a symbolic system of common associations", but that these spaces constitute an interlocking functional system. If television circulates the images of commodified desire to be found in the mall, the mall itself is "television you can walk around in" and the freeway is the ultimate home of the subjectivity of mobile privatisation. Thus, she argues, "just as television is the main source of shared images … there is a 'national weather' within the enclosed spaces of mall and home and auto – the even temperature of the comfort zone".[9] She speaks of "the growing dominance of a differently constituted kind of space … an *elsewhere* which inhabits the everyday" (original emphasis) and she argues that freeways, shopping malls and television share a number of critical features. They are not, in her terms, truly places, but rather constitute a kind of in-between zone of "non-space" characterised by the inculcation of a distracted state of mind on the part of the driver/shopper/viewer. For Morse, then, "the practices of driving, shopping and television viewing are dreams become habit" in which we navigate the "non-space of privatised mobility".[10]

(Non) place, home and identity

These radical transformations in the geography of our lives pose substantial problems for established academic disciplines. Thus Marc Augé notes that, traditionally, anthropology has always dealt with the "here and now". Direct observation of the culture of a discrete physical setting (e.g. a village, treated as a metonym for a whole culture) has long been the discipline's primary methodology. The difficulty, nowadays, he argues, is that "an increasing proportion of humanity lives, at least part of the time, outside territory" in the "non-places" (the airport lounge, the motorway, the housing estate, the supermarket) which characterise, for him, the era of "supermodernity".[11] In hyperbolic spirit, J.G. Ballard claims that "the great airports are already suburbs of an invisible world capital, a virtual metropolis whose faubourgs are named Heathrow, Kennedy, Charles de Gaulle, Nagoya; a centripetal city whose population forever circles its notional centre".[12]

According to Augé we are in an era characterised by an "overabundance of events" (constantly brought to our attention by the media) and by an "excess of space" – in so far as the era is characterised by profound changes of scale. Not only have rapid means of transport brought any capital within a few hours' travel of any other but now, more even than in the time of which Marinetti spoke, "in the privacy of our homes … images relayed by satellites can give us an instant, sometimes simultaneous vision of an event taking place on the other side of the planet". By these means, we are inserted into universes (or cosmologies) of recognition, totalities which are nonetheless effective for being partly fictional, in which the small screen establishes a familiarity between the ordinary viewer and the actors of big-scale history "whose profiles become as well known to us as those of soap-opera heroes and international artistic or sporting stars … we may not know them personally, but we recognise them". To this extent, Augé argues, we have to abandon the traditional anthropological approach, with its focus on "the idea of a culture localised in time and space" as inappropriate to our era, with its changes of scale and parameter.[13] Thus we must also abandon that "indigenous" fantasy of a closed world founded once and for all, long ago (and perhaps it always was, in part, a fantasy): the fantasy of each ethnic group living in isolation, on its own separate territorial island.

As Augé notes, traditionally, anthropological place is a "principle of meaning for the people who live in it, and also a principle of intelligibility for the person who observes it". It is formed by "complicities of language, local references, the unformulated rules of living know-how". These are places invested with meaning – places of identity, of relations, of history – in which "place of birth is a constituent of individual identity" and the inhabitants do not so much make history as live in it.[14] "Place", then, marks the materialised idea of the relations that its inhabitants have with each other, with their ancestors and with outsiders of various sorts (expressed physically in community halls, graveyards and monuments to the battles fought against the enemy). By contrast, Augé argues, because supermodernity finds its full expression in non-places, in this era people are both always and never "at home", in the traditional sense.

Bifocal visions and telesthesia

Nowadays, as Gupta and Ferguson argue, our "point of view on even the most local of happenings may be as much formed by the mass media as by immediate sensory perception, because the ... media ... form a constitutive part of the experience of face-to face communities".[15] Thus, in his discussion of contemporary forms of cosmopolitanism, Dick Hebdige argues that, while many descriptions of postmodern time–space compression may seem overblown, it is clear that many people are caught up in networks that extend far beyond their neighbourhood or locality. To that extent, he claims, many forms of what he characterises as "mundane cosmopolitanism" are part of ordinary experience. For some immigrant peoples, this amounts to being forced to be "proletarian cosmopolitans, cosmopolitans in spite of themselves".[16] However, even for sedentary majority populations, one does not have to be "design conscious, educated, well-off or adventurous" to be a "world traveller" at the level of cultural consumption, for, as Hebdige notes, "if we don't choose to go and visit other cultures they come and visit us as images and information on television, as snatches of world music or Italian opera heard on the radio, as Indian or Chinese 'take-away' meals".[17]

According to John Durham Peters, the contemporary media provide us with a form of "bifocal vision", in which our immediate sense impressions of our local world are often undercut by media representation of global events. It is not simply that the role of place as a "container" of experience wanes as global forces enter the most local of terrains. As Peters puts it, "the irony is that the general becomes clear through representation, whereas the immediate is subject to the fragmenting effects of our limited experience", and "the local environment is often seen fleetingly, whereas global events – war in Iraq, pollution in Eastern Europe ... are portrayed as coherent, if often violently foreshortened visions for our gaze" by the newly powerful media at our disposal.[18] The central point, he argues, is that, in our mediated world, the "age old limits of locality and truth" are now broken and "local knowledge … is constantly discredited as a guide to living in the modern world – for being too concrete, too mired in immediacy" compared with what the available media can tell us.[19]

What then does it mean to be "at home" in a landscape of this sort? Here we might return to Vincent Descombes' definition of a "rhetorical country": the place where a person feels at home – in the sense that there they are able, by virtue of a shared rhetoric, to make themselves (relatively) easily understood and to understand others.[20] As Augé notes, the paradox of the cosmology of supermodernity is that this sense of a familiar rhetorical territory is now, for many people, supplied globally by the stable forms of international consumer culture. Thus,

> a foreigner lost in a country he does not know (a "passing stranger") can feel at home there only in the anonymity of motorways, service stations, big stores or hotel chains. For him, an [international] oil company logo is a reassuring landmark; among the supermarket shelves he falls with relief … on products validated by multinational brand names.[21]

In his account of the impact of reunification on East German cities, Ulrich Mai rightly stresses the importance of naming in the socialisation process through which people learn to symbolically appropriate their environment. Correspondingly, as he observes, when the old familiar place names are transformed (and as strange new symbols and cultural forms invade all spheres of life, as they have in East Germany in recent years) people often come to feel undermined, as if they were now strangers in what has been their home.[22] Here Mai also locates one possible source of the new surge of racism and attacks on foreigners witnessed recently in East Germany: as he puts it, what we see here is a process in which "those who themselves are made strangers at home … seek to improve their status by rigidly ascribing the quality of strangeness to the weakest" – i.e. foreign workers and asylum seekers.[23]

For McKenzie Wark, nowadays in the emerging "virtual communities, unanchored in locality", which are made possible by the "ever more flexible matrix of media vectors criss-crossing the globe", "we no longer have roots, we have aerials" and "we no longer have origins, we have terminals".[24] Wark acknowledges that, of course, we still physically exist in our familiar terrain but also now, simultaneously "in another terrain, equally familiar: the terrain created by the television, the telephone, the telecommunications networks criss-crossing the globe". These technologies offer a new kind of experience, which Wark defines as that of "telesthesia" – perception at a distance. This, he says, is our "virtual geography" – the experience of which "generally permeates our experience of the space we experience first hand". In Wark's view this virtual geography is no more or less real than that of rivers and mountains, but is rather a different kind of perception, not bounded by proximity, and involves the "expanded terrain from which experience may be instantly drawn" via the media which offer us access to an "instantaneous global dialogue in a virtual narrative space".[25]

However, it may be as well to exercise some caution here. In her critique of the overblown claims of McLuhan, Meyrowitz *et al.*, Marjorie Ferguson argues that while, of course, it must be acknowledged that new communications technologies are producing new definitions of time, space and community, these are not necessarily erasing but rather overlaying our old understandings of distance and duration.[26] Neither is it a matter of physical geography somehow ceasing to exist, or ceasing to matter. It is rather a question of how physical and symbolic networks become entwined around each other. At a very material level, Peter Wollen notes, the network of "global cities" identified by Saskia Sassen exists not only in a virtual mode, but simultaneously functions as "agglomerations of new service industries, as communications centres and as magnets, to which immigrant workers cross, in reverse, the bridges built to their ex-homelands by migrating capital".[27]

This insistence on the material dimensions of the globalisation process is crucial. If the trope of mobility in general (and of air travel as an exemplary instance) is central to accounts of globalisation, and if, as Augé and Rosler argue, the airport itself is one of the emblematic non-places of supermodernity, we must recognise nonetheless that it too is part of a very local world – for some particular categories of people. First, as Tomlinson points out in his critique of Augé's own account of Roissy Airport, there is still the "entirely different experience of Roissy that belongs to its more permanent denizens – the check-in clerks, baggage-handlers, cleaners, caterers [and] security staff ... who work there". Moreover, "pressed hard up against the perimeter fence of the airfield" are the homes of the poor who have no part in the world of "connexity" which the airport is seen to symbolise. Paradoxically, as Maspero and Frantz report, it is very hard for those living in the immediate vicinity of the airport to get anywhere at all, as the only transport facilities around are those designed for the benefit of the international travellers on their way between the airport and the city.[28] Other forms of what Augé designates as non-places, such as supermarkets, can, in fact, also be places where social relations are re-embedded. Thus for example, a British lesbian woman interviewed in Bell and Valentine's study of shopping habits reports that

> It's funny going to Sainsbury's ... I never go there without seeing a lot of dykes ... which is nice! And people you haven't seen for ages, so you ... end up ... what was going to be ... twenty minutes nipping in and getting a few things ... you end up chatting to people ... I do enjoy that.[29]

Clearly, generalisations about de-territorialisation, disembedding and nomadology as dimensions of some undifferentiated postmodern experience must be handled with great care.

Mediated strangers

Our analysis here is concerned with the movement of both people, goods and information.[30] In his review of Robert Sack's analysis of the ways in which the consumption of mass-produced goods transforms the contemporary experience of the highly industrialised societies, Joshua Meyrowitz argues that historical transformations in the dominant mode of communication have resulted in an important corresponding transformation in our modes of experience of alterity. In Meyrowitz's view, although traditional societies exhibited an awareness of a "vast mysterious external world filled with faceless others" which functioned as the boundary to reinforce the limits of the known world, in practice strangers were not, on the whole, often encountered in everyday life.[31] His argument is that with the development of modern urban, literate societies, there was an increasing degree of contact with (and more explicit awareness of) various forms of alterity, so that it became much more common to have at least some degree of interaction with (or various forms of more precise knowledge about) strangers from different social worlds. Furthermore, he argues that under the conditions of contemporary postmodernity, increased mobility (both physical and virtual) means that people frequently

> travel through or "inhabit" electronic settings and landscapes that are no longer fully defined by the walls of a house, neighbourhood blocks or other physical boundaries … strangers become partial neighbours in a "19-inch neighbourhood" of shared mass-mediated communications and mass-produced products.[32]

In a more sociological account of changes in contemporary patterns of residence, Graham Allan also notes that the social conditions which in the past created tightly knit networks of relationships with particular localities no longer exist in contemporary neighbourhoods. As he puts it:

> as geography has become less constraining with the development of more effective transport systems … many people come to rely less and less on those who live in the locality … Neighbours usually do not work together; they are not related through kinship; they often did not grow up in the same area; they have separate social networks and different leisure interests. What they share is a common locality, but for many this does not mean that they have any need to be embedded in a set of local relationships. The neighbourhood is just a place to live.[33]

In the end, Meyrowitz's overall scheme of historical development is perhaps too much of a broad-brush picture, relying on an overly simplistic and Eur-Amcentric set of (de-spatialised) periodisations, and is too close for comfort to technological determinism in the explanatory weight it gives to changes in modes of communication. Nonetheless, and despite the substantial force of these qualifications, his attempt to make these links between questions of residence, mobility and communication in the production of our contemporary definitions and experiences of alterity is a commendable one. Thus, in relation to the role of the telephone and computer technology in the construction of "psychological neighbourhoods", he points to the extent to which it no longer makes sense to conceive of community so much in terms of locality but rather in terms of the networks of social relationships, whether local or distant, directly experienced or mediated, which we knit together to construct a sense of "personal community". As Wurtzel and Turner put it, the extended family is now in many cases "strung out on the telephone wires", and in this context the social role of the telephone is "not only as a means of immediate interaction but of what might be called imminent connectedness" so that the primary psychological function of the medium is "the maintenance of symbolic proximity".[34] In relation to this idea of "imminent" connection, Meyrowitz also notes that the mere knowledge of the existence of the "shared arena" of national broadcasting functions in many ways "like the knowledge of the existence of the 'family home', where relatives can ... gather at times of crisis or celebration. It does not have to be used everyday to have constant presence."[35]

Certainly all of this has profound implications for how we must conceive of the home. As Meyrowitz notes, as the social functions of physical location become fuzzier, "the family home ... is now a less bounded and unique environment".[36] If communications technologies are simultaneously both potential exits from and entrances to our intimate living spaces then, as Tomlinson observes, the corollary of our increased ability to keep in touch with others via these technologies is that we are more constantly "on duty" as communicational agents. As Meyrowitz observes, "constant availability" to others (especially for many professionals, whose mobile phone functions much as the electronic tag on the prisoner under home surveillance) is increasingly the tacit norm and to be "out of touch" (once upon a time, not to have a phone – now, not to have a mobile phone) is increasingly seen as abnormal or even a form of misanthropy, or at least unco-operativeness.[37]

Centrally, Meyrowitz's argument is that our contemporary experience of alterity is a result of a dual transformation, in which relationships based on physical contiguity decline in importance, so that neighbours become more like strangers at the same time that electronic media continually bring news of "foreign" people and lands into our lives and homes. Meyrowitz's portrait of this situation, in which we are increasingly familiar via the media, in a superficial sense, with various forms of alterity while simultaneously alienated from immediate community, carries clear echoes of Heidegger's famous question, when he asks:

when any incident whatsoever, regardless of when and where it occurs, can be communicated to the rest of the world at any desired speed; when the assassination of a King in France and a Symphony in Tokyo can be "experienced" simultaneously; when time has ceased to be anything other than velocity, instantaneity and simultaneity, and time as history has vanished from the lives of all peoples ... through all this turmoil a question still haunts us like a spectre: What for? Whither? What then?[38]

In a closely related observation, Raymond Williams commented that the central issue is one of the relationship between distance, familiarity and alienation. As he put it:

The central claim of television is that it can show us distant events. The hybrid name selects this quality, following telescope, telegraph, telephone, telepathy – with "tele" as the combining form, from the Greek for "afar" ... Yet in most everyday television, distance, in any real sense is not the leading factor. We are in one place, usually at home, watching something in another place: at variable distances, which however do not ordinarily matter, since the technology closes the gap to a familiar connection ... [The] argument that now needs to be stated, with a patience determined by its urgency, is about the culture of distance, the latent culture of alienation.[39]

It is to this issue of the "culture of distance" that we must now turn.

Fellowmen, compatriots and contemporaries

Anders Johansen, from whom I take my sub-heading in this section, offers a cogent analysis of the role of communications media in the construction of our sense of the space of contemporaneity, in the "expanding now" of the broadcast world.[40] Drawing on the work of the anthropologist Johannes Fabian on time and alterity and on that of the philosopher Alfred Schutz on the "structure of the life world", Johansen offers a useful reformulation of Meyrowitz's schema of the relationship between modes of social organisation, models of communication and the perception of alterity.[41] Ultimately, Johansen's concern is with the role of the modern media in widening the circle of our potential "consociates" and in combating what Fabian has called the "denial of coevalness" to others. Johansen starts from the proposition that, in the "generalised now" of the media's "news world", a far larger variety of strangers are encountered (if in a mediated form) than the members of a traditional community ever came across.[42]

In Schutz's schema of the life world, the core area consists of that within my actual reach, "which I ... can have direct perception [of] ... without the aid of

instruments.. which acts upon me immediately and upon which I can act".[43]
For Schutz, this is the *Umwelt*, populated by my immediate "consociates" and
"fellowmen", and around this is the *Mitwelt* – the world of contemporaries who
"coexist with me in time without … being with me in reciprocal spatial reach" –
although various communication mechanisms enable me to feel my mediated
togetherness with them as a form a shared experience of living through a
common present time. As Johansen argues, in societies relying exclusively on
oral communication, the world of one's consociates is restricted to one's immediate neighbours, who one meets and talks with, so that the "now" of
communication equates with the "here" of a specific, narrowly bounded place.
For such people,

> the perceived horizon of the world is also the horizon of the present –
> which has the same limits as the "space of life", so that the dimensions
> of time and space are not differentiated, and equally, the history of the
> kinship group is fastened to its territory.[44]

In such a situation, in a society exclusively dependent on oral communication, in which there is no sense of time separate from space, it is impossible to
conceive of remote strangers as consociates: their very distance in space allocates
them to a correspondingly different status in time. Conversely, the introduction
of broadcasting into such closed rural societies is described by Peter Narvaez as
constituting a bewildering destabilisation of this "contractionist" world view,
limited by known places. These new media foster an expansionist involvement
in a quite different sense of a "spatially continuous world" of various places
existing simultaneously.[45]

In most cosmologies, if more explicitly in those of earlier historical periods,
the here and now, as Johansen observes, is surrounded by regions of increasing
remoteness, pastness and strangeness, so that those far away are often perceived
as not really human. Thus, "the periphery, seen from any point of orientation is
barbarous and, at the limit, fantastically harmonious or (more probably)
chaotic". We must beware, notes Johansen, that "in the informal cosmologies
of everyday life" the "West" is still synonymous with the present and its future.
Correspondingly, the South and the East still often are taken to "represent the
crudeness and helplessness, or the virtuous simplicity and mysterious wisdom of
some earlier stage of development".[46]

The time of the Other

Just as the ancient Greeks defined barbarian tribes as both "chronologically
anterior … [and] spatially marginal", Zia Sardar *et al.* note that, historically, the
cosmology of the West has worked on the model of a concentric set of circles,
with Athens, Rome or some other European capital at the centre, and the
degrees of primitivity or barbarousness of others increasing as one moves out

through the peripheries.[47] The culture of the civilisation at the centre defines the idea of human nature against which the various degrees of wildness, barbarity and savagery of its Others is measured. However, it is a matter not only of spatial but also of temporal difference. The people of the "primitive" peripheries have also been defined as living in the time of Europe's past – as people "without history", marooned statically in a pre-modern age, which Europe itself has transcended, while the West lives in a future which the Other has still to enter.[48] It is, of course, on this basis that, as Fabian puts it, the Now of the primitive is placed in the Then of the Western Adult, and the familiar equation is drawn between primitives, lunatics and children – as all equidistant from mature Western Adulthood.[49]

In his pathbreaking analysis of the role of anthropology as a "time machine", which has functioned to provide temporal distance between itself and its objects of study, Fabian argued that the key issue is the way in which what he calls "coevalness" (or co-presence in time), the sense of the "common, active 'occupation' or sharing of time", has been denied to the objects of anthropological analysis. In this respect, he argues, what we see is "a persistent and systematic tendency to place the referent(s) of anthropology in a time other than the present". In all of this, Fabian notes, anthropology has effectively provided the West with a political cosmology in which We are "here and now" and They are "there and then", according to a system of co-ordinates emanating from the Western Centre in which other societies "may be plotted in terms of relative distance from the [Western] present".[50]

Sadly, this point is of more than merely historical interest. Olu Oguibe argues that, even today, the condition of the visibility of the work of many African artists in the West is a process of "neo-primitivising" in which they are introduced "as circus-animals, curiosities from the Dark Continent".[51] Their "primitiveness" or naivety (and their habitation outside the West, which makes it possible for them to be "discovered") is in fact still the condition of their entry to the prestigious spaces of the Western Art World. In this, their coevality with the West is denied: the main interest of their work is, in effect, deemed to be the insight that it offers into the workings of the primitive mind of some (supposedly, in the West at least) distant era. The geographical distance of their peripheral location from the West's centre stands as some analogy for their temporal distance, as marked from the time of Western contemporaneity. In a similar vein, in his discussion of Australian Aboriginal art, Gordon Bennett notes that Aborigines

> are manufactured in ontological ... terms as an essence which exists in binary opposition to non-Aborigines and which is not subject to historical change ... [and] are ... recast as the living embodiment of the "childhood of humanity", that which is the evidence of the progress of history and of Western culture.[52]

181

At one point Fabian poses the question as to "what would happen to the West ... if its temporal fortress were suddenly invaded by the Time of the Other".[53] In this connection, in his comments on the mutual inscription of our geographical and temporal schemas, Naoki Sakai notes that the West is a temporal concept just as much as the past is a geographical one.[54] Drawing on Sakai's work, Robins and I have attempted to explore the significance of the panic and destabilisation which occurred in the West in the period in the early 1990s when Japan and, later, other South East Asian economies looked set to dethrone the West from its dominant position in the global economy.[55] At least for the period before the economic crash of these economics in the mid-1990s, which was the occasion of so much Western *schadenfreude*, one of the major traumas for Western commentators arose from the potential of these economic developments to rewrite the traditional temporal schema which Fabian and others have described. If, in short, the possibility arose that They might be *more* modern (or even postmodern) than Us, then it followed that, for the first time, it might be They who represented Our future, rather than vice versa. In such contexts, as Appadurai notes, the complexities of contemporary global flows "play havoc with the hegemony of Eurochronology".[56]

Robins and I have noted elsewhere the importance of Wilk's analysis of the role of satellite television as an "instrument of global time".[57] If Wilk's analysis is perhaps overoptimistic in its estimation of the potential effects of satellite communications, he is nonetheless right to identify it as in principle working to overcome the segregation of time zones of previous eras. If, given the largely one-way nature of its programming flows, satellite television does not represent the invasion of the West by the time of the Other, as envisaged by Fabian, it certainly allows a variety of others to participate on more coeval terms in the representational time of the West. [58]

Screening the Other

Various forms of electronic communication, from the telegraph onwards, have had the effect of creating a greater sense of such coevalness, in so far as they produce a wider sense of a shared present across geographical space through a sense of broadcast liveness as a form of fellowship. This entails an awareness of having been among those who have listened to and seen broadcast events together, and of passing together through the events which are, in Hayden White's terms, the "content" of a given historical time.[59] As Johansen observes, if going to the movies is like passing into a dream world apart from ordinary existence, the common location of the television set, in the very centre of the home, profoundly integrates televisual experience into the time of everyday life. As a result of this, via television's transmission into the home, the coevalness of alterity is more strongly established than ever before, as that which is far away is made to feel both very much "here" – right in our sitting rooms – and precisely "now". As he notes, one does not in any sense need to share McLuhan's naively

Saint-Simonian view that enhanced technical means of communication necessarily lead to consensus or mutual understanding, in order to recognise that the new electronic media make faraway others appear increasingly coeval with Us in a much more interconnected way than in any previous historical period.

However, against any easy presumptions concerning the mediated production of coevalness, Nigel Thrift, drawing on Adam Smith's ideas concerning the "geography of sympathy", poses the question of place and distance as a moral problem, in relation to the question of whether distance in space may weaken our capacity for sympathy for others. On Thrift's argument, even if the modern media make other places and peoples seem less distant, we may still care less for others the further away they seem to be, whether in geographical or cultural terms.[60] It is worth recalling here Zygmunt Bauman's argument that the very idea of that which is near is commonly associated with the familiar and reassuring world of unreflexive and unproblematic habit, a place where one seldom feels at a loss or uncertain how to act. The far away, by contrast, often connotes a space of anxiety and hesitation, in so far as it is a world where

> things happen which one cannot anticipate or comprehend and would not know how to react to once they occurred: a space containing things one knows little about, from which one does not expect much, and regarding which one does not feel obliged to care.

As Bauman argues, as a result of the typical mode of the representation of these distant others to us via the mass media, the people of this faraway world are often closely associated with a world of trouble – of social and natural disasters, murders, epidemics and the breakdown of social order. Thus, as Bauman ironically observes, on the basis of their media representations it is as if "given their monstrosity, one cannot but thank God for making them what they are – the *far away* locals, and pray that they stay that way".[61]

In the context of the global media's role in increasing our knowledge of faraway places, John Thompson argues that via these media we

> find ourselves drawn into issues and social relations which extend well beyond the locales of our everyday lives ... not only ... observers of distant others and events, but also ... involved with them in some way ... [We] are called on to form a view about, even to assume some responsibility for, issues and events which take place in distant parts of an interconnected world.[62]

However, as Robins and I have argued elsewhere, if the media present these distant places to us, they simultaneously "screen" them from us, in so far as the method of presentation inevitably distances us from the images we see.[63] As Jonathan Miller noted in his early critique of Marshall McLuhan, the fact the "television screen reduces all images to the same visual quality" and that "atrocity and entertainment alternate with one another on the same rectangle of bulging glass", along with the fact that "the viewer sits watching them all in the drab comfort of his own home, cut off from the pain, heat and smell of what is actually going on", serves to distance the viewers from what they see. As Miller observes, this can easily mean that they fall into the "unconscious belief that the events which happen on television are going on in some unbelievably remote theatre of human activity", so that the medium tends to act as a cordon sanitaire, emotionally insulating us from the very events that it shows.[64]

As Robins notes in his comments on Regis Debray's analysis of the contemporary media, these technologies of seeing allow us to maintain a considerable distance from what we see and thus to acquire an anaesthetised form of knowledge. The viewer thus achieves a certain detachment and remoteness from what is seen, and the significance of what they see is often, as Robins puts it, "derealised" as the screen insulates the viewer from the bombardment of experience. Thus even if, at times, television has "opened hearts and minds to suffering and oppression that was previously invisible and in so doing … created a … global public opinion with some influence in the world", nonetheless, more often, as viewers, in the end it allows us to "magically control our position *vis-à-vis* the world and its spectacles … to maintain a distance, never becoming actors in it".[65]

The geography of sympathy

In his discussion of the extent to which "our social and technological capacities to extend relations across distance" have "outstripped our moral/imaginative capacity to live our lives in regard to … all the distant others with whom we have necessarily become connected", John Tomlinson offers a critical reading of both Robins' and my own positions on these issues. In his view, we rely too much on an outmoded "morality of proximity" which presumes that Adam Smith's "geography of sympathy" (which determines how far afield our moral concerns can run) still applies in our contemporary mediated world.[66] I would accept the force of Tomlinson's critique to the extent that I would not want to unproblematically valorise a traditional conception of local face-to-face communications over mediated ones. As Tomlinson notes, Iris Marion Young and Doreen Massey have both taken issue with the tendency to romanticise the notion of the traditional community concentrated in contiguous space and characterised by immediate face-to-face communication. To unproblematically privilege physical co-presence and immediacy over mediation in that way may be to labour under what Young defines as the metaphysical illusion of the possibility of the unmediated co-presence of subjects to each other. As Young notes, "even a face-to-face relation between two people is mediated by voice and gesture, spacing and temporality", and, as Massey puts it, we must recognise that the "place called home was never an unmediated experience". To that extent there are no good grounds for considering face-to-face relations as some pure realm against which to counterpose relations mediated across time and distance as thereby inauthentic.[67] However, one can accept that point while still recognising that there are very significant differences between encounters mediated by communications technologies of varying degrees of complexity and immediacy.[68]

Drawing on the work of John Thompson, Tomlinson concedes that although technology brings representations of distant events right into our living rooms, they do remain "for the most part ... distant from the practical contexts of daily life" and it is usually hard to see how we could conceivably engage with or intervene meaningfully in these events, beyond calling the Freephone number given by the television to contribute to charity appeals.[69] While Tomlinson himself (like Johansen quoted earlier) argues an optimistic case for the potential capacity of television to produce meaningful forms of planetary consciousness (in relation, for example, to ecological issues), I am inclined to the more pessimistic conclusion that majority audiences in the "cultures of contentment" of the affluent West are mainly interested in their own local affairs, not least because of their feelings of impotence to affect events in the wider world.[70] It is not only a question of distance (whether physical, moral or emotional), but also of power.

The regime of the fictive "We"

In his classic analysis of how national television news makes itself pleasurable for its audience, Robert Stam argues that one of the keys to understanding this puzzle lies in television's capacity to allow us to share the literal time of people who are physically elsewhere. Thus, he argues, what television provides crucially for "His or Her Majesty the Spectator" are the voyeuristic satisfactions of seeming omniscience and instantaneous ubiquity.[71] To this extent television offers a prosthetic extension of human perception, "granting an exhilarating sense of visual power to its virtually 'all-perceiving' spectator, stretched to the limit in the pure act of watching". In Stam's argument, television news flatters its "armchair imperialist viewers" into adopting a subject position as "the audio-visual masters of the world", and the "guarantee" which television offers them is the "illusionary feeling of presentness, this constructed impression of total immediacy", which, in Stam's point of view constitutes "a televisual metaphysics of presence". Moreover, and centrally for the purposes of my argument, Stam notes that the sense of community thus promoted by national television news (what he calls the "regime of the fictive We") is premised on the simultaneous construction of its excluded Outside. As he notes, if the mutually flattering implicit dialogue between newscaster and spectator constructs a strong sense of shared community, this fictive We can not only "then speak warmly about 'Ourselves' but also speak correspondingly coldly about whoever is posited as Them".[72]

If, in John Ellis' well-worn phrase, domestic television is the "private life of the nation-state", this is nowhere more so than in the realm of daytime television, characterised as it is by a tone of syrupy intimacy, in-jokes and gags apparently shared by people who all seem to be on familiar first-name terms.[73] Thomas Elsaesser has argued that the best starting point for the analysis of how ideas of national identity and belonging are addressed on and through television would be to pay attention to how its programming is attuned to "locality, language, the conjugation of the day, the seasons and the generations".[74] What national audiences want – and mainly get, according to Elsaesser – is "the familiar – familiar sights, familiar faces, familiar voices … television that respects and knows who they are, where they are and what time it is". As Johansen puts it, broadcasting plays a crucial role in supplying the members of a modern nation with "a stock of tacit knowledge that foreigners do not even suspect, constituting implicit premises, and a sounding board of commutations for conversations among countrymen".[75] Daytime television is then perhaps, par excellence, the world of Stam's fictive We, even if its ambivalent relation (of horror and fascination) with the world of alterity means that its bread-and-butter topics are increasingly drawn, for our edification, from the realm of the Freak Show or the Cabinet of Curiosities. Against this backdrop, one sees all the more clearly the significance of the tendencies of nation-states (and thus of national broadcasting systems) to draw lines between friends and enemies, so that in their representations, the recalcitrant elements in our midst (such as the stranger) are seen to pose a major problem. However, we have thus far only considered the role of communications in reconfiguring the virtual geography of our world in relation to print and broadcasting technologies. It is now time to turn to the question of computer technologies and their effects in the reconstitution of our ideas of place and community.

The boundaries of cyberspace: access to the Net

A number of commentators have taken a somewhat utopian view of the possibilities offered by computing technologies for the transcendence of all forms of spatial and social limitation in the realm of cyberspace. Ideologists of the Internet argue in their wilder moments that in this global village there is no such thing as abroad, and that home is wherever your Internet feed is. However, even John Perry Barlow, an early Net enthusiast, raises the sociological question of what (or who) is missing from cyberspace.[76] Among the notable absences he lists, besides that of women, are "old people, poor people, the blind … the illiterate and the continent of Africa". As he notes, "there is not much human diversity in cyberspace which is … [still largely] populated by white males under 50 with plenty of computer terminal time, great typing skills and strongly held opinions". For all the talk of the global on-line community, and despite the fact that the Net is undoubtedly now used by all kinds of minority and oppositional groups from the Zapatistas to the Digital Diaspora network, statistically the Internet is still American dominated and is still perhaps best described (despite these important exceptions) as the "YanquiNet".[77]

Against the sociologically naïve fantasies of the ideologists of the Internet, Julian Stallabrass suggests that the socially self-selecting exclusiveness of the Net has, in fact, been crucial to its success. Thus, he suggests that "until very recently, many of the advantages of networking were derived from its very exclusiveness: it was open only to people who had access to a computer and a modem, and using them was quite a technical matter".[78] That is to say that the space of the Internet is in fact more socially homogenous than that of the physical world, because those who have access to it have already been selected by ethnicity, nationality, class and gender. Access to the Internet is not free – while certain privileged categories of people (such as students in universities and colleges and employees of various types of organisations in the affluent West) have free access through their institutions, for many others access to the Net remains an expensive luxury. Even in the affluent West, the better off are still much more likely to own a computer than the poor.[79] In the Third World, on the whole, only the affluent can afford Net access. As a result, as Ziauddin Sardar observes, "most of the people on the Internet are white, upper and middle-class Americans and Europeans and most of them are men".[80]

The effect of all this is evident in the statistics summarised by Victor Keegan, in his commentary on Net access, who reported in 1997 that "96 per cent of all Internet sites are located within the rich 27-nation OECD area ... with English as its *lingua franca*".[81] Still in 1999 it was estimated that 80 per cent of the Internet was operated in English, a language spoken by only 10 per cent of the world's population. Ironically for a technology which has been lauded for its capacity to transcend geography, the Internet turns out to have a very real geography which replicates and reinforces existing patterns of social, economic and cultural division.[82] To take one example of this geography, Stephen Graham and Simon Marvin report that Manhattan has twice the "domain density" of Internet hosts as does the next most "net-rich" place in the USA (San Francisco) and six times the overall US average. As they go on to note, the disproportionate share of the Internet growth in these cities demonstrates that, rather than weakening the role of the city, "the activities of information-producing cities have been driving the growth of the Internet". In fact, as they observe, the urban dominance of the Internet in the USA has been growing in recent years.[83]

Far from the urban world being transcended by the new technologies of cyberspace, what we see is the emergence of complex combinations of tele-mediated and place-based exchanges, to which the city remains central. Growing flows of electronic information, Graham and Marvin suggest, may in fact require more face-to-face contact to make sense of them, and the reflexive management of electronic risk economy trading requires forms of trust which it seems are hard to sustain without such contact.[84] It is for these kinds of reasons that, for example, the MIT Media Lab continues to be situated in the heart of

Boston and, notwithstanding much talk of decentralisation, the British media industries continue to be centred in a few small areas of London, just as many commercial telecoms firms tend to locate themselves near the kind of concentrated hubs of transport and transactional opportunity that cities offer.[85] In these hub areas it is precisely the interweaving of physical, face-to-face and electronic connections and networks that is the key to their vibrancy. In this situation, rather than telecommunications substituting for other forms of contact, the different modes of connectivity feed off and fuel each other. So much for the capacity of the pure, clean realm of cyberspace to deliver us from the trials of the "polluted, contested finite city".[86]

Rhetorics of the technological sublime?[87]

As Robins notes in his survey of the commercial and political discourses through which the current communications revolution is being articulated, the prevailing tone is one of a striking optimism.[88] The pronouncements made about the beneficial possibilities of new communications technologies can perhaps usefully be seen as what James Carey has called, in his historical study of the hype surrounding previous technological breakthroughs in communications, a "rhetoric of the technological sublime".[89] This is a rhetoric which we would do well to treat with some caution. Thus, in a series of incisive articles, Robins has scrutinised the "politics of optimism" surrounding these new technologies, and their supposed capacity to usher in a post-geographical Eldorado of social harmony, unity and democracy.[90] As he points out, the naive optimism of the advocates of the communications revolution is ultimately a nostalgic and backward-looking perspective, premised on the belief that new technologies will somehow restore us to the world of friction-free *Gemeinschaft* we suppose ourselves to have lost. As Armand Mattelart has argued, this almost religious faith in the capacity of technical improvements in communications to somehow transcend (and even magically mend) social divisions goes right back to the utopian tradition of Saint-Simon.[91] It may well be that for those who can afford to use them, new communications technologies better enable people to "reach out to others", thus transcending the barriers of distance in a "post-geographical" world.[92] However, as it is not only distance that divides us, its transcendence can hardly be expected to necessarily unite those who are divided by more than geographical distance.

It is, as Robins and Webster remark, only within a vision "where geographical distance is presented as the fundamental obstacle to human communication and community" that the "achievement of technological proximity" could appear to be the solution. This is a world where the principal motivating desire is that to "achieve immersive, multisensory telepresence ... to 'make contact' across the world" and where the principal values are those of "immediate communication, 'connectivity' and being in touch". The difficulty, according to Robins and Webster, is that in this world of "presence at a distance" the system works to expel all that is uncertain, unknown and alien – all the qualities of otherness which may attach themselves to distance. Thus, in its simulation of immediacy, the virtual world functions merely as a form of "generalised and globalised intimacy" where "distance and its otherness is turned into illusory proximity and spurious affiliation".[93] Indeed there is a striking analogy between contemporary ideas of cyberspace and the Christian idea of heaven. As Margaret Wertheim puts it:

> Just as early Christians envisaged heaven as an idealised realm beyond the chaos and decay of the material world ... so today's champions of cyberspace hail it as a place where the self will be freed from the limitations of physical embodiment.[94]

In his critique of Barrie Sherman and Phil Judkins' eulogy to Virtual Reality, Robins argues that we must beware of the political implications of the ways in which the new communications technologies cater to our most regressive, narcissistic and solipsistic desires for illusory forms of empowerment.[95] He describes this "feverish belief" in transcendence – a faith that this time new technology will deliver us from the limitations and frustrations of this imperfect world – as ultimately no more than "the fag end of a Romantic sensibility" which now puts its faith in Virtual Reality "as an alternative reality in a world gone wrong".[96]

The further problem here concerns the downside of the new technologies' capacities to enable us to interact all the more easily with like-minded others in distant places. At the same time as they enable us to do this, they simultaneously entice us to withdraw from the noisy physical world of social division, conflict and difference by which we are surrounded. These new technologies can thus be argued to invite a solipsistic mode of retreat from the actual world where we must encounter a variety of others, with all the difficulties that entails, into a computer-space, where we are able to choose to interact only with those like us who share our interests and presuppositions.[97]

To the extent that many potentially troublesome others are screened out of cyberspace by the expense of the entry costs to its (effectively) gated communities, it can be argued that, on the whole, global on-line culture has largely become the international public sphere of the globally privileged, increasingly divorced from disadvantaged members of their own society, communicating mainly with each other. This process is replicated at many scales. Thus, it is often held that electronic communication has the principal facility of enabling communication across great geographical (if not social) distance. While it is true that email has this potential, recent research demonstrates that 60 per cent of all email traffic is in fact between people who work in the same building, so that the actual prime function of email is to further enhance and consolidate communication between people who are already in close contact with each other.[98] This only goes to further emphasise the exclusion of those who are outside the loop of the new technologies and their charms.[99]

Community lite and communitarianism

As I have argued, the attraction of the on-line monoculture of cyberspace and its elective communities is that they protect us from the need to engage with our actual "noisy neighbours" in a pluralist multi-cultural society.[100] Thus, Neil Postman argues that the word "community" on the Net "has exactly the opposite of the usual meaning – a community not of people of shared interests but people of different interests who have to negotiate with each other's interests to achieve harmony".[101] This is also the point of John Gray's critique of the fantasy of virtual community in which we imagine that "we can enjoy the benefits of community without its burdens, without the daily effort to keep delicate human connections intact" in actual places, where people "put down roots and are willing to put up with the burdens of living together".[102] As Ziauddin Sardar notes in his commentary on Gray's analysis,

> cyberspace provides an easy simulation for the sweaty hard work required for building real communities ... The essence of real community is its presumptive perpetuity – you have to worry about other people because they will always be there. In a cyberspace community you can shut people off at the click of a mouse and go elsewhere. One has therefore no responsibility of any kind.[103]

The fact that, in Gray's words, virtual community is "community at zero cost" in relation to the traditional constraints and responsibilities of community life is both its strength and its ultimate limitation. Notwithstanding Young's cautions, noted earlier, about the fact that even face-to-face communications are necessarily mediated by language and culture (rather than being the realm of some unproblematic authenticity), it does seem that in the case of communities in cyberspace, alongside the enhanced potential for relating to those at a distance (whose virtual presence can be "switched off" at will) we see a similarly enhanced (and ultimately disabling) tendency towards disengagement from the disturbing real presence of those others in the locality whose immediate presence can be so troubling.[104]

Robins and Webster note what they call a "strange affinity between virtual futurism and communitarian nostalgia", which both aspire to the transcending of all difference and alterity, so as to achieve the utopian state of a community "copresent" to itself without division. Following Young, they argue that the technoculture of Virtual Reality is but the latest expression of Rousseau's dream of "a transparent society, visible and legible in each of its parts, the dream of there no longer existing any zones of darkness ... zones of disorder".[105] In this vision the security of traditional small-town community is somehow to be transposed to the transnational scale of the global village, rewritten as a form of Disneyland of on-line communion, which is not so much "an alternative society, but an alternative to society."[106] Against this model, in which technology supplies the balm to overcome social disorder, Robins' argument is that we should eschew the "illusion of consensus and unanimity" and develop a perspective that recognises difference and conflict as integral to democratic culture. According to him, there is an elective affinity between virtual technologies and communitarianism, such that in an Edenic Mythology "the illusion of transparency and consensus sustains the Communitarian myth, now imagined at the scale of global electronic *Gemeinschaft*".[107]

The problem is that this kind of idealisation of community involves, as Young notes, the fundamental denial of difference, and represents a naive "urge to see persons in unity with one another in a shared whole".[108] In this context, Robins argues, what we see is the space of virtual community imagined as a compensatory one of order, refuge and withdrawal from the experiences of difference, asymmetry and conflict which are the necessarily constitutive features of actual social life. In the end, as Chantal Mouffe rightly proposes, we must reject the illusory idealisation of some undifferentiated communal experience, based on any presumption of shared interests, consensus and unanimity, in favour of an "agonistic pluralism" which recognises that "a healthy democratic process calls for a vibrant clash of political positions and an open conflict of interests".[109] This is to recognise that democratic culture is necessarily and properly founded on the differences and divisions within any given community. It is to conceive of democratic politics as founded in "a relationship of strangers who do not understand one another in a subjective and immediate sense relating across time and distance".[110] It is also to recognise that the principles of adversarial democracy, which itself involves "a coming together which can only occur in conflict", must be defended against any sentimental ideal of community as necessarily involving consensus, for, as Young puts it, "democracy is neither compromise between interests nor the formation of a common will. Its kind of dialogue is that of a divided community."[111] The question is how such a divided community is to understand itself and how its constituent parts are to come to terms with each other. We shall return to these issues in the concluding chapter, but having outlined some of the key debates about the virtual and cybernetic geographies of our contemporary world it is now time to consider in more detail the work of some of the other critics of simplistic visions of postmodern geography.

Postmodern geographies: a sceptical view

Against the hype of some models of postmodern globalisation, which suggest that all forms of mobility and connectivity are somehow exclusive to the twentieth century, there has been an understandable backlash on the part of scholars with a longer historical perspective, pointing out the existence of previous "world-systems" in earlier centuries and emphasising the extent of earlier forms of "connexity". In this respect Doreen Massey has made a series of critical interventions, aimed at what she sees as the current orthodoxies of postmodern geography.[112] In particular, her criticisms are aimed at the abstracted model of postmodernity as characterised by space–time compression and hypermobility, which is advanced by authors such as Fred Jameson, Ed Soja and David Harvey.[113] In essence, her argument is that the current orthodoxy offers too stark a binary contrast, in which an overly static model of the past is unhelpfully set against an overly frantic model of the present. In this orthodoxy, as she puts it, "an (idealised) notion of an era when places were (supposedly) inhabited by coherent and homogenous communities" is set against an image of de-stabilising postmodern fragmentation and disruption. Her point is that the "past was no more static than the present".[114] This is so, she argues, not least because "it has for long been the exception rather than the rule that place could simply be equated with community, and by that means provide a stable basis for identity", and because, certainly so far as Britain goes, "places have, for centuries been ... complex locations where numerous different and frequently conflicting communities intersected".[115] So much for the settled, homogenous communities of postmodern theory's romantic and nostalgic idyll.

In this connection, Clifford cites Amitav Ghosh's account of his first encounter as an ethnographer with the inhabitants of the Egyptian village which he had come to study, as one cautionary example:

> When I first came to that quiet corner of the Nile Delta I had expected to find, on that most ancient and most settled of soils a settled and restful people. I couldn't have been more wrong. The men of the village had all the busy restlessness of airline passengers in a transit lounge. Many of them had worked and travelled in the Sheikhdoms of the Persian Gulf, others had been in Libya and Jordan and Syria, some had been to the Yemen as soldiers, others to Saudi Arabia as pilgrims, a few had visited Europe: some of them had passports so thick they opened out like ink-blackened concertinas.[116]

As Clifford notes, this might give us the impression that this rural village had only recently been made over into an airline transit lounge, as if it were a specifically postmodern phenomenon of mobility and or rootless history. However, as Ghosh rapidly discovered:

> none of this was new: their grandparents and ancestors and relatives had travelled and migrated too ... because of wars and for money and jobs, or perhaps simply because they got tired of living in one place. You could read the history of this restlessness in the villagers' surnames: they had names which derived from cities in the Levant, from Turkey, from faraway towns in Nubia; it was as though people

had drifted here from every corner of the Middle East. The wanderlust of its founders had been ploughed into the soil of the village: it seemed to me sometimes that every man in it was a traveller.[117]

In a paper on the social and cultural organisation of mobility, Orvar Lofgren poses the question as to what exactly it is that is specific about the ways in which people, ideas and commodities move about today. By way of a framing device, he goes on to quote the observation made by François Deseine, as long ago as 1699, that "today the custom of travelling is so common that a man who has never left his country is held without esteem".[118] It seems that the very idea that "nowadays" we are living in an age of striking mobility, from which we can look back, by contrast, to the sedentary lives of earlier times is itself hardly new. In a similar vein, Lofgren is elsewhere highly sceptical of the tendency to construct a dramatised image of de-territorialised, displaced, rootless Postmodern Man against a mythical backdrop of a stable past in which identities were clearly fixed, rooted and located in space.[119] He is particularly sceptical of sociological attempts such as that of Scott Lash and John Urry to argue that we have somehow moved from an era of place to one of "flow".[120] First, he notes, it is crucial to desegregate this "we" – and ask, more concretely where, how and for whom de-territorialisation is taking place. This is to reframe the question at stake, and to ask for whom is travel an adventure or a disaster? Who experiences new forms of hybridity as enriching or threatening? Clearly one possible contrast is between the privileged cosmopolitans increasingly de-linked from their nation of origin into an international world of business connections, as opposed to marginalised, poorer groups who may respond to the pressures of globalisation by "becoming even more national, regional or home-loving … [opting] for the safeness of place and ritual belonging, and in this nostalgia [becoming] both more inward-looking and more xenophic".[121]

Lofgren's central point is that we should not overstate the postmodern contrast with a mythical past. Drawing on Stephen Kern's work, Lofgren makes a strong case that, in contrast to previous times, the period between 1880 and 1920 was, if anything, a greater era of global migrancy, cultural transformation and hypermobility than is the present day.[122] In arguing for a longer historical perspective on these issues, Lofgren points out that these previous experiences of migrancy and de-territorialisation have much to teach us about our contemporary situation. Indeed, a similar case can be made in relation to contemporary rates of technological change. As Will Hutton has observed, "our great-grandparents had to deal with the change from the horse economy to the motorised world of the car, aeroplane and mass production – and our grandparents to the world of radio and television". As he remarks, besides all that, the development of the Internet, on which so much attention is focused, could in fact be argued to be relatively small beer, as much current technical progress is actually not so much about creating seismic changes in the way we live as upgrading and making more accessible the range of technology we already have, in one shape or another.[123]

On the whole I am very sympathetic to the critiques of the more overblown claims of those who announce the "end of geography". However, one should not underplay the significance of the transformations of the world's transport and communication systems that have taken place in the last century. Mobility may not have begun with postmodernity, and there is plenty of evidence that the past was not as settled a place as some postmodern theorists seem to imagine it to have been, but Tomlinson is surely right to observe that "globalisation does not have deep roots in the pre-modern world". As he points out, not only was it the case that in pre-modern times "the immediate concerns of locality took general precedence over those of connectivity", but also the

> very fact that "connectivity" for the pre-modern world was inevitably centred on the physical mobility of people – individual travellers (merchants ... pilgrims ...) as the embodied carriers of trade, information and cultural influence – was surely a major limitation on the degree and complexity of that connectivity.

Tomlinson's argument is that, in our concern to reject problematic traditional anthropological models of indigeneity, we should not simply rush to the opposite extreme of assuming that rates and degrees of mobility – and thus of the pertinence of locality as the horizon of experience – are unchanged as between modern and pre-modern times. As he rightly puts it, in earlier times locality "in the sense of the significance of local physical environments and climates, features of landscape, customs and practices, linguistic dialects, food culture, particular inflections of wider religious belief systems ... clearly did figure much larger" as a determinant of experience.[124]

The destabilisations of the postmodern period have certainly engendered a variety of defensive and reactionary responses: witness the rise of various forms of born-again nationalism, accompanied both by sentimentalised reconstructions of a variety of "authentic" localised "heritages" and by xenophobia directed at newcomers, foreigners or outsiders. Certainly, as Massey notes, in the face of these developments it has come to seem, to many critics, that any search for a sense of place must, of necessity, be reactionary. Massey rightly argues that this is not necessarily the case and that it is, in fact, possible, if we approach the question differently, "for a sense of place to be progressive; not self-enclosing and defensive, but outward-looking". This is to reject the notion that a sense of place must necessarily be constructed (à la Heritage Industry) out of "an introverted, inward-looking history, based on delving into the past for internalised origins".[125] As Neal Ascherson has noted, that way lie the inanities of phoney distinctiveness, façadism and the attempt to get the contemporary inhabitants of a particular town to "locate themselves by ... landmarks which they may never have seen: biscuits which their regional ancestors (allegedly) used to bake".[126] That way too lies fundamentalist absolutism, and the shadow of ethnic cleansing with its explicit demands for the purification of space. It is a way of thinking about space and identity which is premised on the association of spatial penetration with impurity, and in which any incoming elements (foreign immigrants, foreign commodities, foreign television programmes) are seen to represent matter out of place.

Against this kind of inward-looking definition of place and identity, Massey rightly argues for "a sense of place which is extroverted, which includes a consciousness of its links to the wider world", where what gives a place its identity is not its internalised history, but rather its uniqueness as a point of intersection in a wider network of relations. This is then not simply a bounded, self-contained sense of itself, constructed in antagonism to all that is outside (the threatening otherness of externality), but "an understanding of its 'character' which can only be constructed by linking that place to places beyond" and where it is the "particularity of linkage to that 'outside' which is ... part of what constitutes the place".[127] For her,

> place is constructed out of the melting and mixing of social relations ... This is not to say that the local is irrelevant: uniqueness is constructed (and reconstructed) by combinations of local characteristics with those wider social relations. Place is an articulation of that specific mix in social space–time.[128]

In a similar vein, Suzanne Moore has argued that what we call "local" is "more and more made up by that which comes from beyond its borders" and "what we call 'home' is increasingly defined by what is outside, not by what is within" – including inputs from all kinds of communication networks. " 'Home' is the place where we ingest all this information [or imported goods], all this 'foreignness'."[129] To this extent, different locals are made through a process of indigenisation of originally foreign materials.[130]

Massey's further criticisms of the orthodoxies of postmodern geography concern what she calls, first, the ethnocentricity of the idea that time–space compression is a new phenomenon, and second, "the politics of mobility and access".[131] In relation to the first issue, Massey's argument is that the predominant characterisation of time–space compression as distinctive of postmodernity is very much a Western, coloniser's view, in so far as the sense of dislocation, which those in the metropolitan West only now experience (as the cultures of the Third World are reimported via patterns of migration to London, Los Angeles or Paris) "must have been felt for centuries, though from a very different point of view, by colonised peoples all over the world". As she argues, the question is, "who is it in these times who feels dislocated/placeless/invaded? ... The assumption that this openness, this penetrability of boundaries is a recent phenomenon makes no sense from the point of view of [the] colonised periphery", for whom "the security of the boundaries of the place one called home must have dissolved long ago" in the wake of imperialism's conquests of other people's homes. For them it is perhaps "centuries since time and distance provided much protective insulation from the outside", as for many societies for whom modernity was encountered as irrupting from elsewhere into their indigenous temporality.[132]

The power geometry of "connexity"

The further issue concerns the level of abstraction at which the analysts of post-modernity consider the issue of time–space compression or connexity. The question Massey poses is a simple one: "Who is it that experiences it and how? Do we all benefit and suffer from it in the same way?"[133] For Massey, the politics of mobility and access centrally concern what she calls the "power-geometry" of these issues, in so far as different groups and individuals are placed very differently within the overall field of mobility. The question is, who moves and who doesn't, who has control of their movements and who doesn't? If we consider (voluntary) access to both physical mobility (transport) and information (via communication systems) as forms of cultural capital, then the question is that of the social distribution of access to these goods. As soon as we pose that question, we see that whether in terms of access to physical transport (possession of a car, for instance) or to communications systems (the ability to pay for a cable television subscription or to rent time on the Internet), access is heavily structured by class, by gender, by ethnicity and a whole range of other social factors. The idea that "we" somehow all experience the same form of postmodern nomadology then appears little more than a cruel nonsense. There are, then, many conditions of postmodernity, in so far as groups and individuals are "located in many different way in the new organisation of relations over time–space". This applies even within the First World. As Massey notes,

> amid the Ridley Scott images of world cities, the writing about skyscraper fortresses, the Baudrillard visions of hyperspace, much of life, for many people, still consists of waiting in a bus shelter with your shopping for a bus that never comes. Hardly a graphic illustration of time–space compression.[134]

Critiques of Francis Fukuyama's thesis of the "end of history" have rightly argued that we need to pose the question of whose history, exactly, is at an end and how it has got there.[135] In a similar vein, in relation to what she calls the "cybercelebratory" writings of William Mitchell et al., for whom the new technologies subvert the idea of geography as destiny, Ella Shohat argues that if we are now said to be facing the "end of geography", we might want to pose the question of whose geography is coming to an end. As she notes, while rich people "with access to the new multi-directional media cross oceans with a click ... immigrants and refugees ... who attempt to cross by boat, plane or foot are

bound by their homeland passports" or indeed by "their lack of any passport".[136]

As Zygmunt Bauman argues, we must recognise that distance "is a social
product: its length varies depending on the speed with which it may be overcome (and in a monetary economy) on the cost involved in the attainment of
that speed". The geophysical factors (mountains, deep rivers, etc.) which have
traditionally been taken to constitute the types of natural borders with which
geography has been concerned are, in fact, better understood as "merely the
conceptual derivatives, or the material sediments ... of 'speed limits' ... or ... of
the time and cost constraints imposed on freedom of movement".[137] Borders,
then, have always been, and remain, far from absolute. They are permeable for
those who possess the resources (financial or other) required to transcend them.
Despite his overly voluntaristic tone, Ballard captures something of the
dynamics in play in this situation when he argues that

> A mastery of the discontinuities of metropolitan life has always been
> essential to the successful urban dweller ... a failure to master these
> discontinuities ... leaves some ethnic groups at a disadvantage, forced
> into enclaves that seem to reconstitute mental maps of ancestral
> villages.[138]

For the poor, locality is often a restraining trap. As Tim Putnam puts it, "the
neighbourhood aspect of residence has been transformed to the extent that the
shared experience of work and home life within a local geographical area has
become a sign of social and economic marginality".[139]

While working-class communities in the advanced industrial West are often
homogenous with the spatial confines of a given neighbourhood, by contrast
higher-status groups characteristically

> construct and live in a very different kind of community, usually more
> diffusely defined, with a far wider spatial reach, and rarely coterminous
> with any spatially contiguous neighbourhood ... [which] in addition to
> the environs of the home may include the locale of a summer home ...
> miles away, the private school where the kids are sent, and a whole
> orbit of non-contiguous but habitually visited places.[140]

This pattern was well illustrated in the HICT study reported on earlier,
where we came across the case of a middle-class family with exactly this style of
life. Their inner-city metropolitan home was complemented by a holiday home
(complete with a boat) in a coastal town. The family's way of organising their
life and their conception of their household clearly spanned both these
geographical locations – and their lifestyle was carefully organised so that their
activities in each location served to complement those in the other. Indeed, they
understood the viability of their hectic, "open-door" city household, in which

they led very individualised lives, to be fundamentally premised on their corre-sponding capacity to retreat at other times, as a unit, to the quiet of their holiday home.

As we have seen, Massey's key argument is that some groups are more mobile than others and have more control over both their own and others' mobility – thus we can distinguish between those who are empowered by and those who are on the receiving end of the effects of time–space compression, and are effectively imprisoned by them. However, beyond this, she argues that the very mobility of the "jet-setters, the ones sending and receiving the faxes and the email, holding the international conference calls ... distributing the films, controlling the news, organising the investments and the international currency transactions", itself further undermines the remaining power and control over their lives of the already weak, so that "mobility and control over mobility both reflect and reinforce power".[141]

The vitality of a place, and its potential to renew itself is determined in large part by the richness of the networks of routes and people passing through it. As Liz Greenhalgh argues in her analysis of housing and social policy in the UK, access to a whole range of connections and services is a key form of socio-cultural capital which is very unevenly distributed. For those living in sink estates with little local employment, nothing but poor-quality run-down local shops, no car and with poor (or in some cases non-existent) public transport links to enable residents to get elsewhere, and in situations where those from elsewhere (from doctors to pizza delivery services) are reluctant to enter their territory, it is their very disconnection which is both most symbolic and, in practical terms, constitutive of their material poverty.[142]

Inequalities in access to connections of one sort or another are themselves a crucial factor in reinforcing social inequality. Thus "whilst elite groups are 'super-connected' to phone and IT networks at home, school, in their cars and at work even the ... telephone is an expensive luxury in many ... marginalised urban neighbourhoods".[143] As Graham and Marvin note, in poor inner-city areas in the UK telephone connections can still be as low as only 25 per cent. To take a very different kind of example, the relationship between material poverty and access to the symbolic realm is perhaps most dramatically captured in Celeste Olalquiaga's account of the situation of the residents of the area around the Sambodromo in Rio de Janeiro, where the annual carnival parade is now held. Tickets to the Sambodromo being well beyond the means of the poor, "the biggest paradox of this popular event can be found right outside the Sambodromo's walls, in the very poor neighbourhood whose inhabitants have to watch on TV the spectacle that develops only a few feet away from them".[144]

It is those who do not have connections – those without jobs, cars or phones "who remain attached to, perhaps really trapped within, their territorial communities. For the rest, the majority of city dwellers, the neighbourhood is only one of a number of communities of interest to which they belong".[145] For those who Susan George calls the "fast castes", their power is both reflected in and constituted by their control over greater speeds of motion and activity than enjoyed by most.[146] As Mark Kingwell puts it:

> extreme speeds are not available to most of us. They are the preserve of the elite who get to rise above the slow yet frenetic plodding of the urban lifescape. Sitting in traffic … watching the dollars count them-selves off in the red numerals of the taxi's meter, as helicopters take off from distant office buildings, I realise that speed is the ultimate luxury good.

Moreover, as he goes on to argue (if from within a particularly North American framework of reference and expectations):

> Time for reflection, the indispensable precondition of reading or any other "slow" activity, is possible only with the prior benefit of speed. Leisure time is a luxury good too – the flip side of being able to move fast when you want to … For most of us, precious moments … [of rest] are purchased only at the cost of long, harried hours on the expressway or waiting for connecting flights.[147]

The ultimate issue is not who moves or is still, but who has control – both over their connectivity, and over their capacity to withdraw and disconnect. It matters little whether the choice is exercised in favour of staying still or in favour of movement. The point is that while the poor have to put up with the unpredictability of what is, in many ways, an increasingly chaotic and unstable world, the rich are able to buy control over that chaos, so as to make their lives more manageable. Just as Mike Davis has argued that security is now a posi-tional good and that, in the USA, a person's social status is increasingly marked by the degree of their insulation in residential, travel, working and shopping environments, so likewise with differential access to desirable forms of mobility.[148] Thus the *Toronto Star* reported that the new Highway 407 scheme (advertised as involving "tolls but no jams") which will connect the airport to downtown Toronto, is designed to offer a "congestion free higher speed and lower travel time corridor" through a highly congested region, aimed at "firms operating just-in-time production methods who require high degrees of certainty in travel times for the movement of goods and services". As Graham and Marvin observe in their commentary on the scheme, those who can afford it will be able to literally buy their way out of the traffic jams, but it is a socially exclusionary scheme strictly "designed to meet the needs of large, international corporations and elite users prepared to pay the premium for increased certainty" in relation to travel and transport.[149] Conversely, according to Phil Cohen, the "Home Boy is the nationalist of the neighbourhood par excel-lence", whose macho aggressiveness in relation to the micro territory of his "hood" or turf has to be understood precisely in relation to the poverty of his options in relation to wider horizons. As Cohen notes, "most Home Boys stay at home because they have no jobs ... to go to".[150] The process of territorialisation, through which the "Home Boys" of a particular area "privatise" a public space by declaring it their exclusive preserve, can then be seen as a compensatory strategy for creating some semblance of autonomy among those who in fact control no private domestic space of their own, by virtue of their economic dependency.

Deterritorialisation is uneven in its effects, and as Tomlinson observes is not an experience "which only arrives at a certain threshold of socio-economic advantage, above which is a switch to the hyperspace of a cosmopolitan lifestyle and below which there is ... exclusion from the ... processes of globalisation". As he notes, one might fall into the mistake of seeing things that way if one were to equate globalisation entirely with the economic ability to buy into various technologies of communications. That remains an important consideration, but the use of such technologies is only part of what the more general process of "deterritorialisation" involves. As we have seen, deterritorialisation is nowadays associated with forms of mundane cosmopolitanism which are very widely distributed in the affluent West. Thus Massey points to the case of the "pensioner in a bed-sit in an inner city ... [in the UK] eating British working-class style fish and chips from a Chinese take-away, watching a US film on a Japanese TV" as an example of globalisation also affecting the relatively disadvantaged.[151] Indeed, Tomlinson observes that it is often "the poor and marginalised – for example those living in inner city areas – [who] often find themselves daily closest to some of the most turbulent transformations", while it is the affluent who can afford to retire to the rural backwaters of a preserved and stable locality. As he goes on to argue, disadvantage is not a matter of exclusion from the whole process of globalisation but rather a particular way of being positioned within it. Even the most socially marginalised groups, for whom locality is in a sense destiny, also experience deterritorialisation and the transformation of their locality, as the forces of globalisation intrude into it in a variety of forms.[152]

New geographies and differential mobilities

As Massey notes, beyond simple class differences in degrees of mobility, there are also important differences in its styles. The mobility of choice of the affluent British middle classes, conducted in relative ease, is, as she puts it, "quite different from the mobility of the international refugee or the unemployed migrant as a social experience".[153] However, as she goes on to explain, based on her analysis of a groups of middle-class hi-tech male scientists based at Cambridge University who live thoroughly "internationalised" and highly mobile working lives (communicating by email, fax and phone, travelling to international conferences, etc.) this type of mobility itself is often balanced by a strong commitment to a very settled form of residential localism. Massey observes that, at the end of their thoroughly globalised working days, a very high proportion of these men retreat to a home "in a cottage in an 'Olde Worlde' English village, whose symbolic essence ... is stability and localism". As she notes, just as migrants are known to often get sentimental about home, so it would seem that men such as these, whose working lives take a global span, also seem very strongly to want a settled place of their own to which to retreat. Affluent groups such as these are "the groups which have the most power to ensure that they do have a place of their own ... [for] the power to defend an exclusionist localism is greater for those that are already strong".[154] This particular group are in the happy position to be able to choose a specific combination of mobility and stability which is unavailable to others.

I earlier quoted Johansen's work on the extent to which the historical period in which we live could be characterised, by contrast to earlier ones, by reference to differences in the extent of the geographical "reach" which we can have, via the instruments of different modes of communication, to perceive and act on the world. While that is a useful (if crude) form of historical periodisation, it is evidently premised on a contrast between the extent of that reach for an undifferentiated "We" of today, as compared with peoples of the past.[155] The further question concerns precisely the differentiation of that reach as a form of social power available in structured ways, to greater or lesser extents, to members of different groups within any one society at a given time. These differences are what Massey calls the differential "activity spaces" of members of different social groups and are the axes of the power geometry of the organisation of spatial order. Sometimes these differences can be registered in the simplest – and apparently superficial – forms of appearance. Thus, in his descriptive account of Los Angeles airport, the travel writer Pico Iyer makes the simple but telling observation that there is a clear relation between affluence, mobility and luggage. As he puts it, "people from rich countries ... travel light, if only because they are sure they can return at any time; those from poor countries come with their whole lives in cardboard boxes, imperfectly tied with string".[156]

Tourists and vagabonds

According to Zygmunt Bauman, alongside an emerging planetary process of business and trade flow on the part of international capital and its employees, we see a contrary, localising, space-fixing process, as the weak states necessitated by global capital are required to spatially police their recalcitrant "surplus populations" so as to create the conditions necessary to attract inward investment in the international marketplace.[157] The result, he argues, is a sharp differentiation in the existential conditions of different parts of the population – globalisation for the rich elite and either "incarceration" or vagabondage for the poor.[158] For the rich, entry visas are needed less and less in moving between countries, while for the poor immigration controls of one sort or another (residence laws, zero-tolerance policies) at different levels of geographical scale are, increasingly, in force. From Bauman's perspective, time–space compression emancipates some people from territorial constraints, "allowing them unprecedented ability to move and to 'act at a distance'".[159] For others, there is little choice of ever escaping from the locality in which they live – while the forces which determine the nature of life in that locality operate from further and further away and are increasingly out of the reach of the locals' capacity to influence them.

Manuel Castells argues that while the global market economy notionally covers the whole planet, in actuality it excludes the majority of the world's (disposable) population. For these who are now excluded, there is a significant shift from a logic of exploitation to the finality of their new-found structural irrelevance. Castells thus argues that we now see the emergence of a

> Fourth World of exclusion ... predominantly populated by women and children ... made up not only of most of Africa, and rural Asia and of Latin American shanties, but also of the South Bronx, la Courneve, Kamagasaki or Tower Hamlets of this world.[160]

For Castells, one key dimension of exclusion is that of access to the information networks which are, as he puts it, the prerequisite of effective participation in the affluent societies of the West. He foresees a multimedia world, inhabited by "two essentially distinct populations; the interacting and the interacted, meaning those who are able to select their multidirectional circuits of communication and those who are provided with a restricted number of pre-packaged choices".[161] From this perspective, societies are also increasingly stratified with respect to time, being divided between the over-employed, who spend money to save time, and the under-employed who, having no other resource, spend time to save money. Thus Castells argues that "selected functions and individuals transcend time, while downgraded activities and subordinate people endure life as time goes by ... Timelessness sails on an ocean surrounded by time-bound shores, from where can still be heard the laments of time-chained creatures".[162]

The mobile elites can physically leave the squalor of the regions that those who cannot afford to move are stuck in. The point, for Bauman, is that, for the globally mobile, "space has lost its constraining quality and is easily traversed" – both physically and virtually. The locally tied, conversely, are "bound to bear passively whatever changes may be visited on the locality to which they are tied". For them, real space is closing up and virtual space, the more it is commodified, is less and less accessible without a good credit rating. Thus some are admitted to extraterritorial cyberspace and made to feel welcome wherever they wish to shop. Others are deprived of the relevant "transit visas" and are prevented from unproductively roaming about the places reserved for the proper residents under the pass laws of cyberspace.[163] Mobility is increasingly seen as a social good and immobility increasingly acquires, by contrast, the connotation of defeat, of failure and of being left behind.[164]

Addressing the question of the impact of the reunification of Germany on former citizens of the GDR, Ulrich Mai makes the point that life in East Germany prior to 1989 was much more localised than in the West. Not only were car ownership scarce and general rates of mobility low, but much of life (including healthcare and education) was organised around the local factory base of production. Social life was similarly organised, in large part, in stable and close-knit networks of people heavily embedded in their shared locality. However, as he points out, as these networks have been restructured under the impact of reunification, "the old quality of locality becomes less important" and it is only for "the losers in unification – the jobless and the old" that these local networks continue to survive – as their last remaining vestige of security and support, and as the focus of a form of *Ostalgie*, or nostalgia for the security of life under the old regime in East Germany.[165]

Among the mobile, Bauman distinguishes between those he calls "tourists" and those he calls "vagabonds". The tourists – the members of elite groups – travel by choice, taking advantage of all forms of mobility available. The vagabonds – the "mutants of postmodern evolution, the monster rejects of the brave new species" – know that they won't stay in a place long, however much they wish to, since they are not guaranteed a welcome anywhere. If tourists "move because they find the world within their (global) reach increasingly attractive, then vagabonds move because they find the world within their (local) grasp unbearably inhospitable".[166] Behind these differential experiences, Bauman argues, there lies a process in which, now it has been emancipated from space, capital no longer needs itinerant labour (it will go wherever labour is cheap). To this extent "the pressure to pull down the last remaining barriers to the free movement of money and money-making commodities and information" goes hand in hand with the pressure to erect new barriers to the movement of all those people who are themselves uprooted, or displaced by the movements of capital.[167] Let us now turn to consider the dynamics of this supposedly borderless global economy and culture.

9

BORDERS AND BELONGINGS
Strangers and foreigners

Global culture: a borderless world?

For some commentators it seems that the combined effects of global flows of information, investment, trade and people across national borders mean that we are heading in the direction of a "borderless world", in Kenichi Ohmae's phrase.[1] At its crudest, this argument is represented by Ohmae himself as a matter of technology making natural borders obsolete, as the process of what he calls "California-isation" produces universally homogenous forms of consumer culture, focused on global brands. In a world where global capital markets set severe limits to what any national government can do, the idea of the nation-state as the basic form of organisation of human affairs is, for Ohmae, "increasingly a nostalgic fiction". In this scenario, he claims, we face a global logic which is slowly but surely "dissolving the fabric holding nation states together" alongside the "progressive globalisation of markets for consumer goods".[2] In this vision, the nation-state has simply been by-passed by history and operates at a level of aggregation which makes it dysfunctional for the organisation of economic activity in the global marketplace.

Ohmae argues that if economic borders have any continuing meaning at all, it is as the "contours of information flow". For him information flow is decisive in reshaping our world, away from one based on "things like the location of raw material deposits, energy sources, navigable rivers, deep-water ports, railway lines, paved roads and national borders". Rather, he argues, the salient contours of today's maps are the "footprints cast by television satellites, the areas covered by radio signals ... the geographic reach of newspapers and magazines", and "information has replaced both propinquity and politics as the factor most likely to shape the flow of economic activity". In his image of it, our world is increasingly full of uprooted people who have metaphorically migrated (via the medium of their "shared exposure to the English language, to the Internet, to Fox TV, the BBC, CNN and MTV and interactive communication tools") from citizenship of the nation-state to a quite different sort of "country" – "the global economy of the borderless world".[3] However, even Ohmae stops short of declaring this borderless world to be quite without patterning of any sort. In fact, he argues that if the nation-state is withering away, its place in the organisation of economic affairs is increasingly being taken, at a different level of geographical scale, by what he calls the new "region states", which span existing national borders.[4]

Against Ohmae's somewhat apocalyptic vision, we find Hannerz querying whether the nation is quite as outmoded (for everyone, as opposed to the highly mobile business elite) as might appear.[5] In the first place, there is the question of the extent to which the global consumer culture of which Ohmae makes such play can truly "put down roots among the populations of the world" to the extent that national loyalties will be displaced.[6] If, as Hannerz notes, the nation has long been a thing of "great cultural resonance" it may be well to ask for whom it is still so, as opposed to assuming that the whole population has necessarily ceded from the nation, along with Reich's elite of mobile workers such as "symbolic analysts". Certainly, for them, working in corporations which have loosened their ties with any particular country, the corporation itself may offer a denationalised "source of solidarity and collective identity" and the nation in which they are based at a given moment perhaps functions as little more than a temporary operating environment. In that case, as Hannerz rhetorically formulates it, the question (for the rich, at least) would be "what can your nation do for you that a good credit card cannot do?"[7] But if the nation as an idea has become culturally impoverished, for some people at least, it is not clear by what it might be replaced (for those not in a position to identify with The Company). Despite the fact that many people have links (of various sorts) which transcend the space of the nation, these do not often, as Hannerz puts it, "coalesce into any single conspicuous alternative to the nation". Clearly something important is happening here: as Hannerz notes, among those countries of the West centrally involved in the supranational restructuring of the global economy, if the "nation is not really withering away … it is changing" – but he rightly argues it is not, in the simple sense that Ohmae seems to suggest, "being replaced by any single transnational culture".[8]

Here we might note that, as Michael Mann points out,

> the national basis of production and trade seem undiminished. Ninety per cent of global production remains for the domestic market. Almost all the so-called "multinational corporations" are still owned overwhelmingly by nationals in their home-base country, and their headquarters and research development activities are still concentrated there.[9]

According to Mann, the "nation-state is not in any *general* decline" but, rather, on the whole "still strides dominant across the world", and "European talk of the death of the nation-state sounds odd in other parts of the globe". Indeed, the "Western European weakenings of the nation-state" by virtue of the transfer of some of its powers to the European Union is a development,

205

Mann argues, which is thus far particular to that region – a unique "European novelty [that] does not represent the future of the world".[10]

A rather different perspective on these matters is supplied by the American foreign policy analyst Samuel Huntingdon. Like Ohmae, he also believes that we are now moving beyond the period of the nation-state, which has itself been the norm in the organisation of international affairs "since the Treaty of Westphalia in 1648".[11] However, in contrast to Ohmae's vision of a move towards a borderless world, Huntingdon foresees a move towards a world where borders are still crucial. The difference, he argues, is that the key borders of the future will be those between different civilisations, rather than those between nations (and these borders do to some extent parallel the outlines of Ohmae's transnational "regional states"). Fundamentally, Huntingdon's argument is that what we see emerging is a "civilisation-based world order ... [where] societies sharing cultural affinities co-operate with each other" and, of course, vice versa – as cultural (or civilisational, in Huntingdon's terms) difference becomes the crucial fault line in generating conflict.[12] In this sense Huntingdon does for the analysis of civilisations what Kristeva (see below) does for the analysis of nations and Sibley for the analysis of suburbs: he traces the process through which conflict is generated in the attempt to expel alterity beyond the boundaries of the ethnically, culturally or civilisationally "purified" homogeneous enclave.[13]

Unsettling motion

For much of history, the most pervasive political units have been tribes, villages, city states, feudal settlements, dynastic empires or loose moral communities based on religion. By contrast, as Geoff Eley and Ronald Grigor Suny point out, the modern nation involves the imagining of a "desirable future of harmonious living and collective self-determination, within the sovereign space of a well-integrated and solidaristic social and political order ... with the ... ideal of a coherent and well-organised common culture". Moreover, they argue, this vision of modern nationality requires a "grounding of the national community in a specific and more definitively delineated territory, with harder boundaries".[14] As they note, it also involves both the effacing of internal differences and the emphasising of the external ones which differentiate this community from others. In this neat and idealised scheme, humanity is divided between fictively unified ethnic groups and each individual is allocated to (only) one of these groups. Equally, each individual body (the site of the unique personality) is safely encased within one homogenous territorial community – the site of national identity. As Mark Augé puts it, in this connection "the ideal, for an ethnologist wishing to characterise singular particularities, would be for each ethnic group to have its own island, possibly linked to others but different from any other; for each islander to be an exact replica of [their] neighbours".[15] In the territory of the nation-state, represented to itself as "a place that functions as the site of homogeneity, equilibrium and integration", differences either have to be assimilated, destroyed or

> assigned to ghettos ... demarcated by boundaries so sharp that they enable the nation to acknowledge the apparently singular and clearly fenced off differences *within* itself, while simultaneously reaffirming the privileged homogeneity of the rest, as well as the difference *between* itself and what lies over its frontiers.[16]

From this kind of artificially fixed perspective, globalisation is seen to threaten the integrity of authentic and indigenous cultures and thus to weaken the sense of cultural unity that holds such groups together. At the same time, immigration is seen to dilute (or pollute) forms of cultural purity. The first difficulty here is evidently that not everybody can fit into this kind of schema. Speaking of his novels, the Tanzanian writer Abdulrazak Gurnah, now based in England, has explained that he is "interested in explaining what happens to people who are in every respect part of a place, but who neither feel part of a place, nor are regarded as being part of a place".[17] One important dimension of the migrant experience is well captured in the description of the effects of the mid-air explosion at the beginning of Salman Rushdie's *Satanic Verses*:

> mingling with the remnants of the plane, equally fragmented, equally absurd, there floated the debris of the soul, broken memories, sloughed-off selves, severed mother-tongues, violated privacies, untranslatable jokes, extinguished features, lost loves, the forgotten meaning of hollow, booming words, land, belonging, home.[18]

Those whom Rushdie has called "translated men" inevitably problematise any neat system of boundary fixing.[19] They are, as Stuart Hall puts it

> people who belong to more than one world, speak more than one language (literally and metaphorically) inhabit more than one identity, have more than one home; who have learned to negotiate and translate between cultures and who, because they are irrevocably the product of several interlocking histories and cultures, have learned to live with, and indeed to speak from, *difference*. They speak from the "in-between" of different cultures, always unsettling the assumptions of one culture from the perspective of another, and thus finding ways of being the same as and at the same time different from, the others amongst whom they live.[20]

For such people identity is not rooted in one single original homeland, but rather depends on their ability to inhabit different imaginary geographies simultaneously. Thus Michael Ignatieff reports a conversation with a man called

Husseyn, who came to Germany from Turkey as a child. Husseyn is confused and says, "I don't know where to go … I grew up here, I speak German, I love Turkey … I'm not at home there any more … But I'm always thinking of going back." For Husseyn, even the prospect of being granted German citizenship offers little prospect of hope "What am I supposed to do with a German passport? Hang it round my neck?" As he observes, having a German passport will not necessarily make people stop calling him a "Dirty Turk", nor make his co-workers more likely to socialise with him in their lunch break. He feels that his fate is written in his Turkish face and appearance, and that any formal rights which a passport might offer will not necessarily change the way Germans look at him. As Ignatieff observes, even if one day he is able to belong to the German state, he is unlikely to ever be able to feel that he belongs to the German nation in anything like its current form. At the same time, this is not to deny the importance of formal nationality, argues Ignatieff. In his account of his trip through the Ukraine, he explains that the connection between nationhood and personal dignity is self-evident to those without the former. As he puts it, from their point of view "without nationhood, people sneer at you on the bus; people jeer at you for what you are. It is not enough to be a people. In order to have respect, you must have a nation."[21] Commenting on Zygmunt Bauman's observation that nationalism has to be understood as one particular modality "of the big family of we-talks", Ghassan Hage points out that, unlike other modalities of such discourse, nationalism's specificity is that it is necessarily territorial, in so far as to be national is to possess a territory – without which there can be no national existence.[22] Hage argues that for a people to constitute a nation, two crucial ingredients are required: the possession of both a mother tongue and a national territory. In order to become an internationally recognised entity there is, according to Hegel, a further requirement, for as he puts it, "only those people can come under our notice which form a state".[23] That is to say that "only a nation which has a bodily integrity, which has recognised borders … can confidently appear as a recognised 'we' on the international scene".[24]

However, as we have noted, nowadays nations do not appear as confident as they used to be. The weakening of the nation-state has complex consequences. Among other things it means, according to Etienne Balibar, that "masses of the population feel unsafe in the very state that is meant to protect them", and many tend to compensate for this anxiety by becoming particularly hostile to strangers or foreigners.[25] Indeed, as Balibar argues elsewhere, in this situation "all the conditions are present for a collective sense of identity panic to be produced and maintained", not least because while people "and especially the most deprived and … most remote from power, fear the state … they fear still more its disappearance or decomposition".[26]

Citizenship and belonging

The arrival of postcolonial people from the periphery of empire into the metropolitan centres has to be understood as doing rather more than simply making the question of immigration controls on incomers politically decisive.[27] This movement of people also necessitates a reconceptualisation of how these metropolitan centres are now to conceive of themselves and their borders. In this connection Phil Cole addresses the issue of the "constitutive outside" of Western liberal political theories of citizenship, in relation to questions of race and immigration.[28] Cole's analysis concerns the difficulties arising within the UK at the point in 1998 of the celebrations of fifty years since the ship the *Empire Windrush* docked in London, carrying the first large cohort of West Indian immigrants to enter the UK in the post-war period. He notes that much of the debate surrounding the anniversary of the *Windrush*'s arrival focused on the difficulties that these migrants and their descendants have subsequently faced in their efforts to establish themselves in British society. However, as he points out, from this perspective

> the issue of citizenship is taken to be a question of participation, rather than admittance – an internal question, rather than an external one. The problem of who is a member of the political community in the basic legal sense ... is taken to be settled, and the challenge is ... [then] to spell out what that membership entails

– and to spell out how all the members of the multi-cultural community are to co-exist as equally respected citizens.[29] Against this, Cole argues that the neglect of the question of how people are admitted to (or excluded from) the political community renders incoherent the project of the construction of multi-cultural equality within that community. As he notes, global migration exposes the theoretical limits of liberal political philosophy, in so far as the latter cannot coherently justify those arbitrary "practices of exclusion which constitute 'outsiders'". The irony is that, at the same time, the "existence of a liberal polity made up of free and equal citizens rests upon the existence of outsiders who are refused a share of ... [its] goods".[30] Moreover, the creation of a more internally integrated and coherent community often goes alongside the creation of even more exclusive policies along the borders of that community. As we shall see later, the European Union's simultaneous relaxation of its internal borders along with the tightening of its peripheral borders is a clear current example of exactly this tendency.[31] Beyond this, there is also the question of the impact on internal policing of the way in which the external boundary is controlled – in so far as any group which shares characteristics with those identified as outsiders will themselves be in a vulnerable position. Their [community] membership will be constantly questioned; they will be subjected to forms of surveillance from which other members are free, and their access to the public sphere of citizenship will become hazardous.[32]

It seems that, far from strict immigration controls being the necessary price of good "race" relations, it may be that a tightening of a community's external boundaries, and the "racialisation" of various categories of outsiders may well in fact lead to increased hostility and racism targeted at members of such groups (and their descendants) who have been allowed in. To put it at its simplest, one cannot separate these questions of exclusion from those of the subsequent dynamics of the community constituted by such exclusions. The dynamics of exclusion (and/or of grudging or partial inclusion) have their own effect on the subsequent development of the community's internal relationships.

Pilgrims and nomads: from (rapid) journeys to Generalised Arrival

In his analysis of postmodernity, which he characterises as the "cosmopolitic era", a nomadic universe of migration, Zygmunt Bauman distinguishes between "post-modern nomads" and their predecessors, whom he characterises as "modern pilgrims". The difference, according to Bauman's schematic model, is that whereas the pilgrim's journey is a planned form of progress, the nomad's is more likely to be a series of improvisations, moving through time/space and, simultaneously, through a series of reinvented identities. The most secure form of belonging that such a nomad can aspire to in this unsettled world is, according to Bauman, membership of what Maffesoli calls a "neo-tribe" – a brittle and evanescent form of collective life all the more "hypochondriac and quarrelsome" for being deprived of all the things from which old-style tribes derived their security.[33] Turning from the realm of the personal experience of geographical mobility to the development of the technologies which provide the communicative context in which mobility can be understood, Virilio offers a parallel distinction to that which Bauman draws between pilgrims and nomads. Thus Virilio moves beyond the account of time–space compression given by authors such as David Harvey, arguing that what Harvey describes is only the first stage of this process, in which the individual still moves, even if with increasing rapidity, from one location to another. Virilio's argument is that the new electronic communications technologies enable, via their "instant transmission", a new form of "generalised arrival", in which the individual is, in effect, in two places at once, and the element of a journey across space is lost, in a "crisis of the temporal dimension of the present".[34]

However, in the context of all this hypermobility, Iain Chambers notes that despite the optimistic theorising of nomadism and rhizomatic becoming, the mystery of that sense of belonging – deposited in the desire, the need to be a part of a historical social and cultural unit that is called "home" [or] "homeland" – refuses to fade away.[35]

In the realm of the postmodern, Chambers argues, we no longer have available the choice between the domestic and the exilic, as polar alternatives, but must rather learn to dwell in what Bhabha has described as a "third space", where the familiar and the foreign are conjoined, where it is less clear where home concludes and the foreign begins – where we must dwell in home as itself a hybrid space of coeval times and lives. The classical sense of home was that of the place from which the hero ventures out, and which supplies the constant domestic anchoring place to which he (sic) will return, at journey's end. This space, argues Chambers, where "the journey always confirms the point of departure, secured in the presumption of eventual homecoming" is now quite undone. Rather, he argues, in the new space of postmodernity, we necessarily move in a space of "multiple sites of coeval temporality and histories that ground us in a differentiated communality, in which the Australian Aboriginal, Chicano city dweller and Anglo Suburbanite reoccupy a shared, if asymmetrical world".[36]

This is a space inevitably populated by strangers of one sort or another, but it is important, Zygmunt Bauman argues, to distinguish their different forms of strangeness. Thus, in his analysis of the changing place and function of the stranger in the transition from the order of modernity to the disembedded and de-territorialised flux of postmodernity, he argues that "under the pressure of the modern order-building urge" strangers lived "in a state of suspended extinction. They were, by definition, an anomaly to be rectified. Their presence was defined, a priori, as temporary."[37] Strangers were either to be excluded or assimilated, so that the pragmatics of permanently co-existing with the differences and otherness which they represented did not have to be "faced point blank as a serious project". By contrast, Bauman argues, in the "atmosphere of ambient fear" which characterises the deregulated realm of the new world disorder, all positions and identities, including our own, are unfixed and destabilised – and the postmodern strangers are, by contrast to earlier times, here to stay. Moreover, such strangers are "no longer ... preselected, defined and set apart" but are as "unsteady and protean as one's own identity". To this extent, the differences between "the normal and the abnormal, the expectable and the unexpected, the ordinary and the bizarre, domesticated and wild" are blurred, as are those between "the familiar and the strange, 'us' and the strangers".[38]

Continuing difficulties with differences

The various functions performed for the civilised by the barbarians of one sort or another who lie beyond the boundaries of their community are now well recognised, and the derivation of the term "barbarian" from the Greek word for those who could not speak the Greek language is now well-rehearsed. What is less often remarked is first, why the linguistic criteria was so particularly important in the Greek definition of alterity and, further, the significance of the particular historical circumstances under which this definition was articulated. In the first case, Edith Hall argues that the priority given to the linguistic criteria in the Greeks' definition of their identity derives historically from their extensive geographical dispersal as a diaspora throughout the eastern Mediterranean and beyond, as people living in the context of a variety of different cultures and ways of life.[39] As she notes, had they all lived together on a single mainland, the original criteria of Hellenic ethnicity might well not have been language, but perhaps some other criteria, such as one based on lifestyle or habitat. This Greek discourse on barbarianism was, of course, an exercise in self-definition, in that the barbarian was usually defined as the opposite of the Ideal Greek. Barbarians were defined as those who "fall short of the standards of Hellenic virtue" by being "emotional, stupid, cruel, subservient or cowardly". They were the "universal anti-Greek", against whom Hellenic (and especially Athenian) culture was defined".[40] However, Hall's central point is that this polarised self-definition was largely invented in the specific period of the early fifth century BC, in the context of the Greek wars with the Persians. According to Hall, it was only when many Greek-speaking communities came under threat from the rise of Persian power that Hellenic self-consciousness was heightened. It is at that point that the archaic Greek definition of alterity – as the "Not Human" (the realm of the monstrous or supernatural) was transposed into an ethnic definition – of the "Not Greek". If the story of the invention of the barbarian is inseparable from the story of the Greeks' conflict with the Persians, it is nonetheless a story with continuing ramifications for us today, in relation to contemporary debates about ethnicity and alterity.

Notwithstanding our contemporary sense of mobility, in many respects it is still common to think of cultures as depending on and being rooted in places – in the stable patterns of interaction of the same people doing the same things, over and over again, in the same places. In this way place comes to act as a generator of cultural belongingness, so that the geographical boundaries round a community also come to carry a symbolic charge in separating out those who belong from those who do not. As Stuart Hall notes, the correlation of culture and place is the basis of the traditional notion of ethnicity – as the expression of a strongly bounded form of cultural identity, based on "shared meaning systems … underpinned by long, historical settlement of a population … in one environment, with strong kinship links as a result of continuous intermarriage, over generations".[41] As we shall see later in the chapter, this identification of culture and place as the constituents of ethnicity can be the basis for powerful forms of "homely racism". The connection between land, community and ethnicity is well captured in Ignatieff's definition of nationalism as "the dream that a whole nation could be like a congregation; singing the same hymns, listening to the same gospel, sharing the same emotions, linked not only to each other, but to the dead buried beneath their feet".[42] In this, the link to the land is sacred precisely because there lie the graves of the ancestors, which must be protected from the danger of profanation by strangers.

The articulation of domestic and national senses of belonging, and the symbolic relation between the domestic house or home and the landscape of the nation is also clear in Ignatieff's account of his interview with a wealthy German couple living in a dormitory village north of Frankfurt. The couple explain that, in effect, they no longer feel at home in the city, now that 30 per cent of the population of Frankfurt is foreign – which is why they moved to the countryside, where there are very few foreigners. The couple have built their house themselves, and Ignatieff describes it "with its heavy nature paintings on the walls ('from my ancestors') and its Brockhaus encyclopaedia and collected works of Schiller and Goethe in the bookcases", as "a humble bourgeois monument to a certain idea of Germany".[43] Clearly this particular domesticated version of their national home functions on a micro-scale as a safe haven from the ravages which they perceive modernity to have wrought in their environment.

This kind of romantic vision of a past Golden Age of national unity often functions in tandem with an alter ego – most usually the vision of a fragmented hybrid, polyglot future, of the type represented in films such as Ridley Scott's *Blade Runner*. As Gilane Tawadros puts it, the choice for the newly destabilised West seems to be twofold – either to "step back into a rose-tinted mythical past, where modernity and migration have yet to be imagined" or, alternatively, to "step forward into a contemporary Tower of Babel – a chaotic, urban and multi-racial nightmare".[44] This Babel-like, chaotic world is replete with (actual or virtual) strangers of one sort or another, and as Zygmunt Bauman notes, the problem with strangers is that they do not fit our cognitive, moral or aesthetic maps of the world, in so far as

> by their sheer presence [they] make obscure what ought to be trans-
> parent, confuse what ought to be a straight-forward recipe for action
> … [and] pollute joy … with anxiety … They befog and eclipse the
> boundary lines which ought to be clearly seen … they gestate uncer-
> tainty, which in its turn breeds the discomfort of feeling lost.[45]

We are accustomed to live in the familiar, obvious space of the "near" – where the physical nearness of our domestic world stands in for its unproblematicness and for its emotional familiarity. However, as we have seen, in our contemporary world the far away is irredeemably mixed in with the space of the near as the processes of migration and of media representation continually bring actual and virtual forms of "foreignness" into jealously guarded home territories of various sorts.

Island boundaries

For long, cities have been the primary site of cultural mixing. In Iris Marion Young's argument, the "unoppressive city" would be one which would move beyond this simple mixing, to become a place in which the fact of difference would be accepted – where there would be an openness to unassimilated otherness. For her, city life embodies difference and, contrary both to the idealised image of the face-to-face interactions of a small close-knit community and to the solipsistic communities of cyberspace (as we saw in Chapter 8), city life necessitates the "being together of strangers".[46] Here the politics of everyday life has to be understood as the working out of viable relationships between strangers who do not necessarily understand each other in any obvious, automatic or immediate sense, without difficulty.[47]

The problem is that outside the realm of Young's ideal vision of the city, in reality the construction and maintenance of purified and internally homogeneous spaces, from which alterity (in the form of minority groups or non-conformist activities) has been expelled, is central to the geography of exclusion of urban life. At its simplest, Massey argues that the social definition of place often involves

> an active process of exclusion. And in that process the boundaries of the place, and the imagination and building of its "character", are part and parcel of the definition of who is an insider and who is not; of who is a "local" and what that term should mean, and who is to be excluded. It is a space of bounded identities.[48]

Sibley describes these processes as being aimed at securing "both protection from and positional superiority over, the external Other".[49]

In order to explore these issues in a more focused way, we now move to consider processes of social "purification" as practised in one particular city – in the East End of London. In doing so we shall also have occasion to consider again some of the issues raised in earlier chapters concerning boundary maintenance in the domestic home, and, from another perspective, some further implications of the gendering of ideas of home. In their analyses of the development of contemporary racism in the UK, both Phil Cohen and Vron Ware have focused on an area of East London known as the Isle of Dogs.[50] The area is a relatively self-contained geographical space which forms, as its name suggests, (almost) an island jutting into the River Thames. In recent years it has been a central focus of "race" politics in the UK, as some of its long-term inhabitants have protested at what they perceive as the growing immigrant presence in "their" area. As Ware notes, the fact that the area is itself an island has allowed its transformation to be constructed as an allegory for that of Britain as a whole, so that developments there have come to carry much more than local significance.

Historically, the area was the centre of the London docks, servicing the empire trade through the eighteenth and nineteenth centuries, with a population of dockers, seamen and their families. The area suffered badly in the Second World War, as the German Luftwaffe bombed the docks in the London Blitz. In the post-war period, the docks were gradually run down to the point of almost total closure by the 1970s, and the remaining local industries gradually declined after that. In this same period, many of the area's previous inhabitants were rehoused in London's outlying eastern suburbs, while there was significant immigration into the area (especially in the early period) from Bangladesh, many of these immigrants being housed in poor quality council accommodation which local white residents considered undesirable. Throughout the 1980s the area was transformed by Mrs Thatcher's Conservative government into an enormous redevelopment site, under the management of the London Docklands Development Corporation, culminating in the construction of the massive Canary Wharf commercial development. Unfortunately, the area's residents perceive themselves as having gained little from this process of "development".

Discursively, the central figure who is held to define the population of the area is the "cockney" – a discursive composite, who represents the cheerful, wisecracking, "salt of the earth" – the very backbone of nation and Empire. As Cohen observes, this figure was constructed in the nineteenth century by distinction from (and in opposition to) the figure of the immigrant as "an alien and corrupting presence, dragging down the natives to their own depraved level", as these "cast-offs of foreign shipping established their habits and vices" and set in train what some feared to be "the insidious deterioration of the British race".[51] The East End is thus characterised, as a result of the effect of these alien influences, as a kind of "Internal Orient, which is also The Other England" – by further contrast to the culturally refined West End of London.[52] The point, as Cohen argues it, is that contemporary forms of racism still frequently draw on the orientalist discourses through which London's East End has been historically characterised, by images of fog, labyrinthine impenetrability and exotic squalor.

Within the confined territory of the Isle of Dogs itself, many of its white inhabitants exhibit an extremely strong identification of themselves with the special qualities of the area in which they live. It is, as Cohen puts it, a sense of belonging focused on their island as the "locus of a fixed, almost biological sense of identity", a genealogy of place "rooted in local custom and circumstance … congenitally linked to one's place of birth and early life". This sense of rooted solidarity is well expressed by one of Cohen's interviewees who says: "It's in your blood. We were born here, we've grown up together, we all help each other, and we stick together." This image of a Golden Age, when all the members of the community lived in a paradisical state of social harmony, is, of course, constructed precisely as the counterpoint to the negative image of "nowadays" – when everything is held to have changed for the worse, under the influence of immigrants and their alien ways. As Cohen argues, "the myth of a golden age ... before the Others came, when the world was a safe and friendly place" is precisely what produces the "rationale for social closure around a racialised model of community".[53] These dying white working-class communities of the East End, virtual enclaves, bounded by the river and the dereliction that surrounds them, according to Sivanandan have "developed a siege mentality and turned to the ... belief that their last 'belonging' is now taken from them by the ... [immigrants]. The only thing left that holds them together now is their race and space." In their despair, he argues, they have turned to racism as "the comfort of the last resort" and attempted to "found an imagined community out of their bloodstock racism".[54]

Boundary, identity and conflict: social and psychological mechanisms

In his analysis of racism in this same area Paul Hoggett draws, in general terms, on Kleinian psychoanalytic theory and specifically on the premise that human development "requires the existence of a benign social medium which is reliable and flexible enough for fear to be contained without being visited upon the other".[55] Hoggett argues that this "containment" constitutes a necessarily bounded space within which fear and anxiety can be dealt with efficiently. In Kleinian terms, while from the paranoid-schizoid position difference is likely to be constructed as a Bad Object (poisonous, persecutory, etc.), conversely, from a position of full subjecthood, differences and anomalies can be more positively construed as enriching novelties offering new possibilities for self-enrichment. If from the first position "unity without difference" is the only thing tolerable, the second position, which allows for both ambiguity and uncertainty, is the positive basis for all self-development. Hoggett's particular interest is in the ways in which periods of rapid social and economic change can have the effect, through their destruction of social networks and traditional patterns of loyalty and security, of triggering, at the individual level, such a strong sense of anxiety that fear can no longer be effectively "contained" but must then be projected outwards on to some demonised other.

For Hoggett, "the problem is not the propensity of groups and individuals to construct boundaries, but the meanings that are ascribed to them once they have been constructed".[56] From this perspective "the existence of differences should not be an analytical or social problem: rather, the problem is the racialisation ... of such differences". Thus, he argues, the white racist response to Bangladeshi immigration in the East End should be understood in the context of the destabilisation of the white community's familial and employment structures during the recent transformations of the area in which they live. As Hoggett notes, there is further pathos in the fact that the resentment the whites feel towards the Bangladeshi community is made poignant by the fact that [far from simply displaying difference] the latter community has many characteristics – extended and intensive kinship networks, a respect for tradition and male seniority, a capacity for entrepreneurialism and social advancement – which the white working class in the area have lost.[57]

While there is clear and troubling evidence of white working-class racism in the area, the situation is a complex one. It is always easy for white liberals, themselves often living in more affluent areas where few immigrant families can afford housing, to decry the racist attitudes of the working-class people who themselves more often have to come to terms, in their daily lives, with all the difficulties of "living with difference". As we shall see later, it is also important to recognise white working-class racism as often a symptomatic expression of the despair of the downwardly mobile at their relative powerlessness to control any aspect of their lives. The question of power is, of course, crucial here. In the earlier period, when the Other, whose intrusion into their area the inhabitants of the Isle of Dogs were resisting, was the powerful London Dockland Development Corporation, their defence of their territory was applauded by many who would nonetheless feel compelled to criticise the racist form of the residents' current defence of their territory against groups even less powerful than themselves.[58]

Homely racism

The discourse of "homely racism", according to Cohen, allows us to imagine that we do not have to share our space with anyone else unless they are of exactly our own kind by virtue of consanguinity. It is a discourse in which there simply is no legitimate space for the Other, in which the organic image of life and landscape blurs together fond memories of happy childhoods and settled ways in a "pervasive sense of privacy invaded as well as tradition undone".[59] As he notes, the anti-immigrant sentiments currently expressed against Bangladeshis in the Isle of Dogs were foreshadowed over a hundred years ago by those opposed to Jewish immigration into the area. As one of their spokesmen put it at that time:

> This great influx is driving out the native from hearth and home … some of us have old associations here of such a nature that we feel it hard to be parted from. And all this is being jeopardised by those who come amongst us with their alien ways, and who dare to claim our native hearth as their own.[60]

Cohen also stresses the particular importance of the role of ideas of the family and of matrilocal residence in areas such as the Isle of Dogs, in combination with ideas of indigeneity, in binding "the transmission of values and patrimonies into a fixed sense of home".[61] In his analysis of "homing devices", he focuses particularly on the role of "domestic metaphors and images of privacy ... in constructing common-sense arguments for the exclusion of those who are held not to belong within the public domains of the body politic". In these metaphors, as he puts it, the barbarians are held to have "already broken and entered the gates ... [and] invaded the privacy of the master bedroom" as well as having "occupied and laid waste desirable residential areas". In this homespun philosophy of habitation, with its recurring analogies between domestic and public order, there is, as Cohen puts it, always "an underlying sense that an environment is being polluted, a generation disinherited, honour or habitat defiled" by immigration. The pervasive metaphor in this discourse is one of domestic privacy invaded, as much as public tradition undone. Underlying it is a heavily gendered image of home as a space in need of protection from defilement by the alien presence. This form of homely racism is, Cohen argues "founded on a deeply held belief in domestic order as the centre of social aspiration", and "the gendering of home, its inclination as a space of threatened privacy ... is a necessary condition for its mobilisation in discourses of racism and nationalism, and these discourses in turn reinforce the patriarchal closure".[62]

Moreover, as the individual comes to feel increasingly threatened by alien influences in the world outside, and the external environment comes to be seen as dangerous, the space "behind the symbolic lace curtains", where "personal standards" can be maintained, has to bear increasing symbolic weight. By this means, as Cohen notes, "the sense of home shrinks to that space where some sense of inherent order and decency can be imposed on that small part of a chaotic world which the subject can directly own and control".[63] In this the Islanders can be held to be producing a racist inflection of a pre-existing and, according to Ray Pahl, specifically English idea of the household, which is distinctive in so far as it crystallises notions of "homeliness, cosiness, domesticity, and a belief that, if one can control just one small part of this large and threatening world, then one has achieved something worthwhile".[64] However, the particularly unfortunate consequence, as Cohen argues, is that "the idealisation of the domestic interior as a space of privatised transcendence serves to intensify the racialisation of the public sphere". This is no merely defensive discourse, but an aggressive one, aimed at preventing immigrants from putting down roots in the area to which they have moved, in so far as their ability to make a home for themselves there is "perceived to threaten the privileged link between habit and habitat on which the myth of indigenous origins rests".[65] Similarly, in her analysis of the role of gender in the construction of a sense of a local exclusively white organic community on the Isle of Dogs, Vron Ware is particularly concerned with what she describes as the voice of beleaguered mothers in the area, which "summons up a version of white femininity that is passively concerned with the task of trying to reproduce the racial purity longed for by their menfolk".[66]

One of the most contentious issues, in recent times, has been the local authority's housing policies in respect of the competing claims on the area's limited housing stock of new immigrants and of the grown-up children of existing council tenants. The white residents of the area complained that their own children were being forced to move away from the area for lack of housing, which was being allocated instead, they claimed, to strangers. In response, the local Liberal Party advocated a "Sons and Daughters" housing policy, designed to meet these anxieties by prioritising the claims of the area's long-term white residents. As Ware notes, this policy effectively constructed "an exclusive white kinship – in the name of local democracy, a kinship which implicitly appeal[led] to a form of matriarchy, in its desire to protect the rights of its offspring". It was, as she observes, a policy tacitly addressed to women as mothers, in its prioritising of the desirability of keeping extended families together on a matrilocal basis. As such, of course, it effectively functioned to exclude all those who were unable to "claim natural kinship with the group". It also served to naturalise that definition of the local community as "both homogenous and rooted organically in the soil", in a form of "mystical white kinship" constructed through the appeal to "family, tradition and association with place".[67]

The central figures in this discourse, in Ware's analysis, are those of the

> embittered cockney "mum", fighting to have her grown-up children re-housed in her own neighbourhood [and] the pale tense young woman held prisoner in a tower-block overrun with cockroaches and foreign smells, or the frail pensioner, afraid to leave her flat for fear of being mugged by blacks.[68]

Ware identifies a succession of press reports quoting local women who complained of immigrants as "dirty pigs who bring disease into the group and spit everywhere", responsible for the invasion of vermin such as cockroaches in the local area and, allegedly, as the source of an "awful smell".[69] These complaints all represent a specifically female point of view, in so far as they refer to the threat of pollution of the sacred space of the domestic home, the proper sphere of traditional feminine influence.

As Wendy Webster observes in her analysis of questions of gender, "race" and national identity in Britain in the post-war period, Enoch Powell's famous "Rivers of Blood" speech, made in 1968, also features the figure of a frail white woman whose "quiet street" has been invaded by immigrants. In the speech's imagery of windows broken and excreta pushed through the letterbox, the invasion of the micro-boundaries of this (fictional) woman's home stand in for the broken boundaries of the nation. The story of the nation which Powell told was also "about powerlessness and vulnerability in an English street, and has at its centre the figure of a white woman".[70]

The racialisation of space

The rise in cockroach infestation in the area has been one of the unintended results of the local council's building modernisation programme (double glazing and central heating ducts providing cockroaches with an ideal environment in which to thrive). As Hoggett notes, "the evidence that the infestation has structural and physical causes cuts no ice with white tenants, for whom the cockroach signifies a complex knot of resentment, fear and hatred". The immigrants were both blamed as being somehow the cause of this unwanted infestation and, at the same time, their very identity was fused with that of the insect itself – as an unwanted Other who "is resilient, small in stature, multiplying fast and impure".[71]

In his analysis of the racialisation of space in British cities, Sibley observes that the threat of the alien, racialised Other escaping from the far territories of empire to the inner city, and then breaking out of that space to invade the surrounding white suburbs may be an old-established cultural script, but it is still one with depressingly contemporary resonance. To turn to a contemporary American example, as a black man driving his car through a white suburb in Los Angeles, Rodney King can similarly be seen to have embodied precisely this threat, in so far as "the mobility provided by the car, in a city built around the automobile was not supposed to extend to black men who might threaten the white suburbs through their movement, resisting containment where only whites were supposed to drive".[72] In a similar vein, Tim Cresswell suggests that the attack on the three black men whose car broke down in the white Howard Beach neighbourhood of New York in 1986 could equally be understood – and was widely reported in the media in these terms – as trouble that had its origin in the local whites' understanding of these young black men as violating the customary laws of the area by being "out of place".[73] Our imaginings of these racialised spaces are still powerful, as we have seen in our earlier discussion of this representation of immigrant districts in the French media: thus, Sibley notes *Le Figaro's* emblematic characterisation of these districts as *banlieues du cauchemar* – the physical spaces where "our" nightmares are embodied.[74]

Nationalism, narcissism and minor differences

In her analysis of images of home and Heimat at a micro-level, Nora Rathzel demonstrates that the more strongly someone holds an image of Heimat as something necessarily stable and unchanging, the more likely they are to be hostile to newcomers.[75] Similarly, in his analysis of nationalism, Ignatieff observes that it seems that "the more strongly you feel the bonds of belonging to your own group, the more hostile, the more violent will be your feelings towards outsiders".[76] Drawing on the work of Hans Magnus Enzensberger, Ignatieff defines the process involved here as a form of autism, in which members of a group become so enclosed in their own sense of self-righteous victimhood, so trapped inside their own mythology, that they become unable to listen to outsiders. The justification of this strategy of self-enclosure is the belief that, as (by definition) no one else can understand you but your own group, there is no point in listening to strangers. What is denied in the autism of this kind of identity politics is the possibility of any communicative empathy across social or cultural divisions. The basis of this form of autism, Ignatieff argues, is best understood as a narcissistic over-valuation of the self which results in the corresponding devaluation of others or strangers, and which thus exacerbates intolerance.[77]

Here Ignatieff draws on Freud's theory of the "narcissism of minor differences", where Freud argues that the smaller the actual difference between groups, the larger it is likely to loom in their imaginations.[78] In this symbolic economy, the hatred of others is also the necessary complement to the narcissistic idealisation of the "national self". In a similar vein, Anthony Cohen points out that the symbolic expression of community (and of its boundaries) tends to increase in importance precisely to the extent that the actual boundaries of a community are undermined, blurred or weakened. Moreover, he notes, following Pitt-Rivers, that the finer the differences between people, the stronger is likely to be the commitment which they have to maintaining them.[79] As Pitt-Rivers put it:

> It is always the people of the next door town who are the cause of the trouble, who came stealing the crops, whose wives are unfaithful, who swear more foully, are more often drunk, more addicted to vice and who do one down in business. In all things they serve as a scapegoat or as a warning.[80]

In Cohen's gloss on this, he argues that the assertion of distinctiveness "is likely to intensify as the apparent similarity between (symbolic) forms on each side of the boundary increases".[81] If identity is necessarily articulated as difference, it is at the boundary that difference is most likely to be articulated in an aggressive form. Thus the geographer David Ley's study of "turf-divisions" between Philadelphian street gangs in the 1970s showed that while at the centre of its territory a gang's graffiti mainly tended to celebrate itself and its exploits, the nearer to its boundary, the more aggressive the graffiti tended to be, often taking the form of obscene insults towards other gangs and their members.[82] It is at the boundary, where territorial control is, in fact, least secure that it is likely to be asserted all the more hysterically.

Kristeva: the problem of "the foreigner"

If the foreigner is "none other than the alter ego of national man" then the form in which that foreignness is defined necessarily follows the particular logic of each national language and culture.[83] However, although its contents and contours may change, what is constant is the way in which, as Kristeva puts it, everywhere "the foreigner concentrates upon himself the fascination and the repulsion that Otherness gives rise to".[84] Foreigners have always constituted a problem. In classical times, while Plato argued that they should be treated with proper civility, he nonetheless also recommended that they be closely monitored and treated with circumspection (and ideally, confined to the port area of the city), on account of the threat they necessarily pose to civic order. Just as it is common for strangers to only be admitted to the hall or lobby of the house, so historically, strangers were often held at the city gates, as a "purifying filter", preventing them contaminating civil society.[85] Plato's concern was that "strangers are always suggesting novelties to strangers" such that their intercourse with the citizens of the places they visit "is apt to create a confusion of manners".[86]

According to Kant, hospitality is best understood as the "right of a stranger not to be treated as an enemy when he arrives in the land of other".[87] However if, as Kristeva notes, during the Middle Ages in Europe a sophisticated code of hospitality was developed to provide for the needs of travellers, it was nonetheless a form of hospitality with clear limits. Just as any travelling Christian had the right to be greeted with hospitality, so this right only extended to him as a member of the broader Christian community. Non-Christian travellers had no such rights, and the local community in which they might arrive understood itself to owe them, as non-believers, no such obligation of hospitality. As she points out, this issue remains resonant in the present day, in so far as it still seems that "in order to found the rights that are specific to the men of a civilisation or nation … one has to withdraw such rights from those who are not citizens".[88]

In her now well-established analysis, Kristeva follows Freud in arguing that it is only on the basis of the recognition of the presence within us (in the unconscious) of strange, frightening and dangerous elements that external forms of strangeness can be stripped of their pathological aspect. Thus, it is only by recognising the internal presence of foreignness that one can avoid projecting on to the foreigner all that we find dangerous or unpleasant in ourselves, and it is only with the knowledge that we are, in her phrase "foreigners to ourselves" that we can attempt to live with others – so that, by recognising the "foreigner" within us we are spared detesting him in himself. As Kristeva puts it: "living with the other, with the foreigner, confronts us with the possibility … of being an other … [which is] not simply … a matter of … accept[ing] the other, but of being in his place … to imagine and make oneself other for oneself". On this argument, community is only possible on the condition that all its members recognise their own foreignness.[89]

Domesticating alterity

In his commentary on Phil Cohen's writings on homely racism as providing a "homespun philosophy of habitation", Ghassan Hage rightly argues that, valuable as it is, Cohen's analysis needs to be supplemented in one crucial respect. Whereas Cohen argues that there is "no place for the Other" in the nationalist or racist conception of the homeland, Hage rightly argues that it is a crucial misconception to believe that "all home/nation-building involves an exterminatory approach to otherness".[90] At its simplest, as Hage argues, many forms of others (slaves, migrant workers, domestic servants) are often positively required, in both the domestic home and the nation. Moreover, at a symbolic level, if nationalism is a masculinist discourse, still at the centre of the symbolic home there is already a gendered Other – the figure of the woman or mother.[91] Thus, Hage argues, the house (or the Motherland) cannot be a place from which otherness is excluded: nor indeed need it be, for the feeling of symbolic plenitude and security to be achieved. It is not the presence of otherness *per se* which is problematic, but only that of undomesticated otherness. Domesticated otherness (the woman under the patriarchal authority of the Father in the home; a subdued and domesticated working class under the hegemony of the dominant class; *Gastarbeiter* confined to particular areas of physical and social space) is welcome and indeed necessary to service the needs of the domesticator. Home-building (at both micro and macro levels), we might then argue, is to be seen as much as a process of domestication as of the exclusion of otherness. Alterity, on this model, is non-threatening as long as it is "in its place", and home-building does not require its absolute displacement but, rather, only its domestication.

In her account of growing up on the wrong side of the railway tracks in a small Kentucky town, bell hooks offers an illuminating exemplification of Hage's argument concerning the necessity of the Other to the functioning of dominant forms of life, and of how that otherness is kept in its place, rather than necessarily being entirely excluded. As hooks puts it, in relation to her own childhood experience:

> to be in the margin is to be part of the whole but outside the main body ... the railroad tracks were a daily reminder of our marginality. Across those tracks were paved streets, stores we could not enter, restaurants we could not eat in, and people we could not look directly in the face. Across those tracks was a world we could work in as maids, as janitors, as prostitutes, as long as it was in a service capacity. We could enter that world but we could not live there. We had always to return to the margin, to cross the tracks to shacks and abandoned houses on the edge of town.[92]

Returning to the question of the gendering of the nation, Hage argues that the Other of the Fatherland is constituted as the non-believer – the one whose lack of commitment (or downright opposition) to the national ideal prevents or precludes its realisation.[93] This other functions as a virus, weakening the nation's capacity to achieve self-realisation and, as such, constitutes a presence which cannot be easily tolerated. This, according to Elias Canetti is the "ludicrousness of order", in so far as while it wants to be total it

> depends on so little. A hair ... lying where it shouldn't, can separate order from disorder. Everything that doesn't belong where it is, is hostile. Even the tiniest thing is disturbing: a man of total order would have to scour his realm with a microscope and even then a remnant of potential nervousness will remain in him.[94]

If we understand nationalist discourse as a modality of this kind or desire for total order, characteristically taking the form of a yearning for some form of national self-realisation not yet (never, in fact) fully achieved, then, Hage argues, paradoxically this Other is, in fact, absolutely necessary to the nationalist project. If the nation is perceived as that whose final realisation we must struggle to achieve, then

> what is needed is something that explains the failure of this possibility to materialise so far. Here lies the importance of the other ... while portrayed as that which comes between the nationalist and his goal, in fact, the other is what allows the nationalist to believe in the possibility of that goal. It spares him the anxiety of having to face the fact that such a goal is impossible ... by the very fact of being posited as that which threatens it.[95]

To confront these issues more directly we must now turn to a more detailed consideration of the questions of cosmopolitanism and hybridity.

10

COSMOPOLITICS
Boundary, hybridity and identity

Cosmopolitics and connexity: the new condition of the world?

In this world of hypermobility not only are we often engaged in border-crossings of one kind or another, but the nature and functions of borders themselves are shifting. Thus Balibar argues that borders "are no longer the shores of politics, but have indeed become ... things within the space of the political itself". However, as he notes, the fact that borders are vacillating does not mean that they are disappearing. On the contrary, he argues, far from Ohmae's vision of the "borderless world" discussed earlier, we see increasingly that "borders are being both multiplied and reduced in their localisation and their function, they are being thinned and doubled, becoming border zones, regions or countries where one can reside and live".[1] The transformation of the means of international communication has, according to Balibar

> relativised the functions of the point of entry and by contrast revalorised internal controls, creating within each territory zones of transit and transition, populations awaiting entry or exit, individually or collectively engaged in a process of negotiation of their ... mode of presence (and ... rights) with one or more states.[2]

In parallel with Bauman's argument noted earlier, Samir Amin notes that the globalisation of the world economy stops well short of allowing any untrammelled mobility of labour from the colonial peripheries to the metropolitan centres, and that while "the mobility of commodities and capital leaves national space to embrace the whole world, the labour force [largely] remains enclosed within the national framework".[3] Indeed, one could argue that, in terms of immigration controls, people are now more tied to their country of birth than at any time this century. As Naficy observes, while technology, media and capital are globalised and easily cross the geographical boundaries of nation-states, simultaneously national governments are almost everywhere tightening their border controls and more vigilantly enforcing immigration laws, often

225

through the effective militarisation of their borders.[4] Thus, Bauman argues that globalisation and (re)territorialisation are in fact mutually complementary processes, so that there is a "mutual conditioning and reciprocal reinforcement between the 'globalisation' of all aspects of the economy and the renewed emphasis on the 'territorial principle'".[5] We should recall that the British ex-Prime Minister Mrs Thatcher, having been persuaded of the advantages of European "free trade", was scandalised when she discovered the possibility that this might also mean some (relatively) higher degree of mobility for people and other unwanted foreign elements. As she put it, "we joined Europe to have free movement of goods ... I did not join Europe to have free movement of terrorists, criminals, drugs, plant and animal diseases and rabies and illegal immigrants."[6]

The fundamental point, as Gupta and Ferguson argue, is that "if we accept a world of originally separate and culturally distinct places, then the question of immigration policy is just a question of how hard should we try to maintain this original order?" However, if we acknowledge that cultural difference is produced and maintained in a field of power relations in a world always already spatially interconnected, then the "restriction of immigration becomes visible as one of the main means through which the disempowered are kept that way" and are spatially incarcerated within the zones of poverty produced within the system of globalised economics.[7] At its simplest, Walden Bello argues that we have to understand that most migrants "are refugees fleeing the wasteland that has been created by the equivalent of a scorched earth strategy by means of which the poor countries of the world's South have in effect been condemned to exile from the global economy".[8] In an attempt to escape this fate, as Hall observes, all over the world

> peoples, drawn inexorably through the laws of uneven development into the networks of a globalised world system, and long accustomed to dwell simultaneously in the "local" worlds of traditional societies and the global worlds of international capital, have simply packed their few belongings and set out – legally or illegally – to cross those visible and invisible frontiers designed to keep them immured in the "backwardness" of their "ethnic particularisims", in search of ... whichever European or American city they can get access to.[9]

The migrant in limbo

In a critique of the "millenialist hyperbole of global fluidity", Vered Amit-Talai offers a "cautionary tale against assumptions that spatial displacement and increased border crossings necessarily or easily engender new forms of imagined community, even when old notions of home lose their salience".[10] Amit-Talai's complaint is that those who enthuse about the positive potential of travel, transit and creolisation confuse the relationship between uncertainty, deterritorialisation and boundary. In celebrating ... interstitiality, they can end up being quite cavalier about the necessary and ... difficult ... work ... required to construct ... new forms of identity and naive about the political or personal costs of failed or stillborn efforts at creating these new boundaries.

This is to argue that in their "precarious traversals of borders, tenuous legal statuses and rights" migrants can often lose the benefits of their old forms of belonging without gaining any replacement or substitute for them, as they are buffeted by economic processes "that treat human beings as disposable: that demand mobility but leave mobile workers impaled on the national borders so easily traversed by capital".[11] Amit-Talai's central point is that many migrants get caught up "in the crossfire between structural pressures towards career and geographic mobility, on the one hand, and worker and citizen entitlements still predicated on the assumption/principle of stable employment and residence, on the other". Many of the migrants Amit-Talai studied in the Cayman Islands have ended up in limbo: they have been away from their homes of origin for too long to feel comfortable going back there. They might still own a house in their country of origin (usually rented out to strangers) but it offers them no more than a default place to be. On the other hand, they have no long-term welfare or residence rights in the Cayman Islands and certainly do not feel at home there: they exist in a state of "tenuous stalemate" in which "they cannot go backwards and they cannot go forwards".[12] As Karen Fog-Olwig puts it, for migrants existing in this kind of interstitial state of displacement, their experience is not at all one of a sojourn abroad which will be redeemed by their ultimate return to the familiar structure of their home life, as it was in traditional societies, where journeys such as pilgrimages served ultimately to consolidate the migrant's sense of belonging.[13] Such migrants can remain stuck in an eternal situation of transience, neither belonging where they work nor having much real sense of connection back to the homes they have left.[14]

As Barry Curtis and Clare Pajaczkowska argue, "if the tourist travels, for the most part, backwards in time, then the immigrant, the exile and the diasporic travel forward with no promise of a restored home".[15] In this respect, the predicament of the migrant worker or the refugee is largely an "inversion of the tourist's experience, on a journey in which the return to the 'present' of home, the lost equilibrium which brings closure, coherence and the security of identification, is hopelessly deferred".[16] Thus, in her study of Turkish workers living in Germany, Ruth Mandel argues that while their Turkishness marginalises them in the German context, when they visit Turkey on their regular visits home the markers of their Germanness entrap them in "a circular quest for an increasingly elusive identity".[17] In a similar sense, as we have seen, Baldassar reports that while their continuing attachment to their place of origin makes the immigrants she studied still identify themselves as Italians, despite their years of settlement in Australia, their years of emigration have nonetheless transformed them into Australians in the eyes of the townspeople of their home town.[18]

The value of mobility: home truths?

As we have seen earlier, all discussions of mobility necessarily tend to have moral overtones of one sort or another. Sometimes travel is seen as enriching, and to be "travelled" means to be sophisticated and experienced. At other times, travel is principally articulated through a discourse of regret at the consequent root-lessness or artificiality of mobile life. Commonsensically in English, one talks of young people "settling down" at the point of marrying and setting up house together: the moral approval of this act as a signifier of maturity is built into the descriptive terminology. Thus Madan Sarup observed the heavily value-laden nature of the very word "home" in everyday discourse, pointing to the burden carried by words and phrases such as "homecoming", "home-made", "make yourself at home", "bought home to me", "home truths" and "home is where the heart is".[19] If the moral economy of a household is grounded in the creation of a home then, vice versa, the absence of the physical structure seems to betoken the absence of a moral framework.[20] Thus Lisa Malkki observes that refugees' loss of bodily connection to their homelands means that they often also come to be seen as having also lost their moral bearings, no longer having the status of honest citizens.[21] It is, in fact, impossible to discuss the issue of mobility without making implicit value judgements, as witnessed earlier in the discussion of Heller's use of the deeply value-laden terms "geographical monogamy" and "geographical promiscuity". To be a vagrant is already, within that conventional vocabulary, a moral if not always a criminal offence.

Conversely, there are many contemporary theorists who would valorise (if not romanticise) ideas of travel and mobility. Thus Scott Malcolmson notes positively that immigrant life, especially at disadvantaged social levels and despite its constrained circumstances, is often a "model of cosmopolitanism. One need not search long in an American city to find a stockroom worker or janitor who can communicate more successfully, in more languages, than most Ivy League college graduates."[22] However, the number of highly qualified bi- or multi-lingual immigrants forced to make a living doing menial work in the affluent West only goes to demonstrate that the terms of trade of cosmopolitan exchange invariably work to favour the already powerful. In this connection, Edward Said has stressed "the danger of intellectuals projecting their own sense of dislocation as a universal cultural condition", and he emphasises the "impor-tance of distinguishing exile as a romanticised trope of intellectual life from the real conditions of displaced or migrant populations".[23] Just as Rob Wilson has queried what he calls the "lyric promise of postnational culture" so Pheng Cheah has argued against the privileging of migrancy as "the most radical form of transformative agency in contemporary globalisation".[24] For Cheah, flux and mobility are not necessarily phenomena to be celebrated. Moreover, in his view,

228

much "hybridity theory" reduces postcoloniality to the space of the metropolis, has no interest in those who do (or cannot) migrate, and has nothing to say to those still dwelling in the post-colonial South, for whom sustaining the stability of their nation, in so far as they can, remains their only effective defence strategy against the ravages of the global economy. In a similar vein to Cheah, Tim Brennan is highly dismissive of what he calls the "almost boastful cosmopolitanism" of those he calls "Third World metropolitan celebrities".[25] In his associated critique of contemporary forms of cosmopolitanism in literature, he claims (somewhat reductively) that this literature principally functions to supply exotica for a reactionary market in the taste for the "picturesque" of a cultural miscellany based on empire.[26] His argument is that much of it, produced by "spokespersons for a kind of perennial migration", has the effect of valorising a rhetoric of wandering and is premised on an epistemological privileging of the "all-seeing eye of the nomadic sensibility".[27] Certainly, the epistemological point at issue is a serious one, and Robbins is rightly critical of the dubious tendency in some recent theories to reinstate the figure of the cosmopolitan intellectual as the equivalent of Mannheim's "free-floating" (and therefore supposedly both more perceptive and more "objective") intellectual.[28] Indeed, this potential analogy is not the only one we might want to make. We might also beware the dangers of constructing migrant(s) as the inheritors, by virtue of their objective place in the global economy, of the epistemological privilege which Lukacs famously bestowed on the proletariat, by virtue of their position in the capitalist system, in an earlier period.

Cheah accuses Clifford of "endowing cosmopolitan mobility with a normative dimension" and of presenting cosmopolitan movements as "exemplary instances of active resistance to localism and cultural homogenisation". According to Cheah, Clifford assumes that all forms of cultural stasis are inherently reactionary, and correspondingly presumes that "physical mobility is the being of emancipatory practice because it generates stasis-disrupting forms of cultural displacement". Furthermore, he argues, "hybridity theorists" (as he calls them), such as Clifford and Bhabha, are "attached to historical cases of migration and diasporic mobility because they see such cases as empirical instances of the flux they regard as the ontological essence of culture", in so far as they equate physical mobility with the "possibility for endless hybrid self-creation and autonomy from the 'given'".[29] In so far as this claim could be substantiated, it would obviously be a serious matter, if Clifford were doing no more than belatedly following Roland Barthes' libertarian valorisation of flux as always progressive (and all forms of stability as thus *ipso facto* reactionary).[30] However, in his response to Cheah's criticisms, Clifford clearly demonstrates his own awareness that there is nothing automatically progressive "about crossing borders or living in diaspora". As he further notes, in the global economy, physical mobility is certainly no longer the necessary precondition for the disruption of cultural stasis: "you do not have to leave home to be confronted with the concrete challenges of hybrid agency ... at least since 1492, the outside world is guaranteed to find you".[31]

The historical roots of "nomadology"

In his erudite essay on the deep historical roots of the contemporary post-modern and post-structuralist tendencies to romanticise "nomadology", John Durham Peters demonstrates the origins of this ideology in Christianity and its continuity through medieval and nineteenth-century romanticism.[32] As he notes, concepts of mobility and narratives of exile, pilgrimage, displacement and dispersion are central to the canon of Western civilisation, from the biblical story of man's expulsion from the garden of Eden onwards. Drawing on Hegel's argument that romanticism is continuous with Christianity, Peters points out that just as the major themes of medieval romance were those of quest, exile and impossible love, so in nineteenth-century romanticism "much of the picture of humans as sojourning pilgrims is preserved without the theo-logical content".[33] To that extent he argues, the postmodern beatification of the nomad is thus caught up in the romance of the quest (or "the road") and in a "dream of radical liberty" in which nomads are identified with not just phys-ical but intellectual mobility, and are seen to "liberate thinking from dogmatism, break through convention to new life and beauty and [to] prize the mobile diversity of being".[34] Nomadic cultures have long been a canvas on to which moderns have projected their romantic idylls, and Western anthropolo-gists and travel writers have often displayed a fascination with them as representing a particularly heroic mode of life.[35]

For the nomadologist, any notion of a fixed identity or home is a dangerous illusion, involving the disavowal or elimination of difference and what Rosie Braidotti calls "the terrifying stupidity of that illusion of unity".[36] Conversely, critics of nomadology such as Durham Peters argue that only from the point of view of a privileged elite does nomadic life take on such a rosy hue, in so far as while "those with political rights and civil securities can extol homelessness all they want ... such talk is profoundly dangerous for those who are in fact home-less". Along with the exoticisation of alterity often goes its oppression, in a process whereby the powerful centre "feeds at a prissy distance on the wild glamour of minorities, while neither alienating their hardships or recognising their autonomy" – as in the case of the gypsies, for whom the romanticisation of their lifestyle by Western cultural elites has done little to protect them from material and legislative oppression.[37]

Discrepant and variable cosmopolitanisms

By contrast to the more traditional valorisation of sedentarism, "settling down" and geographical monogamy invoked earlier, Ignatieff notes that cosmo-politanism makes a "positive ethic out of cultural borrowing" such that within those terms it is then presumed that "exogamy [is] better than endogamy, and promiscuity better than provincialism".[38] However, once one inserts the question of power into the equation, one might equally say that "a cosmopolitan is simply someone empowered to decide who is provincial".[39] The oppositions between home and abroad, staying and moving have often, as James Clifford remarks, "been naturalised along lines of gender (female, domestic space versus male travel), class (the active alienated bourgeoisie versus the stagnant, soulful poor) and race/culture (modern, rootless Westerners versus traditional, rooted 'natives')".[40] Similarly Malcolmson warns that we should guard against the Eurocentric arrogance of the presumption that "I" am in a position to "correct your provinciality with the cosmopolitanism of my terms".[41] As Clifford has observed, "the notion that certain classes of people are cosmopolitan (travellers) while the rest are local (natives)" can perhaps best be seen as "as the ideology of one (very powerful) travelling culture".[42] The figure of the cosmopolitan, like that of the *flâneur*, is clearly masculine, and is often a symbolic figure of the West and its sophistications marked out against a backward other. Thus, in the opposition between the cosmopolitan and the local, the latter is almost inevitable denigrated as "narrow, benighted, parochial, conservative, incestuous, ill-informed".[43] Against the conventional approach, which assumes that there is only one true cosmopolitanism, we must recognise that this lofty creed, for all its detachment from local loyalties, was (and is) nonetheless the expression of a specifically European philosophical universalism, expressing Greek and Enlightenment values.

In his trenchant critique of contemporary forms of cosmopolitan and multi-cultural politics Tim Brennan rightly raises the question of their largely American base and the extent to which they inadvertently serve the interests of a US-dominated free market liberalism. In so far as they override and denigrate forms of postcolonial nationalism which remain necessary foci of struggle against transnational capital, there is a danger that the new cosmopolitanism will serve as an unwitting support for US-centred Transnational Capital.[44] We must also beware the dangers of a specifically (if quite unself-conscious) American cosmopolitanism, which presents itself as though it were simply the proper and fullest expression of uncontroversially universal values. Thus Malcolmson warns of the dangers for American cosmopolitans of dwelling on the "specialness" of their country as a nation of migrants, as "always already cosmopolitan", so that America becomes the global model of (and yardstick for) cosmopolitanism. As he notes ironically, if the immigrant is figured as some kind of global cosmopolitan, the "carrier of some liberal and liberated hybridity", then it is the USA, from this perspective, which represents his or her spiritual home[45] and Americans may thus be able to imagine themselves as simultaneously cosmopolitan and patriotic.[46] For Robbins, the point is that we must recognise that there now exist a whole variety of "discrepant cosmopolitanisms" and that there are "plural and particular ... European and non-European ... weak and underprivileged ... strong and privileged" forms of cosmopolitanism, in different locations. Moreover, we must recognise that they all are (and need to be seen as) *located* – for, as Robbins puts it, "no one actually is or ever can be a cosmopolitan in the full sense of belonging everywhere".[47]

However, notwithstanding all its attendant difficulties, it is important that we rescue what Wilson calls cosmopolitanism's "aesthetic of openness towards otherness".[48] Robbins argues that in doing this, rather than attempting to somehow transcend nationalism in search of some "abstract emptiness of non-allegiance" (or, alternatively, giving all forms of cosmopolitanism a negative evaluation) we should attempt to develop a sense of belonging which "includes the possibility of presence in other places, dispersed but real forms of membership, a density of overlapping allegiances".[49] We should not accept a polarity between cosmopolitanism as meaning an allegiance to the "world-wide community of beings" on the part of people "indifferent to where they live" as opposed to the narrow nationalism of the "old home feeling" of those emotionally rooted in a single place.[50] Rather, Robbins notes, following Yi-Fu Tuan, it might be better to opt for a "cosmopolite" recognition of our multiple rootedness, our multiple attachments and connections (of different types and at different levels), which avoids both the artificial detachment of the one perspective, and the narrow exclusiveness of the other.[51]

Hybridity talk

In the wake of the valorisation of cosmopolitan hybridity within the fields of cultural studies and post-colonial theory, a number of questions have been raised about the possible dangers of these anti-essentialist positions. I am concerned here to take on board some of the basic points of the critique of "cosmo-multiculturalism", in so far as that critique usefully alerts us to the dangers of any romanticised analysis of our situation which fails to address the continuing disparities of power which vitiate any easy celebration of hybridity. However, in doing this I am also concerned to avoid what seems to me the ultimately reductionist perspective into which some of this criticism falls.

Among the critics of the celebration of hybridity in discussions of contemporary art, we find Sarat Maharaj rightly warning against the dangers of hybridity now "becoming the privileged, prime term" of analysis and thus simply "swapping places with the notion of stylistic purity" as the new buzzword of our times. As he notes, in this process the term "seems paradoxically to flip over into its opposite, to function as the label of flattening sameness" or, in effect, undifferentiated Difference (with a capital D) marked unproblematically against a EurAmcentric standard.[52] In a parallel sense, Sardar *et al.* argue that the dominant epistemology of the West lumps together the vast diversity of peoples all over the world into one gigantic category of Otherness, so that "the distinctiveness of a particular Other … [is] lost in the generality shared with all Others, that of being different … from the West".[53] By way of example, in his study of immigrant encounters with Swedish culture, Gunar Alsmark reports one Argentinian refugee who understandably complains that she is

> tired of being exotic. Tired of those who come to me and introduce themselves and say "We want to be friends with you because foreigners are so nice. You sing and you are happy" ... Year after year, Swedes come to me and say "It's so boring here, but you're so nice, you come from hot countries." I try to explain that I don't like the sun. Our tradition is to seek the shade on hot days.

As she notes, the specificity of her cultural difference seems either immaterial or incomprehensible to her Swedish hosts – for them, she simply represents the Exotic Foreigner in general.[54]

In relation to the valorisation of hybridity within cultural studies, Pnina Werbner claims that if hybridity once posed a challenge to modernity's ordered systems, so it must follow that its supposed transgressive powers are diminished to the extent that, within the globalising trends of postmodernity, mixtures and cross-overs of all sorts are now routinised.[55] Similarly, John Hutnyk glosses Gayatri Spivak to the effect that a critique of hybridity is now necessary because that for which "hybridity talk" (as he describes it) was useful "now tends to inhabit other struggles demarcated differently".[56] In the same vein, Werbner claims Spivak's authority in support of her assertion that "too much hybridity ... leaves all the old problems of class exploitation and racial oppression unre-solved", while Hutnyk claims that hybridity talk in its cultural studies form is itself in danger of becoming just another marketable commodity.[57] This is ulti-mately to dismiss the politics of hybridity as a rhetorical (and political) cul-de-sac, serving only to divert attention from what he calls the "real" demands of anti-racist politics.[58]

Just as Peter Van der Veer is critical of what he sees as cultural studies' "extremely romantic notion of nomadism" and its preoccupation with questions of marginality, Freidman takes issue with what he describes as Iain Chambers' "militant attitude against all forms of rootedness" and argues that, for him, as for Homi Bhabha "the enemy is that which is generally bounded and thus, for him, essentialised".[59] Van der Veer pushes the critique of Bhabha even further, arguing that he unwisely "emphasises the potential of migrants to reinvent themselves continuously in the post-colonial situation of cultural hybridity" much in the manner of the traditional romantic trope of the "self-made indi-vidual who invents himself in the marginality of the American frontier", to the extent that the figure of the migrant is then conflated with the romantic image of the pioneer settler.[60] There is certainly a considerable danger in any simplistic conceptual reversal which privileges the migrant's hybrid lifestyle in order to celebrate as central all that was previously defined as marginal. As critics such as Aijaz Ahmad rightly argue, such an attempt to turn the ideological tables on the West fails to deal with the continuing power differentials between (what still are) the centres as against (what still are) the margins and fails to deal with the terms of trade within which the new hybrid mixtures and melanges are produced.[61] We shall return to the question of the valuation of mobility later in the chapter, but first we shall explore the cultural consequences of the commercialisation of hybridity.

The commodification of differences

According to Zygmunt Bauman, ours is, in some respects a "heterophiliac" age, in which "difference comes at a premium" and where, in contrast to the modernist presumption that the "order of the future would have no room for strangers", our postmodern times are "marked by an almost universal agreement that difference is good, precious and in need of protection and cultivation".[62] However, the difficulty here is that, in the West, "difference" is principally available to members of the dominant cultures in the commoditised forms of ethnic musics, cuisines and fashions. Thus, in his trenchant critique of current tendencies in Western music circles towards what he sees as the exploitative marketing of World Music in commodified forms for privileged white audiences, John Hutnyk describes this phenomenon as a "kind of commercial aural travel-consumption", a late twentieth-century "version of the Great Exhibitions of the nineteenth century" in which spectacularised forms of primitivism were displayed for the edification of the West.[63]

For Hutnyk, occasions such as World Music festivals are no more than uncritical appropriations of (at best) half-understood cultural differences which, rather than representing examples of "human harmony and togetherness", are better understood as exploitative and regressive reductions of a variety of forms of musical and cultural differences to "something that mass audiences can comfortably appreciate on a sunny weekend".[64] While Hutnyk is surely right to identify the problematic dimensions of these forms of multiculturalism, his own ultimate reduction of this phenomenon to its potentially exploitative commodity form is unhelpful. Minimally, one could still argue that, notwithstanding his reservations, it is precisely through occasions such as these festivals and the commercial marketing opportunities for non-white, non-Western music to which they have given rise that, in the UK at least, the cultural hegemony of white "Britpop" has, in recent years, been somewhat undermined. However, World Music is but one form of the commodification of difference. Just as Hutnyk critiques the presumption that multiculturalism in music is necessarily any kind of a good thing, so Jon May critiques the parallel presumption that there is anything necessarily progressive in multicultural patterns of residence.[65]

I argued earlier, following Doreen Massey, that there is nothing inevitably reactionary about place-based identities, as long as they are founded on an "extroverted" definition, in which a place is seen as constituted by the flows of people, objects, and symbols passing through it. The implicit presumptions of this position are the subject of May's criticisms. His argument is that the partic-

234

ular form of openness to difference exhibited, for example by the members of the white, urban middle class in their participation in the gentrification of inner-city multi-cultural areas in the UK and in their parallel enthusiasm for exotic foods, amounts in fact to a form of racism which is "anything but progressive".[66] Drawing on hooks, May argues that this is simply a form of commodification of otherness, within which multicultural difference is consumed exploitatively by the privileged white middle classes – as a form of spice or seasoning "that can liven up the dull dish that is mainstream white culture".[67] This is also the force of Adrian Rifkin's argument that, for the privileged "in the modern metropolis travel and slumming have collapsed into one another".[68] May claims that this is essentially a form of exploitative aestheticisation – "part of an agreeable new lifestyle aesthetic for those who would advocate a superficial politics of difference as part of their cultural capital".[69] For him, the white members of this new middle class are best understood as "new urban *flâneur(s)*" projecting their exoticising gaze on to the minority residents of the new global city. In May's view, these people are celebrating not so much a politics of difference as indulging their own sense of the picturesque, as they reduce the reality of other people's lives to "the sights of an afternoon stroll ... for those suitably insulated from the reality of life in a declining inner city neighbourhood".[70]

Certainly, May's last statement here carries a considerable and important force: areas such as the one he studied in London do display a crucial politics of differential access and mobility.[71] As May notes, while members of the area's privileged white group are able to undertake occasional adventurous sorties into the exotic, "when tired of this other world ... [they] can always go home" to their privileged white enclaves.[72] Conversely the members of the area's non-white communities have far less possibility of entry (not least, by virtue of price) into the spaces (restaurants, etc.) that the privileged regard as their home turf. However, the difficulty with May's argument, like that of Hutnyk, lies in its reductiveness. While it is undoubtedly true that these elements of aestheticisation of difference are in play as one of the dimensions of the experience of life in a multicultural area such as that he studies, to reduce everything to this one exploitative dynamic is problematic. Given that, in the end, the logic of May's position would seem if anything most sympathetic to the straightforward prejudices of the area's elderly white residents – who dislike newcomers of all sorts – whether "the blacks" or the white gentrifiers – it is hard to see what positive alternative outcome he could envisage. Presumably, his advice to would-be "gentrifiers" of these exoticised districts would be the same (if less wryly phrased) as that given "for men's ears only" by Adrian Rifkin in the context of his critique of patriarchal discourses – that they should rather "stay at home" and cultivate new arts of reading existing travellers' tales.[73]

Nonetheless, in this connection Ghassan Hage is right to complain that the cosmopolitan experience of tasting other foods at local ethnic restaurants can produce a discourse of diversity in which migrant subjects themselves are erased, and where the central subject is, once again, the Anglo-cosmopolitan consumer. The danger, as he argues, is one of producing a "multiculturalism without migrants" – a culinary landscape in which exotic foods are disconnected from the cultures and places which they symbolise. Multiculturalism needs some other index than the number of ethnic restaurants available in a given neighbourhood. As Hage tartly observes, at present it does indeed sometimes seem that

> in the cosmo-multicultural version of things, if an area is more multicultural than another, this appears to be less to do with who *inhabits* it, who makes a home in it, and the degree of interaction between different cultural subjects within it, and more to do with what multicultural commodities are *available* on its markets, and who has the capacity to appreciate them.[74]

However, it is also worth noting that not all consumers display any such taste for the "exotic". Thus, in their commentary on Daniel Miller *et al.*'s study of shopping in North London, Phil Crang and Peter Jackson observe that what that study found was a strong tendency for many shoppers to draw an unfavourable contrast between familiar local products ("a good old cup of tea, roast beef and all that"; "pure linen" and other British goods, from "nice quality shops") and inferior and shoddy, imported products from further afield ("it's rubbish today: Taiwan, Hong Kong, Jamaica"; "you get stuff from all over the world these days ... foreign muck"). As Crang and Jackson note, these working-class consumers draw heavily on a set of discourses about the defiling potential of foreign products which has a long history in Britain's imperial past. Even the experience of doing their shopping within the controlled environment of a purpose-built modern shopping centre still leaves some consumers anxious about their encounters with the exotic, even in its commodified forms.[75]

Anti-anti-essentialism

In a further critique of hybridity theory, Werbner argues that the deconstructionist critique of all forms of essentialism has gone too far – not only in "denying the ontological grounds of experience as a source of cultural meaning" but in tending to "label all collective representations ... as misplaced essentialisms".[76] For Werbner, the crucial issue is to distinguish between, on the one hand, necessary and enabling modes of objectification (which can be understood as arising from "the way collectivities describe, redescribe and argue over who they are") and, on the other hand, pernicious modes of reification of identity which fail to allow for the fluidity and provisionality of any process of collective naming or labelling. As she puts it at another point, if we are to avoid "essentialising essentialism" we must recognise that "not all collective representations and self-representations are essentialising in the same way".[77] As we shall see in the later discussion of Honi Fern Haber's critique of Young's analysis of the politics of difference, this is a point of some considerable weight.

If solidarities are often ephemeral achievements they are nonetheless crucial to minority groups' strategies of survival in a hostile environment. Thus Werbner argues that "anti-essentialist arguments attacking the false construction of 'culture' or 'community' fail to recognise the importance for participants ... of an imaginative belief in the reality of such achieved solidarities".[78] She accepts that we must recognise the extent to which any community is necessarily constituted through processes of argument, debate and conflict – over who has the right to lead and to name the community, who can claim to represent it, and how it is to be represented. However, as she rightly notes, this process of "self-essentialising is a rhetorical performance in which an imagined community is invoked ... situationally in opposition to other ... communities". It is in this performative rhetoric that people "essentialise their imagined communities in order to mobilise for action".[79]

The fluidity of this process is well captured in Gerd Baumann's analysis of the contested nature of community in the particular multicultural area of London which he studied.[80] Baumann demonstrates how (and why) inhabitants of Southall oscillate between closed and open definitions of the various cultures or communities to which they claim allegiance according to the demands of their situation. If, on some occasions, for particular purposes, people hold to seemingly reified images of community, this is because, as Baumann notes "in a discourse of political contestation ... reification may be desirable, and even ... necessary, to effect mobilisation".[81] At other times, and for other purposes, these same people will undercut these dominant images of community identity and closure with what Baumann calls more "demotic discourses", in the process of negotiating, arguing with others and redefining who they are. The problem is that, as Werbner argues, "in the present deconstructive moment any unitary conception of a 'bounded' culture is pejoratively labelled ... essentialist".[82] In a world where scarce resources have often to be fought for, it can hardly be assumed that appeals to community which, for political purposes, stress a group's shared external distinctiveness, rather than its internal divisions, are necessarily reactionary. Such seemingly essentialising claims by no means preclude, as Baumann shows, more open and fluid modes of identity-making being utilised at other moments.

Differential hybridities

Just as we might distinguish between forms of mobility and their significance depending on the context of power and choice within which they occur, so we must distinguish between different forms and modalities of hybridity in different contexts, most especially in relation to the degree of choice or control that people have over their living circumstances. Thus, Massey notes that while we might want to reject a future in which local cultures protect their distinctiveness by restricting any invasions from outside ... it is necessary to remember that the alternative to "endless mixing" will be a mixing on unequal terms. And each form of mixing will have its own geography of power.[83]

Life in many cities is now conducted in a manner in which each culture is compressed against others. As Sandra Wallman puts it,

whether modern migrants are "pulled" by better economic prospects, [or] "pushed" by persecution ... they are rarely moving to vacant homes ... they fetch up in cities with an already high density of population. Inevitably, those in search of new homes press up against "locals" of that place who already have homes to defend ... [and as] the supply of homes is finite: what you take, I lose.[84]

Thus one of Salman Rushdie's characters delivers a brief lecture on the modern city as the new *locus classicus* of colliding realities, describing how

lives that have no business mingling with one another sit side by side upon the omnibus. One universe, on a zebra crossing, is caught for an instant, blinking like a rabbit, in the headlamps of a motor-vehicle in which an entirely alien and contradictory continuum is to be found.[85]

Commenting on Swyngedouw's argument that what we see around us is "the resurrection of locality in an age of hyperspace", Erhard Berner argues that in a modern metropolis the First World is directly confronted with the Third. However, largely because of the ways in which kinship networks determine patterns of migration and settlement, it is also a situation in which, in the metropolis' different districts, "Korea borders on America, Mexico on Vietnam, Louisiana on Samoa and wars are possible between all these 'tribes'."[86] As Castells puts it, in the contemporary city, we are increasingly confronted by "a variety of social universes, whose fundamental characteristics are their fragmentation, the sharp definition of their boundaries, and the low level of communication with other such universes".[87]

In his critique of Dick Hebdige's and Celeste Olalquiaga's analysis of the lower East Side of New York, Tim Brennan criticises their tendency to valorise the various forms of hybridity which they identify there.[88] His concern is that theirs is an elite and aestheticised view of the matter – as if it were only a matter of struggles at the level of representation. Against this perspective, Brennan quotes the views of a long-standing lower East Side community activist who contends that

COSMOPOLITICS

despite the cultural mixing in New York City, migrant groups strive to maintain a culture they can call their own. The vision that emerges is not one of cosmopolitan hybridity but of immigrant communities longing for their own national cultures and imprisoned in the USA by economic circumstance.[89]

In a similar vein, Freidman poses the important question of "who can afford a cosmopolitan identity?", in the context of Werbner's claim that the "real voices from the margins want no truck with hybridity".[90] Notwithstanding the considerable difficulties begged by Werbner's valorisation of "real" (as opposed, presumably, to unreal) voices, Freidman's question remains an important one. As he puts it, hybridity means different things to people in different contexts, and he claims that

the urban poor, ethnically mixed ghetto is an area that does not imme- diately cater to the construction of explicitly new hybrid identities ... [where] the problems of survival are more closely related to territory and to creating secure life spaces ... just as the area itself may be divided into gang territories.

As he observes, in the context of the increased "ethnification" of public space there is often "little room for the hybrid identification discussed ... by cultural elites ... [as] ethnification entails the reinforcement of boundaries ... in a feedback process whereby increasing conflict leads to increasing closure, which in turn leads to increasing conflict".[91]

Nationalism and conjuncturalism

Just like mobility and hybridity, nationalism likewise depends for its significance on its context. Appadurai notes that it is increasingly common in the advanced West to regard nationalism as some kind of unwanted Third World import and to see it as if it were some kind of "disease, especially when it is someone else's nationalism".[92] Eley and Suny point out that, in the history of nationalism, it is an ideology which is seen to have degenerated as it moved further east, from its heroic origins in revolutionary France, throughout the nineteenth century, with its irrationalist and organicist elements increasingly predominating as it moved away from its point of origin. Nowadays, as Partha Chatterjee has it, nation- alism is seen increasingly by the West as some kind of

dark elemental, unpredictable force of primordial nature threatening the orderly calm of cultural life. What had once been banished to the outer peripheries of the earth is now seen as picking its way back toward Europe, through the long-forgotten provinces of the Hapsburg–Tzarist and ... Ottoman empires. Like drugs, terrorism and

239

illegal immigration, it is one more product of the Third World that the West dislikes but is powerless to stop.[93]

Thus, in his analysis of the way in which nationalism is now often demonised in the West, Tom Nairn argues that it is often presented as if it is only the re-emergence of the "mysterious, unfinished business of Eastern nationality ... this ... blood-based ... heroic and exclusive cult ... [the] atavistic force of the ethnic revival" which has somehow unfortunately wrecked the "New Order" of world affairs so optimistically heralded when the Berlin Wall came down in 1989.[94] As Stuart Hall notes in this connection, while many of the nationalisms which emerged in the course of the fragmentation of Communism were driven by ethnic absolutism, it ill behoves Western Europe to criticise them, in so far as its own historical development also occurred in the form of nationalisms which were racially and ethically exclusive. Moreover, as he notes,

> it is not a surprise that the Croatians, Slovenians, Latvians and Estonians should regard the construction of a little nation of their own as a passport to the west. These emergent nationalisms are not simply revivals of the past but reworkings of it in the context of the present.[95]

While these new forms of nationalism may seem to simply represent a return to a pre-1914 historical agenda, they also function, as Hall observes, as a way of evading the past and making a bid for modernity, in the form of entry to the Euro-Club. Similarly Nairn notes that nationalism, "far from being an irrational obstacle to development", was for most societies "the only way in which they could compete without being either colonised or annihilated". As he argues, if they "turned to the past (figuratively, to the "blood") in these modernisation struggles, it was essentially to stay intact as they levered themselves into the future" and their reliance on "ethnos" offered the only way of ensuring the cohesion necessary to this task. To this extent, Nairn (following Gellner) claims that nationalism is therefore "as much a native of modernity as are democracy and the capitalist motor of development. It is as inseparable from progress as they are."[96]

There is no more reason to assume that nationalist forms are always and inevitably reactionary than there is to assume that "crossover" practices and hybrid forms are always liberatory. The politics of these issues is always conjunctural and "what matters politically is who deploys nationality or transnationality, authenticity or hybridity against whom, with what relative power".[97] Describing his difficulties in delivering a speech denouncing nationalism on the occasion of his return to Bulgaria in 1981 after a long period of exile in France, Tzvetan Todorov observed that

> condemning national values has a different meaning depending on whether one lives in a little country ... in the orbit of another larger

one, or whether one lives abroad, in a third country, where one is ... free from any threat from a more powerful neighbour. Paris is undoubtedly a propitious place for a euphoric renunciation of nationalist values, Sofia much less so.[98]

In this connection, Ignatieff offers a powerful caution when he says that

If patriotism, as Samuel Johnson remarked, is the last refuge of a scoundrel, so post-nationalism, and its accompanying disdain for nationalist aspirations of others, may be the last refuge of the cosmopolitan ... and cosmopolitanism is the privilege of those who themselves can take a secure nation-state for granted.[99]

In the context of all this discussion of, as he puts it, "hybridity, collage, mélange, hotchpotch, synergy, bricollage, creolisation, mestizaje, mongrelisation, syncretism, transculturation, third cultures and what have you", Hannerz rightly argues for what he describes as "some rather unexciting caution". Against the more hyperbolic models of global flows, Hannerz contests Appadurai's argument that the new global culture is now so decentred that it can no longer usefully be understood in terms of "existing centre–periphery models, even those which allow for multiple centres and peripheries". Hannerz fully accepts that cultural flows run in more than one direction, rather than simply outwards to the peripheries, from Hollywood or the World Bank.[100] However, as he notes acerbically, it is as well to recognise the continued existence of "net asymmetries of flow". He argues, similarly, that it is important to observe that "some cultures are more Creole than others" and concludes that varieties (and disjunctures of) postmodern flux notwithstanding, we are still not "at a point when it has become entirely impossible to tell centres and peripheries apart".[101] In an important respect his argument echoes Nelly Richard's critique of postmodern theory from a Latin American perspective, where she notes that even within the discourse of "decentring" Eurocentric perspectives on modernity, it is often still the intellectuals of the powerful nations who stand at its centre.[102] Similarly, Gerardo Mosquera offers a simple but effective corrective to naive visions of a decentred, de-territorialised world, where multicultural flows move in all directions.[103] As he points out (based, in his case, on some years' experience of the practical difficulties involved) the best way to travel from one African country to another is usually via one of the capital cities of Europe. The point is simply that globalisation has not produced "a planet in which all points are interconnected in a reticular network". On the contrary, Mosquera argues, the connections only take place

inside a radial and hegemonic pattern around the (Northern) centres of power, where the peripheral countries [of the South] ... remain disconnected from each other, or are only connected indirectly via –

and under the control of – the centres ... [in a] structure of axial globalisation and zones of silence ... [where] globalisation ... [operates]
from and for the centres, with limited South–South connections.[104]

In this respect, as Paul Willemen observes,

> although we can all agree that cultural zones are far from unified,
> homogenous spaces, this should not lead us to deny or unduly rela-
> tivise the existence of borders. The existence of borders is very real,
> and although their meaning and function are changeable, their effective-
> ness has not diminished in the least.[105]

Having now, hopefully, gone some way towards establishing the necessarily
conjunctural significance of discourses of hybridity, cosmopolitanism and
nationalism as they are mobilised in the context of varying power relations, we
turn to reconsider the dynamics of community building at a variety of micro
and macro scales.

Nation, community and household: the fuzzy logics of solidarity

From a sociological point of view Michael Schudson questions the extent to
which social solidarity necessarily depends upon some form of unified value
consensus.[106] In his critique of the prevailing models for understanding the role
of culture in the integration of nations, Schudson argues that cultural unity is
neither the sole, nor a sufficient, nor perhaps even a necessary condition for
national integration.[107] In line with Lockwood's distinction between social integration and system integration, Schudson insists that not only must we
recognise the role of other factors (such as economic interdependence) in the
maintenance of social integration but that "it may be better to suggest not that
there are several forces that help societies to cohere, but that there are several
different ways in which a society is integrated". The point is that members of a
society do not need to all be members of one coherent community of shared
values for it to be viable. As long as they are coherently co-ordinated "people of
different roles, interests and values ... [can] manage through various formal and
informal mechanisms to interact peacefully".[108]

Some of the cruder sociological models of community, solidarity and identity
are the object of a perceptive critique from an anthropological point of view by
Anthony Cohen, in his analysis of the symbolic dimensions of processes of
community construction.[109] Cohen argues firstly that the conventional sociological contrast between *Gemeinschaft* and *Gesellschaft* (in Tönnies' terms) or
between mechanical and organic forms of solidarity (in Durkheim's terms) is
quite unhelpful if these distinctions are treated as representing a unilinear
historical schema of development. The point, argues Cohen, is that these are

242

not best seen as the exclusive schemas of successive periods of social development, but rather as "different modalities of behaviour within any society at a given period of its history", as mechanical and organic forms of solidarity are likely to co-exist in different areas of social life.[110] Second, Cohen is equally at pains to stress the versatility and flexibility of symbols and the crucial positive role of ambiguity in allowing the simultaneous expression of identity and difference at different levels of social scale. It is the versatility (or multi-accentuality, in Volosinov's terms) of the symbolic markers by which a community distinguishes itself from others which is crucial. By virtue of this indeterminacy "people of radically opposed views can find their own meanings in what nevertheless remain common symbols".[111] The symbols supply a common currency for the expression of meanings rather than necessitating any consensus of sentiment, and are in Douglas and Isherwood's terms "good to think with".[112] Thus it is the shared vocabulary of value, rather than any necessary orthodoxy of value content which enables the integrity of a community's distinctive identity and self-image to be sustained, in so far as this vocabulary allows people to share conceptual forms without, at the same time, necessarily requiring them to share their meanings.[113]

Cohen argues that what is at stake is how, if societies can be said to cohere, they do so around a commonality of forms of meaning rather than of contents. This is to regard community as an aggregating device rather than as an integrative mechanism and to see that "the triumph of community is to so contain ... variety that its inherent discordance does not subvert the apparent coherence which is expressed by its boundaries". It is by this method that the common forms of a culture reconcile individuality and community without necessarily subordinating its members to a tyranny of orthodoxy. The common symbolic repertoire of a community aggregates

> the individualities and ... differences found within ... and provides the means for their expression, interpretation and containment ... [and] transforms the reality of difference into the appearance of similarity. It unites them, in their opposition both to each other and those "outside". It thereby constitutes and gives reality to the community's boundaries.

The same complexities attach to expressions of community identity produced for external consumption. In a comment which echoes Gayatri Spivak's remarks on the role of strategic essentialism, Cohen notes that general statements of belief or position presented on behalf of "the community", if "not exactly fictions, are often sufficient distortions of individuals' aspirations that they would not pass within the community". Such expressions nonetheless have a crucial role to play in many forms of inter-community communication and negotiation, as they are the political means by which the community expresses its identity for particular purposes, on particular occasions.[114]

If we move the analysis to a different level of socio-geographical scale, we find strong parallels between Cohen's analysis of large-scale societal processes and Scott K. Phillips' analysis of similar phenomena at a micro level. In his analysis of relations between "natives" and "incomers" in a Yorkshire village, Phillips demonstrates convincingly that while the distinction between these two groups is central to the life of the village it is, nonetheless, a boundary which is both porous and mobile, and which is marked by different people, in different ways, for different purposes, at different times. This boundary then, while important, is far from fixed – indeed it is, he says, "anything but hard and fast".[115] Just as Gerd Baumann argues in the case of Southall, Phillips suggests that rather than thinking in terms of a single inside/outside boundary demarcating the community, we should note that the local/incomer distinction is simply what he calls a "cultural shorthand" used for particular purposes, on particular occasions. Alongside this shorthand there also exists what he calls the "cultural longhand" in which both incomers and locals, in everyday contexts, communicate and represent themselves and others as "belonging to the community less in dualistic terms and more in qualified ways … [placing] themselves … at various points along a *scale* of localness".[116] The scalar qualifications, Phillips notes, are also likely to contain temporal qualifications, relative to how local a person is deemed to be *now* – i.e. after some specific period of time.[117] To this extent, the village is best understood not so much as a unified and homogeneous cultural entity, clearly defined against all outsiders, but as a nodal point on a cultural continuum of belonging – on which scale a person's place will vary, depending on the context and function of the questions posed as to their identity, in that particular instance.

In relation to questions of ethnicity, Cohen argues that for some purposes it is best to "regard ethnicity as a strategy, based upon choice and influenced by a calculus of advantage".[118] Of course, people do not always have such a choice, in so far as categories of ethnicity are often imposed on one group of people by another more powerful one. However, in some situations people do make such choices of self-ascription. In this respect, at a micro level, Sandra Wallman's analysis of a group of London households offers a valuable caution against the essentialising of ethnicity. As she observes, while from the outside (in the eyes of various observers) a household's ethnic origin is often hypostatised (so as to give it a necessarily defining role), from the inside, considering ethnicity as a resource, sometimes it is of relevance, sometimes it is a liability, sometimes, and for some purposes, it is irrelevant. As Wallman observes, we should not assume that:

> people of the same ethnic origin use the ethnic tie in the same way all the time and that the livelihood of ethnic minority households will be dominated by ethnicity … Age and family stage can be better predictors of a household's organisation and work patterns … and employment or locality more important loci of its identity.

Conversely, neither is locality always important in the same way, rather "its significance varies according to which of the household's resources are vested in the local area, and which are vested outside it, in other geographic domains".[119]

At a yet more microscopic scale, in relation to the household, Allan demonstrates that the boundary round the domestic home itself is a similarly complex phenomenon.[120] As we have seen, Phillips argues that the village he studied is better understood by mobilising a scalar continuum of degrees of localness, rather than a rigid and fixed division between outsiders and locals. In a similar vein, to return to the issue of domestic boundaries discussed in Chapter 2, Allan argues that the question of who is allowed into the home, under what circumstances, for what purposes (and of who, correspondingly, is excluded – and when) is much more complex than might first appear.[121] As Allan observes, even the question of whose home it is does not necessarily allow of a simple answer, as not all those living in a house may think of it equally as their home (elderly parents, step-children, au pairs, lodgers, etc.) and some of them will have more control over its use than others. He argues that even the primary distinction between insiders and outsiders is less clearly marked than is often assumed, so that there are "different degrees of outsiders", and conversely "insiders are not always as cohesive, or as 'revealing' to one another as the category implies". To this extent the somewhat rigid geographical connotations of the term "boundary" need counterbalancing by some recognition that the limits of the home are often "somewhat permeable, fuzzy and liable to alter".[122] Indeed, an examination of the relative rigidity of such boundaries – as between different types of home, for example – is a key terrain for research. Precisely to the extent that the home is the family's private territory, which outsiders of one sort or another "enter only when invited and then only for reasonably well-defined purposes", so "privileged access to the home symbolises the solidarity of kinship".[123] Nonetheless, even the access of close or primary kin to the home is itself carefully policed: they may be granted access to rooms beyond the front parlour in which visitors are normally received, but they should not prove too nosey, nor should they outstay their welcome. Even inside the family and its close kin, and within the very realm of the *heimlich*, trouble and conflict still lurk, ready to erupt even on the most sacred occasions designed to symbolise family solidarity (the family row that sometimes breaks out over Christmas dinner, for example).

11

POSTMODERNISM, POST-STRUCTURALISM AND THE POLITICS OF DIFFERENCE

At home in Europe?

Nostalgia, belonging and fear

Today we see the rise of a variety of reactionary particularisms attempting to "salvage centred, bounded and coherent identities – placed identities for place-less times" or to (re)invent "primordial" places, in which a group's culture is held to be historically rooted, for which people are willing to die or kill others.[1] In this context it is sometimes hard to resist the idea that the very idea of home is itself reactionary and should simply be ceded to the political Right. Certainly, as Rapport and Dawson observe, there is a widespread nostalgia for a vision of homeliness which "posits an idyllic past of unified tradition, certainty, stasis and cognitive and behavioural commonality ... an 'original life world' of traditional absoluteness and fixity, where the individual is ... first and 'truly' at home". In this mythical vision the home is "socially homogenous, communal, peaceful, safe and secure" and people can be "reintegrated within all-embracing, meaningful structures and social, physical and metaphysical solidarity".[2] As we have seen, there is plenty of evidence of those with the necessary resources attempting to reconstruct for themselves (within gated communities and the like) private, enclosed havens which will serve to produce a refuge of exactly this kind.

In the light of such developments, Celeste Olalquiaga argues that, today, the "notion of home endures solely as an icon of itself; home is now a nostalgic yearning, a burning desire for a romanticised sense of belonging whose segregative appeal is apparent in the current resurgence of fanatic nationalisms".[3] However, against this perspective, Wendy Wheeler argues that these forms of what she terms "postmodern nostalgia" are not necessarily regressive and senti-mental, but are rather to be understood as the "affective expression of the desire for community".[4] She argues that rather than seeing the

> intensification of nostalgia in postmodernity as a regressive sentimen-talism, or as a symptom of the loss of any sense of history as real, it is perhaps more useful to see it as an intense cultural expression of the desire for social forms capable of representing what is lost in the expe-rience of enlightenment modernity.

Nostalgia, according to Wheeler, represents not simply an "unbearably intense and 'uncanny' yearning for the homely comforts of a settled way of life" but, more generally, a nostalgia for all those things which are the Other of Enlightenment Reason, and which are "excluded, lost or repressed as a condition of modernity and the subjectivity it produces".[5] If such nostalgic feelings are, of course, ultimately directed towards an imaginary past of plenitude and security, their strength is no less pertinent for the fact that their object is imaginary.

Wheeler argues that we badly need to develop a better political response to these nostalgic desires – by "articulating a politics capable of constituting a 'we' which is not existentialist, fixed, separatist, divisive, defensive or exclusive".[6] In this connection Jonathan Rutherford has argued that the success of the political Right in many Western societies throughout the 1980s was attributable precisely to the way in which they "responded to the destabilisations and uncertainties of popular feelings in this post-modern era by promising well-policed frontiers against the transgressive threat and displacements of difference".[7] As he notes, in the UK the Right mobilised images of the family and the nation as central themes of its hegemonic strategy (while simultaneously denying, in Margaret Thatcher's case, the existence of such a thing as "society"). Thus, Mrs Thatcher proclaimed, "the family and its maintenance really is the most important thing, not only in your personal life, but in the life of any community, because this is the unit on which the whole nation is built".[8] In this formulation, then, "society" is replaced by "nation" (with connotations of a corresponding singularity of ethnicity and culture) and the individual is subsumed into the regularising structure of the (implicitly heterosexual and nuclear) family. Those who do not fit this model (e.g. single parents) are to be reformed by social policies which eliminate internal difference, while external boundaries are to be strongly policed. The key problem, according to Rutherford, is that "the Right, in its articulation of order and the yearning for familiarity and a sense of belonging, addresses a little part of all of us".[9]

Cultural fundamentalism and Homo Xenophobicus

It may be helpful here to try to explicate some fundamental theoretical and conceptual points in relation to questions of alterity and difference. It can be argued that ethnocentrism is an inevitable tendency in human affairs, which should not be conflated with racism.[10] Thus racism, ethnocentrism and xenophobia might be distinguished along the following lines, in so far as racism can be seen as a

> discourse and practice of inferiorising ethnic groups … [while] ethnocentrism occurs when one's own culture is taken for granted as natural, and is characteristic of all ethnicities to a greater or lesser extent. Xenophobia, or the dislike of the stranger or outsider … becomes racism when there are power relations involved.[11]

It is on this conceptual framework that my argument is premised.

In relation to the contemporary political pertinence of these issues, Verena Stolcke observes that not only has the loosening of its internal borders been accompanied by a progressive tightening of Europe's external barriers but, at the same time, immigrants (and especially blacks, or those from the poor South) have come to be increasingly regarded as undesirable, threatening strangers, and have become the targets of hostility.[12] In parallel with Cole's argument quoted earlier, concerning the relationship between citizenship and racism, Stolcke observes that populist anti-immigrant feeling of this kind has been fuelled by a political rhetoric which extols the virtues of a form of national identity which is predicated on cultural exclusiveness. She notes that advocates of immigration control often justify their arguments by reference to what ethnologists call the (natural) "territorial imperative" – the idea that populations of animals (and thus, by extension, they argue, humans) will automatically defend their territory against intruders, when these latter increase above a certain maximum level. This idea is certainly fundamental to British anti-immigrant discourse: *vide* Enoch Powell's famous "Rivers of Blood" speech in the UK, to the effect that "an instinct to preserve an identity and defend a territory is one of the deepest and strongest implanted in mankind".[13] In this connection, Bhabha has noted that "etymologically ... 'territory' derives both from *terra* (earth) and *terrere* (to frighten), whence *territorium* – a place from which people are frightened off."[14]

In this new theory of xenophobia, likened by many to a "racism without race", as Stolcke notes, "the demand to exclude immigrants by virtue of their being culturally different 'aliens' is ratified through appeals to basic human instincts ... in terms of a pseudobiological theory".[15] The presumption of this approach is that people naturally prefer to dwell among their own kind, and this preference is assumed to be part of an instinctively negative response to the presence of people with a different culture. Thus, miscegenation (in physical or symbolic form) is defined as the key issue in the struggle of a community to preserve its own original, pure, biocultural identity. This form of contemporary cultural fundamentalism emphasises differences of cultural heritage and the incommensurability of different cultural identities. Cultural fundamentalism thus "legitimates the exclusion of foreigners [or] strangers ... [on] the assumption that relations between different cultures are by 'nature' hostile and mutually destructive". The presumption is that people have a natural propensity to distrust, fear and reject strangers, simply because they are different, and to be hostile to all that is foreign. The idea of a natural, inherent xenophobia (rather than simple ethnocentrism) in humankind is to cultural fundamentalism what the concept of "race" is to racism – "the naturalist constant that endows with truth value and legitimates the respective ideologies".[16]

Cultural fundamentalism, in Stolcke's account, assumes that humanity comprises a multiplicity of ultimately distinct and incommensurable cultures, the relations between which are inevitably conflictual. Thus the argument for the exclusion of immigrants is justified by reference to a natural trait in humanity. Simultaneously, culture is territorialised:

> instead of ordering different cultures hierarchically, cultural fundamen-
> talism segregates them spatially, each culture in its place ... [and] the
> "problem" of immigration is construed as a political threat to national
> identity and integrity on account of immigrants' cultural diversity,
> because the nation-state is conceived as founded on a bounded and
> distinct community, which mobilises a shared sense of belonging and
> loyalty, predicated on a common language, cultural traditions, and
> beliefs ... In [which] respect, nationality is not all that different from
> the kinship principles that operated in so-called primitive societies to
> define group membership.[17]

Contemporary cultural fundamentalism thus roots nationality and citizenship in an idea of a bounded, compact, distinct and territorially located cultural heritage, and cultural differences are reified. For Stolcke, this is quite the wrong approach: as far as she is concerned it is not cultural diversity *per se* that should interest us "but the political meanings with which specific political contexts and relationships endow cultural difference".[18] These issues must be examined conjuncturally. Cultural relativism itself, she argues, "when it was first defended by Boas against racist and other ethnocentric determinisms, was progressive in the colonial context". Conversely, "in the contemporary, crisis-ridden postcolonial world, radical cultural relativism spells exclusion".[19]

A number of criticisms of Stolcke's arguments can be advanced, the most interesting perhaps being those made by Peter Fitzpatrick and Terence Turner.[20] Fitzpatrick points out that in practice, as far as most cultures are concerned, "not all strangers are equally strange".[21] Thus, in Britain anti-immigrant discourse is not, on the whole, targeted at white immigrants, but predominantly at black people.[22] Turner approaches the problem from the other direction, posing the question of why the politics of xenophobia should appeal more strongly to some sections of a society than to others. As he puts it, the issue is why cultural fundamentalism and the aggressive assertion of cultural identity "has emerged as the idiom of choice for expressions of social discontent by marginalised or downwardly mobile elements of national populations". Turner's argument is that what needs to be accounted for is the populist character of the various fundamentalist cultural nationalist movements which have to be understood as "the social and political protests of subordinate social strata against the dominant political–economic and cultural order that excludes them from full participation in national life".[23] From this point of view, these groups' opposition to immigrants, and the demand for the "cultural cleansing" of the nation through the expulsion of foreigners, is not so much an end in itself as rather a means to an ultimate end: "their own fuller integration into and more equitable participation in the social and economic life of the nation". In this way of looking at it, immigrants are simply the most "visible, accessible and vulnerable extensions of the hegemonic system that the protesters feel oppresses and excludes them". This is to reverse the terms of the usual perspective on these matters, and to argue that

> cultural nationalism is not merely, or even primarily, exclusionary and xenophobic, and the foreign immigrants and *gastarbeiter* towards whom it is ostensibly directed are not its primary targets. It is a claim for inclusion and integration on more favourable terms directed at dominant ... groups by relatively disenfranchised ... elements of the national population.[24]

Certainly, such a perspective on forms of working-class racism is likely to be ultimately more productive than any ethical denunciation of racism in the abstract.

In the context of the widespread popular appeal of right-wing forms of cultural absolutism, fundamentalism and racism, there has also recently been a new interest in the philosophy of "communitarianism", which has been adopted by many on the Left, and especially within the "New" British Labour Party, as their guiding philosophy. However, one of the key problems with communitarianism is its implicitly authoritarian perspective; another is that it too tends to be premised on a conception of community as a necessarily homogenous entity, which allows little room for cultural difference. Behind this there again lies a deeply problematic assumption about the naturalness of xenophobia. In his discussion of David Selbourne's work on communitarian philosophy, Kenan Malik notes that, from that perspective, the struggle for individual and collective rights is sacrificed to the need to maintain "community values".[25] Thus, Selbourne operates from an unexamined premise that since a community cannot bear social differentiation, so immigrants must conform to the dominant values of their host culture, or face the consequences. "The individual ethnic stranger," Selbourne writes, "is also an ethical stranger to the civic order of which he is a member." Thus, for Selbourne, if any minority group fails to assimilate to dominant values, then, "the civic order will justly react against them".[26] Communitarianism, it seems, is, in this formulation at least, an exclusive and intolerant creed which falls into all the intellectual traps that Stolcke is concerned to lay bare.

Beyond identity politics?

The politics of identity have been a key area of concern in recent cultural theory, and one of the most powerful approaches to these issues has been that provided by various forms of postmodern and post-structuralist theory, which have given rise to what is often referred to as a new "politics of difference". One key text in the construction of this discourse is Iris Marion Young's critique of what she terms the "metaphysics of presence" implicit in the idea of community.[27] Despite the fact that, in earlier chapters, I have drawn heavily on some of the positive aspects of Young's work, nonetheless I offer here a critique of one particular aspect of her argument, based on the work of Honi Fern Haber.[28]

Just as deconstruction and post-structuralism warn us against the universalisation of totality, so Haber argues, we must also avoid universalising difference. Her point is that such a universalisation of difference would amount, in effect, to the denial of the possibility of any structure – a position which is incoherent, for, as she notes, "without some notion of structure [or unity] and some allowance for a legitimate recognition of similarities between ourselves and others, there can be no subject, community, language or culture". Her argument is that, crucially, "in insisting on the universalisation of difference, post-modern politics forecloses on the possibility of community and subjects" – which are, she notes, "necessary to oppositional politics".[29] In short, post-modern theory's own Grand Narrative – that of the universalisation of difference (which is often held to follow from a rejection of the metaphysics of presence) – leads only, Haber argues, to a "metaphysics of difference" which precludes any sense of identity or community. Similarly, in their warnings against "the relativism that often bedevils identity politics", Michael Keith and Steven Pile argue that we risk a "Babel-like world where truth claims ... [and] ethical claims ... offer no external criteria of refutation". In this situation, they note the danger that "in articulating complexity" we could end up simply "celebrat[ing] incoherence".[30]

The conventional post-structuralist position follows Lyotard, in equating any form of "unity" with terror. Thus any assertion of structure or identity is equated with totalitarianism and viewed as an instrument of repression, and all forms of closure (or unity, consensus or community) are similarly reduced to forms of terrorism. As we saw earlier, with reference to Werbner's critique of anti-essentialism, the central problem with this position is that it risks precluding the identity formations necessary to political activity. Haber's argument is that while it is imperative that we recognise all forms of identity as necessarily provisional, this provisionality does not in itself invalidate these identities. Haber is happy to recognise that all structures (or identities) are temporary (and socially) produced, and thus always open to redescription (to do otherwise would be to reify the concept of structure). However, she insists that "any viable political theory necessitates structure(s) ... and communities, even if these are themselves plural, internally inconsistent, open ended and always amenable to deconstruction". Haber fully recognises that the self, far from being a coherent unity, is "a product of plural narratives" and that the "subject which is a product of one community will also be a product [or member] of many others, not all of whose interests are compatible".[31] However, the repression of difference which is logically implied by any imposition of structure is not (contra Lyotard et al.) necessarily terroristic, if we abandon the idea of structures (or identities) as timeless or unchanging.[32] Thus we can recognise that, in any particular formulation of an identity, "something will always be excluded ... [for that] is simply how language operates".[33] However, this is simply the condition of any minimal coherence which would allow the subject or community to formulate any sense of itself, at all. In Haber's terms, the "subject-in-community" can only have a vocabulary in which to form thoughts by virtue of membership of a community, given that language is social. The alternative is an incoherence which is not only politically but existentially immobilising, in which we are finally impotent, because speechless.[34]

In particular, Haber argues that Young's influential analysis implicitly proposes a false dichotomy: either similarity or difference. According to Young, the ideal of community necessarily denies difference between subjects, so that "the desire for community relies on the same desire for social wholeness and identification that underlies racism ... ethnic chauvinism ... and political sectarianism".[35] For Haber, Young's model "assumes that members of a community see themselves as a non-conflictual, monadic unit, and that identification with others in the community can work only by erasing ... differences". This is clearly premised on a "model of empathetic understanding which forces the silencing of experiences different from one's own". However, Haber argues that there is little reason to presume that "community understanding" (or the recognition of sufficient similarity to allow identification) should preclude the simultaneous recognition of difference. Just as Cohen argued that a community may be held together by a common vocabulary, rather than by a common stock of shared valuations, so Haber argues that "unity (the requirement that a thing be at least minimally coherent enough to be identified and redescribed) does not necessitate 'unicity' (the demand that we speak with one voice)".[36]

Haber recognises that the "logic of difference reveals the artificiality of any and all closure (structure)".[37] Her argument is that rather than this meaning that we should abandon all forms of closure as repressive, we must simply acknowledge their necessary provisionality.[38] Deconstructionists are right to remind us that the definition of any identity has, as its necessary price, the production of a "remainder", which is not assimilated. However, if Haber's arguments are accepted, this in itself has none of the potentially disabling consequences that are often held to follow – as long as the process of identification/remaindering is not itself reified.[39] In this connection Yuval-Davis advocates what she calls a "transversal politics", which involves participants in recognising their own various forms of rootedness and their variable interests – avoiding both the reification of community as an essentialist fixed construction and equally eschewing the groundless flux of some forms of post-structuralism which would not allow the construction of any kind of community as a bulwark for defence of (temporary, negotiated) group interests.[40] In a formulation which both guards against the dangers of reification and yet recognises the necessity of strategic essentialism, Stuart Hall puts matters this way:

it may be true that the self is always , in a sense, a fiction, just as the kind of "closures", which are required to create communities of identification – nation, ethnic group ... are arbitrary closures ... temporary, partial ... [All] identity is constructed across difference ... but doesn't the acceptance of the fictional or narrative status of identity ... also require, as a necessity, its opposite – the moment of arbitrary closure? Is it possible for there to be an action or identity in the world without arbitrary closure ... without ... what one might call the necessity to meaning of the end of the sentence? Potentially, discourse is endless, an infinite semiosis of meaning, but to say anything at all, in particular, you have to stop talking. Of course, every full stop is provisional. The next sentence will take nearly all of it back. So what is this "ending"? ... It is not forever ... not underpinned by any infinite guarantees, but just now, this is what I mean; *this* is who I am.[41]

Community, difference and Heimat

In her own perspective on these questions, Young proposes the idea of a coalition, in which "each of the constituent groups affirms the presence of the others, as well as the specificity of their experience" as a means of overcoming the deficiencies of the concept of community.[42] The problem, according to Haber, is that Young's position logically implies an inescapable infinite regress, in which all of her criticisms of the concept of community must also apply to that of a coalition, in so far as such a coalition would comprise a set of groups – whose formation must involve exactly the processes of identity-recognition which Young herself decried earlier. As Haber notes, "within the coalition lurks the spectre of identity and community" which Young wishes to banish.[43] The central point is that we should not equate community with the denial of difference. Rather than repudiate all closure (an impossible exhortation – for there can logically be no discourse in which all differences can be simultaneously expressed) we must recognise both its necessity and its provisionality.[44] Only thus can we arrive at an understanding not only of "subjects-in-communities", but of "communities-in-difference".

These questions cannot be entirely resolved at a theoretical level. In her empirical study of attitudes to Heimat and *Ausländer*, in Germany, Nora Rathzel's research, as we have seen earlier, goes some way to demonstrating that people who hold a reified, harmonious image of Heimat, as something necessarily stable and unchanging, are particularly likely to be hostile to newcomers – who are held to be the cause of all manner of disorientating forms of change.[45] For these people, Rathzel argues, this is because they think of their cultural identity as something stable, connected with the place in which they live, in such a way that this place must never change. If it does, it seems to them that they will lose their sense of orientation and they may attack those whom they see as responsible for this change.[46] I noted earlier that Rathzel's research revealed that, at a micro level, given their anxieties about both public and private spaces, the women in her study could only even generate a harmonious image of home by means of the radical deletion of its population. The image of this harmonious place is, like a mirage, always receding from direct grasp. Thus, one group of Rathzel's respondents initially suggested that Heimat was not related to anything they currently experienced, but rather something they had known as children. However, when pressed on the point, it transpired that their childhoods had not, in reality, been like that either – their sense of loss was an emblem of a psychic yearning, rather than a historical, empirical experience.

Rather than abandon the idea of community altogether, what we need to do is to abandon the reification of any particular idea of it. Rathzel's study shows that what makes images of *Ausländer* threatening is precisely that they "make our taken-for-granted 'identities' visible as specific identities and deprive them of their assumed [or reified] naturalness" so that "once we start thinking about them, becoming aware of them, we cannot feel 'at home' any more".[47] In this spirit, Begag argues that an immigrant "is a person designated as such by someone living in a particular place who sees the presence of the other as a threat to his own sense of being within that territory".[48] Thus, Marc Augé notes: "perhaps the reason why immigrants worry settled people so much is that they expose the relative nature of certainties inscribed in the soil".[49] Elsewhere Augé remarks that now that the other "of postcards and tourist trips" (the Other, as Augé puts it, "dear to Msr Le Pen") is on the move and can no longer "be assigned to a specific place", it seems perhaps that "in the eyes of those who cling to the ideal of having 'their' land and 'their' village" the example of successful immigration is perhaps more terrifying than that of illegal immigration, in so far as "what's frightening in the immigrant is the fact that he [sic] is also an emigrant".[50] In a similar vein, Iain Chambers, drawing on the work of Levinas, writes of the difficulty created by the "question of the Other", the outsider who "comes from elsewhere and … inevitably bears the message of a movement that threatens to disrupt the stability of the domestic scene". In Levinas' terms, this threat is represented by "the stranger who disturbs the being at home with oneself".[51]

In an essay on his experience of exile from Nazi Germany during World War II, Julian Amery contends that home is security, and without it "one becomes subject to disorder, confusion, desultoriness" so that "it is not good to have no home".[52] However, Dan Stone argues that the key issue is to distinguish between homeland and identity, in so far as the loss of the former does not necessarily entail the loss of the latter. This is to argue that we should not conflate the need for a home with the desire for Heimat. Stone follows Jean-Luc Nancy's argument that Heimat fever has its roots in the West's long obsession with the "loss of community". As Nancy puts it, "at every moment in its history, the Occident has given itself over to the nostalgia for a more archaic community that has disappeared, and to deploring a loss of familiarity, fraternity and conviviality".[53] For Nancy, Nazism was simply the limit case of this phenomenon, "the grotesque ... resurgence of an obsession with communion" – the logic, in effect, Stone argues, of community *in extremis*: the myth of the racially purified, homogenous community from which all polluting elements have been eliminated. For Stone it is the confusion of community with nation that contains the danger. As he puts it, "the house can be shared [with others] ... it does not have to be eulogised in the shape of a homeland", and the security which home offers does not need to be expanded to encompass some mythic notion of homogenous community. Indeed "only the vision of a non-exclusive community – a community open to the plurality of modes of being – offers any viable alternative to self-destruction".[54]

As we saw in the last chapter, the shrinking of effective distance and the emergence of complex forms of interdependence in the globalisation process result in various forms of what we might call enforced proximity and cultural compression in the increasingly crowded social and cultural space of the global neighbourhood, where different (and contradictory) cultures have to live side by side. Clearly the only options are either the building of high fences of one sort or another, as different groups retreat into various forms of "entrenched nationalist, ethnic, religious, gender, sexual or even environmental 'localist' fundamentalisms", or else the development of some way of getting along with what James Donald calls our potentially "Noisy Neighbours".[55] Donald poses the question of what makes living together possible, and offers a critique of approaches that assume that the answer is community. Most particularly, Donald is critical of Raymond Williams' celebration of settled, "positive and unquestioned" community, based in (ideally, for Williams, rural) place. As he points out, Williams displays a "desperate investment in the authenticity of place" and in the rooted settlements and the commonalities of feeling which they might secure. This investment is perhaps the basis of Williams' seeming sympathy, in his comments in *Towards 2000*, with the racialised antagonism towards newcomers expressed by the white working-class members of such settled communities in Britain, as Paul Gilroy pointed out in his well-known critique of Williams.[56]

Crucially Donald argues that Williams "gets community wrong" in so far as he confuses the intractable singularity of the fact of origin with the idea that "community, the question of how we live together, must take the form of collective belonging, affiliation or identity" of a singular, homogenous form. Rather, Donald suggests, we should "start from the question of living in the present with strangers" to ask how that form of commonality might be socially sustainable, and address the modalities through which the (not necessarily homogenous) members of any community manage the business of talking, negotiating and living with each other.[57] In this connection Donald offers an insightful account of Spike Lee's *Do the Right Thing*, as a portrait of just such a divided urban community under pressure, having to confront the question of whether, or in what sense, it is a community. As Donald notes, "at the heart of the film is a rondo of racial invective addressed to camera by different

characters" and the film, he argues, can be seen as "an almost anthropological study of the way that what Freud called 'the narcissism of minor
differences' between ethnic, racial and national groups is invested in icons,
objects and anthems". In the film, as tempers fray in a heatwave, the routines of
co-existence begin to break down and "people ask, are you one of us or not? If
not, what are you doing here?"[58] As he observes, the film reveals "the violence
of the constitution of any community based on the principle of a common existence", because from such a definition inevitably follows the question of the
drawing of the boundaries – of defining who "we" are by excluding the others.
Drawing, like Stone, on the work of Jean-Luc Nancy, Donald argues that,
contrary to Williams' image of community as a lost home (or of a home to be
regained in some common culture to be built in the future), community should
not be conceptualised as some shared essence, but as a process of "being in
common". This is, to return to Iris Marion Young's terminology, the "openness
to unassimilable difference" through which we can deal civilly with each other,
while acknowledging that both "they" and "we", as Kristeva argues, are ultimately strangers, as much to ourselves as to each other.[59]

Donald rightly argues that "publicness is more important than community
and dialogue ... more important than identity". His central concern is with the
politics of how "strangers" of various sorts can work out how to live together in
the compressed space of the contemporary metropolis as a "community
constantly undergoing the experience of its sharing".[60] At stake here are the
rules and grammar of urban living. As Dick Hebdige demonstrates in his
account of his own local dispute with a set of neighbours in Stoke Newington,
it is whether these rules are followed or not which makes local life bearable – or
not.[61] The problem that Hebdige encountered when the young musicians in his
street woke him and his neighbours up in the night by playing loud music was,
as Donald observes, that they initially failed to "respond to his complaints ... as
neighbours", and Hebdige had to insist, in effect, that they "respond before the
question of community, as people having to find a way of living in common".[62]
As Michael Walzer notes, even for those "well-entrenched in their own commitment of pluralism" in the abstract, there will always be "some particular
difference – perhaps a form of worship, family arrangement, dietary rule, sexual
practice or dress code" which they find hard to tolerate and live with in
practice.[63] It is precisely when we run up against these limits that we need
recourse to the pragmatic rules of neighbourliness which make the project of
"living with difference" viable. We must not assume that communication will
necessarily produce consensus: our neighbours' differences will ultimately
remain unassimilable. In the end, the question is one of how to nurture the
mundane pragmatics of neighbourliness in relation to others, rather than
imagine that we can ever live free of alterity, except as a regressive fantasy.

Rather than offer any abstract, theoretical conclusion to my overall argument, having now drawn together as many as I can of the threads from which a
viable understanding of the idea of home and community might be wrought, I

end by attempting to concretise the issues at stake by turning to the question of Europe and its cultural future. The question is for whom Europe is to be a home, and how (and by whom) that home is to be defined.

Europe: living on the ethnic faultlines

The destabilisation of national frontiers in Europe, to the extent that it has in fact occurred outside the wish-fulfilment dreams of European Union bureaucrats, has not simply led to a new definition of the "European state", but also to the development of an enlarged zone of chaos and uncertainty. Crucial to our enquiry here is the extent to which the process of the "Balkanisation" of the West into separated enclaves and the associated rise of nationalisms and ethnic absolutisms can be understood primarily as a fear-driven, defensive process.[64]

At stake here are questions of how we see our past (and our future) as constitutive of, or at odds with, our present sense of who we are. In these matters, it is not always clear what tense we are in. Thus Neal Ascherson has written of the phenomenon of the "Volga Germans" who came home to Germany in the wake of reunification – their ancestors having settled several hundred years ago in Russia, and their communities having then been deported by Stalin to central Asia.[65] Ascherson describes these people as rather like the "living dead", taking on the role of ghosts come to life, in a community of which they consider themselves to be a part, but which had itself (till recently) forgotten about them. He reports contemporary citizens of the cities of (West) Germany describing the experience of meeting these people as "like talking to the dead of another century". As he notes, they

> come to Germany, "their" country [but one] … which is utterly unfamiliar to them. They speak antique German dialects, whose vocabulary has withered over the centuries, tongues almost or completely incomprehensible to modern Germans. From 6,000 miles away, they bring values from the German past … [and] are puzzled to find that actually – existing Germany is not like this at all … and their "fellow-countrymen" are not always pleased to see them.

Nonetheless, their relief at "coming home" is epitomised, for Ascherson, by the rapture of a German woman from Kazakhstan, arriving at Frankfurt airport, who simply declared, "We are in heaven."[66]

The confusion surrounding the "return" of these people to Germany is described by Ignatieff in similar terms. Like Ascherson, he notes that the older generation speak an antique form of German which has been artificially preserved in exile, and that some of the younger generation speak no German at all, but only Russian:

These people look Russian, and their habits and mentality are Soviet. Their ancestors left Germany 300 years ago, to settle and colonise the eastern Slavic border regions beyond the then Holy Roman Empire. Intermarriage has thinned the tie that binds to vanishing point. Yet if you ask them where their *Heimat* is, they look around the cramped rooms of their Frankfurt hostel, and they say proudly "Here". For the eldest among them, they are coming home to die.

However, the reality of contemporary Germany contains many surprises for them, especially the number of foreigners. One of the younger returnees complains (in Russian, because she speaks no German): "I thought I was coming to Germany … Instead, it's Turkey."[67]

However, when a group of young musicians (calling themselves Cartel), who are Turkish by ethnic origin but born and raised among the *Gastarbeiter* community in Germany, visited Istanbul, they reported that " in our homeland [which is how they still think of Turkey], we are thought of as being from Germany and here [in Istanbul], we are called foreigners".[68] As indicated in Ignatieff's example, quoted earlier, of the German couple who had retreated to the countryside to get away from foreigners, it is not only a matter of the past and the future, but also of how these dimensions are symbolically associated with the realms of the country and the city respectively. Elsewhere, Ascherson talks of the city as the citadel of difference: as he notes, it is the

> big cities that are … multi-ethnic: the place where immigrant communities settle and seek work. The villages and small towns and countryside, in contrast, still represent the "nation" – the mythical single *Ethnos* that is supposed to be the real national community. Waves of xenophobia and racialism are "national" rebellions against the reality of what the European cities have become, but it is in those cities that a new idea of community is being painfully worked out and defended … a place of new identities, which transcend frontiers.[69]

In a similar vein, Dominique Le Gilledoux reported from Marseilles on how the tendency of second-generation immigrants in Marseilles to identify themselves with the city itself was symbolised by a craze in the early 1990s for learning the regional language of Occitan.[70] This form of city-based, rather than national (or racial) identification is similar to that espoused by the Turkish–German novelist Jakob Arjouni who, when pressed by an interviewer, settles for identifying himself as "a Frankfurter" rather than anything else, explaining that "to say that you come from a certain town, that means something. To say you're German [or Turkish] that means nothing."[71] Likewise, in Le Gilledoux's account of Marseillaise youth cultures, the point is that not only does any second-generation immigrant necessarily have a Marseilles accent, but, despite the way they are viewed by the rest of France, these young people, who are by ethnic origin African, Senegalese, Spanish or Italian, "are also from Marseilles, and most of them feel it is their home town".[72] For Arjouni, the deconstruction of the myth of ethnicity is paramount. He explains that when his novel *Happy Birthday, Turk!* was published in Germany it came in for particularly strong criticism from the Left. The leftists complained that the hero of Arjouni's novel was "not a real Turk": to which Arjouni's reply was "so who is this 'real Turk'? – I don't know him". Arjouni is incensed by this form of ethnic absolutism, militantly insisting in response that "a character is not determined by his 'origins' … His life is determined by whether he has a big apartment or a small one, if he has love or not, enough to eat or not." He is also deeply resistant to any notion that he somehow represents or might be presumed to speak for "the Turkish community". As he puts it,

> I grew up in a Turkish family, I have friends who are Turkish, but I don't know about "the Turkish community". There is a left and a right, people who read books and people who don't like it, or more likely, don't read it.[73]

Evidently, this is to return to the question addressed earlier as to whether the establishment of community need entail the elimination of difference and whether "difference" itself should be written with a small or a large D. This is the question, as Ahmad poses it, of whether difference is to be treated as "something local and empirically verifiable" or as an "epistemological category or perennial ontological condition".[74]

Amidst the current tide of resurgent nationalisms and ethnic absolutisms, Misha Glenny's television documentary on the fate of ethnic Hungarians living in disputed territory in southern Slovakia poignantly reported one elderly woman's complaint, when confronted with the contentious dilemma of her community's identity: for myself, she said, "I do not want to be a pure identity person."[75] In a similar polyglot spirit, Umberto Eco has rightly argued that Europe must find a "political unity across a polyglot culture" and recognise that the "real unity of Europe is a polyglot unity", rather than pursue false dreams, imposing some "Euro-Esperanto" as a unifying language across the continent.[76]

The making of EuroCulture

Over the last few years we have seen a concerted attempt by the European Union to construct the equivalent of a transnational EuroCulture, enshrined in concepts and cultural institutions such as the European Audiovisual Sphere, based on a geographically expanded version of the conventional model of national broadcasting. These cultural strategies have been intended to create a synthetic pan-European identity which will transcend the narrow limits of national particularisms.[77] However, Shore notes "that new Europe is being constructed on precisely the same symbolic terrain as the old nation states themselves ... Flags, anthems, passports, trophies, maps and coins all serve as icons for invoking the presence of the emergent [EU] state." In this respect, Robins argues that what we see here is the recreation of the conditions of the national community at a higher level of geographical scale.[78]

If we are unable to transcend a notion of Europe as anything more than a nation-state writ large, the project of creating a European AudioVisual Sphere of Culture risks simply replicating, on a larger scale, all the corresponding problems of nationalism. As Robins notes, the discourse of EuroCulture emphasises cohesion, integration, union and security – values equally central to the kind of belonging associated with the problematic history of the nation-state. This is centrally characterised by a form of "identitarian" thinking, "centred around the ideal of social integration ... a sense of coherence and bounded culture". The dark side of this kind of national project is that it involves "the elimination of complexity and the extrusion or marginalisation of elements that compromise the 'clarity' of national attachment. Monolithic and inward-looking, the unitary state has seemed to be the realisation of the desire for purity and integrity of identity".[79] In this model of identity, difference is always deemed problematic, in so far as it portends the threat of fragmentation of the symbolic territory, continuity and psychic coherence of the community – thus any impure elements in the culture are automatically deemed to require repression or elimination. It is a discourse in which "European culture is imagined in terms of an idealised wholeness and plenitude and European identity in terms of boundedness and containment".[80] The problem here, as Ignatieff has rightly noted, is that "national identity everywhere ... is a site of conflicted meanings, and only our nostalgia for a fictive past leads us to imagine an end to the conflict".[81]

We need to move beyond the singularity of perspective that has characterised this kind of traditional nationalism so as to construct a sense of identity, security and stability which is more open to others, beyond its own narrow confines.[82] Such a sense of identity would need to place a positive value on cultural reciprocity, and an awareness that it is through their valency, or in Pontalis' terms their "migratory capacity", that cultures can revitalise themselves. For Robins, it is not so much a question of the rights of imagined communities to exist but rather a question of how the communities that assert these rights can coexist – for, as Daniel Rieff remarks, "we shall be polyglot in the next century or we will kill each other off".[83]

The problem is exacerbated by broadcasting's tendency, as a medium which has primarily developed to support one form or another of cultural unity, to reinforce what Max Dorra calls the "group illusion ... ferociously eliminating all difference".[84] The solution must be to develop forms of broadcasting which come to terms with the reality of cultural disunity and promote a positive valuation of internal forms of hybridity and an openness to external forms of cultural alterity. To do this is also, necessarily, to reconceptualise our notion of our symbolic home. In this respect Meaghan Morris rightly advocates a conception of home as "always made of mixed components", where the interior space it creates might best be seen as "a filter or a sieve, rather than a sealed-in consistency", so that it is not understood so much as simply a place of origin, enclosure or secure belonging but rather the basis of a "process which it enables … a way of going outside".[85] The question of who is to be allowed in or out through the doors of Europe is a crucial one, most particularly at a moment when its walls themselves are being rebuilt.

Europe as an unresolved issue

At this moment, when the question of which countries are or are not to be admitted to the European Union is still being debated, it is important to recognise, as Balibar does, that "Europe is not something that is 'constructed' at a slower or faster pace, with greater or lesser ease; it is a historical problem without any pre-established solution".[86] The question of where Europe ends is a vital one, as can be seen most dramatically if we consider the case of Italy. I commented earlier both on the forms of racism experienced by North African immigrants in Italy and on the ways in which some of the wealthier regions of the North would happily see the South of their country abandoned to poverty. The argument of those in the Northern League seems to be that only if the Italian (and thus European) border is redrawn just south of Rome will Italy's place within Europe be secure.[87] The "Southern Question" has long been at the heart of the dilemma of Italian politics. As Julian Carmen and Chris Endean put it in mid-1998,

> while the North celebrates and puffs out its chest … the country's South lies prostrate on the brink of economic exhaustion. Living on a combination of tick, crime and black marketeering, it is edging closer to Africa than Brussels. If this … continues it will fall off Euroland's economic map altogether, a melancholy Indian reservation, beyond the pale of Brussels' new harmonised world.[88]

It is not only the borders of Europe that are being redefined. According to Neal Ascherson, its centre of gravity is shifting too, away from Paris or Brussels, towards the east. As he puts it, "in twenty years' time the very epicentre of European gravity will have been shifted eastwards to a point nearly half-way between Moscow and the Atlantic. That point is called Berlin."[89] In Ascherson's view, we shall all need to learn the "new Berlinocentric geography of Europe", which will be far less simply orientated to the West and is perhaps best symbolised by Berlin's position as the place where Europe's main east–west (Moscow to Paris) and north–south (Stockholm to Vienna) rail routes will cross – at the new Lehrter Bahnhof station. Lest anyone should doubt the significance of such transport links in making and remaking the symbolic geography of the continent, one need only point to the significance of the Channel Tunnel and the cross-channel rail link it has enabled, effectively drawing London and the other capital cities of northern Europe closer together. The tighter the links are drawn within the magic circles of affluence, of course, the more dramatic the forms of the exclusion of those left outside.

Fortress Europe

If the formation of NATO can be seen to have constituted "an act of faith in the destiny of Western civilisation" at a time when that civilisation was still clearly defined by reference to Christianity, then in the contemporary context of its post-Communist expansion, NATO is increasingly seen by those outside its charmed circle as "the White Race in Arms" in Martin Walker's words.[90] Just as it makes good sense to see NATO in these terms, so one can regard the contemporary reconstruction of Europe in the same perspective – as an entity whose primary identity is still implicitly defined in both religious and racial terms.

As Martin Walker and his colleague Alan Travis have pointed out elsewhere, if the Schengen agreement to reduce internal border controls within EU territory has come to allow relatively "hassle-free travel between EU countries" for Europe's white citizens, at the same time compensatory measures to strengthen Fortress Europe's external borders have also "started to create a joint European internal security operation" which lays the basis for a tightly defended European super-state.[91] In this context, as Yasmin Alibhai-Brown has argued, "refugees, particularly from the Third World, have been criminalised by European politicians and the popular media. Simultaneously, this white 'Fortress Europe' mentality is creating a state of siege" in relation to all who are either non-white or non-Christian.[92] In this respect Gary Younge's litany of his experiences of discrimination at border crossing points while making a brief post-Schengen tour of Europe makes sorry reading for anyone who might imagine that institutionalised racism is anything other than well-entrenched in the European polity. As he puts it, "when it comes to race, a Europe without borders clearly has its limits". Thus Younge reports his encounter with Ali, an immigrant living in southern Germany, who puts it this way:

> My parents came here in the 60s and I've been here all my life. But here, if you are born to immigrants you will die an immigrant, it doesn't matter if you've read Goethe, wear Lederhosen and do a Bavarian dance, they'll still treat you like an immigrant.[93]

The dominant trend in European policy on these issues has been one which, if not explicitly racist, argues for tighter immigration controls at Europe's external borders on the pragmatic grounds that otherwise the continent will simply be "overwhelmed" by illegal immigration. In 1998 a leaked paper from the EU's secret K4 committee dealing with these issues revealed that the EU was now operating on the assumption that "every other immigrant in the First World is there illegally". In this context, it seems that the asking price for ex-Communist countries along Europe's eastern borders seeking to gain admission to the EU is that they also sign up to a highly restrictive policy on "asylum seekers" and tighter controls on the movements of potential immigrants.[94] In the case of the Czech Republic, the question of borders is clearly not only an external issue but also an internal one. This much was bleakly symbolised by the local government's plans, reported by Ian Traynor, to "ghettoise several hundred gypsies by building a 15-foot wall around their blocks of flats to segregate them from Czech residents" in the town of Usti and Labem.[95] For the local Czechs, the wall was felt to be "the only solution" to protect themselves from the gypsies who "get drunk, make a racket at night ... pile up the rubbish till the rats come and then play with the rats", according to one local resident. The despair of the gypsies can perhaps be felt in the poignant response of their spokesman, who proposed that they would "agree to a wall, but a wall with holes in it, not solid, and not with only one gate. And we'll put flowers on it and decorate it and it won't be a ghetto."[96] Naturally, the local council insisted that it was not being racist: the town's mayor explained that it would be a "multi-purpose" wall, to block out noise and put an end to illegal street trading; and, he added, "they can decorate it anyway they want".[97]

In the end, abstract discussions of the nature of Europe, just as much as those of who belongs in a particular town, do come down to questions of walls and fences. Perhaps the most dramatic symbol of the post-Schengen development of the idea of White Fortress Europe is the £22 million fence which has now been built in North Africa to seal off access to Spain's coastal enclave of Ceuta, in an attempt to block the progress of illegal immigrants who make the short but hazardous sea-crossing from Ceuta to the southern Spanish coast and onwards into other parts of Europe. The 8km fence, similar in concept to that between Mexico and the USA, is being referred to as Europe's new Berlin Wall, controlling as it does the European Union's only direct physical frontier with Africa (except for the other Spanish enclave of Melilla). As Giles Tremlett reports, the fence's expensive price tag (mainly funded directly by the EU itself) "reflects the importance that Europe, and especially the transit-free zone created by the Schengen accord, places on sealing its borders". This is so even if, in the end, the barrier is physically "remarkable only for its fragility" in the face of the desperation of the "poor migrants and exiles who daily find their way over, under or around it on their nightmare journeys of escape from the disaster-zones of sub-Saharan Africa whence they came".[98]

The Other within

According to Balibar, in the future it will be increasingly necessary to conceive of Europe as a cultural space in which "different economic-cultural aggregates ... meet and, if necessary, clash with each other". Principal among them will be "a Euro-American aggregate, a Euro-Mediterranean (mainly Euro-Arab or Euro-Muslim) aggregate and a Euro-ex-Soviet or Euro-eastern aggregate" which will form (to echo Gorbachev's phrase) "not one but several 'common homes' in Europe".[99] As argued earlier, in the absence of the old Communist enemy, it does seem that the principal Other which cannot be accommodated, and against which Europe now, in practice, defines itself is Islam.[100] According to the novelist Tahar Ben Jelloun, while Europe brought millions of Muslim migrants to work in its factories, it has never welcomed them into its culture. As a result Jelloun argues:

> the immigrants took refuge in their faith in Islam, which offers them not only a religion and a moral framework but also a culture and an identity ... They can define themselves by their attachment to the religion ... Even those who might have been less attached to the religion, were they still in their own countries, took to Islam with determination and vigour – because it became, in their eyes, something that would protect them and give them the identity they lacked in the land of exile.[101]

As the hero of Ben Jelloun's story "I am an Arab, I am a suspect" puts it, "before I came to France, I didn't know the word 'fundamentalist'. I think I heard it for the first time on TV."[102] Similarly, one might argue, in the UK, in the wake of the Gulf War, a feeling of beleaguerment among Muslim communities has led to a turning inwards which has created a fertile basis for recruitment by fundamentalist groups such as Hizb ut Tahrir, which forbids even friendship with unbelievers. However, it may be that what worries white Christian Europeans even more than total alterity is an Other who is, in fact, manifestly like them.[103] Thus Ben Jelloun writes of the particular difficulties facing young people of North African origin who attempt to integrate into French society, arguing that in many cases they get a particularly hostile response from their host society. In his view, "the fear springs not from the difference but from the resemblance. The more these young people react like young French people from their own social set, the more het-up the xenophobes get."[104]

A striking example of the particular difficulty of coming to terms with forms of alterity which are nonetheless still "like us" was provided during the war in Kosovo by British viewers' querulous responses to a television interview on Channel 4 with a well-dressed middle-class woman refugee. Afterwards, a number of viewers called the television station, accusing the woman interviewed of being a fake or an actress, on the grounds that her varnished nails and elegant clothes surely precluded the possibility of her being a "real" refugee. As Alex Thomson put it in his account of the incident, "it seems that ... [only] the peasant-type Kosovans fleeing on tractors conform to the notion of what a refugee should be". Anything closer to home is rather more disconcerting for viewers who wish to clearly demarcate the alterity of the disturbing events portrayed from their own lives and identities.[105] It seems that as Homi Bhabha has said, it is in the form of "the strangeness of the familiar" that cultural difference becomes most problematic, both politically and conceptually "when the problem of cultural difference is ourselves-as-others, others-as-ourselves, that borderline".[106] However, as Jonathan Boyarin puts it, the crucial thing is that "We should recognise that the co-presence of ... others is not a threat, but rather the condition of our lives".[107] Facing up to the irreducible presence of alterity, in ourselves and in others, means that there can be for us "No Place Like Heimat".

NOTES

INTRODUCTION

1 G. Flaubert, *Bouvard and Pécuchet*, New York, New Directions, 1954, p. 140. I can only hope that the reader will not feel, in the end, that I have done no more than inadvertently emulate the mock-heroic quest of Flaubert's clerks, as they trawl the human sciences in their ultimately fruitless search for understanding of their place in the world. See pp. 19–20 on the home as a "mnemonic base".

2 P. Bourdieu, "The Berber house: or, the world reversed", in M. Douglas (ed.), *Rules and Meanings*, Harmondsworth, Penguin, 1973. In that analysis, Bourdieu formulates the relation between the domestic and the public as an "opposition between female space and male space on the one hand, the privacy of all that is intimate, and on the other, the open space of social relations". Bourdieu argues that the orientation of the house is fundamentally defined from the outside, from the point of view of the masculine public sphere – as the "place from which men come out", so that the house is "an empire within an empire, but one that always remains subordinate" (op. cit., p. 101).

3 The formulation "EurAm" has an East Asian derivation, from which perspective the distinction between Europe and America is sometimes felt to be of relatively little consequence, the two cultures thus being deliberately collapsed into one concept.

4 M. Foucault, "Questions of geography", in C. Gordon (ed.), *M. Foucault Power/Knowledge*, New York, Pantheon, 1980, p. 149.

5 As Philip Tabor puts it, "A house identified with the self is called a 'home', a country identified with the self is called a 'homeland'"; P. Tabor, "Striking home – the Telematic assault on identity", in J. Hill (ed.), *Occupying Architecture*, London, Routledge, 1998, p. 218.

6 D. Morley, "Notes from the sitting room", *Screen*, 1991, vol. 32(1), reprinted in D. Morley, *Television, Audiences and Cultural Studies*, London, Routledge, 1992.

7 D. Morley, *Family Television*, London, Comedia, 1986; D. Morley and R. Silverstone, "Domestic Communications", *Media, Culture and Society*, 1990, vol. 12(1).

8 cf. D. Morley and K. Robins, "No place like Heimat", *New Formations*, 1990, vol. 12.

9 E. Hobsbawm, "Exile", *Social Research*, 1991, vol. 58(1), pp. 67–8.

10 C. Wright Mills, *The Sociological Imagination*, Harmondsworth, Penguin, 1970, p. 3; original 1959.

11 ibid., p. 162.

12 K. Knorr-Cetina and A. Cicourel (eds), *Advances in Social Theory and Methodology: Towards an Integration of Micro and Macro Sociologies*, London, Routledge, 1981.

13 D. Morley, "Theoretical orthodoxies", in M. Ferguson and P. Golding (eds), *Cultural Studies in Question*, London, Sage, 1997.

14 D. Massey, "Flexible sexism", *Environment and Planning D: Society and Space*, 1991, vol. 9(1), pp. 270–1.

15 M. Douglas, *Purity and Danger*, London, Routledge and Kegan Paul, 1966; H. Bhabha, *The Location of Culture*, London, Routledge, 1994.

16 R. Rosaldo, "Foreword" to N. Canclini, *Hybrid Cultures*, Minneapolis, University of Minnesota Press, 1995, p. xv.

17 P. Chatterjee, *Nationalist Thought and the Colonial World*, Minneapolis, Minnesota University Press, 1998, p. xx; original 1986.

18 Introduction to S. Lash and J. Friedman (eds), *Modernity and Identity*, Oxford, Blackwell, 1992, p. 20.

19 For a history of the exhibition, see Deborah Ryan, *The Daily Mail Ideal Home Exhibition and Suburban Modernity*, PhD thesis, University of East London, 1995. For an excellent collection of critical essays on the "Ideal Home" phenomenon, see Tony Chapman and Jenny Hockey (eds), *Ideal Homes? Social Change and Domestic Life*, London, Routledge, 1999.

20 David Sibley, *Geographies of Exclusion*, London, Routledge, 1995, p. 90.

21 G. Revill, "Reading Rosehill", in M. Keith and S. Pile (eds), *Place and the Politics of Identity*, London, Routledge, 1993, p. 127; C. Lake, *"Rosehill"*, London, Bloomsbury, 1989.

22 On Massey's argument, see Chapter 8.

23 M. Keith and S. Pile, "The politics of place", in Keith and Pile (eds), op. cit., p. 6.

24 N. Smith and C. Katz, "Grounding metaphor", in Keith and Pile (eds), op. cit., p. 69.

25 ibid. pp. 69, 80.

26 cf. S. Moores, *Satellite Television and Everyday Life*, Luton, University of Luton Press, 1996, p. 24.

27 M. Berman, "Why Modernism still matters", in Lash and Friedman (eds), op. cit., p. 35.

28 cf. R. Williams, *Television, Technology and Cultural Form*, London, Fontana, 1974, p. 26.

29 cf. J. Derrida, *Spectres of Marx*, London, Routledge, 1994.

30 S. Wallman, "New identities and the local factor", p. 201 and p. 195 in N. Rapport and A. Dawson (eds), *Migrants of Identity*, London, Berg, 1999.

31 P. Carter, *Living in a New Country*, London, Faber and Faber, 1992, pp. 7–8; N. Rapport and A. Dawson, "Home and movement", p. 22 in Rapport and Dawson (eds), op. cit.

32 A. Appadurai and C. Breckenridge, "Why public culture?", *Public Culture*, 1988, vol. 1, p. 5.

33 J. Clifford, "Mixed feelings", in P. Cheah and B. Robbins (eds), *Cosmopolitics*, Minneapolis, University of Minnesota Press, 1998, p. 369.

34 B. Robbins, "Actually existing cosmopolitanism", in Cheah and Robbins (eds), op. cit., p. 1.

35 N. Rapport and A. Dawson, "Home and Movement", op. cit., p. 8; I. Chambers, *Migrancy Culture, Identity*, London, Routledge, 1994; C. Geertz, "The uses of diversity", *Michigan Quarterly Review*, 1986, vol. 25; J. Clifford, "Introduction – partial truths", in J. Clifford and G. Marcus (eds), *Writing Culture*, Berkeley, University of California, 1986; Keith Hart, "Swimming into the human current", *Cambridge Anthropology*, 1990, vol. 14(3).

36 U. Hannerz, *Transnational Connections*, London, Routledge, 1996, ch. 4.

37 J.F. Lyotard, *The Postmodern Condition*, Manchester, Manchester University Press, 1986, p. 76.

38 Rapport and Dawson, op. cit., p. 25.

39 D. Massey, "The conceptualisation of place", in D. Massey and P. Jess (eds), *A Place in the World,* Milton Keynes, Open University Press, 1995, p. 60.

40 J. Clifford, *The Predicament of Culture*, Cambridge, Mass., Harvard University Press, 1988, p. 14. Similarly Ashley Bickerton writes of encountering "*Terminator* stickers on river boats in Borneo, *Batman* T-shirts on penis-gourd wearing (but otherwise naked) tribesmen in the highland valleys of Irian Jaya ... [and] a certain bad New Jersey haircut everywhere that I have been", *Documents*, 1993, 3, p. 64. One of my daughters returned from her trekking holiday in the villages of northern Thailand with a photograph of a woman in one of the villages she visited weaving traditional cloth while wearing a Benetton t-shirt.

41 Karen McCarthy Brown, *Mama Lola: A Vodou Priestess in Brooklyn*, Berkeley, University of California Press, 1991, p. 1; quoted in J. Clifford, *Routes*, Cambridge, Mass., Harvard University Press, 1997, p. 56.

42 G. Marcus, "Past, present and emergent identities", in Lash and Friedman (eds), op. cit., p. 315.

43 A. Appadurai, *Modernity at Large*, Minneapolis, University of Minnesota Press, 1996, p. 18.

44 ibid. pp. 54, 63, 154–5.

45 ibid. p.179; cf. J. Meyrowitz, *No Sense of Place*, Oxford, Oxford University Press, 1985.

46 Appadurai, op. cit., p. 22.

47 R. Wilk, "Learning to be local in Belize", in D. Miller (ed.), *Worlds Apart*, London, Routledge, 1997, p. 111.

48 L. Abu-Lughod, "The objects of soap opera", in D. Miller (ed.), op. cit., p. 205.

49 F. Ghannam, "Re-imagining the global: relocation and local identities in Cairo", in A. Öncü and P. Weyland (eds), *Space, Culture and Power*, London, Zed Books, 1997, p. 125. The question of what (or who) belongs where and, conversely, of what constitutes the exotic for whom, in which circumstances, is perhaps best captured in a (possibly apocryphal) story told about the French surrealist writer Raymond Roussell's trip to Africa in the early part of the century. Prior to his departure, Roussell's mother urged him to send her the most exotic thing he could find, as a present. Some months passed after Roussell's departure before a parcel arrived. His mother opened it, in great excitement, to discover within an electric fire. It was, as the accompanying note explained, the most exotic thing he had been able to find in Africa at that time.

50 J. Clifford, *Routes*, op. cit., p. 247.

51 ibid. pp. 9–10.

52 ibid. pp. 5, 84.

53 ibid. pp. 24 and 36.

54 S. Lash and J. Urry, *Economies of Signs and Spaces*, London, Sage, 1994.

55 J. Tomlinson, *Globalisation and Culture*, Cambridge, Polity Press, 1999, p. 9.

56 op. cit., p. 132.

57 J. Durham Peters, "Seeing bifocally", in A. Gupta and J. Ferguson (eds), *Culture, Power, Place*, Durham, Duke University Press, 1997, p. 91. Still only 2 per cent of the world's population live outside the country of their birth – see J. Harding, "The uninvited", *London Review of Books*, 3 February 2000, p. 3.

58 Peter Dickens, *One Nation? Social Change and the Politics of Locality*, London, Pluto Press, 1988, pp. 212–18.

59 D. Warburton, "A passionate dialogue", in D. Warburton (ed.), *Community and Sustainable Development*, London, Earthscan, 1998, p. 16.

60 J. Gray, "Do we really want more US Decadence?", *Guardian*, 27 January 1997; D. Sibley, op. cit., p. 29; K. Worpole, *Towns for People*, Milton Keynes, Open University Press, 1992, p. 26.

61 cf. Anthony Giddens, *The Consequences of Modernity*, Cambridge, Polity Press, 1990; Geoff Mulgan, *Connexity*, London, Chatto and Windus, 1997.
62 J. Tomlinson, op. cit., pp. 9, 119, 150.

1   IDEAS OF HOME

1 In the sense of a fiction as something "made"; cf. C. Geertz, *Works and Lives*, Cambridge, Polity Press, 1988.
2 A. Bammer, "Editorial", *New Formations*, 1992, vol. 17, pp. ix–x.
3 Quoted in M. Morse, "Home: smell, taste, posture, gleam", in H. Naficy (ed.), *Home, Homeland, Exile*, London, Routledge, 1999, p. 68.
4 M. Warner, "Home: our famous island race", *Independent*, 3 March 1994.
5 A. Heller, "Where we are at home", *Thesis Eleven*, 1995, vol. 41.
6 M. Douglas, "The idea of home: a kind of space", *Social Research*, 1991, vol. 58(1), p. 289.
7 ibid., p. 301.
8 cf. P. Scannell, "Radio Times", in P. Drummond and R. Paterson (eds), *Television and its Audience*, London, British Film Institute, 1988; see Chapter 4 on this.
9 Quoted in Krishan Kumar, "Home: the nature of private life at the end of the twentieth century", unpublished paper, University of Kent, 1994, p. 1. A later version of this paper appears in J. Weintraub and K. Kumar (eds), *Private and Public in Thought and Practice*, Chicago, University of Chicago Press, 1994.
10 Kumar, op. cit., p. 8.
11 Descombes quoted in M. Augé, *Non-Places: Introduction to an Anthropology of Super-Modernity*, London, Verso, 1995, p. 108.
12 Heller, "Where we are at home", op. cit., p. 6.
13 ibid., p. 18.
14 Federico Fellini, "Miscellany 1 – I'm a liar but an honest one", in *Fellini on Fellini*, translated Isabel Quigley, London, Eyre Methuen, 1976, pp. 53–4; quoted in John Welchman, "Moving images" *Screen*, 1996, vol. 37(4), p. 347.
15 Mary Jordan, "Divide and rule the roost", *Guardian*, 10 March 1994.
16 Douglas, op. cit., p. 302.
17 ibid. pp. 305–6.
18 ibid. pp. 294–5.
19 cf. British Telecom's special discounts for long-distance family phone calls at Christmas as a form of virtual homecoming.
20 Janet Susskind, "The invention of Thanksgiving – a ritual of American nationality", *Critique of Anthropology*, 1992, vol. 12(2), pp. 167 and 175.
21 Susskind, op. cit., pp. 176 and 168. Susskind wryly observes that the turkey eaten at the Thanksgiving meal might be taken to symbolise the Native Americans who were "consumed" in the course of the foundation of the nation.
22 G. Bachelard, *The Poetics of Space*, Boston, Beacon Press, 1994, pp. vii–viii, xxxxvi.
23 Defined as the "topography of our intimate being" or as the "systematic psychological study of the sites of our intimate lives", ibid. p. xxxvi and p. 8.
24 R. Bowlby, "Domestication", in D. Elam and R. Wiegman (eds), *Feminism Beside Itself*, London, Routledge, 1995, p. 77.
25 D. Wood and R. Beck, *Home Rules*, Baltimore, Johns Hopkins University Press, 1994.
26 Wood and Beck, op. cit., p. 61; cf. Mary Douglas quoted in Chapter 6 on "dirt".
27 ibid. p. 154.
28 ibid. pp. 7–8.
29 ibid. p. 1.

30 ibid. pp. xvi–xviii and 2–5.

31 W. Rybczynski, *Home: A Short History of an Idea*, London, Heinemann, 1986.

32 Rybczynski, op. cit., pp. 75 and 18.

33 Philip Tabor goes so far as to argue that the "home of the home" in the sense that we now know it in the West was seventeenth-century Holland – P. Tabor, "Striking home", in J. Hill (ed.), *Occupying Architecture*, London, Routledge, 1998, p. 218.

34 For a contemporary parallel, see Mary Bouquet's "You can't be a Brahmin in the English countryside", in A. Cohen (ed.), *Symbolising Boundaries*, Manchester, Manchester University Press, 1986.

35 Rybczynski, op. cit., p. 66.

36 P. Ariès, "The family and the city in the Old World and the New", in V. Tufte and B. Meyerhoff (eds) *Changing Images of The Family*, Princeton, Yale University Press, 1979.

37 Kumar, op. cit.

38 D. Chaney, *Fictions of Collective Life*, London, Routledge, 1993, ch. 2.

39 T.J. Clark, quoted in Chaney, op. cit., p. 70.

40 Chaney, op. cit., p. 65.

41 Z. Bauman, *Globalisation*, Cambridge, Polity Press, 1998, pp. 36, 42.

42 Quoted in M. Facos, "The ideal Swedish home", in C. Reed (ed.), *Not at Home*, London, Thames and Hudson, 1996, p. 86.

43 L. Davidoff and C. Hall, *Family Fortunes*, London, Hutchinson, 1987.

44 M. Daunton, "Public place and private space", in D. Frazer and A. Sutcliffe (eds), *The Pursuit of Urban History*, London, Edward Arnold, 1983.

45 J. Lukacs, "The bourgeois interior", *American Scholar*, 1970, vol. 39(4).

46 Lukacs, quoted in Rybczynski, op. cit., pp. 35, 36, 39, 51.

47 Rybczynski, op. cit., p. 75.

48 Bowlby, "Domestication", op. cit., p. 83.

49 A. Heller, *Everyday Life*, London, Routledge and Kegan Paul, 1981, p. 239.

50 As Bird quotes from the story, before our hero "closed his eyes, he let them wander round his old room, mellow in the glow of the firelight that played or rested on familiar and friendly things which had long been unconsciously a part of him" – K. Grahame *The Wind in the Willows*, London, Methuen, 1944, p. 124; quoted in J. Bird, "Dolce domum", in J. Lingwood (ed.), *House*, London, Phaidon Press, 1995, p. 114.

51 T. Putnam, "Introduction", T. Putnam and C. Newton (eds), *Household Choices*, London, Futures Publications, 1990, p. 8.

52 S. Norve, "The home – materialised identity and household technology" in K.H. Sorensen and A.-J. Berg (eds), *Technology and Everyday Life*, Oslo, Norwegian Research Council for Science and Humanities, 1990, p. 52.

53 J. Carsten and S. Hugh-Jones (eds), *About the Home*, London, Jonathan Cape, 1995, p. 7, drawing on the work of Lévi-Strauss.

54 R. Feldman, "Psychological bonds with home places in a mobile society", unpublished paper, University of Illinois; quoted in Putnam and Newton (eds), op. cit., p. 12.

55 Carsten and Hugh-Jones (eds), op. cit., p. 44, cf. the English aristocracy's ideas of physical houses as the embodiment of family history and their corresponding snobbery about the "bought" houses/furniture of the *nouveau riche*.

56 cf. J. Goldthorpe, D. Lockwood, F. Bechhofer and J. Platt, *The Affluent Worker in the Class Structure* (three volumes), Cambridge, Cambridge University Press, 1969.

57 A. Oakley, *Housewife*, Harmondsworth, Penguin, 1976, p. 65.

58 A. Franklin, "Variations in marital relations and the implications for women's experiences of the home", in Putnam and Newton (eds), op. cit., p 57; cf. also A. Tomlinson (ed.), *Consumption, Identity and Style*, London, Comedia, 1989.

59 G. Allan, "Insiders and outsiders: boundaries around the home", in G. Allan and
    G. Crow (eds), *Home and Family: Creating the Domestic Sphere*, London, Macmillan,
    1989, p. 143.
60 S. Laing, *Representations of Working Class Life 1957–64*, London, Macmillan, 1986,
    p. 29; cf. also T. O'Sullivan, "Television memories and cultures of viewing", in J. Corner
    (ed.), *Popular Television in Britain*, London, British Film Institute, 1991.
61 Kumar, op. cit., pp. 10–11.
62 Kumar, op. cit., p. 20. In what might be seen as a symbolic reflection of the decline
    in the status of the "family meal" in the UK, the Oxo stock cube manufacturing
    company decided in the early autumn of 1999 to finally stop the production of the
    advertisements featuring a traditional mum ("Katy") providing a meal for her whole
    family, seated round the table. A spokesman for the company explained that Oxo had
    come to feel that the representation of family eating habits enshrined in the advert
    (which had run, on British television, in suitably updated versions over a sixteen-year
    period) was now out of synchronisation with today's lifestyles – D. Rowe, "A brief
    history of meal time", *Guardian*, 1 September 1999.
63 D. Hebdige, "Redeeming witness: in the tracks of the Homeless Vehicle project",
    Cultural Studies, 1993, vol. 7(2).
64 J. Fontaine, "Public or private?", *International Journal of Moral and Social Studies*,
    1988, vol. 3(3).
65 M. Davis, *City of Quartz*, London, Verso, 1990, p. 23.
66 J. Bird, "Dolce domum", in J. Lingwood (ed.), *House*, London, Phaidon Press,
    1995, p. 119.
67 Neil Smith, "Homeless/global: scaling places", in J. Bird, B. Curtis, T. Putnam,
    G. Robertson and L. Tickner (eds), *Mapping the Futures*, London, Routledge, 1993,
    p. 89; Wodiczko designed a futuristic "Homeless Vehicle" providing shelter, storage,
    security and mobility, which was exhibited in New York in the 1980s and dramatised
    the practical and emotional difficulties facing homeless people very effectively.
68 M. Torgovnick, "Slasher stories", *New Formations*, 1992, vol. 17, p. 145.
69 M. E. Hombs, "Reversals of fortune", *New Formations*, 1992, vol. 17, p. 114.
70 S. Jeffers, "Victimography: framing the homeless", in Putnam and Newton (eds), op.
    cit.
71 See M. Rosler, *Positions in the Life World*, Birmingham, Ikon Gallery, 1998; S. Haar
    and C. Reed, "Coming home", in C. Reed (ed.), *Not at Home*, London, Thames
    and Hudson, 1996, p. 263.
72 Whiteread's sculpture was constructed in Bow, a poor part of East London, in the
    autumn of 1993 and rapidly became the focus of both national and local media
    attention. Whiteread was awarded the prestigious Turner Prize for *House* (along with
    her other work) but local politicians nonetheless voted to demolish it, despite a
    national campaign to prevent them doing so. *House* was demolished in January 1994
    and its site turfed over: all that now remains of it (besides the photographic records)
    is a piece of featureless public parkland.
73 Bird, op. cit., p. 118.
74 D. Massey, "Space-time and the politics of location", in J. Lingwood (ed.), op. cit.
75 N. Couldry, "Speaking up in a public space: the strange case of Rachel Whiteread's
    House", *New Formations*, 1995, vol. 25, p. 109.
76 Simon Watney, "On *House*, iconoclasm and iconophobia", in J. Lingwood (ed.), op.
    cit., p. 99.
77 G. Allan and G. Crow, "Introduction", in G. Allan and G. Crow (eds), op. cit., p. 4.
78 See T. Chapman, "Spoiled home identities: the experience of burglary", in T. Chapman
    and J. Hockey (eds) *Ideal Homes?*, London, Routledge, 1999. Equally, the greater
    "ontological security" displayed by those who own their own homes seems to be less

to do with the economic benefits of ownership and more to do with the greater degree of autonomy from external regulation that private ownership enables. In the case of those who buy their own flats on public housing estates, this autonomy is often clearly signalled to the outside world by the owner's changing the style and colour of their front door, to distinguish it from the drab uniformity of the surrounding publicly owned properties – see P. Saunders, "Beyond housing classes: the sociological significance of private property rights", *Journal of Urban and Regional Research*, 1984, vol. 8, pp. 202–27.

79 W. Benjamin, "Louis Philippe and the interior", in his *Charles Baudelaire: A Lyric Poet in the Era of High Capitalism*, London, Verso, 1973, pp. 167–8. As Stuart Jeffries notes, had Benjamin lived to see *The Simpsons* he would have seen a representation of a domestic interior itself dominated by just such a box: the television set. For the Simpsons, "home is where the television is". However, Jeffries observes that the Simpsons' drawing room is "hardly a box in a world theatre" in so far as television, for them as for so many, offers a very localised experience, where "the world beyond Springfield's city limits hardly merits a mention" – S. Jeffries, "Tune in, turn on, freak out", *Guardian*, 4 January 1997.

80 b. hooks, "Homeplace as site of resistance" in her *Yearning: Race, Gender and Cultural Politics*, Boston, South End Press, 1990.

81 D. Massey, "A place called home", *New Formations*, 1992, vol. 17, p. 10.

82 hooks, op. cit., p. 47. As we shall see later (in Chapter 3) the further irony is that, at a macro level, within the household itself such autonomy or privacy is least available to the figure – the housewife – most associated with the symbolism of the domestic sphere. If the home offers privacy to the family group as a whole, it rarely does so for the woman who performs the central role in maintaining the household.

2 HEIMAT, MODERNITY AND EXILE

1 M. Keith and S. Pile, "The Politics of Place", in M. Keith and S. Pile (eds), *Place and the Politics of Identity*, London, Routledge, 1993, p. 20.

2 Z. Bauman, *Globalisation*, Cambridge, Polity Press, 1998, p. 117.

3 M. Goldman, "The fine line between hatred and home", *Communal/Plural*, 1997, vol. 5, p. 153. In a particularly poignant example of this process, after 1945 foreign-born Japanese, pressurised into repatriating to Japan after their release from internment camps by the Canadian or American governments, were then scorned by their compatriots and labelled as *Kimin* – throwaways, people who, by virtue of their foreign birth were impure, and thus of no value.

4 J. Kristeva, *Nations Without Nationalism*, New York, Columbia University Press, 1993, p. 3.

5 A. Johansen, "Fellowmen, compatriots, contemporaries", in J. Peter Burgess (ed.), *Cultural Politics and Political Culture in Postmodern Europe*, Amsterdam, Editions Rodopi, 1997, p. 171.

6 L. Malkki, "National Geographic", in A. Gupta and J. Ferguson (eds), *Culture, Power, Place*, Durham, Duke University Press, 1997.

7 E. Hobsbawm, "Exile", *Social Research*, 1991, vol. 58(1), p. 67.

8 Y.-F. Tuan, *Space and Place*, London, Edward Arnold, 1977, p. 156. It is perhaps worth observing that the Heimat tradition does take on unusually articulate tones in the case of South Tyrol, not itself in Germany but a German-speaking part of the Austro-Hungarian empire which was annexed by Italy in 1918 and then settled, not to say colonised, by Italian speakers from the Mezzogiorno. I thank Gerd Baumann for his clarification of this point.

9 J.G. Herder, "Auch eine Philosophie der Geschichte zur Bildung der Menschheit", in his *Werke*, Bd. 1, Munich, C. Hanser, p. 619; quoted in H.R. Wicker, "From complex culture to cultural complexity", in P. Werbner and T. Modood (eds), *Debating Cultural Hybridity*, London, Zed Books, 1997, p. 34.
10 Jeffrey Peck, "Racing the nation", *New Formations*, 1992, vol. 17, p. 78.
11 C. Applegate, "The question of Heimat in the Weimar Republic", *New Formations*, 1992, vol. 17, pp. 66 and 73.
12 Ghassan Hage, "Nation-building-dwelling-being", *Communal/Plural*, 1993, vol. 1, p. 80; Paul Chilton and Mikhail Ilyin, "Metaphor in political discourse", *Discourse and Society*, 1993, vol. 4(1).
13 Peck, op. cit., p. 78.
14 At the time of writing (October 1999) the "Freedom Party" in Austria had just achieved considerable electoral success by campaigning under the slogan that their country was *überfremdung* – overpopulated with foreigners.
15 Tim Cresswell, *In Place/Out of Place*, Minneapolis, University of Minnesota Press, 1996, pp. 85–7.
16 P. Stallybrass and A. White, *The Politics and Poetics of Transgression*, London, Methuen, 1986, pp. 128–9; H. Mayhew, *London Labour and the London Poor*, London, Frank Cass (four volumes.), 1967; original 1861–2.
17 Z. Bauman, "The making and unmaking of strangers", in P. Werbner and T. Modood (eds), *Debating Cultural Hybridity*, London, Zed Books, p. 46.
18 cf. L. Holy, "The metaphor of Home in Czech nationalist discourse", in N. Rapport and A. Dawson (eds) *Migrants of Identity*, Oxford, Berg, p. 129.
19 Holy, op. cit., p. 130. Using this schema, Holy then argues that after the annexation of the Sudetenland in 1938 the Germans were seen by the Czechs as "squatters", while after the full-scale invasion of Czechoslovakia in 1939 they came to be seen as "burglars", just as the Russians were, after the invasion in 1968. The Vietnamese who arrived as a result of the then Communist Czech government's agreement with the Vietnamese state in the 1970s were initially understood, in the terms of this schema as "servants" in so far as they came to do particular jobs. The many who have stayed after being made redundant in the wake of the collapse of the old regime in 1989 are now widely regarded as "squatters". The tourists who currently flood Prague, in particular, he argues, are not simply seen as "guests" in so far as their presence has the effect of pushing up local prices, so that the Czechs themselves are less "at home" in their own land. The tourists are thus a problematic category, but less so than the gypsies who are, after the post-war expulsion of the German-speaking minority, almost the only exception to the homogeneity of the Czech population (apart from the small number of Vietnamese referred to above). The gypsies are, as Holy notes, not only the Czechs' single most significant internal Other and as such the object of much racial hostility, but also unlike all other varieties of foreigner, in so far as they do not have a home of their own, somewhere else to go to. See p. 263.
20 M. Billig, *Banal Nationalism*, London, Sage, 1995, p. 74.
21 M. Foucault, "Space, knowledge and power", in P. Rabinow (ed.) *The Foucault Reader*, New York, Pantheon, 1984, p. 244.
22 E. Dimendberg, "The will to motorisation – cinema and the autobahn", in J. Miller and M. Schwarz (eds), *Speed – Visions of an Accelerated Age*, London, Photographers Gallery, 1998, p. 62.
23 Dimendberg, op. cit., pp. 65 and 66.
24 Dimendberg, op. cit., pp. 68–9.
25 O. Lofgren, "Materialising the nation in Sweden and America", *Ethnos*, 1993, vol. 3–4.

26 cf. L. Berlant, "The theory of infantile citizenship", in G. Eley and R. Suny (eds), *Becoming National*, Oxford, Oxford University Press, 1996. For a fuller account of Berlant's work, see her *The Anatomy of National Fantasy*, Chicago, University of Chicago Press, 1991, and her later *The Queen of America goes to Washington City*, Durham, Duke University Press, 1997, where she develops her theory of what she calls the "Intimate Public Sphere".

27 See C. and A. Painter, *At Home with Constable's Cornfield*, London, National Gallery, 1996.

28 C. and A. Painter, op. cit., pp. 24, 44, 5, 11.

29 cf. Patrick Wright, *On Living in an Old Country*, London, Verso, 1985; see also J. Okely, "Picturing and placing Constable country", in K. Fog-Olwig and K. Hastrup (eds), *Siting Culture*, London, Routledge, 1997.

30 Andrew Wilton (ed.), *Constable's English Landscape Scenery*, London, British Museum Prints and Drawing Series, 1979, p. 24.

31 cf. I. Grewal, *Home and Harem*, Leicester, Leicester University Press, 1996, pp. 35–6. A recent correspondent to the *Guardian*, writing from Hong Kong, confirmed the longevity of this imagery: "To many an 'expat' ... rural Britain is what we think of as 'home', with its countryside, village pubs and traditional way of life"; *Guardian*, 30 November 1999.

32 B. Schwarz, "An Englishman abroad and at home", *New Formations*, 1992, vol. 17, p. 95.

33 P. Scott, *My Appointment with the Muse: essays 1961–75*, London, Heinemann, quoted in Schwarz, op. cit., p. 102.

34 P. Carter, *On Living in a New Country*, London, Faber, 1992.

35 Quoted in Ien Ang, "Identity, culture and globalisation", paper to the Researching Culture conference, University of North London, September, 1999.

36 Goldman, op. cit., p. 153.

37 Jean Duruz, "Cuisine nostalgia", *Communal/Plural*, 1999, vol. 7, pp. 97–101.

38 F. Allon, "Home as cultural translation: John Howard's Earlwood", *Community/Plural*, 1997, vol. 5, p. 1.

39 Jason Yat-Sen Li, Australian Unity Party spokesman, quoted in Christopher Zim, "One Nation revives disunity", *Observer*, 6 September 1998. Evidently, from the point of view of Australian Aboriginal culture, this "older version" of the culture is itself but an upstart newcomer with a massive historical blind spot concerning its own origins.

40 In a similar spirit, Charlotte Brunsdon's analysis of public debates in the UK about the first appearance of satellite dishes on the outside of houses in the late 1980s traced how a set of substantive issues about class, taste and citizenship were displaced on to ostensibly architectural questions about the supposed effect of satellite dishes in "spoiling" the appearance of an area's housing stock and thus, indirectly downgrading the national heritage. In Brunsdon's example, the satellite dish was seen to function as a visual symbol of the "taste poverty" of the consumers of such downmarket forms of popular culture – see Charlotte Brunsdon, "Satellite dishes and the landscapes of taste", in her *Screen Tastes*, London, Routledge, 1997.

41 Allon, op. cit., pp. 3 and 19.

42 *Sydney Morning Herald*, 2 March 1996, p. 16, quoted in Allon, op. cit., p. 2.

43 Allon, op. cit., pp. 15 and 22.

44 cf. John Travolta's disquisition on international burger-buying at the beginning of Quentin Tarentino's film *Pulp Fiction*; O. Lofgren, "The nation as home or motel? Metaphors of media and belonging", unpublished paper, Department of European Ethnology, University of Lund, 1995, p. 11.

45 A. Linde-Laursen, "The nationalisation of trivialities", *Ethnos* 1993, 3–4, p. 277.

46 Lisa Malkki, "National Geographic", in A. Gupta and J. Ferguson (eds), *Culture, Power, Place*, Durham, Duke University Press, 1997, pp. 42, 62.

47 Malkki, quoted in D. Hebdige, "On tumbleweed and bodybags: remembering America", in B.W. Ferguson (ed.), *Longing and Belonging: From the Faraway Nearby*, New York, Distributed Art Publishers, 1995, p. 100.

48 Malkki, op. cit., p. 67.

49 G. Bisharat, "Exile to compatriot", in Gupta and Ferguson (eds), op. cit., p. 217.

50 Tuan, op. cit., *Space and Place*, p. 153. It was for this very reason, Tuan notes, that the conquerors of ancient cities razed them to the ground – because in this act they thus appropriated the conquered people's gods, by rendering them homeless. By the same token, the worst fate that could befall anyone was to be exiled, because they would then be deprived of the protection offered by the laws guaranteed by their local gods and would walk among strangers, who would offer them no recognition of their language and customs.

51 In his study of merchant seamen, Robert Davis notes that although they have opted for a life of mobility, they often display a craving for some permanent locality, as an "anchor" for their imagination while at sea: "They had a craving for a headquarters somewhere along the shore, a place where they could leave their trunk, if they had one; a place to which they might project their minds, wherever they might wander and visualise the position of furniture, and imagine just what the inmates of the place to which they looked were doing at different hours of the day; a place to which they could send a picture postcard and bring back a curio; a place to which they could always return and be sure of a welcome"; Robert Davis, "Some men of the merchant marine", quoted in Tuan, op. cit., p. 158.

52 R. Wilk, "Learning to be local in Belize", in Miller (ed.), *Worlds Apart*, London, Routledge, 1995, p. 110.

53 Fog-Olwig, quoted in D. Miller, "Introduction", in Miller (ed.), op. cit., p. 12. In this connection, in her study of transnational migration patterns centred on the Caribbean island of St Kitts–Nevis, Karen Fog-Olwig reports that many households which are dependent on remittances sent to them by family members working abroad "keep herds of goats and sheep around the house, not for their own consumption but … so … they can give members of the family a 'taste of home' during their brief stays on Nevis". As she notes, when these migrants visit home they want to relive the culture of their childhood (if without the poverty historically associated with it) and to this extent their remittances contribute to preserving some aspects of traditional village life which would otherwise have disappeared; K. Fog-Olwig, "Defining the national in the transnational", *Ethnos*, 1993, vol. 3–4, p. 372.

54 *A Day in the Life of Africa*, Tx BBC2, 6 August 1995. In the conclusion to his essay on nation-building, Ghassan Hage quotes a line from a classical genre of nomadic pre-Islamic poetry which involves the "nomadic poet sitting by the remaining traces of a previous encampment and composing a poem in which he mourns camping there with the rest of his tribe". Hage's point is the simple but telling one that we must recognise, against the celebrations of postmodern nomadology, that "even nomads mourn their 'home'" and that "while this era could be that of nomadism, it does not make it in any sense an era where people stop yearning for home"; G. Hage, "Nation-building-dwelling-being", *Communal/Plural*, 1993, vol. 1, p. 102.

55 However, as we have seen, Heller's choice of terminology – geographical monogamy vs geographical promiscuity – is itself so heavily value-laden as to at least partly vitiate the argument she wishes to make.

56 A. Heller, "Where we are at home", *Thesis Eleven*, 1995, vol. 41, pp. 1, 3, 6.

57 ibid. p. 3; cf. Ann Tyler's novel *The Accidental Tourist* (London, Chatto and Windus, 1985). In a similar vein, in his analysis of the lifestyles of the new global business

elite, Castells concludes that the compression of space enabled by the contribution of aeroplanes and information technology leads to an increasingly homogenous lifestyle among the information elite, consisting of "the mandatory diet of grilled salmon and green salad; the 'pale chamois' wall colour intended to create the cosy atmosphere of the 'inner space' ... [and] the combination of business suits and sportswear"; M. Castells, quoted in D. Ladipo, "http://www.global.pillage", *City*, 1997, vol. 7, p. 132.

58 Heller, op. cit., pp. 2 and 16. See earlier Ch. 1 note 11.
59 Nikos Papastergiadis, *Dialogues in the Diasporas*, London, Rivers Oram Press, 1998, p. 7.
60 Nestor Garcia Canclini, quoted in Papastergiadis, op. cit., p. 15.
61 P. Gilroy, *The Black Atlantic*, London, Verso, 1994, p. 198.
62 Dag Elvin, cited in R. Paine, *Herds of the Tundra: A Portrait of Saami Reindeer Pastoralism*, Washington DC, Smithsonian Institution Press, 1994, p. 145.
63 Papastergiadis, op. cit., p. 9; cf. also Wendy Wheeler, "Nostalgia isn't nasty", in M. Perryman (ed.), *Altered States*, London, Lawrence and Wishart, 1994.
64 R. Rouse, "Mexican migration and the social space of postmodernism", *Diaspora*, 1991, vol. 1(1).
65 Rouse, op. cit., pp. 9, 14.
66 Rouse quoted in G. Yudice *et al.* (eds), *On Edge: The Crisis of Contemporary Latin American Culture*, Minneapolis, University of Minnesota Press, 1992.
67 R. Rouse, "Questions of Identity", *Critique of Anthropology*, 1995, vol. 15(4), pp. 352, 363.
68 Heidegger, quoted in O. Lofgren, "The nation as home or motel?", unpublished paper, Department of European Ethnology, University of Lund, 1995, pp. 8–9.
69 Gillis, quoted in Lofgren, op. cit., p. 10; cf. Rybczynski, quoted earlier on this.
70 Shabbir Akhbar, "Notions of nation and alienation", *Times Higher Education Supplement*, 25 April 1997.
71 cf. Patricia Seed, "The key to the house", in H. Naficy (ed.), *Home, Homeland, Exile*, London, Routledge, 1999.
72 G. Bisharat, "Exile to compatriot: transformations in the social identity of Palestinian refugees in the West Bank", in Gupta and Ferguson (eds), op. cit., p. 214.
73 J. Berger and J. Mohr, *The Seventh Man*, Harmondsworth, Penguin, 1975, p. 179.
74 cf. Papastergiadis, op. cit. – although he notes that this possibly apocryphal story is contradicted by Arendt's biographer.
75 I. Rogoff, "Terra infirma", inaugural lecture, Goldsmiths College, London, 1998. See also her *Terra Infirma*, Routledge, 2000.
76 Said, quoted in Maya Jaggi, "Out of the shadows", *Guardian*, 11 September 1999.
77 Meera Syal, *Anita and Me*, London, Flamingo, 1997, p. 267.
78 ibid. p. 267.
79 Lofgren, "The nation as home or motel?", op. cit., p. 10.
80 R. King, "Migrants, globalisation and place', in D. Massey and P. Jess (eds), *A Place in the World*, Milton Keynes, Open University Press, 1995, p. 29.
81 Ayse S. Caglar, "German Turks in Berlin: social exclusion and strategies for social mobility", *New Community*, 1995, vol. 21(3).
82 A. Begag, *North African immigrants in France*, Loughborough, European Research Centre, Loughborough University, 1989, p. 18.
83 A. Hargreaves, *Immigration, "Race" and Ethnicity in Contemporary France*, London, Routledge, 1995, p. 133. The final shots of Taieb Louhichi's 1982 film *L'ombre de la terre (Dhil al-Ardh)* portray exactly this scenario as the migrant's coffin is shipped home to North Africa. As Tahar Ben Jelloun puts it in his novella *Solitaire*, "Today a body will journey home in a metal box ... the dregs of a life gathered together, bound up with string and sent back", London, Quartet Books, 1988, p. 2.

84 J. Berger, *And Our Faces, My Heart, Brief as Photos*, London, Writers and Readers Press, 1984, p. 64.

85 cf. A. Bammer, "Editorial", *New Formations*, 1992, vol. 17.

86 Quoted in J. Daniel, "Temporary shelter: Adorno and the language of home", *New Formations*, 1992, vol. 17, p. 26.

87 cf. *Minima Moralia*, written while Adorno was living in Los Angeles; Daniel, "Temporary shelter", op. cit., p. 31.

88 cf. Ruth Mandel, "Turkish headscarves and the 'foreigner' problem", *New German Critique*, 1989, vol. 46.

89 Daniel, op. cit., p. 32.

90 Quoted in interview with Papastergiadis, op. cit., p. 203. Similarly, Revill argues that in a world where the question is how to create a home in a highly destabilised, impoverished and unstable environment, the stories of an author such as Carol Lake "build bridges between self and locality", and such certainty and security as there is comes from "possessing the means to describe oneself" and "doing this in a way that is shared by the group and unavailable to outsiders"; Revill, op. cit., in Keith and Pile (eds), p.137; cf. Carol Lake, *Rosehill – Portraits of a Midlands City*, London, Bloomsbury, 1989. However, in a further parallel, it is interesting to note that, just as the Turkish–German novelist Jakob Arjouni (of whom more later) principally identifies himself with his city – as a "Frankfurter" rather than as either a Turk or a German – in the end, when Adorno wanted to "go home", it was not simply to Germany but to his own particular city – Frankfurt. As Daniel observes, Adorno wanted to return so that he could live and work in the context in which he felt most "at home" – and "this context was not the German language in and of itself, but specifically Frankfurt, the city of the 'beautiful perfect life' of his childhood" to the place where, as he puts it "whatever was most specifically mine was mediated to the core" – J. Daniel, op. cit., p. 32.

91 Papastergiadis, op. cit., p. 2.

92 Descombes, quoted in M. Augé, *Non-Places*, London, Verso, 1995.

93 A. Begag, op. cit., pp. 8–9.

94 J. Berger and J. Mohr, *The Seventh Man*, Harmondsworth, Penguin, 1975, p. 215.

95 Papastergiadis, op. cit., p. 6; Heller, op. cit., p. 6.

96 J. Kristeva, *Strangers to Ourselves*, New York, Columbia University Press, 1991, p. 20.

97 J. Durham Peters, "Exile, nomadism and diaspora", in Naficy (ed.), op. cit., p. 19.

98 K. Ganguly, "Migrant identities", *Cultural Studies*, vol. 6(1), pp. 29–30.

99 Kristeva, op. cit., pp. 9–10.

100 L. Baldassar, "Home and away", *Communal/Plural* 1997, vol. 5, pp. 74–7.

101 Nandy interviewed in Papastergiadis, op. cit., p. 110.

102 H. Naficy, "Exile discourse and televisual fetishisation", in H. Naficy and T. Gabriel (eds), *Otherness and the Media*, Harwood, 1993, p. 102.

103 Naficy, op. cit., p. 111.

104 ibid. pp. 91, 86. But cf. Richard Wilk, quoted in Chapter 8, on the function of satellite television in constituting a greater sense of the "coevalness" of different cultural time zones, in so far as the technology allows a greater sense of "real time" connection to geographically distant places.

105 Marie Gillespie, *Television, Ethnicity and Cultural Change*, London, Routledge, 1995, p. 180.

106 Balkan historian Ivo Banac, quoted in S. Jansen, "Homeless at home: narrations of post-Yugoslav identities", in Rapport and Dawson (eds), op. cit., p. 98.

107 Jansen, op. cit., p. 86.

108 Dubravka Ugresic, quoted in Jansen, op. cit., p. 92.

109 D. Ugresic, quoted in Jansen, op. cit., p. 107; cf. Marc Augé on airports as "non-places" in Chapter 8 below.
110 Mandy Thomas, "Discordant dwellings: Australian homes and the Vietnamese diaspora" in *Communal/Plural*, 1997, vol. 5.
111 Thomas, op. cit., pp. 95–6.
112 Thomas, op. cit., p.100. However, what is for the migrant the reassuring smell of "home cooking" is sometimes to their new neighbours precisely the "bothersome" smell of threatening cultural difference. Thus. in France, Jacques Chirac was reported as complaining that the "noise and smell" of foreigners was driving 'decent' French people "understandably crazy" – Chirac, quoted in S. Hall, "Globalisation: Europe's other self", *Marxism Today*, August, 1991.
113 Thomas, op. cit., p. 102.
114 Gary Younge, "Are my roots showing?", *Observer*, 12 September 1999; see also his *No Place Like Home*, London, Picador, 1999.
115 U. Hannerz, *Cultural Complexity*, New York, Columbia University Press, 1992, p. 39.
116 L. Baldassar, "Home and away: migration, the return visit and 'transnational' identity", in *Communal/Plural*, 1997, vol. 5. G. Baumann, *Contesting Culture: Discourses of Identity in Multi-Ethnic London*, Cambridge, Cambridge University Press, 1996.
117 cf. the English definition of a cockney as someone born within the sound of Bow church bells.
118 Baldassar, op. cit., p. 76.
119 ibid., p. 90.
120 But cf. D. Kolar Panov, *Video, War and the Diasporic Imagination*, London, Routledge, 1997, for an example of the potentially negative effect of such communications in splitting rather than consolidating erstwhile communities, in some circumstances.
121 Baldassar, op. cit., p. 82.
122 Farha Ghannam, "Re-imagining the global: relocation and local identities in Cairo", in A. Öncü and P. Weyland (eds), *Space, Culture and Power*, Zed Books, 1997, p. 126.
123 Bisharat, op. cit., p. 214.
124 A. Dawson, "The dislocation of identity: contestations of 'home community' in Northern England", in Rapport and Dawson (eds), op. cit., p. 217.
125 K. Fog-Olwig, "Contested homes", in Rapport and Dawson (eds), op. cit., p. 230.
126 Karen Fog-Olwig, "Defining the national in the transnational: cultural identity in the Afro-Caribbean diaspora", *Ethnos*, 1993, vol. 3–4, pp. 367–9; cf. also K. Fog-Olwig, *Global Culture, Island Identity*, London, Harwood Academic Press, 1993.
127 Trinh T. Minh-ha, "Other than myself/My other self", in G. Robertson, M. Mash, L. Tickner, J. Bird, B. Curtis and T. Putnam (eds), *Travellers' Tales*, London, Routledge, 1994, pp. 13–14.
128 Appadurai, op. cit., p. 6; H. Naficy, "Framing exile", in H. Naficy (ed.), *Home, Homeland, Exile*, New York, Routledge/American Film Institute, 1999, p. 4.

3   THE GENDER OF HOME

1 L. Rainwater, "Fear and the house-as-haven in the lower class", *Journal of the American Institute of Planners*, 1996, vol. 32(1), p. 22–31; quoted in D. Sibley, *Geographies of Exclusion*, London, Routledge, 1995, p. 92.
2 Sibley, op. cit., p. 94.

3 A. Oakley, *Housewife*, Harmondsworth, Penguin, 1976; cf. Lynn Segal (ed.), *What Is To Be Done about the Family?*, and Elizabeth Wilson, *What Is To Be Done about Violence against Women?*, both Harmondsworth, Penguin, 1983; see also L. Goldsack, "A haven in a heartless world? Women and domestic violence", in T. Chapman and J. Hockey (eds), *Ideal Homes?*, London, Routledge, 1999.

4 Sibley, op. cit., p. 94; on this see also Wilson, op. cit., in particular.

5 N. Fraser, "What's critical about critical theory?", in S. Benhabib and D. Cornell (eds), *Feminism as Critique*, Cambridge, Polity Press, 1987, p. 37.

6 Sara Maitland, "Where's the truth serum?", *Guardian*, 9 December 1995.

7 Karen Fog-Olwig, "Contested homes: home-making and the making of anthropology", in N. Rapport and A. Dawson (eds), *Migrants of Identity*, Oxford, Berg, p. 226.

8 K. Worpole, *Nothing to Fear? Trust and Respect in Urban Communities*, London, Comedia/Demos, 1997, p. 4; see also L. Greenhalgh and K. Worpole, *Park Life: Urban Parks and Social Renewal*, London, Comedia/Demos, 1995.

9 N. Rathzel, "Harmonious Heimat and disturbing Ausländer", in K.K. Bhavani and A. Phoenix (eds), *Shifting Identities and Shifting Racisms*, London, Sage, 1994, p. 87.

10 Perhaps most spectacularly in the case of Fred and Rosemary West in the UK; see Gordon Burn, *Happy like Murderers*, London, Faber and Faber, 1998. See also the early work of Gregory Bateson and his colleagues – G. Bateson, D. Jackson, J. Haley and J. Weakland, "Towards a theory of schizophrenia", *Behavioural Sciences*, 1956, vol. 1, pp. 251–63.

11 S. Moore, "Barking up the family tree", *Guardian*, 9 March 1995. At the time they were made, Moore's comments were directed at the then Conservative government's "back to basics" social policy, but the New Labour government has disappointed many of its erstwhile supporters by pursuing an equally ideological set of social policies based on the same glorified image of the "traditional family".

12 A. Palmer, "One big dysfunctional family", *Independent*, 15 June 1994.

13 V. Williams, *Who's Looking at the Family?*, London, Barbican Art Gallery, 1994, p. 13.

14 S. Moore, "Here's looking at you, Mum and Dad and kid", *Guardian*, 27 May 1994.

15 Williams, *Who's Looking at the Family?*, op. cit., p. 19.

16 Quoted in Williams, *Who's Looking at the Family?*, op. cit., p. 41.

17 A. Artley, *Murder in the Heart*, London, Hamish Hamilton, 1993, pp. 139–40.

18 Williams, *Who's Looking at the Family?*, op. cit., p. 30.

19 cf. A. Gupta and J. Ferguson, "Introduction" to Gupta and Ferguson (eds), *Culture, Power, Place*, Durham, Duke University Press, 1997, p. 7.

20 W. Rybczynski, *Home: A Short History of an Idea*, London, Heinemann, 1986, p. 72.

21 D. Massey, *Space, Place and Gender*, Cambridge, Polity Press, 1994, p. 9.

22 Quoted in S. Haar and C. Reed, "Coming home", in C. Reed (ed.), *Not at Home*, London, Thames and Hudson, 1996, p. 258.

23 A. Ainley, "Luce Irigaray: at home with Martin Heidegger", *Angelaki*, 1995, vol. 2(1), p. 143; L. Irigaray, *L'oubli de l'air chez Martin Heidegger*, Paris, Editions de Minuit, 1985.

24 In L. Irigaray, *An Ethics of Sexual Difference*, London, Athlone Press, 1993.

25 Ainley, op. cit., p. 144.

26 R. Bromley, "Traversing identity", in *Angelaki* 1995, vol. 2(1), drawing on Julia Kristeva's *Powers of Horror*, New York, Columbia Press, 1992.

27 Bromley, op. cit., p. 111.

28 N. Papastergiadis, *Modernity as Exile*, Manchester University Press, 1993, p. 144.

29 Bromley, op. cit., pp. 110–12.

30 Moreover, they argue that the further problem with domestic typologies such as Bachelard's, "founded on myths of a universal childhood experience set in an ideal past" is that they "fail to address our contemporary situation, where in multi-cultural societies with diverse populations, there can be no single place like home". Rather, as they note, we must recognise that there are "multiple places that are home for different kinds of people" and we must recognise the diversity of domestic experiences – Haar and Reed, op. cit., pp. 258 and 261.

31 C. Reed, "Introduction", C. Reed (ed.), op. cit., p. 7.

32 cf. C. Baudelaire, *The Painter of Modern Life and Other Essays*, London, Phaidon Press, 1964.

33 P. Sparke, *As Long As It's Pink: The Sexual Politics of Taste*, London, Pandora, 1995, pp. 9, 11, 106, 208–9; cf. Adolf Loos, "Ornament and crime", in his *Spoken into the Void: Collected Essays*, Cambridge, Mass., MIT Press, 1982; cf. also on the "femininity" of mass culture, Andreas Huyssen, *After the Great Divide*, London, Macmillan, 1986.

34 Actually men, evidently; see Reed (ed.), op. cit., p. 9.

35 Benjamin, quoted in Reed (ed.), op. cit., p. 10.

36 J. Attfield, "Inside Pram Town: a case study of Harlow house interiors 1951–61", in J. Attfield and P. Kirkham (eds), *A View from the Interior: Feminism, Women and Design*, The Women's Press, London, 1989, p. 228.

37 Adolph Gottlieb and Mark Rothko, quoted in Reed (ed.), op. cit., p. 11; cf. S. Guilbaut, *How New York Stole Modern Art: Abstract Expressionism, Freedom and the Cold War*, Chicago, University of Chicago Press, 1983.

38 C. Greenberg, "The avant garde and kitsch in art and culture", quoted in Reed (ed.), op. cit., pp. 11 and 15. Julius Meier-Graefe, quoted ibid., p. 11; cf. also Matisse's notion of art as "like a good armchair" – in J. Flam, *Matisse on Art*, New York, Phaidon, 1973, p. 35.

39 Reed, op. cit., p. 15.

40 L. Johnson, "As housewives we are worms", *Cultural Studies*, 1996, vol. 10(3).

41 Johnson, op. cit., pp. 451–3.

42 D. Massey, *Space, Place and Gender*, Cambridge, Polity Press, 1994, p. 71.

43 Johnson, op. cit., pp. 460–61.

44 M. de Certeau, *The Practice of Everyday Life*, Berkeley, University of California Press, 1984, p. 117.

45 ibid., p. 461; see also Shunya Yoshimi, "Made in Japan: the cultural politics of home electrification in postwar Japan", for a comparable account of the role of the housewife in the modernisation process, paper to Pacific Asia Cultural Studies Conference, Goldsmiths College, London, June 1998.

46 G. Rose, "Some notes towards thinking about spaces of the future", in J. Bird, B. Curtis, T. Putnam, G. Robertson and L. Tickner (eds), *Mapping the Futures*, London, Routledge, 1993, p. 71.

47 R. Hoggart, *The Uses of Literacy*, Harmondsworth, Penguin, 1969, pp. 33 and 41; original 1957.

48 Massey, op. cit., p. 10.

49 G. Lloyd, *The Man of Reason*, London, Methuen, 1984, p. 50, quoted in Massey, op. cit., pp. 10–11.

50 Massey, op. cit., p. 180; D. Massey, "A place called home", *New Formations*, 1992, vol. 17, p. 11.

51 See D. Morley and K. Robins, *Spaces of Identity*, London, Routledge, 1995, chapter 5.

52 S. Keane, "Imaginary homelands: notes on Heimat and heimlich", *Angelaki*, 1995, vol. 2(1), p. 86.

53 A. Kaes, *From Hitler to Heimat*, Cambridge, Mass., Harvard University Press, 1989, p. 168.

54 C. Applegate, "The question of Heimat in the German Republic", *New Formations*, 1992, vol. 17, p. 72. See also E. Carter, *How German is She?*, Ann Arbor, University of Michigan Press, 1997.

55 C. Brunsdon and D. Morley, *Everyday Television: Nationwide*, London, British Film Institute, 1978.

56 cf. Ruskin's famous definition of what a home is, first articulated in 1868:

> this is the true nature of home, it is the place of peace; the shelter, not only from all injury, but from all terror, doubt and division … so far as the anxieties of the outer life penetrate into it … it ceases to be a home; it is then only a part of the outer world which you have roofed over and lighted a fire in. And whenever a true wife comes, this home is always round her.
>
> (Ruskin, quoted in Morley and Brunsdon, op. cit., p. 78)

57 Marina Warner, "Home: our famous island race", *Independent*, 3 March 1994; reprinted in her *Managing Monsters*, London, Vintage, 1994.

58 Phil Cohen, *Home Rules*, London, New Ethnicities Unit, University of East London, 1993, p. 15.

59 Celeste Olalquiaga, "Home is where the art is", in S. Vogel (ed.), *Home and the World*, Museum for African Art, New York, 1993, pp. 16–17.

60 B. Harlow, "Introduction" to Malek Alloula, *The Colonial Harem*, Minneapolis, University of Minnesota Press, 1986, p. xvi.

61 I. Grewal, *Home and Harem: Nation, Gender, Empire and the Cultures of Travel*, Leicester, Leicester University Press, 1996, p. 49.

62 Grewal, op. cit., pp. 53–4, drawing on P. Chatterjee, "The nationalist resolution of the women's question", in K.K. Sungari and S. Vaid (eds), *Recasting Women*, New Delhi, Kali for Women, 1989.

63 Trinh T. Minh-ha, "Other than myself/My other self", in G. Robertson, M. Mash, L. Tickner, J. Bird, B. Curtis and T. Putnam (eds), *Travellers' Tales*, London, Routledge, 1994, p. 15.

64 M. Gillespie, *Television, Ethnicity and Cultural Change*, London, Routledge, 1995.

65 M. Gillespie, "Technology and tradition", *Cultural Studies*, 1989, vol. 3(2), p. 229; cf. Hargreaves' findings on the gendering of media usage among immigrant groups in France and Germany reported in Chapter 7.

66 Gillespie, *Television, Ethnicity and Cultural Change*, op. cit., p. 80.

67 Gillespie, "Technology and tradition", op. cit., pp. 188–9. However, in his commentary on immigration patterns in the USA, James Clifford cautions that mobility may have an ambivalent effect on traditional gender relations. On the one hand, "maintaining connections with homelands, with kinship networks and with religious and cultural traditions may renew patriarchal structures" but, on the other, "new roles and demands, new political spaces, are opened by diaspora interactions" as, for example, women increasingly migrate independently of men and achieve forms of economic independence which (if fragile) allow them more autonomy than within traditional patterns. At the same time such immigrant women often remain selectively "attracted to, and empowered by a 'home' culture and tradition which they mobilise in strategic ways in their new circumstances"; J. Clifford, *Routes*, Cambridge, Mass., Harvard University Press, 1997, p. 259.

68 For one example, see Elspeth Probyn's analysis of the 1980s American series *Thirtysomething*, which offers a compelling account of that series' articulation of "post-feminism" with the "new traditionalism" of the reaffirmation of "family

values", in which the moral sanctity of the home turns out, after all, to be the most important thing for everyone, and the home itself turns out, in the end, to be the "natural destiny" of the woman – E. Probyn, "New traditionalism and post-feminism: TV does the home", *Screen*, 1990, vol. 31(2). See also Richard Sennett: "if the suburbanised family is a little world of its own" then all other concerns "can be shut out with the feeling of performing a moral act"; R. Sennett, *The Uses of Disorder*, London, Faber and Faber, 1996, p. 83; original 1971.

69 Janet Wolf, "The invisible flâneuse", *Theory, Culture and Society*, 1985, vol. 2(3), pp. 37–40.

70 J. Wolf, "On the road again: metaphors of travel in cultural criticism", *Cultural Studies*, 1993, vol. 7(2), p. 235.

71 cf. T. de Lauretis, *Technologies of Gender*, Indianapolis, Indiana University Press, 1988.

72 C. Enloe, *Bananas, Beaches and Bases*, London, Pandora Press, 1989, p. 21, quoted in Wolf, "On the road again", op. cit., p. 229.

73 M. Morris, "At Henry Parkes Motel", *Cultural Studies*, 1988, vol. 2(1), p. 12.

74 M. Gordon, *Good Boys and Dead Girls and Other Essays*, London, Bloomsbury, 1991, pp. 6, 17.

75 D. Massey, "Flexible sexism", *Environment and Planning D: Society and Space*, 1991, vol. 9, pp. 47–8.

76 T. T. Minh-ha, op. cit., p. 15; Ashraf Ghani, "Space as an arena of represented practices", in J. Bird, B. Curtis, T. Putnam, G. Robertson and L. Tickner (eds.), *Mapping the Futures*, London, Routledge, 1993, p. 51.

77 Rose, op. cit., p. 76.

78 Wilson, quoted in D. Massey, "Politics and space/time", in M. Keith and S. Pile (eds), *Place and the Politics of Identity*, London, Routledge, 1993, p. 149.

79 N. Smith, "Homeless/global: scaling places" in J. Bird *et al.* (eds), op. cit., p. 104.

80 Similarly, Paul Hoggett argues that in the UK "women have less access to the public sphere than men, Muslim women less than non-Muslim women, and so on. It is legitimate for men to go out at night to go to a voluntary meeting ... less so for women"; K. Worpole, *Towns for People*, Open University Press, 1992, p. 84; Hoggett, quoted in Liz Greenhalgh and Ken Worpole, *The Freedom of the City*, London, Demos, 1996, p. 16.

81 L. Harman, *When a Hostel Becomes a Home*, Toronto, Garamond Press, 1989, p. 10.

82 cf. Anthony Vidler, "A dark space", in J. Lingwood (ed.), *House*, London, Phaidon Press, 1995.

83 cf. T. Cresswell, *In Place/Out of Place*, Minneapolis, University of Minnesota Press, 1996, p. 100.

84 P. Stallybrass and A. White, *The Politics and Poetics of Transgression*, London, Methuen, 1986, pp. 23–4.

85 J. Robinson, "Hi honey, I'm home", in Reed (ed.), op. cit., p. 102.

86 Lisa Tierstein, "The chic interior and the feminine modern", in Reed (ed.), op. cit., pp. 18, 26, 27, 30, 31.

87 G. Allan and G. Crow, "Introduction", in G. Allan and G. Crow (eds), *Home and Family*, London, Macmillan, 1989, p. 2.

88 Greenbaum, quoted in J. Craik, "The making of Mother", in Allan and Crow (eds), op. cit., pp. 54, 62.

89 "Introduction" to S. Jackson and S. Moores (eds), *The Politics of Domestic Consumption*, Hemel Hempstead, Harvester, 1995.

90 Jackson and Moores, op. cit., p. 5.

91 A. Murcott, "It's a pleasure to cook for him: food, mealtimes and gender in some South Wales households", in Jackson and Moores (eds), op. cit., p. 93; cf. also the work of Charles and Kerr, below.

92 Pauline Hunt, "Gender and the construction of home life", in Allan and Crow (eds) op. cit., p. 69.

93 Hunt, op. cit., p. 70.

94 R. Deem, *All Work and No Play*, Milton Keynes, Open University Press, 1986, p. 81.

95 Deem, op. cit., p.137; cf. the evidence that the most likely place for a woman to control the use of a television set is when it is placed in "her" territory, in the kitchen.

96 Hunt, op. cit., pp. 71–2.

97 Hunt, op. cit., pp. 71–2.

98 As Gullestad puts it, "by decorating their home, the family members symbolise their unity and elaborate on the values of sharing and togetherness in the charged context of hearth and home"; M. Gullestad, *Kitchen Table Society*, Oslo, Universitetsforlaget, 1984, p. 7.

99 M. Csikszentmihalyi and E. Rochberg-Halton, *The Meaning Of Things*, Cambridge, Cambridge University Press, 1981.

100 Hunt, op. cit., p. 72.

101 N. Couldry, op. cit., p. 111.

102 M. Bouquet, "You can't be a Brahmin in the English countryside", in A. Cohen (ed.), *Symbolising Boundaries*, Manchester, Manchester University Press, 1986.

103 R. Madigan and M. Munro, "Ideal homes: gender and domestic architecture", in T. Putnam and C. Newton (eds), *Household Choices*, London, Futures Publications, 1990, p. 27.

104 ibid., p. 27.

105 J. Carsten and S. Hugh-Jones (eds), *About the Home*, London, Jonathan Cape, 1995.

106 ibid., pp. 40–41.

107 P. Weyland, "Gendered lives in global spaces", in A. Öncü and P. Weyland (eds), *Space, Culture and Power*, London, Zed Books, 1997.

108 Weyland, op. cit., pp. 85, 86, 91.

109 For contemporary Turkish feminist debates about the renegotiation of the meaning of the house, see Carel Bertram, "Restructuring the house; restructuring the self", in Zehra F. Arat (ed.), *Deconstructing Images of "The Turkish Woman"*, London, Macmillan, 1998.

110 cf. Judith Butler, *Gender Trouble*, New York, Routledge, 1990; cf. also Ien Ang and Joke Hermes, "Gender and/in media consumption", in J. Curran and M. Gurevitch (eds), *Mass Media and Society*, London, Edward Arnold, 1991.

111 D. Gauntlett and A. Hill, *Living Television*, London, Routledge, 1999. See below, Chapter 4.

112 Susan Bordo, "Feminism, postmodernism and gender-scepticism", in L. Nicholson (ed.), *Feminism/Postmodernism*, London, Routledge, 1990.

113 B. Robbins, "Comparative cosmopolitanism", in P. Cheah and B. Robbins (eds), *Cosmopolitics*, Minneapolis, University of Minnesota Press, 1998, p. 251, quoting C. Mohanty, "Under Western eyes", *Boundary 2*, 1984, 12–13.

114 cf. my "Theoretical orthodoxies", in M. Ferguson and P. Golding (eds), *Cultural Studies in Question*, London, Sage, 1997, p.127.

115 As she puts it, while the time that women spend out of the labour market (during their child-rearing years) is shortening, "the time spent outside formal employment is more home-centred than in the past since other women [except those who have had their children at the same time] are not available for companionship. Women caring for children on a full time basis experience a period of short but intense home-centredness"; F. Devine, "Privatised families", p. 93 in Allan and Crow (eds), op. cit.

116 D. Massey, *Space, Place and Gender*, Cambridge, Polity Press, 1994, p. 190.

117 D. Haraway, "Homes for Cyborgs", in E. Weed (ed.), *Coming to Terms: Feminism, Theory, Politics*, New York, Routledge, 1985, p. 194.

118 C. Carter, "Nuclear family fall out", in B. Adam and S. Allan (eds), *Theorising Culture*, UCL Press, London, 1995, p. 188.

119 J. Stacey, "Backward towards the postmodern family", in B. Thorne and M. Yalom (eds), *Rethinking the Family*, Boston, North-Eastern University Press; quoted in Carter, op. cit., p. 194.

120 J. Weeks, "Pretended family relationships", in D. Clark (ed.), *Marriage, Domestic life and Social Change*, London, Routledge, 1991, p. 227.

121 P. Palmer, *Domesticity and Dirt*, Philadelphia, Temple University Press, 1989, p. 139.

122 Frazer Ward, "Foreign and familiar bodies", in J. Fuenmayor, K. Haug and F. Ward (eds), *Dirt and Domesticity*, Whitney Independent Study Papers 2, New York, Whitney Museum of American Art, 1992, pp. 8–9.

123 Palmer, op. cit., p. 138.

124 cf. Jesus Fuenmayor *et al.*, "Preface" to Fuenmayor *et al.* (eds), op. cit.

125 Cara Mertes, "There's no place like home: women and domestic labour", in Fuenmayor *et al.* (eds), op. cit., p. 70.

126 Mertes, op. cit., p. 66.

127 D. Sibley, *Geographies of Exclusion*, London, Routledge, 1995, p. 64.

128 R. Bromley, op. cit., p. 103, glossing Kristeva.

129 A. Linde-Laursen, "The nationalisation of trivialities", in *Ethnos*, 1993, 3–4, pp. 278–9.

130 A. Bammer, "Editorial", *New Formations*, 1992, vol. 17, p. xi.

131 Jon Bird, op. cit., p. 114, glossing Freud. However, a little caution is advisable here, as the German word for the second constellation, "private, friendly, habitual", is, and so far as etymologists know always has been, *heimisch* (*Duden Etymologie*, vol. 7, Mannheim, Wien, Zurich, Dudenverlag, 1963). Moreover, this authoritative etymological dictionary insists on the exceptional rider that "in modern native speakers' feeling for the language, [the word] *unheimlich* is no longer regarded as related to *Heim*" – Duden 1963, p. 257. I am grateful to Gerd Baumann for bringing this issue to my attention.

132 S. Keane, "Imaginary homelands", *Angelaki*, 1995, vol. 2(1), p. 84, glossing Freud, "The Uncanny", in *The Penguin Freud Library*, vol. 14, pp. 335–76. One may perhaps separate the speculative from the etymological arguments by alluding to an English-language parallel: *heimlich* does indeed span the range from that which is private to that which should be kept private, and *unheimlich* is indeed the "uncanny", that is, the Scots-English *unkenny* or what one cannot *ken* or know (German: *kennen*); the unfamiliar, the unknown, and by extension the uncontrollable and even unknowable: the secret in all its shades of meaning. Again, I must thank Gerd Baumann for clarifying these etymological points for me.

133 A. Vidler, "Homes for Cyborgs", in Reed (ed.) op. cit., p. 165.

134 J. Bourne-Taylor, "Re-locations", *New Formations*, 1992, vol. 17, p. 91, commenting on Freud, "The Uncanny", standard edition of *The Complete Works*, vol. xvii, London, Hogarth Press, 1955, pp. 224–5.

135 J.D. Peters, "Exile, nomadism and diaspora", p. 31 in H. Naficy (ed.), op. cit., drawing on R. Emerson, *Selected Writings*, New York, Modern Library, 1981.

136 L. Wainwright, "Robert Rauschenberg's fabrics: reconstructing domestic space" in Reed (ed.), op. cit.

137 Wainwright, op. cit., pp. 196, 197, 193, 200, 199.

138 Vidler, "Homes for Cyborgs", op. cit.

139 ibid., p. 177.

140 See, in particular, his *Room Piece, Instant House* and *Bad Dream House.*
141 V. Acconci, quoted in C. Poggi, "Vito Acconci's bad dream of domesticity", in Reed (ed.), op. cit., p. 250.
142 Quoted in C. Poggi, op. cit., p. 237.
143 Poggi, op. cit., pp. 238 and 249; cf. P. Bourdieu, "The Berber house: or, the world reversed", in M. Douglas (ed.), *Rules and Meanings*, Harmondsworth, Penguin, 1973, on the Kabyle sense that a man who stays at home, hidden from the gaze of other men, is not truly masculine.
144 cf. Sharon Haar and Christopher Reed, "Coming home", in Reed (ed.), op. cit.; cf. also Martha Rosler's (1975) "Semiotics of the kitchen", reproduced in Rosler, *Positions in the Life World*, Birmingham, Ikon Gallery, 1998.
145 Arlene Rowen, quoted in Haar and Reed, op. cit., p. 256.
146 D. Massey, in Lingwood (ed.), op. cit., pp. 36, 42.
147 Simon Watney, "On *House*, iconoclasm and iconophobia" in Lingwood (ed.), op. cit., p. 108.

4 AT HOME WITH THE MEDIA

1 Hereafter referred to as the HICT project. This Economic and Social Research Council (ESRC) funded research project, based at Brunel University from 1987 to 1990, was directed by Roger Silverstone and also involved Andrea Dahlberg and Sonia Livingstone.
2 For a comparable analysis in another European context of the ways in which media consumption is incorporated within, and becomes constitutive of the myths and modalities of domestic life, see Francesco Casetti's ethnographic study of Italian families' uses of the mass media, *L'Ospite Fisso (The Live-In Guest)*, Milano, Edizioni San Paolo, 1995.
3 cf. B. Keen, "Play it again, Sony", *Science as Culture*, 1988, vol. 1(9).
4 cf. R. Silverstone, *Television and Everyday Life*, London, Routledge, 1994; J. Meyrowitz, *No Sense of Place*, Oxford, Oxford University Press, 1985.
5 M. Morse, "An ontology of everyday distraction", in P. Mellencamp (ed.), *The Logics of Television*, Bloomington, Indiana University Press, 1990, p. 139.
6 Morse, op. cit., pp. 198 and 205.
7 K. Robins, "Reimagined communities", *Cultural Studies*, 1989, vol. 3(2), p. 146.
8 E. Hirsch, "New technologies and domestic consumption", in C. Geraghty and D. Lusted (eds), *The Television Studies Book*, London, Arnold, 1998a, pp.160–1.
9 S. Yoshimi, "Made in Japan", paper to Pacific Asia Cultural Studies Conference, Goldsmiths College, London, 1998.
10 ibid., pp. 6–8.
11 Quoted in W. Boddy, "The shining centre of the home: ontologies of TV in the Golden Age", in P. Drummond and R. Paterson (eds), *Television in Transition*, London, British Film Institute, 1985, p. 126.
12 John Postill, "Little by little, a national subculture is made: the role of modern media in the institutional transformation of Iban society", unpublished paper, Department of Anthropology, University College London, 1998.
13 O. Leal, "Popular taste and erudite repertoire: the place and space of TV in Brazil", *Cultural Studies*, 1990, vol, 4(1).
14 D. Morley, "The physics of TV", in C. Jenks (ed.), *Visual Culture*, London, Routledge, 1995.
15 S. Moores, *Satellite Television and Everyday Life*, Academia Research Monograph 18, Luton, University of Luton Press, 1996, pp. 65–6.

16 D. Gauntlett and A. Hill, *Living Television*, London, Routledge, 1999, p. 38.

17 Gauntlett and Hill, op. cit., p. 98.

18 ibid., p. 242. Silverstone, Hirsch and I observed the same phenomenon in the HICT study where the members of one family routinely all watched the same soap opera simultaneously in different rooms.

19 Hirsch, "New technologies and domestic consumption", op. cit., p. 165.

20 Roger Silverstone, *Beneath the Bottom Line: Households and ICTs in an Age of the Consumer*, PICT Research Policy Paper 17, London, ESRC, 1991, p. 5.

21 Silverstone, op. cit., p. 12.

22 Lelia Green, "Communications and the construction of community: consuming the remote commercial television service in Western Australia", unpublished PhD thesis, Murdoch University, 1998.

23 G. Murdock, P. Hartmann and P. Gray, "Contextualising home computing", p. 255 in S. Jackson and S. Moores (eds), *The Politics of Domestic Consumption*, Hemel Hempstead, Harvester, 1995.

24 S. Moores, *Satellite Television and Everyday Life*, Luton, University of Luton Press, 1996, pp. 37–8.

25 Moores, op. cit., pp. 40–42.

26 Hirsch, "New technologies and domestic consumption", op. cit., p. 167.

27 E. Hirsch, "Domestic appropriations: multiple contexts and related limits in the home-making of Greater Londoners", in N. Rapport and A. Dawson (eds), *Migrants of Identity*, Oxford, Berg, 1998b, p. 176.

28 Hirsch, "Domestic appropriations", op. cit., pp. 174 and 177.

29 Hirsch, "Domestic appropriations", op. cit., p. 168.

30 K. Fog-Olwig, "Contested homes", in Rapport and Dawson (eds), op. cit., p. 228.

31 Moores, op. cit., pp. 48–9; cf. Massey's comments earlier on men taking work into the home, but not vice versa.

32 A. Moyal, "The gendered use of the telephone: an Australian case study", in Jackson and Moores (eds), op. cit., p. 271.

33 L. Rakow, "Women and the telephone", in C. Kramerae (ed.), *Technology and Women's Voices*, London, Routledge, 1988; quoted in Moyal, op. cit., p. 265.

34 Moyal, op. cit., p. 14.

35 See below on "the paternal cord".

36 Moores, op. cit., p. 63.

37 cf. D. Morley, *Television, Audiences and Cultural Studies*, London, Routledge, 1992, ch. 11.

38 Linda Rakow and Vija Navarro, "Remote mothering and the parallel shift", in *Critical Studies in Mass Communications*, 1993, vol. 10(2).

39 C. Castelaine-Meunier, "The paternal cord", *Reseaux*, 1997, vol. 5(2).

40 D. Gauntlett and A. Hill, *Living Television*, London, Routledge, 1999, p. 285.

41 D. Morley, *Family Television*, London, Comedia, 1986; A. Gray, *Video Playtime: The Gendering of a Leisure Technology*, London, Routledge, 1992; C. Geraghty, *Women and Soap Opera*, Cambridge, Polity Press, 1991; C. Brunsdon, *Screen Tastes*, London, Routledge, 1997.

42 Gauntlett and Hill, op. cit., pp. 226 and 285.

43 cf. A. Huyssen, *After the Great Divide*, London, Macmillan, 1986, ch. 3 on mass culture as feminine.

44 In relation to my own work in *Family Television*, Gauntlett and Hill do go to some pains to recognise my caution in arguing against the generalisability of my conclusions there (concerning the viewing practices of urban working-class housewives in the UK) to stand in for the activities of some undifferentiated or universalised category of "women" in general. However, in two respects I feel that they do not go far

enough. In the first place I would argue that some part of the difference between their own and my findings concerning the continuing pertinence of gender differentials is attributable less to the passage of time (or social change) than to two other factors, both of which they ignore. In the *Family Television* study I stressed that the strong gender differentials displayed there arose in substantial part from two particular specifications – that the women in the study were (1) housewives with children, and (2) living in lower middle-class or working-class families. There is strong evidence to suggest that, in respect of (1), gender differentials reassert themselves more strongly at this stage of many women's lives, as they take on the full brunt of childcare and domestic responsibilities. Similarly, in respect of (2), there is strong evidence that the impact of feminism in making changes in the culture of gender is still less marked among working-class families than among the middle classes. In so far as Gauntlett and Hill's sample contained (1) far fewer housewives and (2) far more middle-class people than mine, I would argue that it is these factors, rather than any fundamental cultural shift in gender identities over time, that account for many of the differences in the findings of the two studies.

45 Green, op. cit., pp. 170, 175–6 on this; cf. also V. Walkerdine, "Video replay", in J. Donald and C. Kaplan (eds), *Formations of Fantasy*, London, Methuen, 1987.

46 Green, op. cit., p. 172.

47 ibid., pp. 190 and 197.

48 cf. D. Hobson, "Soap opera at work", in E. Seiter, H. Borschers, G. Kreutzner and E.M. Warth (eds), *Remote Control*, London, Routledge, 1989.

49 Moores, *Satellite Television and Everyday Life*, op. cit.

50 N. Charles and M. Kerr, *Women, Food and Families*, Manchester, Manchester University Press, 1988; see also N. Charles, "Food and family ideology", in Jackson and Moores (eds), op. cit.

51 Moores' commentary on their work, in Moores, op. cit., p. 18.

52 Charles and Kerr, op. cit., p. 71.

53 R. Bowlby, "Domestication", in D. Elam and R. Wiegman (eds), *Feminism Beside Itself*, London, Routledge, 1995, p. 86.

54 M. Woollacot, "Communication breakdown", *Guardian*, 28 February 1998; J.G. Ballard, "The mobile phone", in J. Miller and M. Schwarz (eds), *Speed: Visions of an Accelerated Age*, Photographers Gallery, London, 1998.

55 M. Bywater, "The desire for gadgets", *Independent on Sunday*, 31 July 1998.

56 P. Flichy, "Perspectives for a sociology of the telephone", in *Reseaux*, 1997, vol. 5(2), p. 156. As she notes, French society at the beginning of this century

> was wary of the telephone because it provided direct access to the intimacy of a particular person. To avoid this intrusion by the outside world into the private domain, upper-class families soon adopted the habit of having servants answer the phone. They thereby ensured that the telephone did not short-circuit codes of bourgeois social behaviour.

Nowadays, the answering machine takes over the role of the servant (or secretary), protecting access to the time and space of the person being called and restoring the space of their discretion as to whether or not to respond.

57 P.A. Mercier, "Dopo Ze Beep", *Reseaux*, 1997, vol. 5(2), p. 202.

58 See Chapter 8 on the argument that new communications technologies tend to stimulate, rather than substitute for, patterns of physical mobility and face-to-face contact.

59 G. Claisse and F. Rowe, quoted in P. Flichy, "Perspectives for a sociology of the telephone", *Reseaux*, 1997, vol. 5(2), p. 154. See also S. Graham and S. Marvin, *Net Effects*, London, Comedia/Demos, 1998, on this – quoted below, Chapter 8.

60 Vanessa Manceron, "Get connected", *Reseaux*, 1997, vol. 5(2).

61 Manceron, op. cit., p. 240.

62 In one respect, Green's study can be seen to offer a contemporary parallel to Robert Hughes' study of the experience of British convicts transported to Australia for their crimes in the nineteenth century (R. Hughes, *The Fatal Shore*, London, Pan Books, 1988). In that book Hughes offers a moving account of how the sheer time (a matter of some months) involved in communicating by letter across the distance between the UK and Australia often had tragic results for those involved, simply because of the asynchronicity of their experience – in which "news" received was characteristically six months or more out of date. At a smaller scale, but in the same vein, a mother in Green's study reports similar difficulties (if not, in this case, tragic ones) with correspondence from her daughter, studying in a faraway city, from which mail only arrives by post infrequently to her Outback home:

> one day we got mail ... after weeks, and the first letter I opened [she] was thinking of committing suicide, the second she was deliriously happy and the third one ... I'm not quite sure what that was ... and I'd actually opened them, and she hadn't dated them, so I didn't know if she was still feeling like committing suicide or happy ... and it really ... was rather difficult.
>
> (Green, op. cit., p. 246)

63 Green, op. cit., p. 250.

64 ibid., p. xxvii.

65 ibid., pp. 297, 292, 290.

66 ibid., pp. 132, 273, 283; cf. R. Wilk on "satellite time", quoted in D. Morley and K. Robins, *Spaces of Identity*, London, Routledge, 1995, pp. 226–7.

67 Green, op. cit., p. 132. The mere fact of coverage of such places, regardless of its content, is often a cause of positive response:

> You just think, "Oh, my town's on the news" and you get all excited. It's just ... like a big thrill to see your own town. You look in the film clip to see if you can see anyone you know, so you can say "Oh I saw you on television last night." It's just good.
>
> (Green, op. cit., p. 139)

68 ibid., p. 8.

69 Moores, op. cit., pp. 40–41.

70 Moores, op. cit., p. 55.

71 Moores, op. cit., p. 70.

72 Moores, op. cit., p. 53.

73 Indeed, it now seems that the distance which children in Britain are allowed to travel outside the home unsupervised is significantly smaller than in other European countries, despite any objective evidence that British children are in greater danger than those elsewhere. The result is now a secondary panic about the unhealthiness of the "couch potato" lifestyle which parents are, in effect, encouraging in their children. See Sonia Livingstone and Moira Bovill, *Young People and New Media*, London, Sage, forthcoming; cf. K. Worpole *The Richness of Cities*, London, Comedia/Demos, 1998.

74 See D. Morley, *Television, Audiences and Cultural Studies*, London, Routledge, 1992, ch. 11, pp. 239 et seq. In this connection, Silverstone has remarked on "the

fear of unwelcome things crossing the threshold. We now fear that we can no longer control any threshold: neither that of the nation nor that of the home ... The fear of penetration and pollution is intense"; R. Silverstone, *Why Study the Media?*, London, Sage, 1999, p. 91.

75 J. Jouet and Y. Toussaint, "Telematics and the private sphere: the case of French Videotex", paper presented to Communication and Data Communication Conference, Université Libre de Bruxelles, Nivelles, May 1987.

76 D.Z. Umble, "The Amish and the telephone", in R. Silverstone and E. Hirsch (eds), *Consuming Technologies*, London, Routledge, 1992.

77 Umble, op. cit., p. 189.

78 M. Bakardjieva, "Home satellite television: reception in Bulgaria", *European Journal of Communication*, 1992, vol. 7, pp. 483–5, 488.

79 "Dainty dish defies rulers' wrath", *Guardian*, 6 April 1994.

80 "Ban on Islam by satellite", *Independent*, 13 August 1995; we shall return to a more detailed consideration of this particular issue in Chapter 7.

81 Andrew Brown, "Asia tries to censor the Net", *Independent on Sunday*, 10 March 1996; Dan Jellincx, "Behind the bamboo cybercurtain", *Guardian*, 27 November 1997.

82 Chris Bird, "Serb Black Hand moves conflict to cyberspace", *Guardian*, 31 October 1998.

83 Andrew Bunscombe, "Diaspora hear the word on Kurd TV", *Independent*, 19 February 1999.

84 N. Ryan, "Kurdistan is alive and well on TV", *Independent on Sunday*, 21 February 1999.

5   BROADCASTING AND THE CONSTRUCTION OF THE NATIONAL FAMILY

1 J. Keane, *The Media and Democracy*, Cambridge, Polity Press, 1991, p. 164.

2 Marista Leishman, *Dictionary of Scottish Biography*, Irvine, Carrick Media, 1999, quoted in the *Guardian*, 5 March 1999; cf. what Richard Sennett called the regressive fantasy or "wish that diversity and ineradicable differences should not exist in the home, for the sake of social order"; R. Sennett, *The Uses of Disorder*, London, Faber, 1996, p. 65.

3 M. Phillips, "Heritage foundations", *New Times*, November, 1999. For my own earlier comments on who feels excluded by or alienated from the world of television current affairs, see my "Finding out about the world from television news: some difficulties", in J. Gripsrud (ed.), *Television and Common Knowledge*, London, Routledge, 1999.

4 cf. Deborah Ryan, *The Daily Mail Ideal Home Exhibition*, London, University of East London, 1995.

5 Da Matta, quoted in D. Dayan and E. Katz, *Media Events*, Cambridge, Mass., Harvard University Press, 1992, p. 128.

6 Quoted in Dayan and Katz, op. cit., p. 129.

7 P. Scannell, *Radio, Television, and Modern Life*, Oxford, Blackwell, 1996; Orvar Lofgren, "The nation as home or motel? Metaphors of media and belonging", unpublished paper, Department of European Ethnology, University of Lund, 1995.

8 Lofgren, op. cit., 1995, p. 12; cf. Jesus Martin-Barbero, *Communication, Culture and Hegemony*, London, Sage, 1993, on the role of the media in the construction of a quotidian sense of national life.

9 Coupland, quoted in Lofgren, op. cit., p. 14.

10 Lofgren, op. cit., p. 20.

11 David Chandler, "Postcards from the edge", in Mark Power, *The Shipping Forecast*, London, Zelda Cheatle Press, 1996, p. i.
12 N. Papastergiadis, *Dialogues in the Diasporas*, London, Rivers Oram Press, 1998, p. 4.
13 Chandler, op. cit., 1996, p. ii.
14 Ambjörnsson, drawing on reminiscences of Swedish radio-listening in the 1940s, quoted in O. Lofgren, "The nation as home or motel?", p. 26.
15 ibid., p. 27.
16 Berlant, quoted in G. Eley and R. Griger Suny, "Introduction" to their edited collection *Becoming National*, Oxford, Oxford University Press, 1996, p. 30; see also Lauren Berlant, *Anatomy of a National Fantasy*, Chicago, Chicago University Press, 1991, p. 20.
17 Eley and Suny, op. cit., p. 29.
18 A. McLintock, *Imperial Leather*, London, Routledge, 1995, p. 357.
19 P. Scannell, "Public service broadcasting and modern life", *Media, Culture and Society*, 1989, vol. 11(2), p. 138.
20 S. Hall, "Which public, whose service?", in W. Stevenson (ed.), *All our Futures, the Changing Role and Purpose of the BBC*, London, British Film Institute, 1993, p. 32.
21 Scannell, 1996, op. cit.; P. Scannell, "Radio Times", in P. Drummond and R. Paterson (eds), *Television and its Audience*, London, British Film Institute, 1988.
22 Braudel, quoted in P. Scannell, *Radio, Television and Modern Life*, Oxford, Blackwell, 1996, p. 175.
23 J. Meyrowitz, *No Sense of Place*, Oxford, Oxford University Press, 1985, p. 6.
24 Quoted in P. Scannell, "Public service broadcasting and modern life", *Media, Culture and Society*, 1989, vol. 11(2), p. 148.
25 H. Sacks, *Lectures on Conversation*, Oxford, Blackwell, 1992; C.D. Rath, "The invisible network", in P. Drummond and R. Paterson (eds), *Television in Transition*, London, British Film Institute, 1985.
26 Scannell, *Radio, Television and Modern Life*, op. cit., pp. 5 and 149.
27 J. Carey, "Political ritual television", in T. Liebes and J. Curran (eds), *Media, Ritual and Identity*, London, Routledge, 1998; B. Anderson, *Imagined Communities*, London, Verso, 1983.
28 C.D. Rath, "Live television and its audiences", in E. Seiter, H. Borschers, G. Kreutzner and E.M. Warth (eds), *Remote Control*, London, Routledge, 1989, pp. 82–3.
29 cf. D. Morley, *Television, Audiences and Cultural Studies*, London, Routledge, 1992.
30 Scannell, "Public service broadcasting and modern life", op. cit., pp. 158 and 136.
31 Scannell, *Radio, Television and Modern Life*, op. cit., p. 4; original emphasis.
32 ibid., p. 4.
33 S. Moores, "Don't criticise VictimVision", *Independent*, 8 May 1998. In the same vein, in his comments on his work recording the songs of the American poor for the Library of Congress in the 1930s, Alan Lomax observed how very much the mere fact of having their songs tape-recorded mattered to the singers that he worked with – see the Notes to the CD *The Alan Lomax Collection*, Rounder Records, 1997.
34 M. Morse, *Virtualities*, Bloomington, Indiana University Press, 1998, p. 46.
35 S. Moores, "Don't criticise VictimVision", *Independent*, 8 May 1998; as its name implies, "Class War" is a fundamentalist Marxist organisation in the UK.
36 P. Scannell, "The merely sociable", University of Westminster, unpublished paper, 1990, p. 20.
37 A. Hargreaves and A. Perotti, "The representation on French television of immigrants and ethnic minorities", *New Community*, 1993, vol. 19(2). For a detailed discussion of Hargreaves' work, see Chapter 7.

38 For a comparable analysis of the relative visibility of ethnic minorities on British television, see G. Cumberbatch and S. Woods, *Ethnic Minorities on Television*, London, Independent Television Commission, 1996. See also the later section of this chapter on the "whiteness" of the public sphere.

39 Or "reasonableness" – cf. Scannell, "Public service broadcasting and modern life", op. cit., p. 160.

40 Dana Polan, "The public's fear; or, Media as Monster in Habermas, Negt and Kluge", in B. Robbins (ed.), *The Phantom Public Sphere*, Minneapolis, Minnesota University Press, 1993, p. 36.

41 P. Carpignano, R. Anderson and W. DiFazio, "Chatter in the Age of Electronic Reproduction" in Robbins (ed.), *The Phantom Public Sphere*, op. cit., p. 93. One of the best-known critiques of Habermas is that by Oskar Negt and Alexander Kluge, who address the question of the limits of Habermasian model and explore the possibilities for the construction of an oppositional, proletarian public sphere in their *Public Sphere and Experience*, Minneapolis, University of Minnesota Press, 1994. Negt and Kluge correctly observe that the bourgeois public sphere was always much more penetrated by the interests of capital than Habermas ever acknowledges. However, there are significant difficulties with their approach, as Polan notes. In the first place there is their romanticisation of the production process and their neglect of the sphere of consumption as an active process. Second, their own perspective is in some ways even bleaker than that of Habermas in their "image of a contemporary world infiltrated by media at every level"; Polan, op. cit., p. 39.

42 Robbins, "Introduction", to Robbins (ed.), *The Phantom Public Sphere*, op. cit., pp. viii–ix.

43 Derrida, quoted in Thomas Keenan, "Windows: of vulnerability", in Robbins (ed.), op. cit., p. 135.

44 Robbins, op. cit., p. viii.

45 Robbins, op. cit., pp. xv and iii.

46 cf. R. Deutsche, "Men in space", *Artforum*, February, 1990.

47 Thus, to take one historical example, Miriam Hansen suggests that early silent cinema functioned as a kind of proletarian counter-public sphere, in so far as it "provided a social space, a place apart from the domestic and work spheres, where people of a similar background and status could find company"; Hansen, quoted in Robbins, op. cit., p. xviii.

48 cf. Chantal Mouffe quoted later on this point – see Chapter 8 on "Community lite and communitarianism", p. 190.

49 N. Fraser, "Rethinking the public sphere", in Robbins (ed.), op. cit., p. 6.

50 L. Abu-Lughod, "The objects of soap opera: Egyptian TV and the cultural politics of modernity', in D. Miller (ed.), *Worlds Apart*, London, Routledge, 1995, p. 191; J. Meyrowitz, *No Sense of Place*, Oxford, Oxford University Press, 1985.

51 Fraser, op. cit., p. 8.

52 Iris Marion Young, "Impartiality and the civic public", in S. Benhabib and D. Cornell (eds), *Feminism as Critique*, Minneapolis, University of Minnesota Press, 1987, pp. 59–60.

53 M. Warner, "The mass public and the mass subject", in Robbins (ed.), op. cit., p. 240.

54 Joke Hermes, "Gender and media studies: no woman, no cry", in J. Corner, P. Schlesinger and R. Silverstone (eds), *International Media Research*, London, Routledge, 1997, p. 73. On the "Public Knowledge" project see J. Corner, "Meaning, genre and context: the problematics of public knowledge", in J. Curran and M. Gurevitch (eds), *Mass Media and Society*, London, Edward Arnold, 1991. I have also addressed the question of "the gender of the real" in my essay "To boldly

go: the 'third generation' of reception studies", in P. Alasuutari (ed.), *Rethinking the Media Audience*, London, Sage, 1999.

55 Hermes, op. cit., p. 87; G.-J. Masciorotte, "C'mon girl: Oprah Winfrey and the discourse of feminine talk", *Discourse*, 1991, no. 11.

56 Winfrey, quoted in S. Livingstone and P. Lunt, *Talk on Television*, London, Routledge, 1994, p. 43; Masciorotte, op. cit., p. 90.

57 S. Livingstone, "Watching talk", *Media, Culture and Society*, 1994, vol. 16.

58 Fraser, op. cit., pp. 14 and 15.

59 Carpignano *et al.*, op. cit., p. 96.

60 Carpignano *et al.*, op. cit., pp. 109–11.

61 Livingstone and Lunt, op. cit., p. 172.

62 cf. Angela McRobbie, "Postmodernism and popular culture", *Journal of Communication Inquiry*, 1986, vol. 10(2).

63 Fraser, op. cit., p. 17.

64 In the following section I draw heavily on materials originally collated by my ex-PhD student, Arun Kundnani. I thank him both for access to these materials and for his helpful comments on this chapter. For his later, published, work, see his article "Where do you want to go today? The rise of information capital", in *Race and Class*, 1998/99, vol. 40(2/3), and his "Stumbling on: race, class and England", *Race and Class*, Spring 2000, vol. 41(4).

65 G. Orwell, *Inside the Whale and Other Essays*, Harmondsworth, Penguin, 1957, p. 66.

66 D. Morley and C. Brunsdon, "Introduction" to *The* Nationwide *Television Studies*, London, Routledge, 1999, p. 12. For the contemporary televisual manifestation of this "heritage of the ordinary" in the UK, see daytime shows such as the highly successful *This Morning* and its presenters "Richard and Judy".

67 cf. P. Scannell, *Radio, Television and Modern Life*, op. cit., p. 37; I am grateful to my colleague, Bill Schwarz for drawing this example to my attention.

68 As Homi Bhabha describes it, in this process "the scraps, patches and rags of daily life must be repeatedly turned into the signs of a national culture, while the very act of the narrative performance interpellates a growing circle of national subjects"; H. Bhabha, in H. Bhabha (ed.), *Nation and Narration*, London, Routledge, 1990, p. 297.

69 cf. T. Modood, "The end of a hegemony: from political blackness to ethnic pluralism", paper to Commission for Racial Equality Policy seminar, London, 1995; cf. also Errol Lawrence, "In the abundance of water the fool is thirsty", in CCCS (ed.) *The Empire Strikes Back*, London, Hutchinson, 1982.

70 C. Hall, *White Male and Middle Class*, Cambridge, Polity Press, 1992, p. 205.

71 R. Dyer, "White", *Screen*, 1998, vol. 29(4), p. 45.

72 P. Scannell, "Public service broadcasting and modern public life", in P. Scannell, P. Schlesinger and C. Sparks (eds), *Culture and Power*, London, Sage, 1992, p. 138.

73 Y. Alibhai-Brown, "Whose Beeb is it anyway?", *Global Thinking: Foreign Policy Centre Newsletter*, London, September, 1999.

74 A. Sreberny, *Include Me In: Rethinking Ethnicity on Television*, London, Broadcasting Standards Council, 1999, p. 27.

75 A. Kundnani, "Scheduling the nation", unpublished paper, Department of Media and Communications, Goldsmiths College, 1995.

76 cf. campaigns about the misuse of the police's "stop and search" powers – which because of their racist application mean that the physical public sphere is not in fact equally available to all; likewise, campaigning over policing practices which do not extend respect for the privacy of the domestic space to Asians and blacks. On this, see A. Hurtado, "Relating to privilege: seduction and rejection in the subordination of white women and women of colour", *Signs: Journal of Women in Culture and Society*, 1989, vol. 14(4).

77 Kundnani, op. cit., p. 19.
78 cf. Whitelaw's comments, quoted in Lawrence, op. cit., p. 52. On the debates surrounding the establishment of Channel Four, see S. Blanchard and D. Morley (eds), *What's This Channel Fo(u)r?*, London, Comedia, 1982.
79 A. Barry, "Black mythologies – the representation of black people on British television", in J. Twitchin (ed.), *The Black and White Media Book*, London, Trentham Books, 1988, p. 9.
80 P. Gilroy, "Channel Four – bridgehead or Bantustan?" in *Screen*, 1982, vol. 24(4), p. 39. On the visibility of blacks on television in the USA after the riots there in the late 1960s, see A. Bodgrokhozy, "Is this what you mean by color TV?", in L. Spigel and D. Mann (eds), *Private Screenings*, Minneapolis, University of Minnesota Press, 1992; cf. H. Gray, *Watching Race*, Minneapolis, University of Minnesota Press, 1995; see also Chapter 7 on the visibility of immigrants in French cities and on French television.
81 Clearly, the danger here is that such "alternative" public spheres might be established in such a way that a central (and implicitly white) public sphere might thus remain intact, untransformed, as the privileged space of authentic national citizenship – cf. Kundnani, 2000, op. cit.
82 For the debates surrounding the launch of the channel, see S. Blanchard and D. Morley (eds), *What's This Channel Fo(u)r?*, London, Comedia, 1982.
83 cf. Janine Gibson, "Jackson's vision for Channel 4", *Guardian*, 10 June 1999; Ed Shelton, "Breaking out of the ghetto", *Broadcast*, 21 May 1999.
84 Sreberny, op. cit.
85 A. Sreberny-Mohammadi and K. Ross, *Black Minority Viewers and Television*, Leicester, Centre for Mass Communication Research, 1995, p. 11.
86 M. Gillespie, *Television, Ethnicity and Cultural Change*, London, Routledge, 1995.
87 Respondent quoted in S. Moores, "Satellite television as a cultural sign", *Media, Culture and Society*, 1993b, vol. 15(4), p. 635.
88 cf. D. Hebdige, "Towards a cartography of taste", in his *Hiding in the Light*, London, Comedia, 1988, and K. Worpole, *Dockers and Detectives*, London, Verso, 1983, for the same kind of dis-identification with the dominant national culture on the part of some white working-class consumers.
89 G. Cumberbatch and S. Woods, *Ethnic Minorities on Television*, London, Independent Television Commission, op. cit. *Television: Ethnic Minorities' Views*, Independent Television Commission, London, 1994.
90 J. Halloran, A. Bhatt and P. Gray, *Ethnic Minorities and Television*, Leicester, Centre for Mass Communications Research, 1995, p. 23.
91 Sreberny and Ross, op. cit., p. 51.
92 ibid., p. 54
93 Sreberny, op. cit., p. 42.
94 Sreberny and Ross, op. cit., p. 50.
95 ibid., p. 53.
96 Sreberny, op. cit., p. 16.
97 ibid., p. 42. See Chapters 6 and 7 for parallels in the USA and in Europe.
98 Alex Spillius, "Pirate Telegraph", *Guardian*, 28 January 1995.
99 Phillips, quoted in J. Pines (ed.), *Black and White in Colour: Black People in British Television since 1936*, London, British Film Institute, 1992, pp. 149–50. The argument returns to this focus on the "whiteness" of the public sphere in Chapter 7.
100 I.M. Young, "Polity and group difference", *Ethics*, 1989, vol. 99(2), p. 257.
101 cf. C. Husband, "The multi-ethnic public sphere", paper to European Film and Television Studies Conference, London, 1994, p. 6.
102 Young, "Polity and group difference", op. cit., p. 261.

103 S. Castles, "Democracy and multicultural citizenship", paper to Aliens to Citizens Conference, Vienna, November 1993, quoted in Husband, op. cit., p. 11. In his commentary on the Macpherson Report into the murder of Stephen Lawrence in London, Arun Kundnani notes that the report rightly rejected the police claims that their policy of treating all crimes and suspects in the same way exonerated them from the charge of racism. On the contrary, as Macpherson concluded, it was the police force's "colour blind" approach which had led them to fail to recognise that they were investigating a racist murder – cf. Kundnani, "Stumbling on", op. cit.

104 To take one example, as Kristin Koptivich observes, Korean Americans can rent last week's news broadcasts by Korean networks in many Korean-run corner stores in North American cities. cf. Kristin Koptivich, "Third Worlding at home", in A. Gupta and J. Ferguson (eds), *Culture, Power, Place*, Durham, Duke University Press, 1997, p. 245.

105 D. Dayan, "Media and diasporas", in J. Gripsrud (ed.), *TV and Common Knowledge*, London, Routledge, 1999, p. 19; cf. A. Appadurai, *Modernity at Large*, Minneapolis, University of Minnesota Press, 1996, p. 4, on the conjunction of "moving images and deterritorialised viewers".

106 J. Curran, "The crisis of public communication", in T. Liebes and J. Curran (eds), op. cit., p. 180.

107 Khaching Tölölyan, quoted in S. Huntingdon, *The Clash of Civilisations*, New York, Simon and Schuster, 1996, p. 274; cf. Gerd Baumann's work on the fluidity of appeals to ethnically distinct identities and on accommodations to dominant national discourses among immigrant groups in the UK in his *Contesting Culture*, Cambridge, Cambridge University Press, 1996, discussed later.

108 J. Clifford, "Travelling cultures", in his *Routes*, Cambridge, Mass., Harvard University Press, 1997.

109 cf. Dayan, "Medias and diasporas", op. cit.; cf. Dona Kolar-Panov, *Video, War and the Diasporic Imagination*, London, Routledge, 1997, on the role of video-letters in particular.

110 M.L. Margolis, *Little Brazil*, Princeton, New Jersey, Princeton University Press, 1994, p. 193, quoted in U. Hannerz, *Transnational Connections*, London, Routledge, 1996, p. 177.

111 Roger Rouse, "Mexican migration and the social space of postmodernism", *Diaspora*, 1991, vol. 1(1), p. 13; Clifford, "Travelling cultures", op. cit., p. 256.

112 Aihwa Ong, "On the edge of empires: flexible citizenship among Chinese in diaspora", *Positions*, 1993, vol. 1(3), quoted in Clifford, "Travelling cultures", op. cit., p. 257.

113 P. Cheah, "Given culture", in P. Cheah and B. Robbins (eds), *Cosmopolitics*, Minneapolis, University of Minnesota Press, 1998, p. 296; cf. Chapter 10 below for a more detailed discussion of this point.

114 Deregulation is transforming the material public spaces of our towns and cities every bit as much as it is transforming broadcasting – and in both physical and virtual forms the very word "public" increasingly becomes a synonym for the provision of downgraded facilities of last resort, the preserve of the underprivileged who, unable to afford better, must use inadequate forms of public transport or dwell in hard-to-let council estates and consume free public media. Just as Worpole has argued that, these days, in many parts of the UK "bus transport, the preserve of the elderly, schoolchildren and women with children, has been so downgraded that it is used only under the most desperate conditions", so Ted Turner has predicted that soon "the only people watching broadcast television will be the poor, the elderly and the minorities"; K. Worpole, *Towns for People*, Milton Keynes, Open University Press, 1992, p. 12; Turner interviewed in *METV: The Future of Television*, Tx BBC2, 25 September 1993.

6 THE MEDIA, THE CITY AND THE SUBURBS

1 R. Silverstone, *Television and Everyday Life*, London, Routledge, 1994; R. Silverstone (ed.), *Visions of Suburbia*, London, Routledge, 1997; K. Lury and D. Massey, "Making connections", *Screen*, 1999, vol. 40(3).

2 K. Lury and D. Massey, "Making connections", *Screen*, 1999, vol. 40(3), p. 234.

3 Silverstone, *Television and Everyday Life*, op. cit., p. 57.

4 A. Medhurst, "Negotiating the Gnome Zone", in R. Silverstone (ed.), *Visions of Suburbia*, op. cit., p. 244.

5 Silverstone, *Television and Everyday Life*, op. cit., p. 64.

6 R. Williams, *Television: Technology and Cultural Form*, Fontana, 1974, p. 26; see below the section on "Exclusion, withdrawal and mobile privatisation".

7 Buttimer, quoted in Silverstone, *Television and Everyday Life*, op. cit., p. 27.

8 J. Meyrowitz, *No Sense of Place*, Oxford, Oxford University Press, 1985, p. 238; cf. Worpole's comments, quoted earlier, on the increasing house-boundness of children in the UK.

9 Silverstone (ed.), *Visions of Suburbia*, op. cit., pp. 14 and 69.

10 ibid., p. 257.

11 Reeves, quoted in N. Duncan and J. Duncan, "Deep suburban irony", in Silverstone (ed.), *Visions of Suburbia*, op. cit., p. 162.

12 John Patterson, "The colour bar", *Guardian*, 2 September 1999.

13 L. Spigel, "From theatre to space ship: metaphors of suburban domesticity in post war America", in Silverstone (ed.), *Visions of Suburbia*, op. cit., pp. 233, 236.

14 H. Bhabha, "Bombs away in front-line suburbia", in Silverstone (ed.), *Visions of Suburbia*, op. cit., p. 299.

15 S. Frith, "The suburban sensibility in British rock and pop", in Silverstone (ed.), *Visions of Suburbia*, op. cit., p. 270.

16 J. Hartley, "The sexualisation of suburbia: the diffusion of knowledge in the post-modern public sphere", in Silverstone (ed.), *Visions of Suburbia*, op. cit., pp. 186 and 209.

17 ibid., p. 182.

18 Medhurst, op. cit., pp. 241, 250, 251.

19 V. LeBeau, "The worst of all possible worlds", in Silverstone (ed.), *Visions of Suburbia*, op. cit., p. 292.

20 M. Young and P. Wilmott, *Family and Kinship in East London*, London, Routledge and Kegan Paul, 1957, p. 123.

21 Pierangelo Sapegno, "Where the grass may be greener", *Guardian*, 18 February 1994.

22 A. Öncü and P. Weyland, "Introduction" to their *Space, Culture and Power*, London, Zed Books, 1997, p. 15.

23 Quoted in A. Öncü, "The myth of the ideal home travels across cultural borders to Istanbul", in Öncü and Weyland (eds.), op. cit., p. 56.

24 The precariousness and vibrancy of life in these areas is well-captured in the portrait offered in Latife Tekin's novel *Berji Kristin – Tales from the Garbage Hills*, London, Marion Boyars, 1996.

25 Öncü, op. cit., pp. 63 and 69.

26 ibid., pp. 68 and 61.

27 ibid., p. 60.

28 T. Tufte, "Television, modernity and everyday life", unpublished paper, Department of Film and Media Studies, University of Copenhagen, 1998.

29 cf. D. Morley and R. Silverstone, "Communication and context", in K. B. Jensen and N. Jankowski (eds), *A Handbook of Qualitative Methodologies for Mass Media Research*, London, Routledge, 1991, p. 4.

30 Tufte, op. cit., pp. 1 and 2.
31 ibid., p. 7; see also Tufte's later *Living with the Rubbish Queen*, Luton, University of Luton Press, 1999.
32 Which are more strictly comparable to the impoverished banlieues of France, see Chapter 7 below.
33 Tufte, op. cit., p. 13.
34 J. Martin-Barbero, *Communication, Culture and Hegemony*, London, Sage, 1993, p. 201.
35 P. Barker, "Malls are wonderful", *Independent on Sunday*, 25 October 1998; J. Garreau, *Edge City*, New York, Anchor/Doubleday, 1992.
36 Barker, op. cit.
37 J. Lichfield, "No particular place to live", *Independent on Sunday*, 15 November 1992.
38 D. Sudjic, "Nightmare on Acacia Avenue", *Guardian*, 14 April 1994.
39 J. Jacobs, *The Death and Life of Great American Cities*, Harmondsworth, Penguin, 1994.
40 Barker, op. cit.
41 M. Davis, *Beyond Blade Runner: Urban Core Control and the Ecology of Fear*, New Jersey, Open Media Pamphlet Series, 1992.
42 H. Naficy, "Framing exile", in H. Naficy (ed.), *Home, Homeland, Exile*, New York, Routledge/American Film Institute, 1999, p. 6.
43 It is also the case that in some American cities, as property values rise in gated communities in the suburbs, in the inner city, where bars on windows also provide security in Davis' sense, property values have declined. The meanings of gates and bars have differential value organised by class, place and race. I am grateful to Herman Gray for this observation and for his other helpful comments on this section.
44 Davis, op. cit., p. 5.
45 K. Worpole and L. Greenhalgh, *The Freedom of the City*, London, Demos, 1996, p. 23. In many American cities, where climate is an important consideration in the quality of life, access to desirable conditions (to heated spaces in the North or to air-conditioned spaces in the South) is largely determined by factors such as class and ethnicity. Again, I am indebted to Herman Gray for this observation.
46 Davis, op. cit., p. 16.
47 M. Foucault, *Discipline and Punish*, New York, Pantheon, 1977, p. 141.
48 K. Worpole, "The new city states", in M. Perryman (ed.), *Altered States*, London, Lawrence and Wishart, pp. 169–70.
49 Richard Lacayo, "This land is your land", *Time*, 18 May 1992, p. 29.
50 cf. Melinda Whittstock, "For those watching in black and white", *Media Guardian*, 2 March 1998, but cf. also J. May, "A little taste of something more exotic", *Geography*, 1996, vol. 81, on the problems of the aestheticised consumption of cultural difference by privileged groups. For an exemplary study of the representation of "race" on American television in "the Reagan years", see H. Gray, *Watching Race: Television and the Struggle for "Blackness"*, Minneapolis, University of Minnesota Press, 1995.
51 Whittstock, op. cit. For an earlier, parallel analysis see John Carlin, "Black and white in America", *Independent on Sunday*, 28 May 1995. The exceptions to this overall pattern of segregated viewing concern the fields of sports and music programming. Especially in the latter case, and particularly among youth groups, viewing across racial categories (at least in the white to black direction) is more fluid. For comparable figures on the differences between white and ethnic minority viewers' "top

tens" in the UK, see the 1994 Independent Television Commission report *Television: Ethnic Minorities Views*, referred to earlier.

52 John Patterson, "The colour bar", *Guardian*, 2 September 1999.

53 Patterson, op. cit. This is not to say that BET is without its problems. A recent *Washington Post* report indicated that there is substantial disenchantment with BET's programming among part of its target audience, who feel that the channel is trafficking in the same stereotypes that blacks have complained about on other channels. BET's management is also in dispute with both performers and employees over the company's pay policy and its resistance to unionisation. See Paul Farhi, "The question of BET and the payoff", *Washington Post*, 22 November 1999. For further views on these issues see the Black Radical Congress website (http://netnoir.egroups.com /group/brc-news).

54 L. Ziener, "Small-mind, small-town, small-world America", *London Evening Standard*, 29 August 1996, pp. 12–13. This *Evening Standard* report of contemporary blinkered attitudes to the outside world among citizens of present-day Peoria is interestingly foreshadowed by Yi-Fu Tuan's account of the incuriousity towards the outside world and the absence of any desire for mobility manifested by an American farm family in north-western Illinois, whose interviewer reports them as explaining:

> My dad never travelled far and I don't have to. We have so many nice kinds of recreation right on our own farm ... I don't have to travel ... Some people don't have a very good life because they don't settle down in one place and don't stay very long ... I like ... my home state ... It's so unreal to be gone.
> (quoted in Y.-F. Tuan, *Space and Place*, London, Edward Arnold, 1977, p. 160)

It is estimated that only 9 per cent of citizens of the USA hold passports.

55 R. Kapuscinski, "We live in a global village: so why doesn't this woman give a darn what's on the news?", *Guardian*, 16 August 1999; A. Culf, "BBC news chief bemoans slide in foreign coverage", *Guardian*, 30 May 1997; M. Whittstock, "Hi there! And here's tonight's non-news", *Guardian*, 19 January 1998.

56 Quoted in Culf, op. cit.

57 A. Cleasby, *What in the World Is Going On? British Television and Global Affairs*, London, Third World and Environment Broadcasting Project, 1995, quoted in J. Tomlinson, *Globalisation and Culture*, Cambridge, Polity Press, 1999, pp. 171–2.

58 M. Ignatieff, "Identity parades", *Prospect*, April, 1998.

59 R. Patel, *Making Difference Matter*, London, Comedia/Demos, 1998, p. 14. These patterns of separated residence are, of course, long established. In an autobiographical account of growing up white in New York, James Clifford tells a poignant story concerning how the anxiety he experienced as a boy about the possibility of getting off at the wrong subway stop and ending up in Harlem was brought back to him by a scene in the film *Brother from Another Planet*. In the film, as Clifford recounts,

> the subway train pulls into 96th Street station and a white kid tells the black alien that he is going to perform a magic trick: "I'm going to make all the white people disappear!" The doors open and all the whites exit, including the magician, who waves goodbye as the doors of the Harlem express close.
> (J. Clifford, *Routes*, Cambridge, Mass., Harvard University Press, 1997, p. 94)

60 L. Mumford, "What is a city?", *Architectural Record*, 1937, New York; quoted in Patel, op. cit., p. 2.

61 Patel, op. cit., p. 4; recently there have been reports in the UK press concerning an initiative under discussion between Muslim housing associations and

the government's Social Exclusion Unit, whereby Muslim "faith communities" might be encouraged to set up what are referred to as "Medina neighbourhoods ... based on Islamic principles" to regenerate derelict areas in British inner cities – cf. James Meek, "Muslim neighbourhoods proposed to revive rundown city suburbs", *Guardian*, 12 November 1999.

62 In C. Lasch, *Revolt of the Elites*, London, Norton, 1995.

63 Phil Reeves, "To have and have not in Zvenigorod", *Independent on Sunday*, 15 August 1999.

64 Will Hutton, "Real cost of the property boom", *Observer*, 15 August 1999.

65 R. Thorney, "A world apart", *Guardian*, 29 August 1998; Jonathan Glancey, "Rich – and excluded", *Observer*, 20 September 1998. On a different geographical scale, witness the phenomenon of rich regions campaigning for "withdrawal" from their nations, such as the Northern League in Italy.

66 M. Dejevsky, "Disney celebrates first birthday of town they built out of the American dream", *Independent*, 23 August 1997. For a more detailed analysis of this Disney community, see Andrew Ross, *Celebration Chronicles: Life, Liberty and the Pursuit of Property Values in Disney's New Town*, New York, Ballatine Books, 1999.

67 Pierangelo Sapegno, "Where the grass may be greener", *Guardian*, 18 February 1994.

68 cf. Kevin Robins, "Cyberspace and the world we live in", *Body and Society*, 1995, vol. 1(3–4), on the appeal of cyberspace in this self-selecting respect.

69 Although geodemographic analysis is now widely used in the market research industry it has not always been used simply for commercial purposes. For example, in 1979 Richard Webber, a Cambridge economist and transport planner, was commissioned by Liverpool Council and the Department of the Environment to see if he could develop a geodemographic model to predict which precise neighbourhoods in Liverpool would be likely to be most affected (and thus need the most intensive policing) in the case of riot (cf. Rosalind Sharpe, "M is for market research", *Observer*, 4 May 1997).

70 Decca Aitkenhead, "Urban meltdown", *Guardian*, 23 August 1999. What makes this process of social segmentation by area all the more crucial, in the British case at least, is the close relationship between residential area and quality of schooling. Clearly, those children who receive the best schooling are then heavily advantaged by their better qualifications in the competition to enter higher education and thence the labour market. What makes the circle of advantage so vicious is that increasingly the best schools, in the best areas, only take children from within a very small radius of the school gates. If only those who can afford to buy property in the relevant catchment areas can gain access for their children to the best schools then, as Peter Preston observes, residential neighbourhoods themselves become the motors of the educational selection process; cf. Peter Preston, "Keep your eyes wide open in the schooling debate", *Guardian*, 23 August 1999.

71 cf. M. Hodgen, *Early Anthropology in the Sixteenth and Seventeenth Centuries*, Philadelphia, University of Pennsylvania Press, 1964; V.Y. Mudimbe, *The Idea of Africa*, Bloomington, Indiana University Press, 1994.

72 Perin quoted in D. Sibley, *Geographies of Exclusion*, Routledge, 1995, p.14.

73 Sibley, op. cit., p. 63.

74 Sibley, op. cit., p. 72; M. Foucault, "Of other spaces", *Diacritics*, 1986, vol. 16(1), pp. 22–7.

75 R. Sennett, *The Uses of Disorder*, London, Faber and Faber, 1996, p. 47.

76 Sennett, op. cit., pp. 48, 36, 70, 83.

77 M. Douglas, *Purity and Danger*, London, Routledge and Kegan Paul, 1966; B. Bernstein, "On the classification and framing of educational knowledge", paper to

British Sociological Association Conference on the Sociology of Education, London, 1970.

78 D. Sibley, "The purification of space", *Environment and Planning D: Society and Space*, 1988, vol. 6, p. 409.

79 Sibley, "The purification of space", op. cit.,, p. 410, summarising Douglas.

80 Douglas, *Purity and Danger*, op. cit., p. 35. For an extension of Douglas' argument see Judith Williamson, "Three types of dirt", in her *Consuming Passions*, London, Marion Boyars, 1985, on the role of consumer advertising in the production of differentiated sub-categories of uncleanliness.

81 Douglas, quoted in Sibley, *Geographies of Exclusion*, op. cit., p. 37; Douglas, *Purity and Danger*, op. cit., p. 36.

82 Douglas, *Purity and Danger*, op. cit., p. 55.

83 F. Ward, "Foreign and familiar bodies", in J. Fuenmayor, K. Haug and F. Ward (eds), *Dirt and Domesticity*, New York, Whitney Museum of American Art, 1992, pp. 29–30.

84 M. Sarup, "Home and identity", in G. Robertson, M. Mash, L. Tickner, J. Bird, B. Curtis and T. Putnam (eds), *Travellers' Tales*, London, Routledge, 1994, pp. 101, 103. Worse still, from this perspective, is miscegenation. In his analysis of the work of the South African writer Bessie Head, Rob Nixon recounts the story of how she came to be born in a mental hospital. Head's mother was from an affluent white South African family, her father a black worker from their estate. On discovering their daughter's pregnancy, Head's mother's parents had her committed to a mental asylum (where she later died) on the grounds of premature senile dementia. As Head herself puts it, "the reason for my peculiar birthplace was that my mother was white, and she acquired me from a black man. She was judged insane and committed to the mental hospital while pregnant" – B. Head quoted in R. Nixon, "Refugees and homecoming", p. 119 in Robertson *et al.* (eds), op. cit.

85 In a dramatic example of this process, in 1994 the Russian parliament decided that all foreigners entering the country would be required to have an AIDS test, in an attempt to "seal the borders to dirty foreign bodies", *Guardian*, 12 November 1994, quoted in Sibley, *Geographies of Exclusion*, op. cit., p. 25. "Foreignness" can be experienced at many different levels. Thus Johnny Speight, the creator of the fictional character Alf Garnett, famous to British audiences for his comic racist tirades (and perhaps to US audiences in the form of Archie Bunker), explained that, essentially, "Alf" was a "racist about everyone else – to him a 'foreigner' was someone who lived four streets away"; Johnny Speight, interviewed on *What's It All About, Alfie?*, Tx BBC2, 5 January 1997. Clearly Speight's fictional character had roots in reality: not long ago a British newspaper reported an incident in which a resident of Much Wenlock (a small town in Shropshire) alerted police that two men speaking with "foreign" accents could perhaps be illegal immigrants from the Balkans. When the police investigated, they discovered that the men came from Cornwall, a distance of no more than 300 miles away; *Guardian*, 30 September 1998.

86 Martin Walker, *Guardian*, 26 May 1990.

87 S. Flusty, "Building paranoia", in N. Elin (ed.), *Architecture of Fear*, New York, Princeton Architectural Press, 1997, pp. 51–2, quoted in Z. Bauman, *Globalisation*, Cambridge, Polity Press, 1988, p. 21. This is not to suggest that these things are entirely new. Writing in the 1930s of his self-imposed "exile" as a tramp, George Orwell reported that until then, although he had "been in London innumerable times ... till that day I had never noticed one of the worst things about London – the fact that it costs money even to sit down"; G. Orwell, *Down and Out in Paris and London*, quoted in Ashraf Ghani, "Space as an arena of represented practices", in Bird *et al.* (eds.), op. cit., p. 55.

88 Sibley, "The purification of space", op. cit., pp. 415, 418–19.

89 ibid., p. 416.

90 Bauman, op. cit., p. 47.

91 Bauman, op. cit., p. 97. See Chapter 9 for an explication of Kristeva's theories in this respect. In the UK a renewed campaign to remove the problem of homelessness from sight was reported by Martin Bright, "Sweep the homeless off the streets", *Observer*, 14 November 1999.

92 Alain Corbin, *The Fragrant and the Foul: Odour and the French Imagination*, Cambridge, Mass., Harvard University Press, 1986, pp. 134–5.

93 Responding to the warning issued in 1996 by Dr Hiroshi Nakajima, then Director General of the World Health Organisation, on the spread of a new generation of infectious diseases, David Bodanis rightly observes that the "infection metaphor" in which the health of an organism (an individual or a group) is threatened by the invasion of "foreign" elements has a very long history. One can trace that history back to nineteenth-century ideas of the "infectious masses" of the urban poor as the breeding ground of disease, through the many varieties of anti-Semitism and racism. Bodanis notes that "Kitchener's forces at Omdurman in 1898 were regularly described [in the press] as taking the field against a huge number of bacteria, worthily eliminated by his army's machine guns". Later it was the turn of Communists to be treated in a similar way: Lenin was a dangerous bacillus that had to be transported across Europe in a sealed train; Communism itself was seen to be an evil that required containment by means of geographical cordon sanitaire placed around it. The poor, and especially poor foreigners, are readily mixed up with the diseases they may carry – so that foreigners may come to be seen, principally, as a source of possible contagion (of either a viral or moral nature). As Bodanis notes, in the fight against such diseases and their potential "carriers", all forms of borders are felt to need strengthening – "for microbes it will be labs, international surveillance, hygiene controls. For immigrants, it will be similar: computer checks, passports, tougher borders"; D. Bodanis, "A sick metaphor plagues us", *Independent*, 21 May 1996.

94 P. Stallybrass and A. White, *The Politics and Poetics of Transgression*, London, Methuen, 1986, pp. 130–5.

95 Quoted in Worpole and Greenhalgh, *The Freedom of the City*, op. cit., pp. 22–3. As Katherine Shonfield observes, the point about the car is that it carries "the contained privacy of the house right to the front door of work"; K. Shonfield, *At Home with Strangers*, London, Comedia/Demos, 1998, p. 3; cf. Raymond Williams' comments on "mobile privatisation".

96 Stallybrass and White, op. cit., pp. 5, 25, 137, 139, 191.

97 Sibley, *Geographies of Exclusion*, op. cit., p. 108.

98 see Pollard's *Pastoral Interlude*, in Kellie Jones, "Recreation", *Ten: 8*, 1992, vol. 2(3). See also I. Pollard *Monograph*, London, Autograph Publishers/INIVA, n.d. As Worpole *et al.* observe in this connection:

> people of white ethnic origin are much more likely to move out of cities than members of England's ethnic minorities, who in post-war Britain have played an increasingly vital role in urban cultures and economies. Still today … Britain's … ethnic minority population remains highly localised in a number of cities, and has yet to make any serious impact on suburban or rural cultures.
>
> (K. Worpole, K. Greenhalgh, C. Landry and W. Solesbury, *New Departures*, London, Comedia/Demos, 1998, p. 8)

99 In his analysis of the significances of the annual "battle" fought for some years by the British police to keep New Age Travellers from gathering at the historic site of Stonehenge to celebrate the summer solstice, Tim Cresswell notes that what was being "defended" here was a crucial element in the construction of English cultural identity. The guardians of English Heritage base their arguments for keeping these "deviant" people from the site at that particular symbolic time on an idea of the monument's historically central place in the pantheon of English mythology; T. Cresswell, *In Place/Out of Place*, Minneapolis, University of Minnesota Press, 1996.

100 J. Kristeva, *Powers of Horror*, New York, Columbia University Press, 1982, p. 69.

101 Cresswell, op. cit., pp. 38–40.

102 ibid., pp. 42–3.

103 K. Koptivich, "Third Worlding at home", in Gupta and Ferguson (eds), op. cit., p. 241.

104 J. Goytisolo, *Landscape after the Battle*, London, Serpents Tail, 1987, pp. 1, 2, 3, 5, 85, 120.

105 M. Gilsenan, *Recognising Islam*, Pantheon Press, New York, 1982, p. 195, quoted in Jan Nederveen Pieterse, "Travelling Islam" in Öncü and Weyland (eds), op. cit.

7   MEDIA, MOBILITY AND MIGRANCY

1 R. Williams, *Resources of Hope*, London, Verso, 1989, p. 171; quoted in S. Moores, "Television, geography and mobile privatisation", *European Journal of Communication Studies*, 1993a, vol. 8(3), p. 376; cf. the earlier account of Wodiczko's "Homeless Vehicle" project which literalises Williams' description of the "shell you can take with you".

2 S. Moores, "Television, geography and mobile privatisation", op. cit., pp. 365 and 336.

3 S. Moores, "Satellite television as a cultural sign", *Media, Culture and Society*, 1993b, vol. 15(4), p. 623; see also, in this connection, Torsten Hagerstrand's work on patterns of communication and time–space paths, "Space, time and human conditions", in A. Karlqvist, L. Lundqvist and F. Snickars (eds), *Dynamic Allocation of Urban Space*, Farnborough, Saxon House, 1975.

4 J. Carey, *Culture as Communication*, London, Unwin Hyman, 1989, p. 160.

5 A. Giddens, *The Consequences of Modernity*, Cambridge, Polity Press, 1990, p. 18, quoted in Moores, "Television, geography and mobile privatisation", op. cit., p. 371. If Giddens' formulation perhaps also overstates the contrast – for instance, by failing to allow for the importance of long-distance relations with absent others in the history of colonialism – it is nonetheless a useful starting point. See the note concerning similar problems with Johansen's formulation of this issue in the section on "Fellowmen, compatriots and contemporaries" in Chapter 8.

6 Andrea Ashworth, *Once in a House on Fire*, London, Picador, 1998, p. 255.

7 Edward Relph, quoted in Colin Ward, "Moving house", *Freedom*, 29 May 1999, original emphasis.

8 Romesh Guneseka, *Reef*, London, Granta Books, 1994, pp. 39–40.

9 Hamid Naficy, "Phobic spaces and liminal panics", p. 124 in R. Wilson and W. Dissonayake (eds), *Cultural Production and the Transnational Imaginary*, Raleigh, Durham, Duke University Press, 1996.

10 cf. Sky Television's "No turning back" advertising campaign in the UK in the 1990s, whose visuals cleverly associated "old-style" national broadcast television with the dead hand of Stalinism and, conversely, equated satellite television with the brave march of consumer freedoms initiated by Mrs Thatcher.

11 A. Bodroghkozy, "Is this what you mean by color TV?" in L. Spigel and D. Mann (eds), *Private Screenings*, Minneapolis, University of Minnesota Press, 1992, p. 156.

12 ibid., p. 156.

13 P. Batty, "Singing the electric", in T. Dowmunt (ed.), *Channels of Resistance*, London, British Film Institute, 1993, p. 110.

14 A. Sreberny and K. Ross, *Black Minority Viewers and Television*, Leicester, Centre for Mass Communications Research, 1995, p. 30.

15 Bruce Gyngell, quoted in Andrew Culf, "Popularity of Australian soaps based on British racism fix?", *Guardian*, 2 November 1993. In their report for the Independent Television Commission, Guy Cumberbatch and Samantha Woods note that in their sample of four weeks of prime-time television, "people from ethnic minority groups were least frequently seen in Australian productions"; *Ethnic Minorities on Television*, London, Independent Television Commission, 1996, p. 19. See also A. Sreberny, *Include Me In*, Leicester, Centre for Mass Communications Research, 1999, p. 27.

16 A. Sreberny *Include Me In*, Leicester, Centre for Mass Communications Research, 1999, p. 27.

17 E. Shelton, "Breaking out of the ghetto", *Broadcast*, 21 May 1999.

18 S. Westwood and J. Williams, "Introduction" to their (edited) *Imagining Cities*, London, Routledge, 1997, p. 11.

19 Quoted by Trinh T. Minh-ha, "Other than myself", in G. Robertson, M. Mash, L. Tickner, J. Bird, B. Curtis and T. Putnam (eds), *Travellers' Tales*, London, Routledge, 1994.

20 Gunnar Alsmark, "When in Sweden", in J. Frykmer and O. Lofgren (eds), *Force of Habit*, Lund, Lund University Press, 1996, pp. 88–90.

21 L. Baldassar, "Home and away", *Communal/Plural*, 1997, vol. 5.

22 Phil Cohen, "Homing devices", in V. Amit-Talai and C. Knowles (eds), *Resituating Identities*, Peterborough, Ontario, Broadview Press, 1996, p. 75.

23 K. Worpole, "We must end this war of town v country", *Independent*, 23 October 1995; Albert Square is the fictional centre of the BBC soap opera *Eastenders*, Coronation St that of the eponymous ITV soap opera; Ambridge is the fictional location of the long-running rural BBC radio soap opera *The Archers*.

24 See Susan Marling, "Fantasy architecture", *Independent on Sunday*, 19 September 1999; cf. the Australian debates about architecture, ethnicity and memory reported in Chapter 2.

25 A. Appadurai, *Modernity At Large*, Minneapolis, University of Minnesota Press, 1996, p. 4. To give an example from the UK, a recent commentary on communications patterns among migrant families from South Asia reported that, at a quotidian level, "In the North-West of England … no-one in Oldham uses the postal system to send their mail home to South Asia, because they know that someone is going to be going there – it is a sub-movement, not a movement between nation-states"; Virinder S. Kalra, quoted in Sanjay Sharma, "Dissing the Orient", *New Times*, 18 January 1997.

26 Appadurai, op. cit., p. 4.

27 ibid., p. 4.

28 ibid., p. 6.

29 Nicola Mai, "Italy is beautiful: the role of Italian television in Albanian migration", in R. King and N. Wood (eds), *Media and Migration*, London, Routledge, forthcoming.

30 cf. C.D. Rath, "The invisible network", in P. Drummond and R. Paterson (eds), *Television in Transition*, London, British Film Institute, 1985, on the role of Western media in East Berlin before the fall of the Berlin Wall.

NOTES

31 G. Campani, "The maid and the prostitute: media representations of immigrant women in Italy", in R. King and N. Woods (eds), op. cit., cf. J. Okely, *The Traveller–Gypsies*, Cambridge, Cambridge University Press, 1983, on public perceptions of gypsy women as unclean.

32 B. Riccio, "Following the Senegalese migratory path through media representation", in King and Woods (eds), op. cit.

33 Senegalese migrant in Italy, quoted in Riccio, op. cit., p. 10. Page numbers to Riccio's article are to the mss copy, for access to which I thank the author.

34 Riccio, op. cit., p. 11.

35 These migrants display an interesting parallel with the practices of the Christianised Jews of Spain who, at the time of the Inquisition, would carry a tiny edition of the Old Testament to church concealed up their sleeve, so that they could maintain their own sense of their moral purity by secretly touching this talismanic object while outwardly seeming to follow the Mass which they were forced to attend; cf. Edmund Jabes, *A Foreigner Carrying in the Crook of his Arm a Tiny Book*, Hanover, New England, Wesleyan University Press, 1993.

36 U. Hannerz, "Bush and Beento: Nigerian popular culture and the world", paper to American Anthropological Association Conference, Chicago, November 1987.

37 Quoted in Riccio, op. cit., p. 10.

38 My ambition here is certainly not to offer any fully developed analysis of migrant and minority cultures in France, as I have neither the data nor the expertise to do so. The materials below concerning the experience and representation of migrancy in the French case are simply offered by way of illustration of some of the book's overall themes.

39 Alec Hargreaves, "Satellite viewing among ethnic minorities in France", in *European Journal of Communication*, 1997, vol. 12(4), p. 460.

40 This usage seems to have been imported into France from North Africa, where the dishes were originally labelled thus by Islamists, on account of their doing "the devil's work" by bringing Western broadcasts into the cultural space of Islam. I am grateful to Alec Hargreaves for his clarification of this point.

41 Quoted in Hargreaves, op. cit., p. 461.

42 cf. Mary Dejevsky, "The angry sound of the suburbs", *Independent*, 26 October 1995.

43 Hargreaves, op. cit., p. 461.

44 Alec Hargreaves, "Satellite television and France's Magrehbi minority", in King and Wood (eds), op. cit.

45

Percentage of each ethnic group in Habitations à Loyer Modère (HLMs) *i.e. local authority schemes*	
French born	13.7
Algerians	43.4
Moroccans	44.3
Tunisians	34.4
Other Africans	36.6

Percentage unemployment by ethnic group

	All	Male	Female
French	10.4	7.5	14.1
Algerian	27.5	23.1	42.3
Moroccan	25.4	20.7	42.5
Tunisian	25.7	22.0	41.7
Other African	27.6	21.5	45.2

46 Published in France in 1983 as *Le thé au harem d'Archi Ahmed*, and in English in London, by Serpents Tail in 1989.

47 For the screenplay of the film *La Haine*, see Kassowitz's contribution to Georgia de Chamberet (ed.), *Xcités*, London, Flamingo, 1999. The *beurs* are the children (or grandchildren) of North African immigrants who settled in France during the post-war economic boom. Their experience has been of growing up with a bi-cultural identity, being both Arab and French, and yet belonging fully to neither culture. They are the children of the sub-proletariat of migrant manual workers who grew up on the poor banlieues, although nowadays a very small number of them (sometimes referred to as the *beurgeoisie*) have gone on to become more economically successful – as demonstrated in the case of the brothers Abdelhafidi in the film of that name directed by Colin Prescod, Tx BBC2, 12 August 1999. For a perceptive commentary on filmic representations of these issues, see Ginette Vincendeau's "Designs on the banlieue: Mathieu Kassowitz's *La Haine*", in S. Hayward and G. Vincendeau (eds), *French Film: Texts and Contexts*, London, Routledge, 2000.

48 Quoted in John Lichfield, "Lost generation makes its voice heard", *Independent*, 20 December 1997.

49 Mary Dejevsky, "The angry sound of the suburbs", *Independent*, 26 October 1995.

50 Allan Horsfall, "Why bus rage?", *Guardian*, 30 December 1996.

51 Ken Worpole, *Towns for People*, Milton Keynes, Open University Press, 1992, p. 27.

52 As the novelist Frederic Raphael melodramatically put it in another context, "I come from suburbia and I don't want to go back. It's the one place in the world that's further away than anywhere else." Anderson and Raphael are both quoted in Peter Hetherington's, "Suburbia has entered crisis of neglect", *Guardian*, 5 February 1999. See also Simon Frith's, "The suburban sensibility in British rock and pop", in R. Silverstone (ed.), *Visions of Suburbia*, London, Routledge, 1997, on the particular poignancy of the adolescent experience of suburbia.

53 Devejsky, "The angry sound of the suburbs", op. cit.

54 K. Ross, "La Belle Américaine", in J. Miller and M. Schwarz (eds), *Speed*, London, The Photographer's Gallery, 1998, p. 80.

55 Francois Maspero, *Roissy Express*, London, Verso, 1994, p.178.

56 Maspero, op. cit., pp. 170 and 143.

57 ibid., p. 159; cf. Z. Bauman, *Globalisation*, Cambridge, Polity Press, 1998.

58 Maspero, op. cit., p. 35.

59 Alain Faujas, quoted in Maspero, op. cit., p. 136.

60 Maspero, op. cit., pp. 40, 156, 172, 252; interestingly, Akim and his friends reject the label *beur*, as imposed on them by "outsiders".

61 B. Campbell, *Goliath*, London, Methuen, 1993.

62 Campbell, op. cit., pp. 317 and 48.

63 ibid., p. 3.

64 D. Morley and K. Robins, *Spaces of Identity*, London, Routledge, 1995, ch. 8.

65 cf. J. Helcké, "Television, ethnic minorities and mass culture in France", in S. Perry and M. Cross (eds), *Voices of France*, London, Pinter, 1997, p. 137.

66 "La France profonde", in Braudel's terms, perhaps – see F. Braudel, *The Identity of France (vol. 1) History and Environment*, London, Fontana, 1989.

67 A. Hargreaves, "A deviant construction: the French media and the banlieues", *New Community*, 1996, vol. 22(4), pp. 607 and 611.

68 Hargreaves, op. cit., p. 609; cf. S. Hall, C. Critcher, T. Jefferson, J. Clarke and B. Roberts, *Policing the Crisis*, London, Hutchinson, 1978.

69 "Journeys into the barbarian estates", *Le Figaro* 27 November 1990, quoted in Hargreaves, "A deviant construction", op. cit., p. 615; cf. Edith Hall, *Inventing the Barbarian,* Oxford University Press, 1991.

70 L. Greenhalgh and K. Worpole, *The Freedom of the City*, London, Demos, 1996.

71 From Worpole's 1992 study, *Towns for People*, op. cit., p. 48; cf. my earlier comments on the role of local pirate radio "shout-outs" in consolidating local subcultures.

72 Saskia Sassen, *The Global City*, Princeton University Press, 1991, p. 101.

73 cf. K. Worpole and L. Greenhalgh, *The Richness of Cities*, London, Demos/Comedia, 1998 on the development of "offices of time" in some European cities to address these issues.

74 Marguerite Duras, quoted in C. Holmland, "Displacing limits of difference", in H. Naficy and T. Gabriel (eds), *Otherness and the Media*, Langhorne, Pennsylvania, Harwood, 1993.

75 S. Selvon, *Moses Ascending*, London, Davis–Poynter, 1975, p. 11; quoted in Susheila Nasta, "Setting up home in a city of words", in A. R. Lee (ed.), *Other Britain, Other British*, Pluto Press, 1995, p. 49.

76 J. Hargreaves, "The representation of immigrants and ethnic minorities of Third World origin", *New Community*, 1993, vol. 19(2), pp. 254–60.

77 cf. C. Husband, *White Media, Black Britain*, London, Arrow Books, 1975.

78 See Chapter 5. For a comparable analysis to Hargreaves', concerning which programme genres ethnic minorities have greater or less access to in the UK, see G. Cumberbatch and S. Woods, *Ethnic Minorities on Television*, Independent Television Commission, London, 1994. While the report is positive about the progress made in UK television in this respect, it nonetheless notes (p. 34) the absence of ethnic minorities from a range of programme types which I would argue are central to the constitution of ideas of English national heritage and ethnicity: classic arts, country pursuits (cf. the comments on Ingrid Pollard's work earlier), war commemorations and defence issues.

79 M. Syal, *Anita and Me*, London, Flamingo, 1997, p. 165.

80 Sreberny, op. cit., p. 37.

81 A. Appadurai, "Disjuncture and difference in the global cultural economy", *Theory, Culture and Society*, 1990, vol. 7, p. 306.

82 cf. my earlier comments in Chapter 3 on Gillespie's findings: British Asian women in the Southall community she studied were more housebound. Having less contact with the outside, a poorer grasp of English and being expected, by virtue of their feminine role, to be the carriers of certain aspects of domestic cultural tradition, they too displayed an enhanced interest in media material in their language of cultural origin. Hargreaves' later study of viewing patterns among Turkish immigrant groups in Germany reveals a similar pattern, with women much more likely to view Turkish language channels – cf. A. Hargreaves, "Transnational broadcasting audiences: new diasporas for old?", paper to Council of Europe Workshop on Media in Multilingual and Multicultural Settings, Klagenfurt, Austria, November, 1999. In an interesting transposition of this perspective, Rivki Ribak argues that if immigrants to a new country (beyond a certain age) tend to rely on their children, who are more easily

NOTES

able to learn the language skills necessary to communicate in their new environment, something of the same process occurs in relation to shifts in communication technologies. Thus, as one of Ribak's respondents observes in her study of gender and generational differences in relation to computing technologies in Israel, to some extent parents often become dependent "like immigrants" on their children's superior facility with new technologies such as the computer – R. Ribak, "Like immigrants: negotiating power in the face of the home computer", unpublished paper, Department of Communication, University of Haifa, 1998. Also Sreberny, op. cit., pp. 42 and 63.

83 Sreberny, op. cit., pp. 42 and 63.
84 A. Hargreaves, "Satellite television viewing among ethnic minorities in France", *European Journal of Communication*, 1997, vol. 12(4).
85 Hargreaves, op. cit., p. 475. Hargreaves also reports anecdotal evidence of these young viewers turning the direction of the satellite dish, when their parents go out, so as to receive American rather than North African programming. One could perhaps speculate that one part of the possible attraction of American culture for young Arabs is because it includes at least some positive representations of non-whites – as sports or music stars. At a more detailed level, comparing Hargreaves' findings with those of the HICT study referred to earlier, one might also want to pose further, more detailed questions concerning whether the children watch in the bedroom because they want to watch French television, or vice versa – i.e. do they simply prefer to watch separately from their parents and, as a consequence, end up watching French television because their sets do not have satellite? A second question concerns gender differences. Just as in the HICT research, Hargreaves reports (private communication) that the boys were more likely to watch television separately in their rooms and girls to watch with the family in the living room, the boys thus enjoying considerably enhanced independence from their parents in their viewing choices.
86 In H. Kureishi, *Love in a Blue Time*, London, Faber, 1997; cf. also the film version directed by Udayan Prashad, BBC Films, 1997.
87 Of which more later. See Tahar Ben Jelloun's comments quoted in Chapter 11.
88 A. Hargreaves, *Immigration, "Race" and Ethnicity in Contemporary France*, London, Routledge, 1995, p. 139. See also Paul Gilroy, *The Black Atlantic*, London, Verso, 1993; M. Kokoreff, "Tags et Zoulous", *Esprit*, 1991, vol. 169; O. Roy, "Les immigrés dans le ville", *Esprit*, 1993, vol. 191.
89 cf. the research on these issues by Ingolf Ahlers and Marx Behrendt at the Institute für Politische Wissenschaft, University of Hannover, financed by the Lower Saxony Ministry of Science and Culture.
90 K. Robins, "Negotiating spaces: media and cultural practices in the Turkish diasporas in Britain, France and Germany", ESRC-funded research project, Department of Media and Communications, Goldsmiths College, as part of the ESRC's Transnational Communities Research Programme.
91 cf. K. Robins, "Negotiating spaces: Turkish transnational media", in King and Wood (eds), op. cit.
92 Ayse S. Caglar, "German Turks in Berlin", *New Community*, 1995, vol. 21(3), p. 320.
93 R. Wilk, "Colonial time and television time", in *Visual Anthropology Review*, 1994, vol. 10(1); for a commentary see Morley and Robins, 1995, op. cit., pp. 226–7.
94 In a different context, but in a parallel fashion, it seems that young British men most frequently use their mobile phones to call their mothers: another example of a new technology being utilised to reinvigorate a thoroughly traditional pattern of behaviour cf. "Sons and mothers", *Guardian*, 15 January 1998.

95 cf. D. Morley and K. Robins, "Yamanci, Albanci", in *Cultural Studies*, 1996, vol. 10(2), on the young Turkish–German rap group Cartel.
96 cf. the German–Turkish novelist Jacob Arjouni's comments on refusing to be seen as a representative of "the" Turkish community, quoted in Chapter 11 below.
97 R. Mandel, "Fortress Europe and the foreigners within", paper to Anthropology of Europe Conference, Goldsmiths College, 1992, p. 4.
98 Mandel, "Fortress Europe and the foreigners within", op. cit., p. 2; cf. Neal Ascherson and Michael Ignatieff's comments on the "returning Germans" quoted in Chapter 11.
99 Mandel, op. cit., p. 5.
100 cf. D. Morley and K. Robins, *Spaces of Identity*, London, Routledge, 1995, ch. 5; cf. M. Bernal, *Black Athena*, London, Free Association Books, 1987, on the importance of ideas of classical Greece in the construction of ideas of the Aryan people; see also M. Herzfeld, *Anthropology through the Looking Glass*, Cambridge, Cambridge University Press, 1987, ch. 2 on the interpenetration of Turkish or Ottoman elements in Greek popular culture.

8 POSTMODERN, VIRTUAL AND CYBERNETIC GEOGRAPHIES

1 F. Marinetti, "Destruction of syntax–wireless–imagination–words in freedom", quoted in J. Miller, "Rejectamenta", in J. Miller and M. Schwarz (eds), *Speed*, London, Photographer's Gallery, 1998, p. 105.
2 R. Arnheim, *Film as Art*, Faber and Faber, 1933, reprinted 1958; quoted in C.D. Rath, "The invisible network", in P. Drummond and R. Paterson (eds), *Television in Transition*, London, British Film Institute, 1985, p. 199.
3 Reprinted in M. Geller (ed.), *From Receiver to Remote Control*, New York, New Museum of Contemporary Art, 1990, p. 129.
4 In *The New Citizen*, London, Council for Education in World Citizenship, 1944:

> The world of rapid aerial transport – and of almost instantaneous communication – is clearly shrinking fast, and it is really quite different from the world of yesterday. This world of air travel cannot help but be an international world. The airman moves too fast for national borders ... A narrow national spirit, pretending that there is something sacred and magical about a frontier, with its old fashioned paraphernalia of customs sheds and passport examinations, is clearly out of place in such a world.

(J.B. Priestley, quoted in Kevin Davey, *English Imaginaries*, London, Lawrence and Wishart, 1999, p. 73)

5 M. McLuhan and Q. Fiore, *War and Peace in the Global Village*, New York, Bantam Books, 1967; A. Giddens, *The Consequences of Modernity*, Stanford, California, Stanford University Press, 1991, p. 140.
6 P. Virilio, "The last vehicle", in Miller and Schwarz (eds), op. cit., pp. 34 and 41.
7 K. Marx, *Grundrisse*, Harmondsworth, Penguin, 1973, p. 524; see also p. 539.
8 Yves de la Haye, *Marx and Engels on the Means of Communication*, New York, International General, 1980, pp. 28–9.
9 M. Morse, "An ontology of everyday distraction", in P. Mellencamp (ed.), *Logics of Television*, Bloomington, Indiana University Press, 1990, pp. 212, 195, 208, 197, 200.
10 Morse, op. cit., pp. 195, 213, 197, 209, 212; for Morse's more recent work see her *Virtualities: Television, Media Art and Cyberspace*, Bloomington, Indiana University Press, 1998.

11 M. Augé, *Non-Places: Introduction to an Anthropology of Supermodernity*, London, Verso, 1995, p. 112. For a development of many of these themes see also Augé's later works: *A Sense for the Other: The Timeliness and Relevance of Anthropology*, Stanford, California, Stanford University Press, 1998; and *The War of Dreams: Studies in Ethno Fiction*, London, Pluto Press, 1999.

12 J.G. Ballard, "Going somewhere", *Observer*, 14 September 1997. In her photographic study of the contemporary experience of air travel, Martha Rosler offers a disturbing portrait of the airport not simply as a "space of flow" but as a container space for the experience of uneasy delays and anxious passages for the "glazed nomads" who suffer the combination of rushing and waiting which is the peculiar characteristic of air travel – Martha Rosler, *In the Place of the Public: Observations of a Frequent Flyer*, Ostfildern–Ruit, Cantz Verlag, 1998, p. 13, 44, 63. The airport, according to Stephen Spender, is a "landscape of hysteria" (Spender, quoted in Rosler, op. cit., p. 17) and it is characterised for Rosler by the "combined discomfort of demoralised waiting and anonymous passage" where, even among many of those who merely suffer the "vicarious and temporary homelessness of privileged nomadism", there is some creeping anxiety about ever getting to their "proper" destinations. The imperatives of crowd-control, and the beguilement of the passengers experiencing this movement of multiple bodies through badly lit and ill-signposted corridors, lead to the "effacement of the experience of travel ... by constructs designed to empty the actual experience of its content", which in the end "puts the traveller nowhere" – Rosler, op. cit., pp. 28, 59, 61. Kristeva has argued that "the space of the foreigner is a moving train, a plane in flight": perhaps correlatively the train or plane, and thus the airport itself, is a site of "foreignness" – J. Kristeva, *Strangers to Ourselves*, New York, Columbia University Press, 1991, pp. 7–8.

13 Augé, op. cit., pp. 31–4.

14 ibid., pp. 52, 101,53.

15 A. Gupta and J. Ferguson (eds), *Culture, Power, Place*, Durham, Duke University Press, 1997, p. 10.

16 A. Appadurai and C. Breckenridge, quoted in D. Hebdige, "Fax to the future", *Marxism Today*, 1990, January, p. 20; or, as Ulf Hannerz describes them, "involuntary cosmopolitans"; cf. U. Hannerz, *Transnational Connections*, London, Routledge, 1996.

17 Hebdige, op. cit., p. 20.

18 J.D. Peters, "Seeing bifocally" in Gupta and Ferguson (eds), op. cit., pp. 79, 81.

19 Peters, op. cit., pp. 81, 82.

20 See Descombes quoted in Chapter 1, note 11.

21 Augé, op. cit., p. 105; cf. recent market research evidence of young people in Europe having more trust in global brands than in national governments.

22 U. Mai, "Culture shock and identity crisis in East German cities", in A. Öncü and P. Weyland (eds), *Space, Culture and Power*, London, Zed Books, 1997, pp. 78–9. For another example, see the scenes at the start of the film *Falling Down*, where the "hero" D-Fens gradually becomes more incensed as he tries to make his way through a city which has now become foreign to him, peopled by Koreans and other "strangers".

23 Mai, op. cit., p. 80. See the section on "Boundary, identity and conflict" in Chapter 9 on this point.

24 M. Wark, *Virtual Geography*, Bloomington, Indiana University Press, 1994, pp. xiv, x.

25 ibid., p. vii.

26 M. Ferguson, "Electronic communities and the redefining of time and space", in M. Ferguson (ed.), *Public Communications*, London, Sage, 1989; see also D. Morley

and R. Silverstone, "Domestic communications", in *Media, Culture and Society*, 1990, vol. 12(1) on the incorporation of new technologies into older communication patterns.

27 P. Wollen, "The cosmopolitan ideal in the arts", in G. Robertson, M. Mash, L. Tickner, J. Bird, B. Curtis and T. Putnam (eds), *Travellers' Tales*, London, Routledge, 1994, p. 194; Saskia Sassen, *The Global City*, Princeton University Press, 1991.

28 J. Tomlinson, *Globalisation and Culture*, Cambridge, Polity Press, 1999, pp. 7, 111, 112; F. Maspero, *Roissy Express*, London, Verso, 1994.

29 D. Bell and G. Valentine, *Consuming Geographies*, Routledge, 1997, p. 138; quoted in Tomlinson, op. cit., p.112.

30 cf. the subtitle of de la Haye's edited collection of Marx and Engels' work, quoted earlier, *The Movement of Commodities, People, Information and Capital*.

31 J. Meyrowitz, "Three worlds of strangers", in *Annals of the Association of American Geographers*, 1990, vol. 80(1), p. 129; R. Sack, "The Consumer's World: place as context" in *Annals of Association of American Geographers*, 1989, vol. 78(4).

32 Meyrowitz, "Three worlds of strangers", op. cit., p. 130.

33 G. Allan, "Insiders and outsiders: boundaries around the home", in G. Allan and G. Crow (eds), *Home and Family*, London, Macmillan, 1989, p. 150.

34 A. Wurtzel and C. Turner, "Latent functions of the telephone", in I.S. Pool (ed.), *The Social Impact of the Telephone*, Cambridge, Mass., MIT Press, 1977, pp. 256–7; cf. also G. Noble, "Individual differences, psychological neighbourhoods and the use of the domestic telephone", *Media Information Australia*, May 1987, vol. 44.

35 J. Meyrowitz, *No Sense of Place*, Oxford, Oxford University Press 1985, p. 90.

36 J. Meyrowitz, "Shifting worlds of strangers", *Sociological Inquiry*, 1997, vol. 67(1), p. 65. However, if we compare Meyrowitz's commentary with that of Ariès, quoted earlier in Chapter 2 on the permeability of the medieval home, perhaps what we have here is not strictly speaking an entirely novel historical development, but rather a return, mediated by electronic technology, to the relative "openness" of the medieval home after the peculiarities of the "bounded"/closed definition of the "model" bourgeois privatised home of the nineteenth century.

37 Tomlinson, op. cit., pp. 116, 161; Meyrowitz, *No Sense of Place*, op. cit., p. 147; cf. the earlier comments on contemporary ideologies and etiquettes of phone usage in Chapter 4.

38 M. Heidegger, *An Introduction to Metaphysics*, 1959, quoted in D. Harvey, *The Condition of Postmodernity*, Oxford, Blackwell, 1989, p. 208.

39 R. Williams, "Distance", in *What I Came to Say*, London, Hutchinson Radius, 1989, pp. 36, 43; quoted in Hebdige, "On tumbleweed and bodybags", in B. W. Ferguson (ed.), *Longing and belonging*, New York, Distributed Art Publishers, 1995, p. 84.

40 A. Johansen, "Fellowmen, compatriots, contemporaries", in J. Peter Burgess (ed.), *Cultural Politics and Political Culture in Postmodern Europe*, Amsterdam, Editions Rodopi, 1997. As the attentive reader will observe, this subtitle refers only to "fellowmen". My main focus in this section is on the articulation of alterity with questions of geographical distance. This is by no means to say that alterity only exists in this modality: my earlier arguments about the inscription of gender in space are picked up later with reference to Ghassan Hage's comments on the "domestication of alterity" in the concluding section of Chapter 9.

41 cf. J. Fabian, *Time and the Other*, New York, Columbia University Press, 1983; A. Schutz and T. Luckman, *The Structure of the Life World*, London, Heinemann, 1974.

42 Clearly, Johansen might be argued to be overstating the contrast, as Doreen Massey has rightly argued (see the section on "Postmodern geographies" later in this chapter) by reference to the impact of the arrival of strangers, in the shape of invading colonists, in many "traditional" societies. Nonetheless, the schema he offers,

if treated with due caution, remains a useful one. See my earlier comments on Giddens in this connection in Chapter 7.

43 A. Schutz, "Structures of the life world", in T. Luckman (ed.), *Phenomenology and the Social Sciences*, Harmondsworth, Allen Lane/Penguin, 1978, p. 62, quoted in Johansen, op. cit., p. 173.

44 Johansen, op. cit., p. 176, drawing on Bourdieu's analysis of the Kabyle. P. Bourdieu, "The attitude of the Algerian peasant towards time", in J. Pitt Rivers (ed.), *Mediterranean Countrymen*, Paris, Mouton, 1963.

45 P. Narvaez, "The folklore of 'Old Foolishness'", *Canadian Literature*, 1986, vol. 108, pp. 128–30; quoted in Johansen, op. cit., p. 181.

46 Johansen, op. cit., pp. 183–5.

47 E. Hall, *Inventing the Barbarian*, Oxford University Press, 1991, p. 54; Ziauddin Sardar, Ashis Nandy and Merryl Wyn Davies, *Barbaric Others*, London, Pluto Press, 1993.

48 cf. E. Wolf, *Europe and the People Without History*, Berkeley, University of California Press, 1982.

49 That is, of course, to be fully explicit about the benchmark from which these things have tended to be measured, white Western middle-class adult masculinity.

50 Fabian, op. cit., pp. 31 and 26.

51 Olu Oguibe, "A brief note on internationalism", in J. Fisher (ed.), *Global Visions*, London, Kala Press, 1994, p. 57.

52 G. Bennett, "The non-sovereign self: diaspora identities", in Fisher (ed.), op. cit., p. 125.

53 Fabian, op. cit., p. 35.

54 N. Sakai, "Modernity and its critique", in *South Atlantic Quarterly*, 1988, vol. 87(3).

55 cf. D. Morley and K. Robins, *Spaces of Identity*, London, Routledge, 1995, ch. 8.

56 A. Appadurai, *Modernity at Large*, Minneapolis, University of Minnesota Press, 1996, p. 30.

57 Morley and Robins, op. cit., pp. 226–7.

58 Fabian, op. cit., p. 35.

59 cf. Hayden White, *The Content of the Form: Narrative Discourse and Historical Representation*, Baltimore, Johns Hopkins University Press, 1987.

60 N. Thrift, "Us and Them: re-imagining places, re-imagining identities", in H. Mackay (ed.), *Consumption and Everyday Life*, Milton Keynes, Open University Press, 1997.

61 Z. Bauman, *Globalisation*, Cambridge, Polity Press, 1998, pp. 13 and 76, original emphasis.

62 J.B. Thompson, *The Media and Modernity*, Cambridge, Cambridge University Press, 1995, p. 233.

63 Morley and Robins, op. cit., ch. 7. Virilio complains of the "banalisation" of a certain type of what he calls the "teletopology" of mediated encounters, as a result of which, he claims, "the bulk of what I can see is, in fact and in principle, no longer within my reach" (P. Virilio, *The Vision Machine*, Bloomington, Indiana University Press, 1994, p. 7). Similarly, in an essay on photography, while Siegfried Kracauer observed that "Never before has an age been so informed about itself", he goes on to qualify that claim immediately with its contrary:

> never before has a period known so little about itself ... The "image-idea" drives away the idea: the blizzard of photographs betrays an indifference to what things mean ... In the illustrated magazines, people see the very world that the illustrated magazines prevent them from seeing.
> (S. Kracauer, "Photography", in *Critical Enquiry*, 1993, vol. 19(3), p. 432, originally 1927; quoted in K. Robins, "Forces of consumption", *Media, Culture and Society*, 1994, vol. 16, pp. 449–68)

64 J. Miller, *McLuhan*, London, Fontana, 1971, p. 126; for a contemporary account of an experience of this sort in the context of the local televising of the war in Croatia, see S. Drakulic, *How We Survived Communism and Even Laughed*, London, Vintage, 1993.

65 Debray, quoted in K. Robins, "Forces of consumption", *Media, Culture and Society*, 1994, vol. 16, p. 458; Gallaz, quoted in Robins, op. cit., p. 461.

66 cf. on this Z. Bauman, *Postmodern Ethics*, Oxford, Blackwell, 1993.

67 I.M. Young, "The ideal of community and the politics of difference", in L. Nicholson (ed.), *Feminism/Postmodernism*, London, Routledge, 1990, p. 314; D. Massey, *Space, Place and Gender*, Cambridge, Polity Press, 1994, p. 164; cf. also Tomlinson's argument that, in some situations, a telephone conversation can be more intimate than a face-to-face one – Tomlinson, op. cit., pp. 162–3. See the later section of this chapter on "Community lite and communitarianism" for a corresponding critique of the romanticisation of virtual communities.

68 See the section on "Community lite and communitarianism" later in this chapter on this point.

69 cf. J. Thompson, *The Media and Modernity*, Cambridge, Polity Press, 1995, p. 228.

70 cf. my comments earlier in Chapter 6 on the increasing insularity of viewing patterns in the West.

71 R. Stam, "Television news and its spectator", p. 27 in E. Ann Kaplan (ed.), *Regarding Television*, Los Angeles, American Film Institute, 1983.

72 Stam, op. cit., pp. 24, 25, 34 and 39.

73 J. Ellis, *Visible Fictions*, London, Routledge, 1982, p. 5.

74 Thomas Elsaesser, "European television and national identity", paper to European Film and TV Studies Conference, London, 1994, pp, 7–8; quoted in K. Robins, "European media culture and the problem of imagined community", paper to Symposium on the Future of Mass Media in Wales, Cardiff, 1997, p. 15.

75 Johansen, op. cit., p. 194.

76 J.Perry Barlow, "Howdy neighbours", *Guardian*, 24 July 1995.

77 See Jim McLennan, "State of the digital nation", *Observer*, 4 June 1995; see below for more recent figures which indicate that this overall pattern still obtains.

78 J. Stallabrass, "Empowering technology", *New Left Review*, 1995, vol. 211, p. 20.

79 In 1997 it was reported that in the UK, while two-thirds of professional households had a computer, only one tenth of households headed by an unemployed or retired person did so. This inequality of access is predictably repeated across all dimensions of social disadvantage.

80 Z. Sardar, "Alt. civilisations. faq: cyberspace as the darker side of the West", in Z. Sardar and J. R. Ravetz (eds), *Cyberfutures: Culture and Politics on the Information Superhighway*, London, Pluto Press, 1996, p. 24.

81 V. Keegan, "What a web we weave", *Guardian*, 13 May 1997.

82 For details see the maps of the distribution of Internet connections and data flows developed by Martin Dodge and his fellow researchers at the Centre for Advanced Spatial Analysis at University College in London, "Atlas of cyberspace" (at www.cybergeography.org/atlas/atlas/html or www.casa.ucl.ac.uk).

83 S. Graham and S. Marvin, *Net Effects*, London, Comedia/Demos, 1998, p.18.

84 Similarly, among the stockbrokers she studied in Sweden, Boden found that routine email and telephone contact was deemed inadequate for the maintenance of the personal trust on which their financial dealings ultimately depended – for these purposes, only face-to-face meetings were felt to suffice, Boden, quoted in O. Lofgren, *In Transit*, Lund, University of Lund, 1996.

85 Graham and Marvin, op. cit., p. 14.

86 ibid., p. 6. In this connection Saskia Sassen offers an account of the thoroughly "placebound" territorial centralisation of top level management and control operations in transnational companies in her essay "Whose city is it?", in O. Enwezor (ed.), *Trade Routes, History and Geography*, Johannesburg, Greater Johannesburg Metropolitan Council, 1997.

87 In this section I am drawing heavily on the work of my colleague Kevin Robins.

88 See K. Robins, "The new communications geography and the politics of optimism", *Soundings*, 1997, Spring, vol. 6.

89 J. Carey, *Culture as Communication*, London, Unwin Hyman, 1989.

90 cf. K. Robins, "Cyberspace and the world we live in", *Body and Society*, 1995, vol. 1(3–4); K. Robins, "The city in question", *Renewal*, 1997, vol. 5(1); K. Robins and F. Webster, *Times of the Technoculture*, London, Routledge, 1999.

91 cf. A. Mattelart, *The Invention of Communication*, Minneapolis, University of Minnesota Press, 1996.

92 B. Gates, *The Road Ahead*, London, Viking, p. 263.

93 Robins and Webster, op. cit., pp. 240, 241, 242, 247.

94 Margaret Wertheim, "The pearly gates of cyberspace", in N. Elin (ed.), *Architecture of Fear*, New York, Princeton Architectural Press, 1997, p. 296.

95 B. Sherman and P. Judkins, *Glimpses of Heaven, Glimpses of Hell: Virtual Reality and Its Implications*, London, Hodder and Stoughton, 1992.

96 Robins, "Cyberspace and the world we live in", op. cit., pp. 139, 147.

97 Thus, in his sceptical analysis of whether "virtual cities" on the Net can give us back the sense of belonging that is said to be vanishing from our urban areas, Stephen Graham argues that what the Net actually does is to allow its dominant users, middle-class suburban Americans, "to keep in touch with carefully screened groups of similar people, right across the world, from the safety of their increasingly fortified homes"; S. Graham, "Flight to the cybersuburbs", *Guardian*, 18 April 1996.

98 cf. Graham and Marvin, op. cit., p. 16.

99 As Neil Smith puts it, "it is not just that the rich express their freedom by their ability to overcome space, while the poor are more likely to be trapped in it: differential access to space [also] leads to differential power"; N. Smith, "Homeless/global", in J. Bird, B. Curtis, T. Putnam, G. Robertson and L. Tickner (eds), *Mapping the Futures*, London, Routledge, 1993, p. 106. Mike Crang *et al.* rightly caution that it is "unhelpful ... to seek or proclaim a singular character to virtual geographies" or to pass "once and for all verdicts" on their qualities: they are, of course, like any other form of geography, subject to all manner of variation – see the Introduction to M. Crang, P. Crang and J. May, *Virtual Geographies*, London, Routledge, 1999, p. 4.

100 Of which more below – see Chapter 11, on James Donald's use of this phrase.

101 N. Postman, "Identity and technology", *Guardian*, 5 December 1999.

102 J. Gray, "The sad side of cyberspace", *Guardian*, 10 April 1995.

103 Z. Sardar, "Alt. civilisations, faq: cyberspace as the darker side of the West", in Z. Sardar and J. R. Ravetz (eds), *Cyberfutures*, London, Pluto Press, 1996, p. 29.

104 More positively, Katherine Shonfield argues that people's use of the Internet does demonstrate that, besides the desire to commune with those who are "the same", there remains the yearning for safe, convivial encounters with others: the urge to "meet, confront and enjoy difference. It is up to us to provide this safety and conviviality in the real, rather than the virtual world"; Katherine Shonfield, *At Home with Strangers*, London, Comedia/Demos, 1998, p. 11.

105 I.M. Young, *Justice and the Politics of Difference*, Princeton, Princeton University Press, 1990, p. 229; cf. M. Foucault, *Power/Knowledge*, Princeton, Princeton University Press, 1990.

106 Robins, "Cyberspace and the world we live in", op. cit., p. 150.

107 K. Robins, "The city in question", op. cit., p. 78l; Robins, "Cyberspace and the world we live in", op. cit., p. 151.

108 Young, *Justice and the Politics of Difference*, op. cit., p. 229.

109 C. Mouffe, *The Realm of the Political*, London, Verso, 1993, p. 6.

110 Young, *Justice and the Politics of Difference*, op. cit., p. 234.

111 Young, op. cit., pp. 49 and 103. In offering this summary of Young's argument I am drawing heavily on Robins and Webster's commentary in Chapter 11 of their *Times of the Technoculture*, London, Routledge, 1999.

112 See her *Space, Place and Gender*, Cambridge, Polity Press, 1994.

113 F. Jameson, *Postmodernism, or, The Cultural Logic of Late Capitalism*, London, Verso, 1991; E. Soja, *Postmodern Geographies*, London, Verso, 1989; D. Harvey, *The Condition of Postmodernity*, Oxford, Blackwell, 1989.

114 D. Massey, "A global sense of place", in *Marxism Today*, 1991, June, p. 24; D. Massey, "A place called home", *New Formations*, 1992, vol. 17, p. 13.

115 Massey, "A place called home", op. cit., p. 8.

116 A. Ghosh, quoted in J. Clifford, *Routes*, Cambridge, Mass., Harvard University Press, 1997, p. 1; see A. Ghosh, *In an Antique Land*, London, Granta Books, 1992.

117 Clifford, op. cit., pp. 1–2. For an account of the extent of migratory labour patterns in the UK and in Europe from medieval times onwards, see R. Leeson, *Travelling Brothers*, London, Granada, 1979.

118 Quoted in Lofgren, "In transit", op. cit., p. 3.

119 O. Lofgren, "The nation as home or motel? Metaphors of media and belonging", unpublished paper, Department of European Ethnology, University of Lund, 1995.

120 S. Lash and J. Urry, *Economies of Signs and Spaces*, London, Sage, 1994, p. 323.

121 Lofgren, "The nation as home or motel?", op. cit., pp. 4–6.

122 S. Kern, *The Culture of Time and Space 1880–1918*, Cambridge, Mass., Harvard University Press, 1983.

123 Will Hutton, "The familiar shape of things to come", *Guardian*, 28 December 1995.

124 Tomlinson, op. cit., pp. 42 and 130.

125 Massey, "A global sense of place", op. cit., pp. 24 and 27.

126 N. Ascherson, "A diverse England we can shape to our taste", *Independent on Sunday*, 3 October 1993.

127 Massey, "A global sense of place", op. cit., pp. 28–9.

128 D. Massey and P. Jess, "Places and cultures in an uneven world", in D. Massey and P. Jess (eds), *A Place in the World*, Milton Keynes, Open University Press, 1995, p. 222; cf. Salman Rushdie's comments on "how newness enters the world" (S. Rushdie, "Imaginary homelands", *London Review of Books*, 7 October 1982).

129 Suzanne Moore, "Watch this space – it's the community", *Guardian*, 1 December 1994.

130 On this process of "indigenisation" cf. D. Miller, "The young and the restless", in R. Silverstone and E. Hirsch (eds), *Consuming Technologies*, London, Routledge, 1992.

131 Massey, "A global sense of place", op. cit., pp. 24 and 26.

132 ibid., pp. 24, 9, 10; cf. Appadurai, *Modernity at Large*, op. cit., p. 9. See also note 42 above, on this point.

133 cf. G. Mulgan, *Connexity*, London, Chatto and Windus, 1997; Massey, "A global sense of place", op. cit., p. 24.

134 Massey, "A global sense of place", op. cit., pp. 8–9.

135 cf. Morley and Robins, op. cit., ch. 10, commenting on F. Fukuyama, *The End of History*, Harmondsworth, Penguin, 1992.
136 E. Shohat, "By the bitstream of Babylon", p. 220 in H. Naficy (ed.), *Home, Homeland, Exile*, New York, Routledge/American Film Institute, 1999; W. Mitchell, *City of Bits*, Cambridge, Mass., MIT Press, 1995; we shall return to the question of immigration control in the discussion of "cosmopolitics" in Chapter 10.
137 Z. Bauman, *Globalisation*, Cambridge, Polity Press, 1998, p. 12.
138 J.G. Ballard, "Going somewhere", *Observer*, 14 September 1997.
139 T. Putnam, "Shifting the parameters of residence", in Bird *et al.* (eds), op. cit., p. 157.
140 Smith, op. cit., p. 106.
141 D. Massey, "Power-geometry and a progressive sense of place", in Bird *et al.* (eds.), op. cit., pp. 61–2.
142 Liz Greenhalgh, *Habitat: Reconnecting Housing to City Policy*, London, Comedia/Demos, 1998. In areas such as these, where people are locked into forms of geographical isolation, these forms of inequality often also acquire a racialised dimension. As Raj Patel observes,

> People who are affluent and mobile can make the move and decide where to live. The effects ... of higher unemployment amongst many ethnic minority groups (and lower average salaries) also manifest themselves spatially. Conversely ... improved economic opportunities targeted at certain groups can help reduce spatial segregation through improved mobility.
> (R. Patel, *Making Difference Matter*, London, Comedia/Demos, 1998, p. 3)

143 S. Graham and S. Marvin, *Net Effects: Urban Planning and the Technological Future of Cities*, London, Comedia/Demos, 1998, p. 19.
144 C. Olalquiaga, *Megalopolis*, Minneapolis, University of Minnesota Press, 1992, p. 83.
145 W. Solesbury, *Good Connections*, London, Comedia/Demos, 1999, p. 7.
146 S. George, "Fast castes", in Millar and Schwarz (eds), op. cit., p. 115 et seq.
147 Mark Kingwell, "Fast forward", in Millar and Schwarz (eds), op. cit., p. 144.
148 M. Davis, *City of Quartz*, London, Vintage, 1992, p. 227.
149 *Toronto Star*, 29 July 1996 quoted in Graham and Marvin, op. cit., p. 23.
150 P. Cohen, *Home Rules*, London, New Ethnicities Unit, University of East London, 1993, p. 21.
151 Massey, *Space, Place and Gender*, op. cit., p. 149.
152 Tomlinson, op. cit., pp. 133–7; cf. Morley and Robins, op. cit., p. 219. Thus Tomlinson notes, at a quotidian level,

> a white British person in a multi-ethnic working-class community may have as much direct contact with global food culture by shopping in the local Asian store which has replaced the old "corner shop" as a middle-class person cruising the ethnic food aisle in Sainsbury's or Waitrose.
> (Tomlinson, *Globalisation and Culture*, op. cit., p. 133)

Cf. also Anthony King's comments that modernity (and even the dislocated experience of postmodernity) was born – or prefigured – in the experiences of cities on the periphery of empire such as Rio de Janeiro or Calcutta, rather than in the imperial heartlands – A. King, "Introduction", in A. King (ed.), *Culture, Globalisation and the World System*, London, Macmillan, 1991.

153 D. Massey, "Making spaces", in H. Mackay (ed.), *Consumption and Everyday Life*, Milton Keynes, Open University Press, 1997, p. 205.

154 ibid., p. 206, original emphasis; cf. the section on "Differential hybridities" in Chapter 10 below – what these affluent groups achieve is the converse of the experience of "imposed" hybridity, at the bottom of the social scale.

155 cf. N. Thrift, "Us and Them: reimagining identities", in Massey and Jess (eds), op. cit., p. 178, on the geometrical increase in the distance travelled in their lives by successive generations of an English family.

156 P. Iyer, "Where worlds collide", in H. Mackay (ed.), op. cit., p. 209.

157 cf. Bauman, *Globalisation*, op. cit.

158 For a depressing account of the increasing resort to incarceration as a state strategy in the USA, see the section an "When the underclass goes to hell", p. 145 et seq. in Manuel Castells, *End of Millennium*, vol. 3 of *The Information Age*, Oxford, Blackwell, 1998.

159 Bauman, op. cit., p.18.

160 M. Castells, "An introduction to the Information Age", *City*, 1997, vol. 7, p. 8.

161 M. Castells, *The Rise of the Network Society: vol. 1, The Information Age*, Oxford, Blackwell, 1996, p. 371.

162 Castells, quoted in David Ladipo, 'http://www.global.pillage', in *City*, 1997, vol. 7, p. 32.

163 Bauman, op. cit., pp. 88 and 51.

164 ibid., p. 113. To shift out of a theoretical register for a moment, all this was well highlighted in the episode of *The Simpsons*, broadcast in the UK on BBC2 on 1 March 1999 ("The Front") in which Homer was awarded the "All Time Left Behind Loser's Prize", for having succeeded in travelling, over his whole life, the least distance from the school in the locality in which he started out. I am grateful to Wendy Wheeler for bringing this example to my attention.

165 Ulrich Mai, "Culture shock and identity crisis in East German cities", in Öncü and Weyland (eds), op. cit., p. 78; Imre Karacs, "Communist spirit lives on in the Honecker arms", *Independent on Sunday*, 8 August 1999.

166 Bauman, *Globalisation*, op. cit., pp. 92–3.

167 ibid., p. 93.

9 BORDERS AND BELONGINGS

1 K. Ohmae, *The Borderless World*, New York, Harper, 1996a.

2 In K. Ohmae, *The End of the Nation State*, New York, Harper, 1996b, pp. 12, 43, 15.

3 Ohmae, *The End of the Nation State*, op. cit., pp. 25, 28, 38. Much of Ohmae's analysis is comparable to that of Robert Reich in its focus, in the extent to which corporations' activities and global trade flows transcend nationality and national "loyalties"; cf. R. Reich, "Who is Us?", *Harvard Business Review*, January 1990; R. Reich, "What is a nation?", *Political Quarterly*, 1991, vol. 106(2); see also Anthony Giddens' 1999 BBC Reith Lectures on globalisation in a "Runaway World".

4 Those across the borders between San Diego and Tijuana, Singapore and parts of Malaysia and Indonesia, Hong Kong and the Chinese mainland, for instance.

5 U. Hannerz, "The withering away of the nation", *Ethnos*, 1993, vol. 58(3–4).

6 A. Smith, *National Identity*, Harmondsworth, Penguin, 1991, p. 158; quoted in Hannerz, op. cit., p. 379.

7 Hannerz, op. cit., pp. 380, 383.

8 ibid., p. 386.

9 M. Mann, "As the 20th century ages", *New Left Review*, 1995, vol. 214, p. 117.

10 Michael Mann, "The end of the nation state? Prospects for Europe and for the world", text of lecture given at the College of William and Mary, February, 1993, pp. 2, 5, 27, 29, original emphasis.

11 S. Huntingdon, *The Clash of Civilisations and the Re-making of the World Order*, New York, Simon and Schuster, 1996, p. 35.

12 Huntingdon, op. cit., p. 20.

13 For a thoroughgoing critique of Huntingdon's work see U. Hannerz, "Reflections on varieties of culturespeak", *European Journal of Cultural Studies*, 1999, vol. 2(3).

14 G. Eley and R. Grigor Suny (eds), *Becoming National*, Oxford, Oxford University Press, 1996, p. 19.

15 M. Augé, *Non-Places*, London, Verso, 1995, p. 50.

16 Khachig Tölölyan, "The nation-state and its Others", in G. Eley and R.G. Suny (eds), *Becoming National*, Oxford, Oxford University Press, 1996, p. 429; original emphasis.

17 Quoted in A.R. Lee, "Long day's journey", p. 11 in A.R. Lee (ed.), *Other Britain, Other British*, London, Pluto Press, 1995.

18 S. Rushdie, *The Satanic Verses*, Harmondsworth, Viking, 1989, p. 4.

19 S. Rushdie, *Imaginary Homelands*, London, Granta Books, 1991, p. 17.

20 S. Hall, "New cultures for old", in D. Massey and P. Jess (eds), *A Place in the World*, Milton Keynes, Open University Press, 1995, p. 206; original emphasis.

21 Michael Ignatieff, *Blood and Belonging*, London, Vintage, 1994, pp. 68, 102. For a fictional portrayal of some of the dilemmas of the life of a German Turk, see Jakob Arjouni's novel, *Happy Birthday, Turk!*, London, No Exit Press, 1994.

22 Z. Bauman, "Soil, blood and identity", *Sociological Review*, 1992, vol. 40(4), p. 678, quoted in G. Hage, "Nation-building-dwelling-being", in *Communal/Plural*, 1993, vol. 1, p. 76.

23 Hegel, quoted in Hage, op. cit., p. 77.

24 Hage, op. cit., p. 85.

25 E. Balibar, "Race against time", *New Times*, 18 January 1997.

26 Balibar, quoted in Tom Nairn, "Demonising nationalism", *London Review of Books*, 25 February 1993. On this see the section on "Boundary, identity and conflict" later in this chapter, and Terence Turner's comments on the specific appeal of racism to downwardly mobile elements of national populations, discussed in relation to his critique of Verena Stolcke in Chapter 11.

27 cf. H. Bhabha, "The third space" in J. Rutherford (ed.), *Identity*, London, Lawrence and Wishart, 1990.

28 P. Cole, "The limits of inclusion", *Soundings*, 1998, vol. 10.

29 Cole, "The limits of inclusion", op. cit., p. 134.

30 ibid., p. 137.

31 cf. Chapter 11 on this.

32 ibid., p. 140.

33 Bauman, "Soil, blood and identity", op. cit., p. 697; M. Maffesoli, *The Time of the Tribes*, London, Sage, 1996.

34 P. Virilio, "The third interval; a critical transition", in V.A. Corley (ed.), *Rethinking Technologies*, Minneapolis, University of Minnesota Press, 1993, p. 4.

35 I. Chambers, "Stranger in the house", *Communal/Plural*, 1998, vol. 6(1), p. 33.

36 Chambers, op. cit., p. 39; cf. my discussion earlier of Fabian's analysis of *The Time of the Other* and in Chapter 3 on the gendering of this model of mobility.

37 Z. Bauman, "The making and unmaking of strangers", in P. Werbner and T. Modood (eds), *Debating Cultural Hybridity*, London, Zed Books, 1997, p. 48.

38 Bauman, "The making and unmaking of strangers", op. cit., pp. 48, 51, 54.

39 E. Hall, *Inventing the Barbarian*, Oxford, Clarendon Press, 1991.

40 ibid., pp. 17 and 5.
41 S. Hall, "New cultures for old", in Massey and Jess (eds), op. cit., p. 181; cf. my analysis in Chapter 5 of Scannell's reading of Miss Lomas' contribution to the *Harry Hopeful* show.
42 Ignatieff, *Blood and Belonging*, op. cit., p. 95.
43 Ignatieff, *Blood and Belonging*, op. cit., p. 72.
44 G. Tawadros, "The case of the missing body", in J. Fisher (ed.), *Global Visions*, London, Kala Press, 1994, p. 107.
45 Bauman, "The making and unmaking of strangers", op. cit., p. 46.
46 Young, quoted in D. Massey, "The conceptualisation of place", in Massey and Jess (eds), op. cit., p. 83.
47 cf. Descombes' definition of being at home in a "rhetorical place" where you and others understand each other easily, quoted earlier, Chapter 1, note 11.
48 D. Massey, quoted in H. Mackay (ed.), *Consumption and Everyday Life*, Milton Keynes, Open University Press, 1997, p. 204.
49 D. Sibley, "The purification of space", *Environmental Planning, Series D: Society and Space*, 1988, vol. 6(4), p. 410.
50 P. Cohen, *Island Stories: Race, Class and Ethnicity in the Remaking of Eastenders*, London, New Ethnicities Unit, University of East London, 1993a; P. Cohen, *Home Rules*, London, New Ethnicities Unit, University of East London, 1993b; P. Cohen, "Homing devices" in V. Amit-Talai and C. Knowles (eds), *Re-situating Identities*, Broadview Press, 1996; V. Ware, "Island racism", *Feminist Review*, Autumn 1996, vol. 54.
51 Cohen, *Island Stories*, op. cit., pp. 10–11.
52 Cohen, *Island Stories*, op. cit., p. 6.
53 Cohen, *Island Stories*, op. cit., pp. 15–18.
54 A. Sivanandan, "Race against time", *New Statesman*, 15 October 1993.
55 P. Hoggett, "A place for experience: a psychoanalytic perspective on boundary, identity and culture", *Environment and Planning Series D: Society and Space*, 1992, vol. 10(3), p. 345.
56 ibid., p. 353.
57 ibid., pp. 353–4; In this context, consider the claim to local belonging made by this Asian Yorkshireman: "We are proud to be Yorkshiremen ... there is a family- and community-based tradition here and many similarities with the Asian culture of community. There is a good atmosphere in Bradford and people take pride in it. It is a real home"; Ishtiaq Ahmed, Director of Bradford's Racial Equality Council, quoted in Michael Smith, "Faith healing", *Guardian*, 26 August 1998. Again, the claim to "local belonging" is heavily contested in the area; despite the strength of the Asian cricket leagues in the area, Yorkshire County Cricket Club features singularly few Asian players.
58 I am grateful to Doreen Massey for her observations on this point and for her other helpful comments on this section. See also Terence Turner's comments on this point in the section on "Cultural fundamentalism" in Chapter 11.
59 Cohen, "Home rules", op. cit., p. 5.
60 Quoted in Cohen, "Home rules", op. cit., p. 5.
61 Cohen, *Island Stories*, op. cit., p. 17.
62 Cohen, "Homing devices", op. cit., pp. 68, 71, 75, 69.
63 ibid., p. 72.
64 R. Pahl, *Divisions of Labour*, Oxford, Blackwell, 1984, p. 324.
65 Cohen, "Homing devices", op. cit., pp. 72 and 75.

11 ibid., pp. 55–6.

12 ibid., pp. 45, 50–51.

13 K. Fog-Olwig, "Cultural sites", in K. Fog-Olwig and K. Hastrup (eds), *Siting Culture*, London, Routledge, 1997, p. 34.

14 Fog-Olwig, "Contested homes", in Rapport and Dawson (eds), op. cit., p. 234.

15 Barry Curtis and Claire Pajaczkowska, "Getting there: travel, time and narrative", in G. Robertson, M. Mash, L. Tickner, J. Bird, B. Curtis and T. Putnam (eds), *Travellers' Tales*, London, Routledge, 1994, pp. 202–3.

16 ibid., p. 215.

17 R. Mandel, "Shifting centres and emergent identities: Turkey and Germany in the lives of Turkish gastarbeiter", in D. Eichelman and J. Piscatori (eds), *Muslim Travellers*, London, Routledge, 1990.

18 L. Baldassar, "Home and away", *Communal/Plural*, 1997, vol. 5, p. 88.

19 M. Sarup, "Home and identity", in Robertson *et al.* (eds), op. cit., p. 94.

20 cf. R. Silverstone, E. Hirsch and D. Morley, "The moral economy of the household", in R. Silverstone and E. Hirsch (eds) *Consuming Technologies*, London, Routledge, 1992.

21 L. Malkki, "National geographies", in Gupta and Ferguson (eds), op. cit., pp. 62–3.

22 S. Malcolmson, "The varieties of cosmopolitan experience", in Cheah and Robbins (eds), op. cit., p. 239.

23 J. Bourne-Taylor, "Re: Locations", *New Formations*, 1992, vol. 17, p. 92, commenting on E. Said, "The mind of winter: reflections on life in exile", *Harper's Magazine*, September 1984, and Said's "Reflections on exile", *Granta*, 1984, vol. 13.

24 R. Wilson, "A new cosmopolitanism is in the air", in Cheah and Robbins (eds), op. cit., p. 351; P. Cheah, "Given culture" in Cheah and Robbins (eds), op. cit., p. 302.

25 T. Brennan, "The national longing for form", in H. Bhabha (ed.), *Nation and Narration*, London, Routledge, 1990, p. 63. For a further exposition of Brennan's argument see his *At Home in the World: Cosmopolitanism Now*, Cambridge, Mass., Harvard University Press, 1997.

26 T. Brennan, "Cosmopolitics and celebrities", *Race and Class*, 1989, vol. 31(1).

27 cf. E. Said, "The mind of winter: reflections on life in exile", *Harper's Magazine*, September 1984, quoted in T. Brennan, "Cosmopolitics and celebrities", op. cit., p. 2.

28 cf. B. Robbins, "Comparative cosmopolitanism", in Cheah and Robbins (eds), op. cit., p. 254.

29 Cheah, "Given culture", in Cheah and Robbins (eds), op. cit., pp. 296, 297, 298, 301.

30 cf. R. Barthes, "Myth today", in his *Mythologies*, London, Paladin, 1973.

31 J. Clifford, "Mixed feelings", in Cheah and Robbins (eds), op. cit., pp. 363, 367.

32 J. Durham Peters, "Exile, nomadism and diaspora", in Naficy (ed.), op. cit.

33 Durham Peters, op. cit., pp. 28–9.

34 ibid., p. 33.

35 ibid., p. 35; cf. E. Gellner, "Foreword" to A.M. Khazanov, *Nomads and the Outside World*, Madison, Wisconsin, Madison University Press, 1983. For the source of much postmodern nomadology see G. Deleuze and F. Guattari, *Nomadology*, New York, Semiotexte, 1986. For a sceptical commentary on this romantic tendency in anthropology, see R. Rosaldo, "From the door of his tent", in J. Clifford and G. Marcus (eds), *Writing Culture*, Berkeley, University of California Press, 1986; for a classic case of the travel writer's romance of nomadology see B. Chatwin, *The Songlines*, London, Picador, 1987.

36 R. Braidotti, *Nomadic Subjects*, New York, Columbia University Press, 1994, p. 12.

37 Durham Peters, op. cit., pp. 35–6. Nonetheless, while recognising that the vast majority of contemporary migrants, exiles and nomads were in fact forced from their home by economic and political factors beyond their control, in the end Peters is rightly sceptical of the arguments of those who would, as it were, attempt finally to restore everyone to their "rightful" home cultures. He accepts that what he describes as their "militant defence of primordial identity ... [their] rhetoric of rigid naming, and outrage at the poaching of exotics may serve as survival strategies, a salvaging of pride or security in a hostile world", but he argues that we should "eschew the project of assigning everyone a homeland in the world of representations" and the associated "hermeneutics of suspicion" involved in this "critique of portrayals", op. cit., p. 36. On the current fate of the Romany population of Eastern Europe, see Chapter 11.

38 Ignatieff, *Blood and Belonging*, London, Vintage, 1994, p. 7.

39 Malcolmson, op. cit., p. 238.

40 J. Clifford, *Routes*, Cambridge, Mass. Harvard University Press, 1997, pp. 84–5.

41 Malcolmson, op. cit., p. 238.

42 Clifford, op. cit., p. 36.

43 cf. J. Tomlinson, *Globalisation and Culture*, Cambridge, Polity Press, 1999, pp. 181–9.

44 T. Brennan, *At Home in the World*, Cambridge, Mass., Harvard University Press, 1997.

45 Wilson, op. cit., p. 352.

46 Malcolmson, op. cit., p. 234.

47 Robbins, "Comparative cosmopolitanism", op. cit., p. 260. Thus Appadurai calls for a "cosmopolitan anthropology that does not presuppose the primacy of the West" (in his "Global ethnoscapes", quoted in Brett Neilson, "On the new cosmopolitans", *Communal/Plural* 1993, vol. 1, p. iii); Clifford talks of "discrepant cosmopolitanisms" to describe the travelling cultures of migrant worlders, refugees, tourists and other mobile communities (J. Clifford, *Routes*, Cambridge, Mass., Harvard University Press, 1997); Benita Parry speaks of "postcolonial cosmopolitanism" ("The contradictions of cultural studies", *Transitions*, 1991, vol. 53); Cohen speaks of "rooted cosmopolitanism" (M. Cohen, "Rooted cosmopolitanism", *Dissent*, 1992, vol. 39); Homi Bhabha writes of "vernacular cosmopolitanism" ("Unsatisfied notes on vernacular cosmopolitanism", in P.C. Pfeiffer and L. Garcia-Moreno (eds), *Text and Narration*, Columbia, Camden House, 1996); and Anthony Appiah declares the possibility of "patriotic cosmopolitanism", in his "Cosmopolitan patriots", in P. Cheah and B. Robbins (eds), op. cit.

48 Wilson, op. cit., p. 355.

49 Robbins, op. cit., p. 250.

50 Martha Nussbaum, *For Love of Country*, Boston, Beacon Press, 1996, p. 4; Carlyle's phrase about nationalism is quoted in Malcolmson, op. cit., p. 233.

51 cf. Yi-Fu Tuan, *Cosmos and Hearth*, Minneapolis, University of Minnesota Press, 1996, p. 159.

52 cf. S. Maharaj, "Perfidious fidelity: the untransability of the Other", in J. Fisher (ed.), *Global Visions*, London, Kala Press, 1994, p. 29.

53 Z. Sardar, Ashis Nandy and Merryl Wyn Davies, *Barbaric Others*, London, Pluto Press, 1993, p. 89.

54 G. Alsmark, "When in Sweden", in J. Frykman and O. Lofgren (eds), *Force of Habit*, Lund, Lund University Press, 1996, p. 89.

55 P. Werbner, "The dialectics of cultural hybridity", in P. Werbner and T. Modood (eds), *Debating Cultural Hybridity*, London, Zed Books, 1996. See Bauman, quoted below, on postmodernity's "heterophiliac" tendencies.

56 J. Hutnyk, "Adorno at Womad: South-Asian crossovers at the limits of hybridity-talk", in Werbner and Modood (eds), op. cit., p. 121.
57 Werbner, op. cit., p. 20.
58 cf. Hutnyk's approving quote of the Asian Dub Foundation's lyric counterposing the "tourist mentality" of multiculturalism with "real" anti-racism, in their song "Jericho"; Hutnyk, op. cit., p. 131.
59 Peter Van der Veer, "The enigma of arrival: hybridity and authenticity in the global space", in Werbner and Modood (eds), op. cit., p. 94; Jonathan Friedman, "Global crises, the struggle for cultural identity and intellectual porkbarrelling: cosmopolitans versus locals, ethnics and nationals in an era of de-hegemonisation", in Werbner and Modood (eds), op. cit., pp. 76–7.
60 Van der Veer, op. cit., p.95.
61 Aijaz Ahmad, *In Theory*, London, Verso, 1992.
62 Z. Bauman, "The making and unmaking of strangers" in Werbner and Modood (eds), op. cit., p. 55.
63 Hutnyk, "Adorno at Womad", op. cit., p. 108.
64 ibid., pp. 113 and 109.
65 J. May, "Globalisation and the politics of place: place and identity in an inner London neighbourhood", in *Transactions of the Institute of British Geographers*, 1996, NS. 21; J. May, "A little taste of something more exotic", *Geography*, 1996, vol. 81.
66 May, "Globalisation and the politics of place: place and identity in an inner London neighbourhood", op. cit., p. 196. Evidently, Massey's own argument is not concerned simply with the physical co-presence of people of different sorts in the same area, but with the power relations that govern the terms of that co-presence. See the quote from Massey at the start of the section on "Differential hybridities", later in this chapter.
67 b.hooks, *Black Looks: Race and Representation*, London, Turnaround Books, 1992, p. 21.
68 A. Rifkin, "Travel for men", in Robertson *et al.* (eds), op. cit., p. 220.
69 ibid., p. 209.
70 May, "Globalisation and the politics of place", op. cit., pp. 208–9. In the debate reported earlier concerning Rachel Whiteread's *House* sculpture, Couldry notes that the local councillors arguing for its demolition also dismissed its supporters in similar terms – as "gentrifiers" who had no legitimate place in the area – N. Couldry, "Speaking up in a public place", *New Formations*, 1995, vol. 25, p. 109.
71 I should note that the area of London which May studied is the one where I live myself. It may be that my antipathy to May's analysis is in some part informed by my own investment in locality, as much as by my sense that he has over-exaggerated the significance of what is but one geological layer of the area's identity – the highly visible influx of "yuppies" over the last ten years or so.
72 May, "A little taste of something more exotic", op. cit., p. 63.
73 A. Rifkin, "Travel for men", in G. Robertson *et al.* (eds), *Travellers' Tales*, London, Routledge, 1994, p. 223.
74 G. Hage, "At home in the entrails of the West", in H. Grace, G. Hage, L. Johnson, J. K. Langsworth and M. Symonds (eds), *Home/World: Space, Community and Marginality in Sydney's West*, Annandale, Pluto (Australia) Press, 1997, p. 132, original emphasis.
75 cf. P. Crang and P. Jackson, "Consuming geographies", in David Morley and Kevin Robins (eds), *British Cultural Studies*, Oxford, Oxford University Press, forthcoming.
76 P. Werbner, "Essentialising essentialism, essentialising silence", 1996b, in Werbner and Modood (eds), op. cit., pp. 226 and 228.

77 ibid, pp. 228, 229 and 249.
78 ibid, p. 240.
79 ibid, p.230.
80 G. Baumann, *Contesting Culture*, Cambridge University Press, 1996.
81 G. Baumann, "Dominant and demotic discourses of culture", in Werbner and Modood (eds), op. cit., pp. 212–13.
82 Werbner, "The dialectics of cultural hybridity", op. cit., pp. 3–4.
83 D. Massey, "The conceptualisation of place", in D. Massey and P. Jess (eds), *A Place in the World?*, Milton Keynes, Open University Press, 1995, p. 71.
84 S. Wallman, "New identities", in N. Rapport and A. Dawson (eds), *Migrants of Identity*, Oxford, Berg, 1998, p. 201.
85 S. Rushdie, *The Satanic Verses*, Harmondsworth, Penguin, 1988, p. 314.
86 E. Berner, "The metropolitan dilemma", in Öncü and Weyland (eds), op. cit., p.101; cf. James Donald's discussion of Spike Lee's *Do the Right Thing*, referred to in Chapter 11 below.
87 M. Castells, *The Informational City*, Oxford, Blackwell, 1991, p. 226. It is in just this spirit of trepidation about intercommunal relations in the city that the fiction-alised teenage Latino hero of Paul Simon's *Capeman* musical declares that the boundaries of his *barrio* are, in effect, the boundaries of his "nation": he fears leaving the *barrio* to cross into other neighbourhoods given the ferocity with which antagonistic cultures are territorialised in the city – Paul Simon, *Songs from the Capeman*, Warner Bros Records, 1998.
88 D. Hebdige, "Redeeming witness: in the tracks of the Homeless Vehicle Project", *Cultural Studies*, 1992, vol. 7; C. Olalquiaga, *Megalopolis*, Minneapolis, University of Minnesota Press, 1992.
89 Brett Neilson, "On the new cosmopolitanism", *Communal/Plural*, 1999, vol. 7(1), p. 116; review of T. Brennan, *At Home in The World: Cosmopolitanism Now*, Cambridge, Mass., Harvard University Press, 1997.
90 Friedman, "Global crises", op. cit., p. 81; Werbner, "The dialectics of cultural hybridity", op. cit., p. 12.
91 Friedman, "Global crises", op. cit., p. 84.
92 A. Appadurai, *Modernity at Large*, Minneapolis, University of Minnesota Press, 1996, p. 19.
93 P. Chatterjee, *The Nation and its Fragments*, Princeton, New Jersey, Princeton University Press, 1993, p. 4.
94 T. Nairn, "Demonising nationalism", *London Review of Books*, 25 February 1993; on the "New Order" see Francis Fukuyama, *The End of History and the Last Man*, Harmondsworth, Penguin, 1992; for a good collection of responses to and critiques of Fukuyama's position, see Alan Ryan (ed.), *After the End of History*, London, Collins and Brown, 1992.
95 S. Hall, "Globalisation – Europe's other self", *Marxism Today*, 1991, August.
96 Nairn, op. cit.
97 J. Clifford, *Routes*, op. cit., p. 10.
98 T. Todorov, "Bilingualism, dialogism and schizophrenia", *New Formations*, 1992, vol. 17, p. 22.
99 Ignatieff, *Blood and Belonging*, op. cit., pp. 9–10.
100 cf. A. Mattelart, M. Mattelart and X. Delcourt, *International Image Markets*, London, Comedia, 1984.

101 U. Hannerz, "Flows, boundaries and hybrids: keywords in transnational anthropology", paper to Workshop on Flows, Borders and Hybrids, Department of Social Anthropology, Stockholm University, October, 1996, pp. 9, 4, 10.

102 N. Richard, "Cultural peripheries: Latin America and postmodernist decentring", *Boundary 2*, 1993, vol. 20(3); see also D. Morley, "EurAm, modernity, reason and alterity", in D. Morley and K. H. Chen (eds), *Stuart Hall: Critical Dialogues in Cultural Studies*, London, Routledge, 1996.

103 G. Mosquera, "Some problems in transcultural curating", in Fisher (ed.), op. cit.

104 Mosquera, op. cit., p. 133; cf. Chapter 7 for Maspero's comments on the parallel difficulties, on a smaller scale, of making lateral journeys across the suburbs of a city.

105 Paul Willemen, "The national", in L. Devereux and R. Hillman (eds), *Fields of Vision*, Berkeley, University of California Press, 1995, p. 23.

106 M. Schudson, "Culture and the integration of national societies", *International Social Science Journal*, 1994, vol. 139.

107 cf. also on this, N. Abercrombie, S. Hill and B. Turner, *The Dominant Ideology Thesis*, London, Allen and Unwin, 1984.

108 Schudson, op. cit., p. 65; D. Lockwood, "Social integration and system integration", in G.K. Zollschan and W. Hirsch (eds), *Explorations in Social Change*, London, Routledge and Kegan Paul, 1954.

109 A. Cohen, *The Symbolic Construction of Community*, London, Routledge, 1985.

110 Cohen, *The Symbolic Construction of Community*, op. cit., p. 22.

111 ibid., p. 18; cf. V. Volosinov, *Marxism and the Philosophy of Language*, New York, Academic Press, 1973.

112 M. Douglas and B. Isherwood, *The World of Goods: Towards an Anthropology of Consumption*, Harmondsworth, Penguin, 1979.

113 cf. Justin Lewis, *The Ideological Octopus*, London, Routledge, 1991, for a discussion of how popular television similarly relies on its capacity to function "polysemically", and thus to carry different meanings for different segments of its mass audiences.

114 Cohen, *The Symbolic Construction of Community*, op. cit., pp. 20–21; cf. Gerd Baumann on this, quoted earlier. As Cohen puts it elsewhere, the boundary "represents the mask presented by the community to the outside world; it is the community's public face"; A. Cohen, "Of symbols and boundaries", in A. Cohen (ed.), *Symbolising Boundaries*, Manchester, Manchester University Press, 1986.

115 S.K. Phillips, "Natives and incomers", in Cohen (ed.), *Symbolising Boundaries*, p. 141.

116 ibid., p. 144, original emphasis.

117 At a different geographical scale, see Stuart Hall's comments on "how long" it might take for different categories of immigrants to become "English", S. Hall, "New cultures for old", in Massey and Jess (eds), op. cit.

118 Cohen, *The Symbolic Construction of Community*, op. cit., p. 105.

119 S. Wallman, "The boundaries of household", in Cohen (ed.), *Symbolising Boundaries*, op. cit., pp. 56, 66; for a fuller account of Wallman's work see her *Eight London Households*, London, Tavistock, 1984.

120 G. Allan, "Insiders and outsiders", in G. Allan and G. Crow (eds), *Home and Family*, London, Macmillan, 1989.

121 At its simplest, different types of people enter and leave the house in different ways. In his analysis of domestic life in traditional mining villages in the north-east of England, Andrew Davison observes that

the back door was for everyday usage and was permanently unlocked while the front door was opened only for strangers, high-status groups, the exit of the dead, and the entry of a new child and on wedding days. The front doorstep, an object of copious cleaning with a small, clay "holy stone", is a threshold in the fullest sense of the word, between inside and outside, family and non-family, life and death and community and non-community.

(Andrew Davison, "Ageing and change in pit villages of North East England", unpublished PhD thesis, 1990, University of Essex)

122 Allan, op. cit., p. 143.
123 ibid., pp. 148 and 146.

11 POSTMODERNISM, POST-STRUCTURALISM AND THE POLITICS OF DIFFERENCE

1 K. Robins, "Tradition and translation", in J. Corner and S. Harvey (eds), *Enterprise and Heritage*, London, Routledge, 1991, p. 141. For a recent instance of this dismal tendency, consider the Serbs' fixation on the significance of their nationalist shrines in Kosovo.
2 N. Rapport and A. Dawson, "Home and movement", in N. Rapport and A. Dawson (eds), *Migrants of Identity*, Oxford, Berg, 1998, pp. 31–2.
3 C. Olalquiaga, "Home is where the art is", in D. Frankel (ed.), *Home and the World*, New York, Museum for African Art, 1993, p. 17.
4 W. Wheeler, "Nostalgia isn't nasty", in M. Perryman (ed.), *Altered States*, London, Lawrence and Wishart, 1994, p. 95; see also her *A New Modernity*, London, Lawrence and Wishart, 1999.
5 Wheeler, op. cit., pp. 95–7.
6 ibid., p. 108.
7 J. Rutherford, "A place called home", in J. Rutherford (ed.), *Identity: Community, Culture, Difference*, London, Lawrence and Wishart, 1990, p. 11.
8 Margaret Thatcher, interviewed by Julie Cockcroft, *Daily Mail*, 4 May 1989; quoted in Rutherford, op. cit., p. 12.
9 Rutherford, op. cit., p. 13.
10 cf. J. Friedman, "Global cities", in P. Werbner and T. Modood (eds), *Debating Cultural Hybridity*, London, Zed Books, 1997, drawing on Lévi-Strauss' "Race and culture", in *The View from Afar*, Oxford, Blackwell, 1985.
11 F. Anthias and N. Yuval-Davis, *Racialised Boundaries*, London, Routledge, 1992, p. 12. On these distinctions see also Michael Banton, "The cultural determinants of xenophobia", in *Anthropology Today*, 1996, vol. 12(2), p. 9, where Banton argues that the degree of xenophobia in a society will tend to vary with "the extent to which a people's collective self-conception is of a political or 'volkish' community".
12 V. Stolcke, "Talking culture: new boundaries, new rhetorics of exclusion", *Current Anthropology*, 1995, vol. 36(1).
13 The text of Powell's speech is reported in *The Times*, London, 22 April 1968.
14 H. Bhabha, *The Location of Culture*. London, Routledge, 1994, pp. 99–100.
15 Stolcke, op. cit., p. 14; cf. Paul Gilroy, *Small Acts: Thoughts on the Politics of Black Cultures*, London, Serpents Tail, 1993.
16 Stolcke, op. cit., pp. 5–7.
17 ibid., p. 8.
18 cf. Hoggett on this in Chapter 9.
19 Stolcke, op. cit., pp. 12 and 19; cf. D. Sibley, *Geographies of Exclusion*, London, Routledge, 1995, on the ambivalent significance of mechanisms of exclusion, for groups in differential relations of power.
20 See their comments published as supplements to Stolcke's article in *Current Anthropology*, 1995, vol. 36(1).

21 Fitzpatrick, supplement, op. cit., p. 14.
22 cf. Paul Gilroy's critique of Raymond Williams in his *There Ain't No Black in the Union Jack*, London, Hutchinson, 1987, pp. 49–51.
23 Turner, supplement, op. cit., p. 17, cf. Balibar, quoted earlier, on this point.
24 Turner, supplement, op. cit., p. 17; cf. Cole's argument about citizenship cited earlier in Chapter 9, notes 28–30.
25 K. Malik, "Same old hate is the new byword for bigotry", *Guardian* 12 August 1995, reviewing D. Selbourne, *The Principles of Duty*, London, Sinclair-Stevenson, 1994.
26 quoted in Malik, op. cit.
27 I.M. Young, "The ideal of community and the politics of difference", in *Social Theory and Practice*, 1986, vol. 12.
28 H. Fern Haber, *Beyond Postmodern Politics*, London, Routledge, 1994. For some of the intellectual background to this critique see Shadia B. Drury, *Alexandre Kojève: The Roots of Postmodern Politics*, London, Macmillan, 1994.
29 Haber, op. cit., pp. 4–5; see also Gerd Baumann's discussion of these issues, referred to in Chapter 10.
30 M. Keith and S. Pile, "The place of politics", in M. Keith and S. Pile (eds), *Place and the Politics of Identity*, London, Calder and Boyars, 1966, pp. 31–2.
31 Haber, op. cit., p. 121.
32 cf. the analysis offered by Anthony Cohen in the previous chapter.
33 ibid., pp. 114–17.
34 For a terrifying representation of a fully deconstructed form of subjectivity, see Samuel Beckett, *The Unnameable*, London, Calder and Boyars, 1966.
35 Young, op. cit., pp. 1–2.
36 Haber, op. cit., pp. 126, 120.
37 ibid., p. 127.
38 cf. Gayatri Spivak on the necessity of "strategic essentialism" and the subsequent development of concepts of "identity under erasure".
39 cf. Christopher Norris' account of Derrida on this point: C. Norris, *Deconstruction*, London, Routledge, 1991; see also Stanley Fish, "The young and the restless", in H. Aram Veeser (ed.), *The New Historicism*, London, Routledge, 1989.
40 N. Yural-Davies, "Ethnicity, gender relations and multiculturalism", in Werbner and Modood (eds), *Debating Cultural Hybridity*, London, Zed Books, 1996.
41 S. Hall, "Minimal selves", in L. Appignanesi (ed.), *Identity: The Real Me* (ICA Documents 6), London, Institute of Contemporary Arts, 1988, p. 45, original emphasis.
42 I.M. Young, *Justice and the Politics of Difference*, Princeton University Press, 1990, p. 188.
43 Haber, op. cit., p. 128.
44 cf. S. Fish, "The young and the restless", in H.A. Veeser (ed.), *The New Historicism*, London, Routledge, 1989; cf. Gerd Baumann, *Contesting Culture*, Cambridge, Cambridge University Press, 1996, pp. 3–4 for a very enjoyable account of the moment when his own fieldwork subjects deconstructed his research plan according to exactly this logic.
45 N. Rathzel, "Harmonious *Heimat* and disturbing *Ausländer*", in K.K. Bhavani and A. Phoenix (eds), *Shifting Identities and Shifting Racisms*, London, Sage, 1994; cf. Banton, quoted earlier on this, in relation to degrees of xenophobia among different populations, note 11 above.
46 Rathzel, "Harmonious *Heimat* and disturbing *Ausländer*", op. cit., p. 81; cf. also Cohen and Ware quoted earlier on this in Chapter 9.
47 ibid., p. 91.

48 A. Begag, *North African Immigrants in France*, Loughborough, European Research Centre, Loughborough University, 1989, p. 9.

49 M. Augé, *Non-Places*, London, Verso, 1995, p. 119.

50 M. Augé, *A Sense for the Other*, Stanford, California, Stanford University Press, 1998, pp. 108–9.

51 E. Levinas, *Totality and Infinity*, Pittsburgh, Duquesne University Press, 1969, p. 39; quoted in I. Chambers, "A stranger in the house", *Continuum*, 1998, vol. 6(1), p. 35.

52 J. Amery, "How much home does a man need", in his *At The Mind's Limits*, Schocken, New York, 1986; republished London, Granta Books, 1999, original 1966; quoted in D. Stone, "Homes without Heimats", *Angelaki*, 1995, vol. 2(1), p. 94.

53 J.-L. Nancy, *The Inoperative Community*, Minneapolis, University of Minnesota Press, 1991, p. 10.

54 Stone, "Homes without Heimats", op. cit.; cf. Kevin Robins' comments quoted in Chapter 8 on the dangerous temptations of the solipsistic virtual communities of cyberspace.

55 J. Tomlinson, *Globalisation and Culture*, Cambridge, Polity Press, 1999, pp. 181–2; James Donald, *Imagining the Modern City*, London, Athlone Press, forthcoming, Chapter 6 (page references to Donald's text are based on the mss copy, for access to which I thank the author).

56 Donald, op. cit., p. 177; R. Williams, *Towards 2000*, Harmondsworth, Penguin, 1985; P. Gilroy, *There Ain't No Black in the Union Jack*, London, Hutchinson, 1987, pp. 49–51; cf. my own earlier comments on these difficulties in the earlier chapters.

57 Donald, op. cit., pp. 182–3.

58 ibid., pp. 183–4; cf. Ignatieff on this, quoted earlier.

59 ibid., pp. 186–7; Jean-Luc Nancy, *The Inoperative Community*, Minneapolis, University of Minnesota Press, 1991; Iris Marion Young, *Justice and the Politics of Difference*, Princeton, Princeton University Press, 1990.

60 Donald, quoting Nancy, op. cit., p. 194.

61 D. Hebdige, "The impossible object", *New Formations*, 1987, vol. 1.

62 Donald, op. cit., p. 201.

63 M. Walzer, *On Toleration*, New Haven, Yale University Press, 1997, p. 11, quoted in Donald, op. cit.

64 cf. S. Mestrovic, *The Balkanisation of the West*, London, Routledge, 1994, and D. Morley "EurAm, modernity, reason and alterity", in D. Morley and K. Chen (eds), *Stuart Hall: Critical Readings*, London, Routledge, 1996.

65 N. Ascherson, "The world's living dead who rise out of the past to go home", *Independent on Sunday*, 12 May 1991.

66 Ascherson, op. cit. Similarly, in an account of his travels in Claudio Magris' footsteps along the River Danube, Darius Sanai reports meeting a family of German-speaking farmers living on the border between Hungary and Croatia who were

> descended from the *Donauschwaben*, Germans from the province of Swabia who had migrated 1,000 miles down the river ... hundreds of years ago. They had German books, a German flag in the kitchen and sold wines to Germany. They had never been there.
>
> (Darius Sanai, "One river, nine countries", *Independent on Sunday*, 12 September 1999; C. Magris, *Danube*, London, Collins Harvill, 1990)

67 M. Ignatieff, *Blood and Belonging*, London, Vintage, 1994, pp. 74–5.

68 Bengi, quoted in D. Morley and K. Robins, "Almanci, Yabanci", *Cultural Studies*, 1996, vol. 10(2), p. 248.

69 N. Ascherson, "Britain bucks the trend of strong city government", *Independent on Sunday*, 27 June 1993.

70 D. Le Gilledoux, "The rhythm of Occitan", *Guardian*, 15 February 1994.

71 Arjouni, quoted in J. Williams, "Down these mean strasse", *Independent on Sunday*, 12 November 1994; cf. my earlier analogy between Adorno and Arjouni's feelings for the city of Frankfurt, in Chapter 2.

72 cf. Hargreaves earlier on the multicultural reference points of the young residents of the Parisian banlieues; see Chapter 7.

73 Arjouni, quoted in Williams, op. cit.

74 A. Ahmad, *In Theory*, London, Verso, 1994, p. 90.

75 Interviewee in Misha Glenny's *Living on the Ethnic Faultline*, Tx BBC2, 15 January 1994.

76 U. Eco, "A tongue for Europe", *Guardian*, 2 October 1992.

77 cf. D. Morley and K. Robins, *Spaces of Identity*, London, Routledge, 1995, ch. 3.

78 C. Shore, "Transcending the nation-state?" *Journal of Historical Sociology*, 1996, vol. 9(4), p. 481; K. Robins, "European media culture and the problem of imagined community", paper to Symposium on the Future of the Mass Media in Wales, Open University in Wales, Cardiff, January 1997.

79 Robins, op. cit., p. 10; cf. Baumann, quoted earlier.

80 Robins, op. cit., p. 11.

81 M. Ignatieff, "There's no place like home: the politics of belonging", in R. Porter and S. Dunant (eds), *The Age of Anxiety*, London, Virago, 1996, pp. 97–8.

82 cf. Robins, op. cit., drawing on J. Kristeva, *Nations Without Nationalism*, New York, Columbia University Press, 1993.

83 Pontalis and Rieff, quoted in Robins, op. cit., pp. 13–14; cf. Eco's comment, earlier.

84 Dorra, quoted in Robins, op. cit., p. 15.

85 M. Morris, "On the beach", in L. Grossberg, C. Nelson and P. Treichler (eds.), *Cultural Studies*, London, Routledge, 1992, p. 454; cf. G. Deleuze and F. Guattari, *A Thousand Plateaus*, Minneapolis, University of Minnesota Press, 1987.

86 Balibar, quoted in T. Nairn, "Demonising nationalism", *London Review of Books*, 25 February 1993.

87 cf. Nelson Moe, "Black South, black Italy: imagining the nation between Europe and Africa", paper to Centre for Italian Studies seminar, University College London, April, 1998, featuring an analysis of the song "Figli di Annibale" by the Neapolitan group Almamagretta, satirising the Northern League's racist attitude towards the Italian South by pointing out that, since the time of Hannibal's conquest, the whole of Italy's population have in one sense been "children of Hannibal".

88 J. Carmen and C. Endean, "Mezzogiorno loses its way in Euroland", *European*, 20–26 July 1998. The central problem is that given the extensive costs of its reunification, Germany, increasingly central to the operation of the whole European Union, is now unwilling to subsidise Brussels' aid to the poorer echelon of EU member states. As a result, Italy has found it harder to win subsidies from Rome, and the national government has been forced to cut public spending in order to meet the monetary conditions for membership of the single currency. As a consequence, in the words of Mario Centorimo, an economist at Messina University,

> as the new Europe emerges, with its single currency and its economic norms and new poorer countries start to join it from the east, we are staring disaster in the face. We are heading for the same fate as Africa, struck off any respectable economic map, shorn of investment and left to our own pitiful devices.
>
> (quoted in Carmen and Endean, op. cit.)

89 N. Ascherson, "All roads lead to Berlin", *Guardian*, 16 November 1998.

90 Paul Henri Spaak, Prime Minister of Belgium, quoted in Fareed Zakara, "The rise and fall of an ideal", *Times Literary Supplement*, 25 September 1998; cf. M. Walker, "The White Race in Arms", *Guardian*, 27 October 1998.
91 M. Walker and A. Travis, "Losers in the game without frontiers", *Guardian*, 7 January 1998.
92 Y. Alibhai-Brown, "Strangers, citizens and the siege mentality", *Independent*, 13 April 1994.
93 G. Younge, "Borders of hate", *Guardian*, 17 June 1998.
94 Alan Travis, "Fortress Europe's circles of purgatory", *Guardian*, 20 October 1998.
95 I. Traynor, "Czech town plans wall to isolate gypsy ghetto", *Guardian*, 16 May 1998.
96 I. Traynor, "Czech gypsies fear ghetto wall", *Guardian*, 20 June 1998.
97 Kate Connolly, "Czechs plan 'Berlin Wall' for Romanies", *Observer*, 26 September 1999. Paradoxically, after the "wall of shame" (as its critics refer to it) had finally been built in October 1999, against the wishes of the Czech central government, it transpired that European Union official disapproval of the enterprise (whether on humanitarian grounds, or because of fears of the wall's effect in creating a "flood" of asylum-seeking gypsies at the EU's own gates) might in fact delay the Czech Republic's application for "fast-track" EU membership; Nick Holdsworth, "The wall the Czechs built to keep the Roma away", in *Times Higher Education Supplement*, 12 December 1999. In fact, the wall was subsequently demolished by protesters, and the *Guardian* (27 January 2000) reported that its remains were to be "auctioned off" by the local authority.

Ironically, in another context Günter Grass has argued optimistically that the gypsies have much to teach Europe's other citizens

> by irritating our rigid order a little. Something of their way of life could rub off on us. They could teach us how meaningless frontiers are: careless of boundaries Romanies ... are at home all over Europe. They are what we claim to be: born Europeans.
>
> (Günter Grass, "Losses", *Granta*, 1992, vol. 42, pp. 107–8)

98 Giles Tremlett, "Barbed wire fails to plug leaks in border with Africa", *European*, 20–26 July 1998; Justin Webster, "Fortress Europe gets a new £22 million anti-immigrants fence", *Sunday Telegraph*, 26 July 1998.
99 E. Balibar, "Racism and politics in Europe today", *New Left Review*, 1991, vol. 186, p. 10.
100 cf. reports on the ex-UK Foreign Secretary Douglas Hurd's concern, during the crisis in Bosnia, with the potential emergence there of "the first Muslim state in Europe"; Hurd quoted in Richard Norton-Taylor, "The story of the spy", *Guardian*, 17 December 1998.
101 Tahar Ben Jelloun, "The crusade for tolerance", *European*, 5 November 1993.
102 *The Nation*, 15 April 1991.
103 As Paul Gilroy observes, in another theoretical context, the "butterfly collectors of alterity ... prefer their cultures integral and want their differences to remain absolute"; P. Gilroy, "For the transcultural record", in O. Enwezor (ed.), *Trade Routes: History and Geography*, Johannesburg, Greater Johannesburg Metropolitan Council, 1997.
104 Ben Jelloun, "France and its new impressionists", *Guardian*, 12 June 1991; cf. also Hargreaves' comments on this issue in Chapter 7. As the black North American comedian Chris Rock put it in a recent interview,

it's threatening to white people, ultimately, that we're alike. Tupac [Shakur], Biggie Smalls, whatever – that's not really threatening. You can figure that out. And that's always going to be "over there". *This* is the real threat: me sitting down in the Royalton and being able to afford anything on the menu.

(Chris Rock interviewed in David Bennum, "Ready to rock", *Observer Magazine*, 26 December 1999)

105 Alex Thomson, "The truth war", *Media Guardian*, 12 April 1999; cf. also S. Drakulic, *How We Survived Communism and Even Laughed*, London, Vintage, 1993, p. xiv, for a parallel account of the psychic difficulties in accepting that troubling material transmitted on television can on occasion be very "close to home".

106 H. Bhabha, "Location, intervention, incommensurability", *Emergences*, 1989, vol. 1(1), quoted in Gupta and Ferguson (eds), op. cit., p. 49.

107 Jonathan Boyarin, *Storm from Paradise: The Politics of Jewish Memory*, Minneapolis, University of Minnesota Press, 1992, p. 129; quoted in J. Clifford, *Routes*, Cambridge, Mass., Harvard University Press, 1997, p. 270. Clearly, it is not simply co-presence which is at issue but also the power relations between those who are present.

INDEX

Aborigines 151, 181
Abu-Lughod, Lila 12, 114–15
Acconci, Vito 83, 84
ACORN system 140
Adorno, T. 18, 47
advertising, and remote communities
   99–100
agoraphobia 69
Ahmad, Aijaz 233–4, 259
Ainley, Alison 60
airports 173, 176
Aitkenhead, Decca 140–1
Albanian migrants 154–5
Algeria 66
Alibhai-Brown, Yasmin 120, 262
alienation 179
Allan, Graham 25, 29, 71, 177, 245
Allon, Fiona 37, 38
Alsmark, Gunnar 152–3, 233
alterity 3, 5, 177–9, 247; domestication of
   223–4; and likeness 264–5; virtual and
   physical 151–3
Americanisation 12
Amery, Julian 254
Amin, Samir 225
Amish community 102
Amit-Talai, Vered 226–7
Anderson, Benedict 16, 19, 109
anti-essentialism 236–7
Appadurai, Arjun 9, 11, 55, 153–4, 182,
   239
Applegate, Celia 32, 64–5
Arab migrants, in France 156–61
architecture, modernist 60–2
Arendt, Hannah 44
Arjouni, Jakob 258, 259
Arnheim, Rolf 171

art: and domesticity 62; modernist 60–2
Artley, Alexandra 58
Ascherson, Neil 194–5, 257, 261
Ashworth, Andrea 150
Attfield, Judy 61–2
Augé, Marc 173–4, 176, 206–7, 254
Australia 37–8; Italian immigrants 52–4,
   227–8; television viewing in remote
   areas of 91, 96, 99–100; Vietnamese
   immigrants 51–2

Bachelard, Gaston 19, 28, 59–60
Bad Dream House (Acconci) 83, 84
Bakardijieva, Maria 102
Baldassar, Loretta 49, 53, 54, 153, 227
Balibar, Etienne 208, 225, 261, 263
Ballard, J.G. 97–8, 173, 197
Bammer, Angelika 16, 79
Bangladeshi immigrants 216–17
banlieues 157–61
barbarianism, Greek discourse on 212
Barker, Paul 133, 134
Barlow, John Perry 186
Barry, Angela 120–1
Barthes, Roland 229
Batty, Philip 151
Bauman, Zygmunt 22, 31, 34, 144, 183,
   197, 201–2, 203, 208, 210, 211, 213,
   226, 234
Baumann, Gerd 53, 237, 244
Beck, Robert 20
Begag, Azouz 46, 48, 254
Belize 40
Bell, D. 176
Bello, Walden 226
belonging 3, 17–18, 32, 43, 209–10,
   212–13, 246–7; and cosmopolitanism

331

forms of 196–200; as deviance 33–4; historical perspectives on 191–6; intergenerational 14; of labour 225; and media consumption 100–1, 149–50; styles of 200–1; value of 228–30; of women 68–70
modernity/modernism 42–4; and domesticity 60–3
Mohanty, Chandra 76
Moore, Suzanne 57–8, 67, 111, 112, 121–2,149
Moores, Shaun 71, 89, 97
Morris, Meaghan 68, 260–1
Morrison, Toni 29
Morse, Margaret 87, 111–12, 172–3
Mosquera, Gerardo 241–2
Mouffe, Chantal 191
Moyal, Ann 93, 94
multiculturalism 120, 121, 234–6
Mumford, Lewis 138
Munro, Moira 74
Murcott, Ann 71
Murdock, Graham 91
music, World 234
Muslim communities 264

Naficy, Hamid 49–50, 55, 134, 150, 225–6
Nairn, Tom 240
Nancy, Jean-Luc 254–5, 256
Nandy, Ashis 49
narcissism of minor differences, theory of 221
Narvaez, Peter 180
nation 247; countryside and 146, 258; gendering of 223–4; as Heimat 31–3; as symbolic home 105–8
nation-state: as homogenous unit 206–7; weakening of 204–6, 208
national identity 3, 206, 260
National Symbolic 35, 107–8
national unity/integration 242; media and construction of 106–7, 118–19
nationalism 194, 208, 212–13, 220–1, 223, 224, 239–42
nationhood 208
Nationwide (TV programme) 118–19
NATO 262
Navarro, V. 94
Nazism 255
Neighbours (soap opera) 152
Nevis 40, 55

nomadology 3, 13, 230
nomads 210–11
non-places 173–4, 176
Norris, Steven 145
Norve, Sivi 24
nostalgia 6, 246–7, 254–5; national iconography and 36

Oakley, Ann 25
Oguibe, Olu 181
Ohmae, Kenichi 204–5
Olalquiaga, Celeste 65–6, 198, 238, 246
Öncü Ayse 131–2
Ong, Aihwa 127
Orwell, George 118
otherness *see* alterity
owner-occupation 25

Pahl, Ray 218
Painter, Colin and Ann 35–6
Pajaczkowska, Clare 227
Palmer, Andrew 58
Palmer, Phyllis 78
Papastergiadis, Nikos 42, 47–8, 107
Paris, Texas (film) 60
parks, and privacy 57
Pasolini, Pier Paolo 115
the past, living in 49–50
Patel, Raj 138
Patterson, John 137
Peck, Jeffrey 32, 33
Peters, John Durham 13, 49, 174–5, 230
Phillips, Mike 105
Phillips, Scott K. 244, 245
Phillips, Trevor 124, 165
photography, family 58
Pile, Steven 7, 31, 251
pilgrims 210, 230
Pitt-Rivers, J.A. 221
place: construction of a sense of 194–5; definition of and process of exclusion 214; and ethnicity 212; and non-place 173–4, 176
Plato 222
Poggi, Christine 83
Pollard, Ingrid 146
Postill, John 88
Postman, Neil 190
postmodernity 2–4, 246–7
post-structuralism 250–3
Powell, Enoch 219–20, 248

urban space: delineation of 22; *see also*
    cities
Urry, John 13, 193

Valentine, G. 176
values, embodiment of in domestic
    structures 20–1
Van der Veer, Peter 233
the veil 66
Vidler, Anthony 80, 82
Vietnamese migrants 51–2
Virilio, Paul 172, 210
Volga Germans 257–8

Wainwright, Lisa 80–1
Walker, Martin 143, 262
Wallman, Sandra 9, 238, 244
Walzer, Michael 256
wanderlust 150
Warburton, Diane 14
Ward, Frazer 78, 143
Ware, Vron 214, 218–19
Wark, Mckenzie 175–6
Warner, Marina 16, 65
Warner, Michael 115
Watney, Simon 85
Webster, Frank 188–9
Webster, Wendy 219–20
Weeks, Jeffrey 78
Wenders, Wim 60
Werbner, Pnina 233, 236, 237, 239, 251
Wertheim, Margaret 189
Westwood, Sallie 152
Weyland, Petra 75, 131
Wheeler, Wendy 246, 247
White, Allon 33
White, Hayden 182
Whiteread, Rachel 2, 28–9, 73, 84–5

Whittstock, Melinda 136
Wilks, Richard 11, 40, 182
Willemen, Paul 242
Williams, John 152
Williams, Raymond 9, 129, 149, 179, 255
Williams, V. 58
Wilmott, Peter 131
Wilson, Elizabeth 69
Wilson, Rob 228, 232
withdrawal, into "gated communities"
    133–5, 138–9
Wodiczko, Krzystof 27, 28
Wolf, Janet 67–8
Wollen, Peter 176
woman/women: of Greenham Common
    69–70; as home 63–4; homeless 69;
    mobility of 68–70; role of 23; *see also*
    femininity; gender; the housewife
Womanhouse installation 84
Wood, Denis 20
Worpole, Ken 14, 57, 69, 135, 136, 153,
    159, 163
Wurtzel, A. 178

xenophobia 6, 194, 247–8

Yat-sen Li, Jason 37–8
Yoshimi, Shunya 88
Young, Iris Marion 115, 124–5, 184, 191,
    214, 250–1, 252, 253, 256
Young, Michael 131
Younge, Gary 52, 262
"Yugo-zombies" 50–1
Yuval-Davis, Nira 252

Ziener, Lanette 137